THE SHAH'S PARTY

ROBERT TEMPLER

The Shah's Party

And the Iranian Revolution that Followed

HURST & COMPANY, LONDON

First published in the United Kingdom in 2026 by
C. Hurst & Co. (Publishers) Ltd.,
New Wing, Somerset House, Strand, London, WC2R 1LA
© Robert Templer, 2026
All rights reserved.

The right of Robert Templer to be identified as the author of this publication is asserted by him in accordance with the Copyright, Designs and Patents Act, 1988.

Distributed in the United States, Canada and Latin America by Oxford University Press, 546 Fifth Avenue, New York, NY 10036, United States of America.

A Cataloguing-in-Publication data record for this book is available from the British Library.

ISBN: 9781805265696

EU GPSR Authorised Representative
Easy Access System Europe Oü, 16879218
Address: Mustamäe tee 50, 10621, Tallinn, Estonia
Contact Details: gpsr.requests@easproject.com, +358 40 500 3575

This book is printed using paper from registered sustainable and managed sources.

www.hurstpublishers.com

Printed and bound in Great Britain by Bell & Bain Ltd, Glasgow

To George and Mary Spender and Ed and Jack Templer

CONTENTS

Acknowledgments   ix
Prologue   xiii

1. Before the Party   1
2. The Party Planner   21
3. The Venue   35
4. The Guests   73
5. The Gift   121
6. The Host   131
7. The Hostess   185
8. Ghosts at the Banquet   207
9. The Banquet   269
10. After the Party   309

Postscript   335

Notes   345
Bibliography   355
Index   401

ACKNOWLEDGMENTS

As with all books, this one stands on the shoulders of the many great writers and academics who have gone before and whose works have informed and inspired me. Robert Steele's book on the celebration was enormously helpful, as were some of the biographers of the Shah, particularly Abbas Milani and Gholam Reza Afkhami. Other works had a considerable influence on *The Shah's Party*, including those by these prolific and remarkable academics and writers: Ervand Abrahamian, Abbas Amanat, Ali Ansari, the late Michael Axworthy, Pierre Briant, Hamid Dabashi, Christopher de Bellaigue, Cyrus Ghani, Talinn Grigor, Lloyd Llewellyn-Jones, Afshin Matin-Asgari, Ali Mirsepassi, Hamid Nafisy and Ahmad Rahnema.

I am very grateful to the staff of the Richard Nixon Presidential Library and Museum, the UK National Archives at Kew, the Library of Congress, the New York Public Library, Harvard Library, and, above all, the British Library, for their invaluable assistance over the years.

There are many Iranians inside the country and around the world whom I wish to thank for their help and generosity. I am not going to name any Iranians here, other than the well-known authors above, as one never knows what will get anyone into trouble. I owe you all an enormous debt of gratitude. I have never

ACKNOWLEDGMENTS

experienced hospitality as I have in Iran: my admiration for the country, its culture and its people is limitless. I wish I knew more, could read more, and learn more. I know I will never stop feeling that. One word: *Azadi*.

I would like to thank Minh Bui Jones for all his editing as well as his support, and Michael Dwyer and everyone at Hurst.

Over the years many others have helped me with writing, editing, research or such necessities of life as encouragement, hospitality, food and friendship. I owe many thanks to: Kimberly Abbott, Hannah Barbash-Taylor, Jasper Barbash-Taylor, Gregory Beals, Blair Blackwell, Kate Bourne, Will Bourne, Kate Carey, Lucien Castaing-Taylor, John Chalmers, Sarah Chalmers, Dominique Chambless, Melinda Chan-Butts, Kathy Charlton, Gina Chua, Sam Clendon, Pippa Considine, Nick Crosby, Jim Della-Giacoma, Marty Dorfler, Charles Emmerson, Galen Englund, Gareth Evans, Magdalen Evans, Shehryar Fazli, Simon Finley, Katya Garcia-Anton, Leah Gary, Will Gibney, Gonzalo Gomez-Montoro, Nimmi Gowrinathan, Jeremy Grant, Valerie Gregori McKenzie, Susan Groce, Jeff Grocott, Peter Harling, Sonya Heppinstal, Richard Horsey, Chris Hougie, Frances House, Kristin Huckshorn, James Huntington-Whiteley, Sarah Jackson-Han, Cynda Johnston, Tim Jones, Sidney Jones, Tom Judge, Tim Karr, Maïssa Khattab, Stephanie Kleine-Ahlbrandt, Bernard Knoll-Tudor, Michael Kovrig, Stephen Laifer, Marcos Lampert, Karen Landgren, Mark Lattimer, Frankie Lawe-Davies, An-My Le, Jennifer Leonard, Vincent Lepinay, Heather Li, David Lindgren, John MacDougall, Peter Mares, Leo Mares, Samantha Marshall, Ian Martin, Philip McClellan, John Miller, Jonathan Miller, June Miller, Nhu Miller, Tom Miller, Charlotte Montpezat, Mark Munger, Sarah Murray, Joanna Nathan, John Norris, Julian Okwu, Verena Paravel, Vasek Pecha, Charles Petrie, Nga Pham, Elizabeth Pisani, John Poirier, Mark Jude Poirier, Marko Prelec, Teresa Raffo, Steve Rasin, Temple

ACKNOWLEDGMENTS

Richardson, Jacob Rinck, Candace Rondeaux, Jason Rosenbaum, Thierry Sanders, Alexandra Sauvegrain, Anya Schiffrin, Dick Schumacher, Adam Schwarz, Tom Scurlock, Michael Shaikh, Julie Sheils, Mark Sidel, Rob Stenekes, Joe Stiglitz, Edy Sri, Aude Thibaut de Maisières, Bella Thomas, Barbara Tierney, Armenak Tokmajyan, Zach Vertin, Natasha Walter, Teresa Whitfield, Doug Williams, Francie Williamson, Kirk Williamson, Ceri Willmott, Xie Yanmei, and, of course, my family: Catherine, Henry, George and Mary Spender, and Bill, Caroline, Ed and Jack Templer.

PROLOGUE

In October 1971, the Shah of Iran threw a party, and before it had even begun, it was declared the Party of the Century. Before it was over, it had been written off as a disaster.

Newspapers reported that it was the most expensive such event ever held, costing as much as two billion dollars. At the ruins of Persepolis, the ceremonial capital of the Achaemenids—the dynasty that founded the Persian Empire and ruled it for 220 years—what passed for the great and the good at the start of that troubled decade gathered in a city of tents. Amid the monarchs, former monarchs, and sundry lesser royals were an array of tyrants, thieves, and some low-rung envoys, including a pair of awkward Chinese diplomats trying to survive the perils of the Cultural Revolution. Ancient dynasts, communist apparatchiks, arriviste crooks, dowdy bicycling monarchs, and self-promoting socialites all came together somewhat uncertainly to mark a fictional anniversary. The American magazine *Newsweek* summed up the attitude of many when it wrote the Shah "invited virtually everybody who was anybody—but mostly nobodies showed up." The event marked the anniversary of Cyrus the Great's establishment of the Persian Empire. It was also a coming-out party for Iran and its Shah.

Speaking at the empty tomb of Cyrus at Pasargadae, another Achaemenid capital about 40 kilometers from Persepolis, the

PROLOGUE

Shah paid homage to the man who had built the first great empire, eventually extending from the Balkans and Libya in the West to India in the East. Cyrus the Great was the most admired Persian in history, founder of a great dynasty, disciplined and ruthless, but also the king who freed the Jews from bondage in Babylon and earned rare acclaim in the Bible as Cyrus the Messiah. His empire would last from 550 BCE to 330 BCE until it was broken up by the Macedonian, Alexander the Great, who marked his own triumph by burning Persepolis to the ground.

This event was to focus more on Cyrus than Alexander, a reviled figure in Persian history, emblematic of a lingering toxicity between Iran and the West that goes back to the complicated and long relationship between the Persians and the Greeks. In 1971, geopolitics was a never-ending source of concern in the Shah's palaces. He had felt his country and his crown had been in a precarious state for decades. This was changing, and a new era of confidence was emerging, even if some dangers lurked. The British were retreating from "East of Suez," handing over to the Shah responsibility as the main power in the Persian Gulf. Oil prices were rising, and the exploitative deals made by Western companies had been rewritten. Richard Nixon was encouraging allies to look after their own security, mostly by allowing them almost limitless access to American weapons. The United States president and his National Security Advisor, Henry Kissinger, had anointed the Shah as their key surrogate in the Middle East.

This was the moment the Shah emerged as a new force. He had started his reign in 1941 as a shy and skinny prince, looking like someone who needed to grow into his suits and his job. By 1971, he was not that different in some ways. A sometimes-insecure man with a taste for call girls from Madame Claude's in Paris, he was still often stiff and unsmiling, lacking a light touch and yet not inspiring the fear that his father aroused. He was born the son of a former army sergeant in a Persian Cossack

PROLOGUE

regiment and would die as an emperor-in-exile. The years in between were dramatic. Three wives; two nearly deadly assassination attempts; coups, exile, and return; a plane crash; moments of humiliation and years of adoration. He knew many of the key figures of the twentieth century and indeed became one himself. But throughout all of this, he was never able to provide a convincing rationale for his aims and ambitions. In a land of storytellers, he never controlled the narrative.

Today, the Shah is often remembered for the brutality of his reign and his overthrow by Ayatollah Ruhollah Khomeini, the Shia cleric whose idea of religious rule has shaped Iran and the Middle East since. Images of Pahlavi rule established in the 1970s, particularly by emerging human rights advocacy groups, have persisted without much scrutiny, and the Shah remains, somewhat unfairly, as a symbol of tyranny and corruption.

Almost every positive aspect of life in Iran today can be traced back to the fifty-four years of Pahlavi rule, during which a modern nation emerged from a century of neglect and exploitation. In those five decades, the country experienced some of the fastest development anywhere at any time, lifting millions out of poverty. Despite being governed for forty years by a theocratic regime that has suppressed many freedoms, its population is among the best educated in the Middle East, largely due to universities established under the Pahlavis. Mullahs have attempted to limit women's public roles, but they have reemerged as a force for change. Iran boasts the most vibrant cultural scene in the region, thanks in large part to the rise of numerous painters, sculptors, writers, and filmmakers in the mid-twentieth century, as well as the inspiration and education they provided. The country has some world-class museums, created half a century before any of its neighbors recognized the value of investing in culture. Its rich history and heritage were better preserved during that time than before or since. A large diaspora has maintained the

PROLOGUE

diverse religious and cultural traditions that the Islamic government has tried to suppress at home.

Little of this is recognized. Instead, we have tales of excess and greed, corruption and torture. That was undeniably a part of Iran in the 1970s, but it is far from the whole story. It was a moment in which the country took several wrong turns, but it was also a period of cultural growth and innovation, economic surges, and transformation. The Shah developed a taste for the grandiose, and it was that part of his character that would come to the fore in the last decade of his reign, undermining prospects for his dynasty. His choices would shape Iran, for better and for worse, for the next five decades, remaking the landscape of religion, politics, and everyday life across the Middle East, but also establishing a more profound sense of history and identity among Iranians that would prove impossible to erase.

* * *

In October 1971, Walt Disney World opened in Orlando, and Greenpeace was founded in Vancouver. The Peoples' Republic of China joined the United Nations, taking the seat held by the Republic of China on Taiwan. The British parliament voted to join the European Economic Community, as the European Union was then known. Idi Amin came to power in Uganda, and Charles Manson was sentenced to death in California. South Vietnam, with American backing, invaded Laos. *Soul Train* appeared on U.S. television, and China canceled its national day ceremonies in Beijing for the first time since 1949 amid rumors of a coup attempt. Polygamy was banned in Hong Kong, and *Jesus Christ Superstar* opened on Broadway.

That year, Pakistan's military carried out a genocide in East Bengal but was eventually defeated by an Indian intervention that led to the creation of Bangladesh. Rebellion was afoot around the world: the Tupamaros urban guerrillas kidnapped the British

PROLOGUE

ambassador in the Uruguayan capital Montevideo, the Weather Underground bombed a men's room in the United States Capitol, and the Tamil People's Liberation Front began a war against the Sri Lankan government seeking an independent state. Qatar and Oman became independent nations, while a sandy collection of British colonies known as the Trucial States came together as the United Arab Emirates. The Pentagon Papers were published, and the voting age in the United States was lowered to 18. The first Internet chat room opened, the first email was sent, and the first CAT scanner and soft contact lenses were sold. *Foreign Affairs*, the house journal of the Council on Foreign Relations, warned of the problems of affluence. Western countries were "groping uncertainly with the consequences of their own success," including disaffected youth, ruptured societies, and environmental degradation. The Montreux Casino burned down during a Frank Zappa concert, inspiring the Deep Purple song "Smoke on the Water." Elon Musk and Charlotte Gainsbourg were born, and Coco Chanel died.

In Iran, the economy was growing apace, exceeding its target of 10 per cent. Prospects were rosy, according to *The Economist Intelligence Unit*, except for agriculture, which was failing even to match the growth in population. Iran was the fastest-expanding market for imports across Asia outside of Japan, with excellent credit and growing interest from investors. A railway connecting Iran to Turkey and Europe started operations. Tensions built between Arab and Iranian communities in these countries and elsewhere as Iran signaled its intentions to seize three islands in the Straits of Hormuz at the mouth of the Gulf. Nine years of land reforms came to an end, with some 2.3 million families reportedly benefiting.

Decades do not begin or end neatly. What we think of as the 1960s in terms of politics, style, and social change was still going in 1971. It was a time of rebellion and reinvention, marked by

PROLOGUE

the anti-war movement in the United States and burgeoning demands for personal and political freedom around the world. Third World liberation movements were all the rage, particularly among students, while the libertine aspects of the 1960s—drugs, flower power, dropping out, and tuning in—were still essential parts of a youth culture, but one that was taking on a decidedly sour tone. Of course, these co-existed, unhappily mostly, with the conservatism of Richard Nixon, anxieties about terrorism, rebellion, and hijackings, as well as the ripples of something deeper and perhaps even more malign. This was the pushback that would emerge in the 1970s: the transformation of economics, society, and liberalism—the ending of the post-war consensus in Europe and the harsher economic vision of neo-liberalism. Christianity and Islam would resist modernity and re-align themselves, ending their apolitical positions and trying hard to dominate new structures of power.

Trying to locate a tipping point here is a challenge. Sex may have begun in 1963, "between the Chatterley ban and the Beatles' first LP", in the words of the British poet Philip Larkin, but it is hard to put a date on the end of the 1960s. Was it the Manson murders in August 1969 or the killings at Kent State on 4 May 1970? Was it Nixon's landslide in 1972, or was it the deadly Rolling Stones concert at Altamont in 1969? And what does the end of a decade mean, except as a nostalgic marker for baby boomers constantly revisiting their youth? Historians often avoid focusing on events, instead concentrating on the underlying social forces at work. However, there is a recognition that historical time is not always even—tensions build up and then something breaks, much like an earthquake. The world is suddenly re-aligned. In the 1970s, pressures were building up in Iran, great seismic forces from near and afar, of enormous consequence and yet hard to see at the time.

Was the Shah's party a marker? It was a moment in which the Pahlavi dynasty attempted to establish a national identity, a move

PROLOGUE

that ultimately failed in the short term but has proven surprisingly durable. By the time the Shah fled on 16 January 1979, a shrunken figure huddled in a thick coat, barely acknowledging the bowing and weeping flunkies on the tarmac at Mehrabad Airport, he had lost support from almost all segments of Iranian society. Even the military did not back him at the end. Just two weeks later, on 1 February 1979, a crowd of more than a million came out to welcome back Ayatollah Ruhollah Khomeini after fifteen years of exile.

* * *

My interest in Iran began near the end of the Pahlavi dynasty. I was living in Germany. Long before the days of iPads, smartphones, and other ways to entertain bored children, there were magazines. My mother read a stolidly Germanic women's magazine called *Bunte*, a mix of leathery Teutonic sub-celebrities (boring) and astonishingly graphic photographs of wars and disasters such as plane crashes (fascinating). The years of the Revolution, 1978 and 1979, were the time I developed an addiction to the news. *Bunte*, the best-selling magazine in Germany by then, had the most engaging coverage of several horrific events and showed them in all their gory details: the Revolution in Iran, the suicides and murders by followers of Jim Jones at the People's Temple in Guyana, and the deadly collision of two Boeing 747s on the ground on the Spanish island of Tenerife. *Bunte*, founded after the war by the French as a vehicle for de-Nazification, made for compelling reading.

Stacks of old magazines yielded fascinating stories about the Shah and his family. *Bunte* had been obsessed with the Empress, and she must have appeared in every other edition of the weekly. Indeed, she still does. A less-than-exhaustive search of *Bunte* yielded thirty-three issues featuring her on the cover. There, amidst the horoscopes and coverage of paunchy old roués like

PROLOGUE

Gunter Sachs, heir to the Opel car fortune and third husband of Brigitte Bardot, were lengthy features that showed a royal family that was exotic and far less bovine than the British royals. They posed on ski slopes and on motorbikes, had waterside palaces and ruled over a country that seemed more connected to the future than Britain or Germany in that drab decade. Iran had an undeniable glamour in colors of peacock blue and gold that was entirely lacking in the mustard yellow polyester of German life in the 1970s.

I had also developed a precocious taste for airport thrillers—the embossed metal cover school of literature. One of the biggest bestsellers of the time was *The Crash of '79*, an apocalyptic vision of what would happen if an Iranian dictator, a very thinly disguised version of the Shah, tried to use nuclear weapons to control the world's oil supply. With all the economic and social turmoil of that decade and the looming threats of the worsening Cold War, it all seemed horribly plausible.

In 1978, the images in German magazines changed. There were photographs of angry crowds in Tehran and the stern, black-eyed cleric Ayatollah Khomeini. What had seemed like a country charging into the future took a shocking turn to the past. From then on, the image of Iran went from bad to worse. From imprisoning American diplomats for 444 days to the seemingly endless war with Iraq, the country was blighted by chaos and violence. Having once appeared as a sunny and forward-looking place, it now seemed to be populated by scowling men with raised fists. My fascination only grew as I became haunted by the photographs of bodies on makeshift gallows and the stridency of young Iranians such as Masoumeh Ebtekar, the gratingly smug spokeswoman for the hostage takers. I pored over the reporting of the doomed United States hostage rescue effort and the fallout that crushed Jimmy Carter's chances of re-election. The year of the revolution was one of astonishing change:

PROLOGUE

Margaret Thatcher, Deng Xiaoping, and Khomeini came to power, and Ronald Reagan became the frontrunner in the United States presidential race. Millions of us who came of age in the 1980s and afterwards had our lives shaped by these leaders. Meanwhile, the Shah and his wife began their sad odyssey as they were denied refuge by former allies who had once traveled to Tehran to fawn over them. Shuttling from rented houses to hospital rooms secured with guards, Khomeini and the press pursued the Shah, a figure wasting away in every sense. The journey would be chronicled in William Shawcross's compelling book, *The Shah's Last Ride*. It traced his fraught exile through Egypt, Morocco, the Bahamas, Mexico, Panama, and finally Egypt again as Margaret Thatcher, Jimmy Carter, Valéry Giscard d'Estaing, and other former friends averted their eyes.

1

BEFORE THE PARTY

9 OCTOBER 1971

Jaafar Sharif-Emami stepped forward in front of the modern domed building that housed the Iranian Senate and presented a cylindrical leather case to two elaborately bearded and costumed soldiers. Inside, inscribed on deer-skin parchment, was a message to the Shah from Sharif-Emami, the president of the Senate, on behalf of the Iranian people, thanking the monarch for his rule. The two soldiers kissed the cylinder and began a journey on horseback of 800 kilometers from Tehran to Persepolis, once the ceremonial capital of the Persian Empire. Cyrus the Great established the first postal service of similarly attired men on horses to connect his far-flung peoples. Now the two riders would start the relay to deliver the message to a ruler marking his own expansive vision of power.

At Persepolis, a final frenzy was underway to welcome one of the largest gatherings of royalty and political leaders since the Congress of Vienna in 1814, the event that set the tone and to some degree the rules for all such occasions. Two emperors, six reigning kings, nineteen presidents, an array of crown princes, a

THE SHAH'S PARTY

prince of the Church, and a bevy of prime ministers and others were to spend three days in tents in the desert.

As with many things involving Iran and foreigners, the history of the party is rife with gossip, resentments, exaggerations, paranoia, and deceit. A celebration that began with the aim of making the world aware of Iran's rich culture and history led to a backlash that eroded the status of a royal family that craved respect above all else. Excess and decadence combined with vanity, hubris, and tragedy. Something that was supposed to be joyous turned very sour.

The party was declared the party of the century, an appellation applied to many events in the years of excess between the late 1960s and the 1980s. Truman Capote had thrown his Black and White Ball at the Plaza Hotel in New York in 1966, nominally to honor *Washington Post* publisher Katharine Graham, but actually to celebrate his bestseller, *In Cold Blood*. That storied gathering of New York, indeed global, society had been thrown on a budget. Capote spent just $16,000, serving guests Taittinger champagne but saving money by decorating the room with cheap balloons and offering just a late supper of scrambled eggs.

Marie-Hélène Rothschild of the French branch of the banking family held several contenders for the Party of the Century in the 1970s, starting with her famous Proust Ball, thrown to mark the 100th anniversary of the writer's birth. Some 700 guests dressed in fin de siècle finery, fishing out tiaras that had not seen much use during the supposedly egalitarian 1960s. Cecil Beaton photographed the guests as they danced in a glasshouse decorated with 1,500 palms. Rothschild threw an even more infamous affair a year later at the Château de Ferrières. With its Surrealist theme, this masked ball still has conspiracy theorists puzzling over its occult vibe and the extravagant headgear worn by men and women alike. Copulating turtles and mannequins topped the tables, along with plates covered in fur. Audrey Hepburn wore a birdcage over her head. Salvador Dalí attended, dressed in his usual manner and posing in front of his image of Mae West. The entire château was lit to look from the outside as though it were on fire. Invitations had been written so they could only be read in a mirror, and the dessert was a naked woman made of sugar lying on a bed of roses. The party inspired scenes in the Stanley Kubrick film *Eyes Wide Shut* and still stirs the fevered imaginations of those who believe the Rothschilds run the Illuminati.

Malcolm Forbes, the publisher of the eponymous business magazine, hired Concorde and two other jets to fly 600 guests to his seventieth birthday party at his Mendoub Palace in Tangiers in 1989. As the guests disembarked from the jets, 300 Berber horsemen saluted them on the runway, followed by a serenade from kilted bagpipe players. Outrage ensued; conspicuous consumption can always be contrasted with suffering somewhere on the planet. Forbes spent several million dollars on the party, but even so, it was not a great success with the jet set. The hotel had not been finished; it smelled of fish and paint, and the air conditioning was inadequate. Hairdryers caused the power to go out. Celebrities were forced into the horror of sharing rooms; a certain lack of gratitude was expressed to the host. His guests were mostly stodgy corporate figures whose companies advertised in his magazine, mixed in with a few actors and fashion designers to lend some luster to the event. They dined in five tents around his palace before fireworks were set off to Ravel's Bolero, played twice through. Most of the cost was written off as a business expense.

Only the most gauche, tawdry, or unashamedly self-promoting would seek out the title of Party of the Century. Those around the Shah had a more serious aim. They wanted to promote the celebration as one of the most important gatherings of world leaders ever. It would bring together East and West, communist and capitalist, the newly rising powers of the South and the

THE SHAH'S PARTY

ancient monarchies of the North. Haile Selassie, Emperor of Ethiopia, would be able to share his views on China, having just met Mao Zedong a few days earlier. Leaders from the United States and elsewhere would be able to confer with friends and rivals. Monarchs from around the world, bound by their unusual and increasingly precarious status, could compare notes on whatever it is that monarchs care most about. Survival and money were at the forefront of many minds.

Among the guests were some of the oddest figures of the twentieth century. There were great national heroes, like Marshal Tito of the Socialist Federal Republic of Yugoslavia, who had forged their nations and then held them together by force of will. Some were truly awful despots like Nicolae Ceaușescu, whose totalitarian vision would shatter the lives of Romanians. Mobutu Sese Seko, the murderous and obscenely corrupt ruler of Zaire, mingled with the gruff president of apartheid South Africa. Members of dynasties that would die out and those that would endure against the odds mixed with obscure bureaucrats whose names are already lost in the mists of history. Leaders who had put on mantles of enormous power but whose legitimacy would hang by a thread were placed on the same level as elected leaders. The gathering would say much about the politics and those in power in the early 1970s. The idealism of the postcolonial moment was deeply tarnished, and even the moral landscape of the Cold War was foggy by then. It was perhaps the most cynical and corrupt crowd ever to gather in history. In subsequent years, almost all would be tarnished by scandal, be overthrown, or die in disgrace.

And so, on their jets, some piloted by their own hands, they gathered in Shiraz on 12 October 1971, and were driven in fleets of new Mercedes limousines and buses to an enormous city of fifty tents.

BEFORE THE PARTY

12 October 1971

The blue and white helicopters set down in a swirl of pale desert sand. Standing in the heat and dust were members of the Imperial court, wearing Napoleonic hats topped with ostrich feathers and clad in new French-made uniforms, each embroidered with a mile of gleaming gold thread. Women were in evening dress and long gloves, even though it was eleven in the morning, and the temperature at Pasargadae was already over 30 degrees centigrade.

They had gathered at this parched and isolated place to pay tribute to Cyrus the Great, founder of the Persian Empire, King of Kings, The Great King, Emperor of the Rims of the World, King of Babylon, King of Anshan, King of Sumer and Akkad, and King of the Four Corners of the World. Shah Mohammad Reza stepped from the helicopter with his family: his wife, Farah Diba, the young Crown Prince, his three other children, and the Queen Mother. The women were all in long gowns and tiaras. Tiny versions had been made for the two young princesses.

The Shah walked past the 3,000 soldiers and down a ramp to face the tomb of the first Persian monarch. A monolith of rough, pale marble dating to before 500 BCE, the building commands with its simplicity and the vast size of the cut stones that make up the six-stepped platform. At the top of this truncated pyramid is a simple sepulcher with a gabled roof. Inside, it was once lavishly decorated with gold and precious stones, all of which are now long gone. Arrian of Nicomedia, a Greek historian of the second century CE, described Alexander the Great visiting the tomb and reading an inscription: "Passer-by, I am Cyrus, who gave the Persians an empire, and was King of Asia. Begrudge me not this monument." A nice line, but there is no evidence that it ever existed.

The tomb was in what was once the empire's most important city, of which very little survives except this monument, the remains of a fort, and the outline of one of the earliest Persian gardens. For many centuries, the tomb, surrounded then by forests and lush greenery, was believed to be the burial place of King Solomon's mother, Bathsheba. After the Arab conquest of Persia, it was incorporated into a mosque complex that venerated her. The remains of that thirteenth-century construction had been cleared away in preparation for the ceremony. The aim was to take people back far before the Arab conquest and the introduction of Islam to Iran.

"O Cyrus, Great King, King of Kings, Achaemenian King, King of the Land of Iran," the Shah began in a rather thin, quavering voice. "I, the Shahanshah, offer thee salutations from Myself and from My Nation. Cyrus, Great King, King of Kings, Noblest of the Noble, Hero of the history of Iran and the World, rest in peace for we are awake and will always remain awake."

It was an emotional moment for the generally buttoned-down ruler. The speech had been written by the court's cultural advisor, Shojaeddin Shafa, as a way of aligning the two kings across the long stretch of history. Both struggled in their time to establish legitimacy; however, they marshalled enormous ambition and resources to expand their reach far beyond the borders of Persia.

The Shah was never a confident speaker, but he rarely practiced either. This time, he had gone over the speech in detail, knowing that it would not just reach his compatriots but was a statement to the world of Iran's emerging power and his own growing claims as a monarch.

A sandstorm gathered nearby, a beige whirlwind rose from the desert, and then, as rapidly as it appeared, it blew itself out. It was taken as a sign of good fortune for the festivities. Another 101-gun salute was fired, and a large wreath was laid by the tomb. With this short ceremony, the celebrations to mark the 2,500th year of the Iranian monarchy began. The Imperial family returned to their helicopters. The blades kicked up another dust storm, and they were gone. Everyone else had a long car ride back to Shiraz.

* * *

On 16 October 1970, exactly one year before the party, an Afghan family with four children left their village outside Kabul and traveled to the holy city of Mashhad in Iran. They were on a pilgrimage along with others who visited the northeastern city to pay tribute to Imam Reza, the eighth of the twelve Shia Imams, who was martyred there in 818 CE. After a few days, their youngest child developed a rash and was taken to a clinic. While traveling through the border area of Afghanistan, the child had picked up the smallpox virus, *variola major*.

Although a local health worker rapidly diagnosed the girl, the virus had already spread to her two siblings and to other pilgrims crammed together in a poorer neighborhood of the city. Mashhad receives millions of pilgrims each year from across the Shia communities of the Middle East and Central Asia. Many were packed into hostels, sleeping together in wooden beds or on the floor.

The toddler would have suffered from a high fever and aching limbs, similar to the symptoms of a severe case of the flu. Shortly afterwards, an aggressive rash would have spread over her skin, with the pox merging into rafts of painful scabs. Had she survived, she would have had immunity for life, but her skin quite possibly would have been ravaged. The disease was a scourge going back thousands of years that had once killed hundreds of thousands each year and was responsible for a third of cases of blindness. Soon, crusted, pus-filled sores would cover the skin and clog the throat, almost eating the patient alive. About a third of patients died in this phase of the disease. Those that survived would gradually see the pustules scab over and fall off, leaving behind deep scars. Throughout this time,

THE SHAH'S PARTY

sufferers were emitting a cloud of viruses, which were caught in droplets of saliva or mucus, or in the dried pus that soaked clothes and sheets.

The child was patient zero in one of the last conflagrations of the disease. Smallpox, which is unique to humans, has a mortality rate of 30 per cent and is believed to have caused 10 per cent of all deaths in the past thousand years, amounting to as many as a billion people. It had been known for centuries in Iran: the ninth-century Persian physician known as Al Rhazes was the first writer to understand the nature of the dreaded disease, distinguishing between measles and smallpox. He also observed that if you survived, you would never get it again, an insight that underlies vaccination. For centuries, nomads in Iran would milk cows with cuts on their hands, as this was believed to give them immunity to smallpox. Long before Edward Jenner discovered that English milkmaids enjoyed some resistance to the illness, Iranians were inoculating their children against the scourge.

From Mashhad, other pilgrims took the virus back to Iraq. A 38-year-old Yugoslav Muslim cleric called Ibrahim Hoti contracted the illness there and took it back to his home in Kosovo in February 1972. He started to feel achy and unwell with a fever and a rash and took to his bed. However, the illness did not seem severe, and he returned to work a few days later. In early March, a young teacher, Latif Mumdzic, arrived in Hoti's town to start a graduate degree at a teaching institute. He fell ill and was treated with penicillin for his fever at a local medical center. His condition worsened, and he was eventually taken to a specialist hospital in Belgrade, where he was said to be suffering from an allergy to the anti-bacterial drug. In fact, he had smallpox. By the time he died on 10 March, he had infected thirty-eight people, including nine doctors and nurses. Of those infected by him, eight would die.

Yugoslavia declared martial law to stop the spread of the virus. More than 10,000 people were forced to remain in requisitioned hotels under army guard. The entire population of the country was vaccinated again. But of the 175 people who were infected, thirty-five died. The outbreak had moved from Afghanistan through Iran and Iraq, killing an unknown number of people. It was to lead to the last outbreak of the disease in Europe before eradication.

In 1941, the Iranian parliament passed a law requiring all children to be vaccinated and to show certificates before they were admitted to school. The program never took off outside a few wealthier cities. Many villages were inaccessible and lacked electricity for refrigerating the vaccine. Iran still had many nomads who remained unvaccinated unless a medical team happened across them. Central Asia had long been a source of the virus, and the pilgrims, traders, and travelers who crossed the area had for centuries moved it to new populations. Historically, it was a disease that hit children, and it had a significant impact on child mortality. If you survived to adulthood, the belief was generally that you were immune.

Iran had officially eradicated the disease in 1963, but it was not uncommon for the virus to arrive from Afghanistan. As late as the 1960s, tens of thousands were still dying each year around the world. Outbreaks occurred throughout the region, usually brought in from South Asia, where the disease was still endemic. In most cases, they were dealt with swiftly through isolation and vaccination. Still, none of the countries in the Middle East had effective public health systems, and almost all preferred to keep outbreaks under wraps, reporting much lower numbers than experts believed were realistic. Saudi Arabia, for example, did not want to jeopardize the Haj pilgrimages by revealing the extent of outbreaks there each year.

In 1971, Iran reported just twenty-nine cases of smallpox to the World Health Organization. In fact, the disease was spreading across the country. Iran rarely reported the true number of cases, but in comparison to its neighbors, it was a cosmopolitan and open country in which it was hard to hide the disease. Soon, people outside Iran began to hear stories of an outbreak.

Even as reports of a mass outbreak reached the U.S. government, which contacted the WHO in November 1971, asking for details, Iran continued to deny there was a problem. Not only was it under-reporting the illness, but it was also vaccinating vulnerable people with a weak vaccine. Persistent queries from the WHO, then engaged in a massive global eradication program, were met with inconsistent answers. Only after the celebrations were over did Iran finally request the effective freeze-dried vaccine that brought the epidemic to a halt in the country. By that stage, the virus had spread to Iraq, Syria, Yugoslavia, and eventually to Germany.

In August 1972, one of the top WHO officials involved in the eradication effort was finally allowed to visit Iran to investigate the outbreak. The American epidemiologist D.A. Henderson toured the country, interviewing doctors. Many were closed-mouthed, but some defied their fear of the intelligence agency SAVAK to tell him the truth. One told him of his distress at having personally inoculated a young girl in Shiraz who later died of the illness because the vaccine was so weak. Although the official figures spoke of just dozens dead, Henderson would estimate that the disease had struck 8,000 people and 2,000 had died in Iran during the twenty-two months of the outbreak. Those deaths could have been avoided if health officials had not been so fearful of reporting the disease at a time when it might have disrupted plans for the celebrations. Instead, mass vaccinations with an effective vaccine only began in late 1971, once all the guests had left.

It was known by the time of the party that there were some 200 cases in nearby Shiraz; it was reported in passing by *The Washington Post* gossip columnist Sally Quinn. No other journalist seemed to notice. The issue was not taken up elsewhere; indeed, it was almost another year before Professor Henderson could visit and estimate the true extent of the outbreak, which was one of the worst to occur anywhere in the final decade of smallpox's ravages.

It is impossible now to ascertain whether senior officials were aware of the outbreak and what they did to control it. Still, it is hard to imagine that a mass vaccination of millions of people could have been carried out without the top officials in a very centralized government being aware of it. It is also hard to imagine that they did not know of the decision to avoid bringing in the WHO, which could have saved thousands of lives, not just in Iran but in the neighboring countries where the disease soon spread. The eradication of smallpox is one of the greatest triumphs of public health, and it required a level of global cooperation that has never been seen since. But eradication depended on the weakest link: if one country still harbored it, then there was a risk of a new epidemic. Iran, for a moment, was the weakest link. Even in their official reporting to the WHO in 1977, the government tried to hide the scale of the outbreak, saying that only thirty-one people had died in 1971 and 1972.

The response to the outbreak revealed a problem that lay deep in the Shah's Iran. This was a bureaucracy that, for all its claims of modernity, could be indifferent to the suffering of people. It preferred silence, conformity, and the image of modernity to the reality of a country that was still struggling with many aspects of development. An honest assessment of situations and a quick response were not the priority. Instead, there was always an effort to present their best face to the world. There is a similarity to all such regimes; they abhor the realities of the present day, preferring either imagined pasts or fantastical futures. The Shah's favorite point of reference was that Iran would soon be like Japan, prosperous, innovative, and a challenge to the dominance of the West. And yet at Persepolis, at the tomb of Cyrus, and at the monument to Iranian kings he would unveil, he referred to a past that was so distant it only had the remotest connection to the present.

The stifling of voices since the 1950s had narrowed the political world to the point that many once moderate nationalists had been swept up in the global movements of anti-colonialism, Marxism, and forms of liberation theology. The communist Tudeh Party had been crushed, the nationalist movement of the ousted Prime Minister Mohammad Mossadegh had been defeated in 1953, and the Shah believed he had the mullahs on the back foot after the violent suppression of protests in 1963. But underneath the apparent success and calm of the White Revolution, resistance was growing. The celebrations at Persepolis would bring it out into the open.

* * *

In 1971, Iran was emerging from a decade of massive changes in which land reforms, the expansion of education, and rapid industrialization had been pulled together into what Mohammad Reza liked to call "The Shah-People Revolution" or sometimes the "White Revolution", to stress that it was not communist and did not involve bloodshed. From 1961, the Shah had come under pressure from the Kennedy administration to focus more on development to counter the threat of communism, rather than relying solely on military means. The spigots of United States assistance were opened, and the Shah was pushed to focus less on acquiring new weapons and more on dealing with an impoverished population. He bitterly resented the pressure, but he had little choice, given that the economy still depended on aid. Taking land from the feudal families and the mullahs, who often accumulated it through donations and bequests, was a way to enhance the lives of rural people while also helpfully undermining those who might challenge his power.

Land reform and a greater role for women were to be a prelude to both economic growth and industrialization. The policies were supposed to take control away from absentee landlords and give it to farmers, freeing them to grow whatever they wished and to sell it where they could command the highest prices. But the reality did not live up to the hope or hype. While it was touted as a major step forward, with the Shah bragging endlessly that Iran was now "more socialist" than Sweden, land reform unsettled rural life without providing the support that farmers needed. In arid Iran, land was important, but water was more so, and the reforms did not always ensure that farmers got what they needed. The country was, and tragically still is, woefully underdeveloped when it comes to agriculture.

Nearly a decade before the party, the Shah had issued the first of what would be known as the Six Decrees, a series of state orders that would change Iranian society, mostly in ways the Shah did not expect and never understood. This was a 1960s-style development from above, high above, at a time when it was seen as the best way to manage the transformation from agriculture to industry, even though there were as many failures as successes. China had tried it with the Great Leap Forward, the Soviet Union had done it with its First Five-Year Plan, Brazil had launched into its high modernist phase in the 1950s, and Iran after 1962. Vast industrial interventions could transform a society, but they also threw up many unpredictable challenges and imposed heavy costs in social upheaval. The Harvard sociologist Talcott Parsons had predicted that traditional values and structures would fall away as a society modernized. Industrialization, globalization, urbanization, and education would overwhelm the old and usher in the new. This was seen as an unalloyed good.

Reza Shah had used land seizures from the clergy and aristocracy to concentrate power in his hands and bring regional landowners into his fold, whether they liked it or not. The consequence was that security of tenure was weak, and feudal landholders had little incentive to invest in improvements or infrastructure. By the end of his rule, rural Iran was even more insecure as *noblesse oblige* faded. Wealthy landlords moved to the cities, increasingly centers of money and power, leaving behind bailiffs who often acted in arbitrary and cruel ways. Tenants could not save money, and few invested in new tools or seeds. Rural life was harsh at the best of times; the system in Iran made it much worse than necessary.

In 1962, 56 per cent of agricultural land was owned by just 1 per cent of the population, with a third of land owned by just 0.2 per cent. Smallholders had just 10 per cent of the land. The government, crown, and religious establishments owned the most, as well as much of the forest and grazing land. Reza Shah had made a few desultory efforts to improve the lot of peasants, but new laws on water consumption and ensuring that land was kept in productive use were enforced by governors who were from the landowning classes and had no great interest in the people they ruled. In the brief democratic interregnum that followed his ouster by the British, there was little interest in reforms in the Majlis, or parliament, as it was mostly made up of the same landholders. By the early 1960s, the Shah was under both domestic and foreign pressure to make some changes. A law was sent to the Majlis in 1959.

Ayatollah Mohamed Hossein Borujerdi, the leading religious figure of the time and then the sole *marja-e taqlid* (source of emulation for the faithful), complained it was against Sharia because of the threat to religious endowments. Landowners in parliament watered it down, and what emerged was never enforced. The country's largest landowner, the Shah himself, had transferred the land his father had mostly stolen to the government in 1941, and after 1951 began to return it to its previous owners while using the income for an Imperial social services fund. In 1962, the Shah decided it was time to push back against the mullahs. A new law limited the amount of land any owner could hold, giving the government powers to purchase land and redistribute it. Landlords who owned significant concentrations of farmland were forced to give it up. The mullahs feared a loss of income and power.

The Shah took control of the process, ending any pretense at democracy and identifying himself fully with the White Revolution. Alongside the creation of a new class of landowning farmers, the Shah was intent on industrialization. A utopia of wealth and freedom, under the Shah, was up ahead if people just applied themselves. He was all about modernity; those opposed to his plans were considered backward and feudal, and would be dealt with harshly. "Progress" was the *mot du jour*. The Shah repeated it at every opportunity. He was also not shy about denigrating his opponents:

"Of course, we should not be surprised that in this population of the country, we can estimate that several hundred people, don't understand," he said.

> This inability to understand may have several reasons. One is that they simply don't have the capacity for thought and understanding. These people, then brains and thought work in different ways. They call these people shallow. One may also call them many other things, but in any case, maybe they are not really to blame since nature has not allowed their small and tired brains the ability to understand or think.

The White Revolution was a political process to connect a series of reforms to the Shah to consolidate his rule and associate rising living standards with him personally. This was a part of several efforts—including the eventual celebrations at Persepolis—to link the Shah with thousands of years of unbroken monarchy. But even those involved had various views on where it should end up. As the historian Ali Ansari has noted, the three central figures who conceived and implemented the White Revolution all felt it should end in different places. Asadollah Alam, the longtime friend of the Shah and at the time the head of one of his artificial political parties, saw it as a means to consolidate Imperial power. The Agriculture Minister, Hasan Arsanjani, thought it might lead to the eventual departure of the monarch and a real democracy, and Ali Amini, the reforming prime minister imposed on the Shah by the Kennedy administration, hoped it might put the Shah back in his box as a constitutional monarch. The Shah saw it as a means to undermine the landed aristocracy, his primary political foe at the time, and to create a landed peasantry that would support him.

The Shah had a somewhat Thatcherite view of land ownership *avant le lettre*. Ownership would set farmers free and create a class that owed its present and future to the monarchy. "Land reform in Iran has many different meanings. The aim of this work is not only that we give paper documents to some people and say that they have become the owners of land," he said.

> No, they will become free men who will have elevated heads and independent spirits, with hope for the future, they will become not only the owners of the land which they cultivate but also the owners of their own future and their children's and shareholders in the present administration and the future of the nation.

The problem with reform handed down from on high was that all its shortcomings and tensions would ultimately be blamed on the Shah and not on a government, which might at least have been sackable. Haunted by the violent overthrow of other monarchs in the region and the military coup against the Turkish Prime Minister Adnan Menderes in 1960, the Shah realized that if there was to be a revolution, he had to get out in front of it and claim it for himself. Opponents of reform were labeled as "black," for those with religious objections; red for those on the left, and feudal for those who were trying to protect their landholdings. Having an enemy is always helpful for any political leader—it had certainly helped Mossadegh to have imperial oil thieves to rail against—and the Shah milked this hard.

BEFORE THE PARTY

Opponents had some legitimate points. Many complained it would cause significant social dislocation in villages, and it did. Others said it was essentially undemocratic as the laws had not been put in front of the Majlis, which the Shah had closed at the time. While the Shah had a vision of a modern society, not exactly democratic but orderly and productive, realities were very different. Landowners had looked after their tenants to some degree, although the system of management by agents, or *kadkhuda*, could be feudal and brutal. These agents handed out land to sharecroppers but also doled out floggings and demanded free labor for occasional public works. Some landlords provided seed in bad years and helped farmers negotiate their way through hospitals, courts, and bureaucracies when needed. But there was little deep sense of cooperation between landowner and sharecropper. It was mostly a world of mutual suspicion.

Once farmers received the deeds to their land, they were cut off from even the desultory support of landowners, often including water, seeds, and access to markets. While the Shah was handing over documents in much-publicized ceremonies, landowners were burning down the houses of the supposedly newly landed middle class. Feudal arrangements and attitudes did not just disappear because the Shah willed it, nor was the Ministry of Agriculture up to the task of enforcing the law or supporting the new landowners. Old landlords were often able to retain half their land; in many cases, they took the best land, and half of a village found itself dispossessed. Once relatively egalitarian villages found themselves divided between the landed and the landless. Those removed from their farms had to find jobs, but their pay often declined by as much as half.

The reforms also froze land holdings in many villages. Sharecroppers had drawn lots and changed land every few years so that they did not end up being stuck forever with a small plot or a less productive area. Under the reforms, they ended up with the land they were farming at the time, whatever its size or quality. This further divided villages and stoked resentment. Land distribution was often skewed in favor of the agent and his family and friends; they chose the best land for themselves, and under the reforms, they ended up owning it.

Farmers were to become members of cooperatives when they received their deeds, but the process did not go as planned. Many of these co-ops failed and were replaced by multiple groups, primarily based on family ties or proximity to one another. Wealthier villagers bought tractors and combines to rent out, getting ever richer at the expense of their neighbors. Nobody had taught villagers how to run a cooperative, and the group excluded all those who had been made landless; the response was to return to more traditional arrangements.

The religious establishment was not at all happy with the reforms. Its wealth and power came from land and now it had lost much of it. In their view, land reform was not creating patriotic Shah-loving Iranians; it was creating communists who would oppose religion. Up to then, the mullahs had generally supported the Shah, unsurprisingly, given that the government subsidized many of them. It was established Shia practice to render unto Caesar, and they had always seen a monarchy as better than risking communism. Indeed, the religious establishment had been keen on the Shah's father becoming monarch back in 1925 rather than risk a republic and any slide towards a Kemalist-style secularism.

The Shah had often succeeded by adopting the policies and language of his opponents to undercut them. Criticism from the left was addressed by the White Revolution, which co-opted policies and language from communism but, as the Shah often boasted, without the revolutionary violence. But the confiscatory approach to land reform was profoundly unpopular in influential circles and antithetical to the sort of private sector development after which the Shah hankered so deeply. It had a profoundly distorting effect on the rural economy that would also fuel inflation and shortages. What was the point in investing in agriculture if your land could be taken from you at any time? Agricultural productivity would not be raised by weakening land tenure. Some key advisors had hoped to push the Shah towards reforms of taxation that would increase productivity, by, for example, taxing land not at the rate of real output but potential output. That way, there was a strong incentive for owners to invest in the land and increase productivity. However, to the Shah, this was all playacting and politics—he enjoyed handing out land certificates to farmers, but seemingly showed no interest in the complexities of rural life or the realities of economic management.

In 1966, the cultural vizier Shafa published a multi-volume work on "Pahlavism"—an effort to capture the Shah's ideology of monarchy, modernity, and economic progress. It put much emphasis on the ancient nature of monarchy and that Iranian identity was grounded in this. Indeed, the country had retained its identity precisely because it had been a monarchy for 2,500 years. Monarchs were good, except for the Qajars, of course. They were bad: corrupt, lazy, and despotic. Some good people supported the brief constitutional interregnum from 1906, but a good monarchy was restored when the Pahlavi dynasty began its rule in 1925.

Pahlavism did not incorporate any positive thoughts about democracy. Political parties often fell under the influence of an individual or a foreign power—a phenomenon that was true of many young democracies and of political parties in all the surrounding states. Ansari has pointed out that the ideological poverty of Pahlavism is evident in the five pages that the books devote to the subject. Almost half of the volumes cover economics. While much of the world suffers under various economic systems, Iran was lucky enough to have Pahlavism, which was a

THE SHAH'S PARTY

bespoke system suitable for the people. How exactly it was suitable was never laid out.

By the time 1971 arrived, the Shah seemed to have grown tired of domestic matters and was more focused on regional threats—particularly from Iraq—and his assertion of authority over the Gulf. But when you elevate yourself to become the nation, the very embodiment of its successes and ideals, there is an inevitable moment when people see the widening gap between rhetoric and reality.

2

THE PARTY PLANNER

WHOSE IDEA WAS THIS, ANYWAY?

A British Foreign Secretary might have been responsible for the celebrations at Persepolis and hence possibly contributed to the beginning of the end for the Shah. Iranians, conditioned by a century of British interference, might not find it surprising that Perfidious Albion was behind the costly and ultimately damaging venture. But rather than some deliberate effort to get the Shah to undermine himself with extravagance and excess, it was simply a chance remark. In 1969, Michael Stewart, the Labour Foreign Secretary, was on a tour of Iran and visited Persepolis, accompanied by the Minster of the Court, Asadollah Alam.

At a reception after the tour, he was enthusing about the majesty of the site and his views of the Shah. "Your Empire was founded by Cyrus. Darius extended it and Xerxes preserved it," Michael Stewart told his hosts. "Your present ruler seems to me to possess something of the qualities of all three of these mighty kings."

Alam, who liked to come up with daily praise for his monarch and often needed some honey to help bad news slip down, passed the compliment on to the Shah. And thus, the idea for the party at Persepolis was reborn.

The idea had actually originated back in 1958, emerging from the head of publications and radio, Nosratollah Moinian. He proposed a simple celebration involving all strata of society, presenting their contributions to the development of Iran in the manner of the figures bearing gifts depicted on the Persepolis frieze. Shojaeddin Shafa, a poet, intellectual, translator, and cultural entrepreneur at the court, took up the idea but proposed a more intellectual celebration of the 2,500th anniversary of the Persian Empire, which was due to fall in 1959. However, the exact year the empire was founded is a matter of debate. The aim was "to show the world who we are," according to Mehrdad Pahlbod, the brother-in-law of the Shah who was to become minister of culture, but the emphasis was to be on culture and history. Shafa also wanted to put Iran on the global intellectual map, reminding people that while Iran might be a developing country, it had once been a great empire. He was a moderate politically, more nationalist than an ideologue, having previously served as head of information in the nationalist government of Mohammad Mossadegh, which was overthrown in a 1953 coup. He was also notoriously sycophantic towards the Shah, always weighing every move to his own advantage.

Iran was struggling financially in the early 1960s, and the Shah was facing down internal political opposition, mostly from religious elements enraged by his plans for land reform and expanding rights for women. It was no time for a celebration. In 1962, the Shah decided to delay the plans. Subsequently, the planning committee carried on its work in a somewhat desultory manner, with Shafa slowly rounding up support from the UNESCO and national committees established to support Persian studies and the celebration of the anniversary.

Shafa's influence at court grew in the following years as he wrote many of the Shah's speeches and ghostwrote books for him on the White Revolution. He was in thrall not just to the Shah but to the mythology of Cyrus the Great, ensuring that the ancient king's memory was revived and inserted at the center of Pahlavism. As the historian Robert Steele has written, much of this revival was driven by figures like Shafa, who used the court to boost their standing and implement their projects, often with almost limitless budgets. The Shah mostly went along with it all, flattered by the comparisons to Cyrus and mindful of the need to build a supportive ideology around his regime.

Shafa had been inspired by a festival in Israel to celebrate Cyrus's freeing of the Jews from their exile in Babylon in 539 BCE and for permitting them to rebuild the Temple in Jerusalem. Cyrus appears in the Torah as a Lord Messiah, the only non-Jew to be described that way, and his place in the Bible ensured him the fascinated regard of historians in Europe and Iran. The project tied into an idea being pushed by the regime's ideologues: that the first declaration of human rights had come from Cyrus, whose empire was the first to allow religious freedom and cultural diversity. "Such a vast empire was founded by Cyrus the Great on the principles of liberty and tolerance, freedom of individuals and nations to practice any religion, freedom of expression, and freedom of national habits and customs."

Shafa's ambition was to host a series of conferences, publish some volumes of academic papers, and encourage historians to take ancient Iran seriously, rather than viewing it solely through the eyes of Greeks and Romans. Gradually, plans grew to include monuments to Cyrus, stamps, exhibitions, and a military tattoo.

Nothing much happened during the 1960s when the court was occupied with other concerns. In 1967, after twenty-six years on the throne, the Shah held his coronation, placing the crown on his own head in the manner of Napoleon. The ceremony was relatively modest, with no foreign guests and a carriage ride through the decorated streets of Tehran. There were some new

THE SHAH'S PARTY

Austrian-made coaches, expensive clothes from French couturiers, and the Queen's new crown, but the overall budget was less than three million dollars. By the standards to come, it was far from extravagant.

It was also a sign of the changing times. Pahlavism was all about creating a national culture as distant from that of the clerics as possible. Apart from the Shah kissing a Koran, there was no religious content in the ceremony, and the Shah was not crowned by a religious leader or anointed in the name of God, unlike the coronations of British monarchs. Crowning his wife was a sign of the new freedoms granted by a wise and generous Shah. The message was that all good things stemmed from the progressive monarchy, not from political parties or revolutionary movements.

The event seemed to arouse a taste for spectacle, mostly among courtiers, at a time when Pahlavism was emerging with a new vigor, even if there was little public enthusiasm for this. By 1970, Alam, whose comment to the Shah had prompted the resurrection of the anniversary celebration, oversaw many of the arrangements and had decreed that the events would take place in Persepolis and Tehran. Others had warned that there was no way to accommodate the expected thirty heads of state at Persepolis, and even the hotels in the nearby city of Shiraz were inadequate. Although a range of state visitors from Elizabeth II to Josip Broz Tito of Yugoslavia had visited Persepolis, they tended to fly in for a day trip and return to Tehran. Finally, a year ahead of the events, a Celebration Council was formed, bringing together various parts of the government under Alam, and a date was set for October 1971.

Alam was one of the Shah's closest friends, if it can be said that the monarch had friends. As Minister of the Court, Alam was essentially the chief of staff, dealing with most issues directly run by the Shah and overseeing the lives of the wider royal family. It was Alam who dressed down ambassadors and scolded family members for their excesses, their corruption, and their poor choices in spouses. The Shah did not much like confrontation, and so it was left to Alam to say no to his brothers, sisters, and cousins while also marshalling the foreign diplomatic corps.

The minister came from an aristocratic family and was drafted into government service at an early age. Cosmopolitan, intelligent, and self-indulgent, he became a skilled but tough courtier, able to sugarcoat some of the necessary harshness involved in wrangling the often badly behaved family. Aged just 23, Alam had been appointed provincial governor in Khorasan. He found himself ignored by the corrupt and barely competent local officials who saw him as an effete young aristocrat. One tax inspector was known for being a crook. Alam was said to have invited him to his family home, had him tied to a tree in the midday sun, and went off to play tennis. Whether the story is true or not, officials followed his orders after that.

In 1947, he became the youngest cabinet member, aged just 27, and he would be in government in one way or another for the next thirty years. He served as prime minister at a key moment when the last remnants of democracy were discarded and protests in the religious center of Qom were put down violently. Khomeini was arrested and then sent into exile. Alam had been the steel in the royal spine then and would be again. Had he had his own way, he probably would have had Khomeini killed. It was said that he took control of the armed forces and cut off the Shah's telephones during the 1963 protests so that he could not be countermanded. If it had all gone horribly wrong, the Shah could plead ignorance and blame his prime minister. Alam stepped down as prime minister after just two years. He was always the perfect courtier, ending up spending more than a decade as Minister of the Court after 1966.

After Alam died in 1978, his family published his very revealing diaries, which give many insights into the hidden workings of the court, although not, unfortunately, about the 1971 party. The diaries are one of the most important documents of the Shah's rule. A mix of sycophancy and understated, yet devastating, criticisms of the monarch and his family, they provide a view into the nature of power under the Pahlavis. Unfortunately, several volumes went missing, possibly destroyed by Alam's long-suffering wife. It was an arranged marriage without much love, and Alam was a compulsive philanderer, sharing women with the Shah. For much of the year ahead of the celebrations, he was supposedly too busy to write a diary, and so sadly we lack his insights into what led up to the event and who exactly made the key decisions.

His worldview aligned closely with that of the Shah. With his wealth, family background, and regional power base in Khorasan, he could have chosen an independent route into political life. But in the 1940s and early 1950s, when the political arena was open, he remained loyal to the weak monarch. He offered friendship and encouragement of the Shah's ambitions. Alam believed that a strong monarchy was the only way forward for Iran, and that religious forces, whom he despised, should be crushed.

It was the 1963 protests that many involved in the Revolution would cite as a key starting point for their movement: they launched Khomeini's political career and gave him the prominence he would eventually harness to overthrow the Shah. Many Shia clerics tended to go along with those in power, taking subsidies and providing the required religious services. But there was also a strain of political action in the faith, an entitled sense that they were owed power and a place in society. Land reforms initiated by the Shah to undercut what he saw as the threat from communism mostly undermined the wealth of the clergy and their institutions. This came to a head with the 1963 protests in which Khomeini, still a junior figure in the religious hierarchy, made clear his feelings on the changes sweeping the country. For the rest of his life, Alam regarded the crushing of those protests as his greatest moment in government.

THE PARTY PLANNER

Alam's aristocratic background and his influence as Minister of the Court sometimes led him into a cul-de-sac when it came to understanding his country. When an American ambassador expressed concern about the increasing opposition to the Shah from the Islamic clergy, Alam brushed him off.

> Their time has passed; they're powerless in the face of HIM (His Imperial Majesty) .... Following their opposition to land reform we came down on them so hard that never again can they be considered a contender for power. The grumbling of a couple of mullahs should not conceal the fact that such wretches are a complete irrelevance as long as the Shah is at the helm.

But Alam would eventually change his mind. Just before he died in 1978, he wrote to the Shah from France, warning him that unless he acted rapidly and decisively, he was likely to be overthrown. The Shah was dismissive, saying that Alam "had lost his marbles," but the warning from a friend must have stung. A political master had recovered his vision once he no longer served the Shah. Before his death, he asked his family to publish his diaries only after the fall of the Pahlavi dynasty, something he obviously believed was inevitable and would soon come to pass.

Alam was a devout Francophile, having been raised in a household that served food from Fauchon on the Place de la Madeleine and spoke French as much as Persian. He had a French governess, wife of a Russian army officer, as well as a legion of other tutors. But throughout his life, he was, as the historian Abbas Milani put it, "a unique mix of rustic simplicity, aristocratic refinement and Machiavellian guile." After high school, he attended an agricultural college, and his better-educated enemies later suggested he was almost illiterate, an accusation that was far from the truth. He even enjoyed writing poetry, and his diaries have a unique voice: self-inflating and sometimes self-flagellating; icily critical of the Shah on occasion, misogynistic, myopic, and filled with foreboding. He produced the essential document of the Pahlavi era.

His father was close to the British when Reza Shah was on the throne. This would be a stain on Alam's entire life, making him a target of the many Iranians who still bristled at the colonial attitudes of many British diplomats and others. It may well have been a key to his enduring friendship with the Shah. The British had removed his father from power. He did not want them doing the same to him, and holding one of their camp close to him would at least give him a warning of any such plan. After the Shah's fall, Alam's proximity to power was Exhibit A for those who believed that the British had stage-managed the Revolution. When Alam was appointed prime minister in the early 1960s, the United States Embassy suggested in a report to Washington that the Shah might be signaling to the British that they were still relevant in Iran and that he needed their backing for his reforms.

The Shah once told an interviewer that he did not have friends. He dismissively, and gauchely, said he had "people for jokes and whatever" but no person whom he held in such respect and trust that he would follow his advice unquestioningly. In some ways, this was his downfall. Alam, politically ambitious and determined not to succumb to the sudden dismissal that other courtiers and political figures had suffered when they became too powerful, never seemed to tell him the whole truth, even as he excoriated everyone else as sycophants and lamented the quality of those in government, particularly his rival and enemy, Prime Minister Amir-Abbas Hoveyda.

When it came to the celebrations, Alam was skeptical about the capacity of his own people to provide the necessary standard of service to cope with foreign leaders. He is said to have told his staff that if anything went wrong, "I will kill myself and then I will kill all of you." An incident in 1968 in which Yugoslav President Josip Broz Tito was served lunch in Shiraz at an ordinary Iranian restaurant, complete with flies on the kebabs and buckets of stale water in the kitchen, had sent the Shah into a rage when reported back by a flunky. Tito quite possibly enjoyed his brief brush with normality.

As the event approached, Alam took the issue into his own hands. Although preparations had been going on for ten years, almost nothing had been achieved except an interminable series of meetings. In 1970, Alam had been in France on an extended holiday and, while there, consulted with the decorating firm Jansen. It had become increasingly clear that the single hotel near Persepolis was inadequate and those in Shiraz were both too far away and of too low a quality for heads of state. What was needed was an encampment akin to those Persian kings had used when they traveled. The head designer at Jansen was on to it. The various caterers used to managing events in Iran also warned that they would not be able to pull off something on this scale, so Alam spoke to Maxim's, the famous Parisian restaurant.

The Shah's cultural advisor, Shafa, was appalled. His plan was for a series of gatherings of academics to consider the history and culture of Iran. Committees were formed around the world, and various researchers contributed ideas. One prominent American historian of Persian art, Arthur Pope, took to the task with some relish, suggesting a large new library along the lines of the Library of Congress as well as a military parade and the luxurious tent city. Already, the event was slipping away from Shafa.

The celebration was repeatedly postponed in the 1960s, but when it did start to take shape, it was no longer quite the image of academic seriousness Shafa had proposed. Instead, it began to look like a northern Tehran society wedding. Many of the foreign academics told Shafa that the plans were too oriented towards foreigners and the West. When commentary started appearing in the French press on the extravagance of hiring Jansen and Maxim's, he decided to act.

THE SHAH'S PARTY

Taking on a long-standing courtier and bureaucratic knife fighter like Alam was a mistake for an academic, even one as devious as Shafa. He chose a meeting of the organizing committee attended by the Queen to discuss "irregularities." This required some chutzpah on his part, as he was notorious for "irregularities" that had allowed him to amass a property portfolio in the South of France. Alam went white and then red, announced he was resigning as Minister of the Court, and then stormed out. The court minister, who probably had better access to the Shah than even the empress, went straight to him to demand changes. Corruption was never mentioned again.

Shafa was a key figure in providing cultural gravitas to the Pahlavi dynasty. His idea was to associate the Shah and his reign with what he believed to be the greatest ancient dynasty, the Achaemenids. Depending on who you believe founded the dynasty, they ruled from 730 to 330 BCE. In 559 BCE, Cyrus the Great established the Persian Empire, conquering a vast stretch of land. This was the largest empire the world had seen up to that time, incorporating as much as a third of the world's population. It had left behind some astonishingly beautiful ruins but little written history. Those records that have survived are mostly bureaucratic: they list rations and official posts rather than tell a narrative that might capture the imagination. Thus, the Persian empire has been something of a blank slate onto which one could project many contemporary ideas about monarchy, politics, and empire.

The exchange between Shafa and Alam typified life in the Pahlavi court, described in a State Department paper as "artificial and self-conscious." The Shah's first wife, Princess Fawzia, the sister of King Farouk of Egypt, despaired at the suffocating provincialism of life in Tehran compared to the cosmopolitan fleshpots of Cairo. The court was controlled by the Shah's cantankerous mother, Taj al-Moluk, and his twin sister, Princess Ashraf.

THE PARTY PLANNER

She would become emblematic of all the ills projected onto the Pahlavis, some just fantasies and some very real. Farah Diba, an intelligent woman who had abandoned her plans to be an architect to marry the Shah at the age of 21, gritted her teeth around her husband's family and indeed often around her husband, who spent much of his private time escaping into sports, speed, and sexual conquests.

By the time Alam was threatening to resign, the country was locked into the plan. Invitations had been issued, and there was no turning back from the foreign contracts, as Iran had little capability to handle an event of this scale. The rumblings, particularly in the French press, which had always been a bugbear for the Shah, were brushed aside as a growing number of countries sought to participate in the celebrations. Alam's confidence and his dominance of the Palace's bureaucracy meant that he would have his way.

Parties can be a great source of anxiety. Guests do not turn up; people fail to RSVP and then turn up anyway; people bring friends that were not invited. The food is bad, the staff are rude, and the drinks run dry. So many things can go wrong. The Shahbanou, as the queen was known, admitted in her first tentative and discreet autobiography published in 1978 that she had resorted to sedatives to get her through the event.

13 October 1973

For the minister of the court, the arrivals were an exhausting round of greetings and journeys back and forth from the airport to Persepolis. When Haile Selassie arrived at the tent city, Alam extended his hand to help him out of the Mercedes 600 limousine. The Lion of Judah, who was carrying his favored chihuahua Cheecheebee, slapped it away, muttering that he was perfectly capable of getting out by himself. He had arrived from Beijing

THE SHAH'S PARTY

with an entourage of seventy-two, ignoring instructions that a maximum of five people should accompany the main guests. Others turned up with more than a plus one. King Hussein of Jordan, a good friend of the Shah and beneficiary of much Iranian money over the years, came with his sister and her husband; they ended up sleeping on camp beds in his tent.

The Shahbanou, having downed what she would later admit was a fistful of anti-anxiety pills as well as antibiotics to keep an infection at bay, toiled away in a slight daze at the welcoming tent. Over the previous year, she had come to resent the massive effort required to orchestrate the event. Endless details had to be attended to by a bureaucracy that was already overwhelmed with demands. Just coordinating the arrival of jets every twenty minutes at Shiraz airport had been a nightmare that required months of attention from the head of Iran Air.

A cable written by the British Ambassador after the event, gleefully recounted the slips that inevitably occurred at such events. The press was summoned at 5 a.m.

> to ceremonies they did not wish to attend, denied access to those they did, and prevented from taking individual television films of the great parade. It was not surprising that some of their comment was generally acidulous, especially *Le Monde*, whose correspondent suggested that 'either the Shah might abdicate or else there would be a revolution.'

Security had meant that access anywhere required a pass, and many press staff and even officials in delegations were unable to get them. The intense scrutiny of everyone made for a nervous atmosphere. When a television light burned out with a loud bang during a welcoming ceremony for the South African president, "the pressmen and photographers jumped a foot off the ground and there was an awful gasp," the ambassador wrote.

Planning had taken years, and the setup involved hundreds of flights and trucks to get all the materiel to the remote site.

THE PARTY PLANNER

Almost all of this had been handled by the Ministry of the Court, with Alam wielding his power to chivvy others into action. Mehrdad Pahlbod, the Shah's brother-in-law since his marriage to his elder sister Princess Shams, oversaw the cultural events and, along with his brother, an army general, had developed the parade. More than 3,000 soldiers were encamped near the site, having grown out their beards to resemble the Achaemenid men depicted on the stone reliefs of Persepolis.

Maxim's, the Belle Epoque restaurant on the Rue Royale, once favored by 1950s café society, was to provide food for the first full day's formal banquet. When Tehran's tailor of choice on Sepah Avenue lacked the staff to sew new court uniforms, Alam called in the Parisian House of Lanvin and its army of *petites mains*. The overall effect was formal, as were most of the guests as they arrived and wandered among the fountains and thousands of new trees planted across the site. What would the Bulgarian Communist Party General Secretary Todor Zhivkov, a hardline Stalinist and former secret policeman, have to discuss with Princess Grace of Monaco? It was hard not to notice the stilted environment; even *The New York Times* social writer Charlotte Curtis commented on the awkward exchanges. Iranian Prime Minister Hoveyda kept to the weather, asking Prince Makhosini Dlamini of Swaziland, if it was suitable for him. "Oh yes," he responded. "We have the same kind of weather."

As dusk fell, most of the jetlagged guests retired to their tents to eat. Room service was provided from the massive tented kitchen set up by the banqueting hall. As the sun set, fairy lights lit up the columns of Persepolis.

3

THE VENUE

12 OCTOBER 1971

Just after his speech at the tomb of Cyrus at Pasargadae, the Shah and Shahbanou flew to Shiraz, landing at the Baghj-e Eram, a former royal palace that was now open to the public. It was the location for a reception for the visiting Iranologists, scholars, and the media who had been flown to the southern city. Many of the visiting scholars had come with gifts, such as books or scrolls, for the Shah; they stepped forward to present them and chat with the Imperial couple.

The gathering of archaeologists and historians became quite carried away by the royalty in their midst, pressing in until the King and Queen were forced to retire to a room where they drank tea awkwardly while being watched by the crowd outside. Although the event took a slightly comic turn, it had started as a genuine effort to put Iran back on the map. Committees had been established around the world to build links, and many of them were at least symbolically chaired by heads of state such as Richard Nixon and Georges Pompidou. Historians of ancient Persia, long sidelined by their colleagues who studied the Greek,

THE SHAH'S PARTY

Roman, Egyptian, or Chinese empires, enjoyed a rare moment in the sun.

None of this would attract much attention from the 600 journalists covering the gathering, but some of it was of lasting value, repositioning ancient Persia as a subject worthy of attention, as well as making more people aware of the history and monuments of Iran. The Pahlavi court tried to emphasize that the events were about more than the lavish tent city and dinners for heads of state. To mark the anniversary, 2,500 schools were planned. According to the Ministry of Education, 3,200 were built and 110,000 students were added to the rolls.

* * *

The tent poles, today bare of fabric, cast sharp geometries on the tiles beneath them. Circles intersect with triangles that touch upon squares and stars in what looks like the most complex of Islamic designs. However, these tessellations are purely accidental, as they were never meant to be seen. The frames had been covered in thousands of meters of plastic panels and canvas fabric in the Imperial colors of pale blue and white. The frames and the dusty roads are now all that remain of the tent city by Persepolis. It looks like an abandoned Californian suburb, an almost painfully blue sky above a forest of climbing frames set in cul-de-sacs. Next to the massive stone platform with its carvings and columns, it is a flimsy and ephemeral ghost town.

Roads are arranged in a star shape, with a now-empty fountain at the center, tiled in the blue of the sky. Down each cracked road are ten frames, surprisingly undamaged. Surrounding the whole area is a forest of dry pines that have stood up well to the heat and drought of southern Iran. They hide the frames from the visitors who climb the monumental ramps to the remains of Persepolis.

There is no doubt of the majesty of the setting. The site backs up against steep hills, and from their heights, you can see across

THE VENUE

an enormous plain. This was once one of the capitals of the Achaemenid Empire, home to thousands of people who gathered here with the court in celebration of spring each year. Cyrus might have been the focus of the party, but Persepolis was not his town. His capital was at Pasargadae, where his stark tomb still stands and where the Shah had given the speech that opened the celebrations. Construction of Persepolis probably began under Darius, although there is some evidence of Cyrus building there.

The building of the tent city was entirely appropriate to celebrate the Achaemenids. The first Persian kings moved among their capitals at Susa, Pasargadae, and Persepolis, mainly living in tents and using the permanent buildings for ceremonies. Evidence from records of the distribution of food and other goods suggests the emperor moved almost constantly, which must have involved an extraordinary level of organization. The point was for the king to show himself to his people and to exchange gifts with his most important subjects, particularly those who formed the core of the imperial system. This was very different from their Assyrian predecessors, who were equally mobile but tended to be on a constant warpath to terrify those under their rule into acquiescence. Assyrian records indicate that there was at least one war a year; the Persian Empire, although very capable of violence, was generally much more peaceful.

The tents that housed the Achaemenid court would have looked remarkably like those set up in 1971, except they were certainly more lavish. Greek historians expressed astonishment at the scale of their enemy's tents—mobile palaces with an array of reception halls, private dwellings, and accommodations for the harem. At the Battle of Platea in 479 BCE, the Greeks captured the tent of King Xerxes. The structures were beyond the imagination of the much more modest Greeks, draped as they were with cloth of gold and tapestries. "The Greeks dispersed themselves about the Persian camp and found tents furnished with gold and silver, and beds overlaid with gold and overlaid with silver, and mixing bowls of gold, and cups and drinking vessels", Herodotus wrote.

> They found also sacks laid upon wagons, in which there proved to be caldrons both of gold and of silver; and from the dead bodies which lay there they stripped bracelets and collars, and also their swords if they were of gold, for as to embroidered raiment, there was no account made of it.

The retinues of wives, children, courtiers, bodyguards, and camp followers—some Greek historians put the number at around 15,000—were housed in encampments below the 12-hectare stone platform that houses the main halls of Persepolis. Such was the confidence of the Achaemenid rulers that the capitals at Susa, Pasargadae, and Persepolis were not fortified beyond a shallow ditch and low walls. They had no reason to believe they would ever be attacked.

* * *

Asadollah Alam was responsible for the decision to build a tent city. Hotels planned for Shiraz and Persepolis were not expected to be ready, and the original idea of housing some guests in palaces in Shiraz raised security concerns. Bringing most of the VIPs together in one isolated place made them easier to guard, but there was no possibility of building a permanent settlement in time.

The design was from Maison Jansen, the venerable decorators founded in Paris in 1881. For much of the twentieth century, Jansen was emblematic of a certain type of wealth: Francophile, cosmopolitan, and elitist. It was for those whose style was perhaps a little too stuffy and arriviste. They liked their furniture to be French and if they could afford it, with a provenance from Versailles or another seventeenth or eighteenth century palace. Monarchs often hired the house. The head designer for many years, Stephane

THE VENUE

Boudin, had decorated Belgian palaces, the homes of the Serbian royals, and even the White House when it was renovated by Jacqueline Kennedy. Jansen designs were often innovative and very influential in their time, but most clients just wanted French style. It spoke of a few addresses: Fifth Avenue, the 16th Arrondissement, Palm Beach and Cap Ferrat.

Maison Jansen furniture now sells for huge sums but in the 1970s, the house was a fading force in the world of design. Boudin had died in 1967. The style was increasingly at odds with the informality of the age. Gilt and elaborate boiserie seemed dusty in an era of Perspex tables and puffy leather couches. It said much about the flunkies in the Pahlavi court that it was Jansen that was selected for what was its last great commission. The Empress was far more contemporary in her tastes.

The idea of tents was a nod to the nomadic past of the Iranians and a way of providing luxurious accommodation for the guests in time for the event. Jansen was known for its organization of celebrations; Boudin had started his career at the firm by designing special events, such as the 1938 Circus Ball, thrown by Elsie de Wolfe, also known as Lady Mendl, the American actress and socialite who was the first modern interior decorator. That ball was another "Party of the Century"—a last frenzied celebration before World War II brought the world of Parisian elites crashing down.

Persepolis was an enormous challenge for the company, which had to subcontract much of the work. There were to be fifty-four tents—actually 42-foot diameter prefab bungalows that were draped in fabric—as well as a special "Tent of Honor" for the Shah. A banqueting hall would accommodate several hundred people. It all had to be air-conditioned and secure, as well as linked to the outside world by phone and satellite. The original model arranged the guest tents around a five-pointed star—each point representing a continent. Off to one side was a helicopter pad and the Tent of Honor, a large striped marquee used to greet guests. Behind it was the banqueting tent, an enormous room lined in red and blue velvet.

The guest tents, each of which was said to have cost $10,000 (about $75,000 in 2025), were all decorated in different styles. They had two small bedrooms and bathrooms, a sitting room, and a tiny room for a maid or bodyguard. The tents were decorated in bright colors; photographs from the time show interiors of 1970s Technicolor intensity: acidic yellow and green, bright purple and tangerine. Guests were all given a carpet portrait that hung on the tent wall. The hosts had made every effort to accommodate their guests' wishes: one had asked for a metronome in his room, another was said to have demanded space for a bodyguard in the bathroom. A predecessor had been drowned, and he wished to avoid that fate.

Not everyone appreciated the designs: in *The New York Times*, the society columnist Charlotte Curtis wrote: "Yet aside from the handsome Persian carpets, the Porthault linen (for the maids' rooms as well as the distinguished guests' rooms), the Guerlain shaving preparations for the men and the Joy Eau de Cologne and soap for the women, the tents have all the charm of motel rooms everywhere."

The setting, however, could hardly be matched. The thirteen standing columns of Darius's palace loomed above the tent city with the hills rising behind them. There are few more spectacular locations on earth.

* * *

The press quickly dubbed the tent city the Field of the Cloth of Gold after the site in France where one of the first great summit meetings took place. In June 1520, Henry VIII and Francis I met just outside Calais for three weeks of banquets, discussions and bouts of wrestling between the two young monarchs. It was one of the most important and extravagant exercises in diplomacy and competitive consumption ever staged.

THE VENUE

Preparations for the Field of the Cloth of Gold were immense and the costs vastly exceeded those at Persepolis as a share of state wealth. The stakes were much higher as well. The monarchs were young and ambitious, both eager to consolidate power amid the intense, fissile politics of the age. The event was held at Ardres, next to an abandoned castle that was partially rebuilt for the occasion. The French king occupied a huge tent, the height of the White Tower in London, surrounded by thirty-two walls covered with cloth of gold, a fabric made of silk and gold thread. Such was the amount used that the French had to buy all the available stock from across Europe. There were three lateral stripes of blue velvet covered with gold fleurs-de-lis, the emblem of the French crown. The tent was made of a durable canvas with the gold coverings attached with violet taffeta ribbons brought from Genoa. Atop the structure was a life-sized statue of St Michael, patron saint of France, portrayed holding a sword and shield. The rooms were lined with more blue velvet with fleurs-de-lis and gold fringe.

Next to this were three smaller tents of a similar design that were to function as a chapel, a meeting room, and a dressing room for the King. Beyond this was a small village of tents decorated with golden apples and a banqueting hall made from board painted to look like bricks. Decorated with gold brocade and tapestries of astrological signs, its roof was covered with gold stars, completing the very fashionable look. Four days after this had been assembled, rain and high winds damaged the tents, breaking the tall mast that held up the main pavilion. The French king retreated to alternative accommodation in a nearby village.

The English were determined not to be outdone, even with the challenges of shipping everything over from London. The castle near the village of Guines was deemed unsuitably dingy. A new temporary palace was required, but there was no timber available in the area. Trees were floated down the coast from

Holland, and glass was brought in from England. Only stone was quarried locally. Painters were brought in from around the region to provide decorations for the building. This was built around a courtyard and included a gatehouse, towers, and crenellations. A foundation of brick was topped with wooden walls, painted also to look like brick, while a canvas roof was painted to resemble slate. It was the glass and gilded lead windows that most amazed observers; they wrote of being stunned by the light and the sense of almost being outdoors.

The ground floor, comprising windowless rooms, was reserved for offices and kitchens; there was even a room dedicated to baking cakes and wafers. The state rooms were on the glazed floor above and included space for Cardinal Wolsey and the Queen, Catherine of Aragon. A huge amount of what was called "the King's stuffe" was shipped over, including gold and silver plate, tapestries, and all the necessary dressings for beds and rooms. Whatever could be covered in gold had been, to the point that several writers at the time remarked on the excess of it all. Some floors were covered with painted taffeta, but many were just strewn with straw, an English custom dating back many centuries that had yet to go out of fashion, even at court. As fleurs-de-lis covered the French tents, Tudor roses were everywhere in the ornamentation of Henry's palace and its chapel, along with other emblems such as portcullises and pomegranates, representing wealth and fertility. Huge quantities of food and wine were brought in from England. Some 250,000 fish, 98,000 eggs, 2,000 sheep, 700 conger eels, thirteen swans, three porpoises, and 66,000 liters of beer were just some of the foods consumed.

* * *

The history of the ancient world was made in tents. Rulers would move from place to place throughout the year, living in vast moveable cities that became the capital wherever they were. Ancient

THE VENUE

Egypt did not have a formal capital for long periods, nor did Persia. Power was where the king pitched his tent. The royal progress persisted, although it tended to involve moving from palace to palace rather than tented cities: the Shah would move each year among Tehran, the Caspian Sea, the island of Kish in the Persian Gulf, and his chalet in the Swiss ski resort of St. Moritz

Tents satisfy two deep and contradictory human feelings: a desire to move and a need for shelter. Enclosure has its own value even when tents offer little in the way of protection from the elements. Tents developed from simple shelters of animal skins to massive royal or religious structures that would have been carried on large, decorated carts. Many nomadic groups had a tent that was physically and spiritually the center of their universe; the central tent pole marked the star around which they navigated. Tents were aligned with the cosmos so that travel across the land was always linked to astral guidance from above. These camps were the first cities, shaping the way we have since designed urban spaces around the world, particularly in those cultures that centered space on a shrine or palace and built in an orderly grid around it.

Tents linked the earth and the sky, man and the gods. In almost all religions there is some sense of a movement between heaven and earth, this world and another often through a structure that descends in some way from tents: the columned temples of the Greeks or the Kaaba in Mecca which is said to float above the world; the ziggurats and pyramids were not so much houses for gods or tombs for kings but airport terminals through which they passed in a constant progress. Surrounding the temples were an array of special boats, carts, and tents to provide for them as they traveled. These were times when it was impossible to separate any understanding of earthly and heavenly worlds; they were ruled by Gods and Kings who were much alike in their needs and demands.

THE SHAH'S PARTY

Tents were the primary form of architecture for millennia, but they have rarely survived to our time; the oldest are some fragments of tents dating back 40,000 years found in the Russian permafrost. What we know of Persian tents comes to us through Greek historians, mostly because they admired the splendor. After conquering Persia, Alexander adopted many of the fashions and customs he had found in Persepolis.

"The tent of Alexander had one hundred couches and was supported by fifty golden pillars; gilded canopies, stretched out and wrought with very costly embroidery, covered the upper area of the tent," wrote Athenaeus.

> Inside, around it, stood, first of all, the five hundred Persians called the 'apple-bearers', adorned with purple and quince-yellow costumes. After them, there were archers to the number of a thousand: some wore flame-colored garments, other ones of scarlet, and many also had dark-blue mantles. At the head of these were five hundred Macedonians, the Silvershields. A golden throne was placed in the middle of the tent, upon which Alexander used to seat himself and hold court, with his bodyguards standing close on all sides.

Once you go Persian, you never go back. The Macedonian is said to have remarked on entering the tent, "*This*, it seems, is royalty." His embrace of the luxe of the Persian court was controversial. He had captured Darius's tent in 333 BCE—the structure described here and by other writers may well have been that tent as it was almost certainly modelled on the *Apadana* Hall at Persepolis with its hundred columns. Alexander also seems to have taken on Persian bodyguards, and protocol that isolated him from his people. He was no longer a monarch who ate simple meals with his men, but one who issued rulings from a golden throne surrounded by hundreds of bodyguards.

By embracing Persian splendor, Alexander was following an old Greek tradition, even if his adoption of barbarian luxury ruffled feathers. Persians were long-standing rivals and enemies

THE VENUE

but also models of how to establish and run an empire. Persians knew how to live well even if they were barbarians, a tense juxtaposition of ideas that would endure for centuries. Persians have long been seen across Europe as indulgent, excessive, and not entirely civilized, lacking self-control and self-awareness. At the same time, there was a clear admiration for a way of life that exceeded their contemporaries in every manner of sophistication and style.

In the fifth century BCE, the Greeks captured spoils of war from the Persians and took them all back to Athens and other cities. There it was to influence their own material culture, particularly in one area—tents. Although there are no surviving tents, there are many descriptions of tents that were much admired by the Greeks. Tents from the east became a must-have luxury item. They were portrayed on vases with heroes and kings shown sitting inside.

Xerxes' tent, captured by the Greeks in 479 BCE, would form the inspiration for the Odeion, a theater for music built on the Acropolis in Athens. This was a pyramid-roofed wooden building on an 8-meter-high platform that was supposedly built with timbers from Persian warships. For all the culture of scorn that they developed against Persians and expressed extensively in their literature and drama, the Greeks developed an admiring relationship with their luxurious objects. Almost everything about Persia, particularly its kings and their iconography, fascinated them. The historian Herodotus was always keen to tease out the differences between Greeks and other people, all the better to firm up the identity of those living among those scattered Greek city-states. Such is the enduring legend of Xerxes' tent that Playmobil sells a version of it alongside figures of the Spartan King Leonidas and the Persian emperor on his chariot.

Before the sixth century BCE we do not know an enormous amount about either Greek or Persian politics or philosophy but there are suggestions that the pre-Socratic world was much influenced by Achaemenid religion. In the fifth century BCE, a time of deep conflict between the Greeks and Persians, their views of each other were generally negative. But by the fourth century BCE, the Greeks had absorbed an array of Persian influences and spread their own culture far and wide. Greeks, for example, were involved in the construction of the Persian capitals of Susa and Persepolis; records indicate that their sculptors and masons worked on these projects. Exchanges between the civilizations were quite considerable. Persia was no longer just the inevitable and necessary enemy of the Greeks, a way for them to bring together their fractious cities.

* * *

The Achaemenid tradition of political nomadism, which reinforced the bond between ruler and ruled through the king traveling around the kingdom in a constant peregrination of vast tented cities, may have originated hundreds of years before their empire and persisted long after it. *The Book of Wei*, a Chinese chronicle from the sixth century CE, records the King of Pars as having ten palaces that he moved among for most of the year, something extraordinary to the more sedentary Chinese rulers. Gift giving, central to kingship among the Achaemenids and most vividly portrayed along the ramps at Persepolis, continued for thousands of years after their rule right up to Shah Abbas in the sixteenth and seventeenth centuries. He travelled among his capitals of Qazwin, Isfahan, and Farahabad.

When the king moved on, it would have taken weeks to pack up the tents and their decorations, herd the animals together and organize the wagons. To build the tent city at Persepolis for the Shah, something similar was undertaken. The prefab tents were built by Sainte Freres, a company founded in the Napoleonic era to produce jute sacks. The company evolved over the years into a major manufacturer of textiles, eventually being bought by

THE VENUE

Bernhard Arnault, now the owner of LVMH and the richest man in Europe. The tents were first assembled in a hangar at Le Bourget airport, where they were tested to ensure that they could withstand powerful desert winds.

The blue and white reception hall was 112 feet in diameter, while the dining tent was 224 feet long, 82 feet wide, and 43 feet tall, with an interior ceiling that was 19 feet high. It took 4,000 yards of fabric, 25,000 yards of canvas, and 12,000 yards of trimming to make the fifty-four tents. Another massive structure was set up as a clubhouse for guests featuring an informal restaurant, a hairdressing salon, and other facilities. It took more than 100 flights and forty trucks crossing eight borders to ship all this from France to Iran, a logistical challenge completed over three months of summer heat, all supervised by Pierre Delbee, the jolly and eternally patient head of Jansen. Twenty miles of new roads were built along with a reservoir to provide nearly 14,000 gallons of water a day to the tents. The Hessarak Institute, the national center for vaccine and antidote production, was brought in to clear insects and poisonous snakes from a 30-square-kilometer area around the site.

* * *

Among many nomads, when a man is cast out from a group, the central pole of his tent is kicked down by the other men. It represents the dissolution of his life in that group. Romans would throw a spear onto the land of rivals, marking where they would pitch their tent when they had defeated them in the battle to come. Raiders of cattle and sheep would often cut the guy ropes of the main tent in an encampment just to make sure everyone knew they had been there. The taking down of a tent has as much power as putting one up.

By 1979, the Shah was gone but his tents were still standing at Persepolis despite at least one failed attempt to demolish not just the encampment but the ruins as well. Not long afterwards, they were taken over as a military camp. Their bright colors faded in the sun, and weeds grew in the cracks in the concrete.

* * *

Few of the guests arriving to celebrate the anniversary would have known that the majestic ruins of Persepolis had little direct connection to Cyrus the Great, who had ruled from several cities, including Pasargadae, the location of his tomb. Persepolis is believed to have been built between 521 and 486 BCE by Darius I, the third Achaemenid emperor who usurped the throne from Cyrus's heir, and Darius's son Xerxes, the third king of the dynasty. This was their great monument, their most glorious and enduring representation, built at a time when the Persian Empire was at its most expansive. Overall, the Achaemenids did not leave behind much architecture: there are the remains of Pasargadae, much diminished by the centuries, and of Susa, possibly their most important capital among the main settlements the monarch traveled to throughout the year. Persepolis, with the columns of the *Apadana*, or great hall, and the reliefs that line the ceremonial staircase, is its greatest architectural legacy.

This empire was unusual in form and behavior, lacking an aggressive *mission civilisatrice*. It did not push Persian culture onto the world, although Greeks adopted some of it. It pulled tribute, and to some degree people, into its sparsely populated center in what is now southern Iran, but it did not care much to impose itself excessively on its outer colonies. Distances were too large and good administrators too scarce to micromanage an empire, although there probably was much greater control than many historians have believed. Research has shown that letters could probably reach Egypt from the administrative capital in Susa in a matter of weeks rather than months, using a system rather like the nineteenth-century Pony Express in the United States.

THE VENUE

The Achaemenids are thought to have come to Persepolis to celebrate the new year festival, now known as Nowruz, and still the most important holiday in Iran. This gathering of people and their tributes to the king is shown in the great frieze on the walls of the stairs that lead up to the *Apadana*, or great hall. One is a relief of a lioness. She is the only female portrayed at Persepolis. She is among the most touching and beautiful of all the images. She turns to look back at the two Elamites carrying her cubs, and there is something both furious and caring about her face. No other sculpture at Persepolis expresses emotion in this way. She visibly strains on her leash and clearly longs to be free of these men and this stone.

The cubs were probably destined for *paradisos*, the lavish gardens that surrounded the monumental halls, serving as places for rest, leisure, and hunting—a central part of court life. The other tribute served a range of purposes. We know from records found at Persepolis that enormous quantities of food and wine were imported to the city, as well as building materials, horses, and workers from across the empire. Cedars for beams to support the wooden roofs came from the mountains of Lebanon. Goldsmiths from Egypt and Assyria, stonemasons from Ionia, bricklayers from Babylon. Persepolis was the place where the Achaemenids collected the best from around their world.

It is possible that there was a cosmological aspect to this, which is why the process is so elaborately presented in the carvings at Persepolis. By bringing together the most precious objects and materials from around the world, the Achaemenids were creating a perfect world at the center of their empire. Our understanding of religion from those times—the earliest forms of what would later be known as Zoroastrianism—is not well developed; they left behind few texts explaining their views but some evidence suggests that this effort to bring together the most perfect objects was to hold off the "fall"—the idea that the world was in a constant state of decay, teetering near the edge. Restoring its material perfection in their palaces, and even on their banqueting table, was a way to return to the state of completeness first created by the "Wise Lord."

This was reflected in everything they did, down to what they ate. Xerxes was said to have been offered a plate of Athenian figs, a renowned delicacy so highly regarded that their export from the area was banned. He turned them down, saying he would wait until he had conquered the city before including its food on his table. Only when the empire was complete would the banqueting table also be a perfect representation of the world and the Achaemenid order.

* * *

Persepolis haunted the Persian and Western imaginations for centuries. Although it was mentioned in ancient texts, its location was unknown in the West, and it was not until 1618 that the Spanish diplomat Don Garcia de Silva y Figueroa correctly identified the ruins known in Persia as Takht-e Jamshid, or the Throne of Jamshid, as Persepolis. For many centuries, it had taken on almost mythical overtones in the West through its association with Alexander.

Diodorus of Sicily wrote in the first century BCE of a feast held in the ruins of Persepolis by one of Alexander's generals, Peucestas, who was left behind to govern the province of Pars. There is evidence of reuse of stones and decorative carvings in new buildings at the site and nearby, but it was never again used as a key political or ritual center. Instead, it took on mythical tones as memories of its real origins faded.

The Sasanian kings, who ruled from the city of Istakhr, about five kilometers from the ruins, did not seem to know of the origins of Persepolis, referring to it as 100 Columns. However, they were in enough awe of the place, with its majestic setting,

THE VENUE

to leave their mark. There is Sassanian graffiti across the complex, including mention of a visit by Shapur II, the fourth-century CE monarch who was the longest-reigning in Persian history. Two images of princes on horseback were carved into the area known as the Harem of Xerxes. Even the later Islamic rulers after the Arab conquest of 650 CE, saw the ruins as somehow connecting them to an ancient Persian culture, even if they knew little of its history. Persepolis transcended dynasty and religion.

The "mute stones" in "their ineffable pathos of ruin," in the words of nineteenth-century British colonial figure Lord Curzon, have stood for millennia as the understanding of their history changed every few hundred years. The Persian scholar Mohammad ibn Jarir al-Tabari mentions the ruins in his commentary on the Koran in the early tenth century, describing them as both the Throne of Jamshid and a palace occupied by King Solomon. An eleventh-century poem by Omar Khayyam suggests a melancholic vision of the ruins, where nature has taken over: "They say the Lion and Lizard keep / the Courts where Jamshid gloried and drank deep."

A darker view of the monument emerged in the fourteenth century with the scholar Mohammed Ibn Mahmud Hamadani writing that the scale of Persepolis was such that it must have been of demonic creation. Marveling at the scale of the stonework and the carving of the decorative bulls on the gates, he wrote: "If it be said that a genius or a fairy had made it, that would be acceptable to the intellect."

The history of Persepolis was a mystery to the Persians for centuries, but it remained a palimpsest of kingly desires and power, connecting each dynasty back to the origins of the Persian empire as they understood it. The Qajars tapped into pre-Islamic Iranian sentiments by naming the Crown after the mythical "Kayan" dynasty, naming their sons after the heroes of the *Shahnameh*, or the Book of Kings, the tenth-century epic poem by Ferdowsi that encapsulates much of early Iranian mythology and history. They also devoted their energies to discovering genealogical links between themselves and ancient Parthians, as well as celebrating the festival of Nowruz.

The Pahlavis took this to a new level, using archaeology as a tool of nationalism and to develop a new historiography. They took their name from an ancient script, known in English as Middle Persian, first used around the second century BCE, to give some historical depth to a new dynasty founded by a Cossack sergeant elevated to the throne with British assistance. No other dynasty did more to resurrect the ancient history of the Persian empire and develop associations with it, culminating in the party and in 1976, the reorganization of the country's dating system from the start of the Achaemenid Empire. The country shifted overnight from the Muslim year 1355 to the royalist year 2535. The Revolutionary Government immediately changed it back when they came to power. Many women used the confusion to remove a few years from their ages on identity documents.

The eighteenth century marked the start of the colonial looting of the site. James Morier, an Anglo-Swiss diplomat and explorer, arrived at Persepolis prepared to steal the best sculptures for the museums and collections that were opening all over Europe. His activities at the site, cleaving sculptures into two to make them more portable and digging into the tunnels under the platform, provoke horror today, but they were normal behavior in the context of the massive theft of art from the Middle East that persists until this day. Fortunately, the scale and remoteness of the site protected it to some degree from the colonial onslaught.

Persepolis, though, suffered indignities at the hands of foreigners and locals alike. Some of the faces on bas-reliefs were scratched off due to the Islamic injunction against the portrayal of people, an idea that has rarely been honored in Iran over the centuries. Some stones were taken for other buildings and one

THE VENUE

governor of Shiraz is said to have destroyed part of the ruins out of irritation with the number of foreigners visiting the area and taking up his time with their demands.

In 1931, formal excavation work began at Persepolis, a process that would culminate in the preparations for the party forty years later. That the city had remained almost untouched—it was the last such major site in the Middle East—was largely due to Iran having granted France a monopoly on research there. The French had focused on the other Achaemenid capital at Susa and mostly ignored Persepolis. In 1928 the license was revoked, and German and American archaeologists were invited to bring their shovels.

When Mohammad Reza took power, Persepolis became ever more important in the creation of legitimacy for the dynasty. Skipping over millennia of Persian history, those tasked with coming up with a narrative scaffolding to support the Pahlavis looked back to the origins of the empire. When the first plans for the celebration at Persepolis were thought up in the early 1960s, the government began a process of preparing the site. Italian archaeologists were brought in to clear some of the debris from the platform and start piecing together those columns that could be fixed. Some excavation work was done, but the process was mostly one of tidying up. By the 1960s, the ruins were now central to presenting Iran to the world. State visitors were taken there. It was again a place of national importance.

* * *

Sadiq Behdad was a successful lawyer in Tehran in the late 1960s who worked for many of the country's top corporations. He was earning the equivalent of three-quarters of a million dollars in today's money and had become a pillar of the establishment. Lurking in his past, though, was a history of student activism in the 1950s, when Mossadegh's National Front was in power.

In the summer of 1969, Behdad disappeared. For fifty-two days, his family knew nothing about what had happened to him.

THE SHAH'S PARTY

His wife was then summoned by a mysterious man and driven to a house in Tehran, where she found her husband. He was shaken and confused, unable to tell day from night. His wife had already suspected what had happened. He had been held by the secret police SAVAK (the acronym for Sâzmân-e Ettelâ'ât va Amniyyat-e Kešvar or The Bureau for Intelligence and Security of the State) even though he was a wealthy lawyer and fixture of North Tehran business circles. The reasons for his arrest, reported by a journalist to American diplomats and recorded in a State Department cable, were pieced together by the family.

Earlier in the year, one of his relatives had died, and among the condolence letters was one from General Teymour Bakhtiar, the founding head of the Shah's secret police, who was in exile at the time. Fearful that the letter might cause problems, Behdad tore it up and threw it away. A few days later, he was arrested by SAVAK and asked if he had heard from Bakhtiar. He denied he had, unaware that agents had earlier intercepted the letter, copied it and then sent it on. For being in touch with the former head of SAVAK, then seen as a major threat to the Shah, he was sentenced to seven years in prison. His journalist friend, well-connected in the Palace, tried to intervene on his behalf, getting the brush off from the Minister of the Court Alam. "SAVAK's business is SAVAK's business," the minister told him, as wary as anyone else of being drawn into its web.

A month later, Behdad was released, although a cloud of suspicion hung over him, hardly an advantage in the increasingly tense atmosphere that was developing in Tehran at that time.

* * *

Shiraz Airport, with its new terminal and modern Imperial blue pavilion for VIPs, was a long way from a dusty old airfield in a remote corner of Jordan. But the hijackings a year earlier of five jets destined for New York and London to a former British airfield

THE VENUE

in the Jordanian desert was the undercurrent that buzzed through the celebration. The Popular Front for the Liberation of Palestine was a breakaway from the Palestine Liberation Organization, run by two leftist intellectuals, Georges Habbash and Wadi Haddad. Three of the jets ended up at Dawson's Field, as the airfield was known. The PFLP called it "Revolution Airport."

This was the age of hijacking, when it was still possible to board a plane without security checks or encountering armed air marshals. Eight planes were hijacked in a single month in the United States in January 1969. Nothing, however, was as spectacular as the PFLP diversions in 1970 of five planes: three to Dawson's Field, one to Beirut, and another to Cairo. This was the performance of violence at its zenith; all done in a way that seems shocking, even today. More than 350 passengers were taken hostage; fortunately, not one of them died.

The hijackings stemmed from the worsening tensions between Palestinians and the government of King Hussein of Jordan. Palestinian factions had carved out states within the state of Jordan; the PFLP controlled the area around Dawson's Field, which had been built by the British during World War II but was no longer in use as an airfield. Palestinians had begun hijackings in the late 1960s, diverting the jets to friendly Arab states such as Algeria and Syria. There, they ran into a problem: these governments tended to take over, running the negotiations and taking control of the hostages. Attention drifted away from the hijackers and their cause.

By flying the planes to Revolution Airport, the PFLP would maintain control of the situation. King Hussein was too weak to challenge the operation and the PFLP could keep a grip on the hostages. On 6 September, they struck, diverting TWA and Swissair flights out of Frankfurt and Zurich. El Al security foiled the hijacking of a 707 flying from Amsterdam to New York, targeted because the guerrillas believed Yitzhak Rabin, the future prime minister and then Israeli ambassador to Washington, was on board. As they tried to take control shortly after take-off, the captain put the plane into a steep dive to knock the pair off their feet. A melee followed in which security officers shot the Nicaraguan hijacker Patrick Arguello and captured Leila Khaled, a young Palestinian woman who had been inspired to join the PLFP by an earlier hijacking. She was arrested when the plane made an emergency landing in London.

Two hijackers who had been kept off the Israeli jet at Amsterdam Airport took control of a Pan Am 747 instead, flying it first to Beirut and then to Cairo. It was too big to land at Revolution Airport.

The PLFP soon discovered there were no British hostages among the 310 passengers and crew they were now holding and so they had no leverage to free the two hijackers held in the United Kingdom. In what seems like a remarkable improvisation, one of their supporters hijacked a BOAC flight from Bahrain to London to provide them with the leverage to free Khaled, who would emerge as the most compelling icon of the Palestinian cause in the 1970s. By 9 September, three planes were parked in the sand at Revolution Airport. Three days later, they would be blown up simultaneously. It was an astonishing publicity coup for a somewhat chaotic and improvised organization that for most of its existence lacked even a telephone in its office.

Revolution Airport put the Palestinian cause on the map and reshaped the global view of both their struggle and terrorism. Habash had issued a warning that would echo down the years: "It is right for Europe and America to be warned now that there will be no peace for them until there is justice for Palestine." The PFLP would become one of the most significant inspirations for the leftist urban guerrillas in Iran, who emerged on the scene in February 1971.

The government jets landing at Shiraz a year later carried men and women who had not yet come to terms with a new age of urban guerrillas, image-conscious terrorists who worked the media with the skills of practiced movie stars. Even the younger members of the entourages were not part of a youth culture that celebrated the intoxicating possibility of revolution and an emerging sense that any victim was legitimate. The years after 1968 saw a surge of violence among the young, from the astonishing brutality of the Cultural Revolution in China to the new Latin American guerrilla groups that inspired others around the world.

There was undeniable sex appeal in the way this violence was presented. Leila Khaled wore her revolutionary chic well. The American photographer Eddie Adams immortalized her in a keffiyeh, holding a rifle up to her head. Her eyes might have been averted, but her smile was confident, even victorious. Aside from Yasser Arafat, she became the most emblematic Palestinian of the time and one of only a handful of women who stood out in this most masculine of worlds. She was so recognizable that she had six surgeries to change her appearance.

Khaled was a Christian Palestinian born in Haifa but raised in a refugee camp in Lebanon, one of a dozen children. She captured the zeitgeist in a way that Che Guevara had done; that fortuitous combination of image, action, and mostly silence that intensified everything about her. Fame in the 1970s was very different from what it is fifty years on in the age of social media; much more complete, much more difficult to achieve, and therefore much more durable. For many young people, Khaled and her cohort of urban revolutionaries were everything the Imperial Court was not. Motivated, stylish, and of the moment.

The Shah knew he could not afford any issues with security, particularly following urban guerrilla attacks earlier in the year. The combined forces of SAVAK, the military, and the police were mobilized to ensure that there would be no problems.

Embassies had inquired as to what special measures would be put in place, even as some might have been fearful of the answers they might get. By 1971, SAVAK was already notorious, and its sense of menace would only grow in the following years. A combination of events that year magnified its violence and profoundly worsened both its reputation and that of the Shah. Left-wing guerrilla attacks, the massive security operation around the celebrations, and a change in leadership pushed it to a level of violence that had not been seen in Iran for more than a decade.

Embassies had started to understand what security meant in the Shah's Iran. The events of the past nine months had played into the Shah's deep anxieties about communism, internal threats, and his neighbors, all linked in his mind. As the Shah consolidated power after 1953, he ordered the creation of a new security agency, the Organization of State Security and Information, known by its Persian acronym SAVAK. It would grow from its founding in 1957 as an investigative unit aimed at preventing conspiracies against the crown to become a force that somehow magnified its own effects so that the entire country believed it could feel the hot breath of its agents on their necks.

Nobody has any interest in being honest about SAVAK, and the secretive nature of its work makes it difficult to separate the embellishments from the truth. For those opposed to the Shah, it was his instrument of brutality and repression. It showed that far from being a modern monarch, he had returned the country to some form of ancient brutality. For the Revolutionaries, it was a useful weapon against the regime. Still, given that they almost immediately incorporated its structures and personnel into their new and much more oppressive system, they tended to prefer to keep it in the background. Some of its men were tried and put to death after the Revolution, but most of its torturers simply changed sides. Why waste all that expensive training from Mossad and the CIA? The continuation of the structures of Pahlavi Iran into Revolutionary Iran ran deepest in its secretive systems of control and repression, which would only worsen as Khomeini consolidated power.

THE VENUE

Many of the men who had put the Shah back on his throne in 1953 would end up opposing him. Inevitably, a certain resentment always brews inside a ruler who has had to rely on others to ensure their own power. The Shah, like so many monarchs, wanted to believe that not only had he been somehow selected by God for this role but that all his nation's achievements were his own. The presence of the men who had not just returned him to his throne but given him real power was a reminder of his early days of weakness.

They also represented something of a threat, the most dramatic coming from the founding leader of SAVAK, General Bakhtiar. The general, from a powerful tribal family in Isfahan, was to become a key figure in the Shah's rise to absolute power, first as military governor of Tehran and then in the secret police. Aided by a small group of American advisors, he started SAVAK with the aim of ensuring the security of the regime. Many years later, he would die at the hands of its agents in one of the most dramatic operations it ever organized.

Bakhtiar had been essential not just in putting the Shah back on his throne in 1953 but in keeping him there in the difficult years after the coup. Widely seen as weak and now deeply unpopular with the emerging middle class that had supported Mossadegh, the Shah needed mechanisms to assert his authority. In the aftermath of the coup, Bakhtiar suppressed any opposition and then dismantled the Tudeh party, erasing the inroads it had made into the military. It was a chance for the Shah to purge the top brass, replacing confident and independent-minded officers with toadies, as he would repeatedly do in the coming decades. He positioned Bakhtiar, a popular and charismatic officer, in charge of the new intelligence force.

The general graduated from the French military academy St Cyr in the 1930s but had an undistinguished career in what was an undistinguished army. In 1945, he helped push the Soviets out of the Iranian province of Azerbaijan and stifled demands for independence there. His niece, Soraya, married the Shah in 1951, bringing him into royal circles. In 1953, he was appointed military governor of Tehran, in command of a motorized division. If everything went south in the coup, he was to take control. It turned out he was not needed, but the Shah had taken note of his abilities and loyalty.

Bakhtiar was pushed forward by the British who saw him as effective and supportive. The Americans envisioned the new security agency as a blend of the FBI and CIA, recruiting the smartest minds in Iran, often while they were still studying at universities in Europe or the United States. It would be a small, elite force that could prevent subversion. Bakhtiar's two deputies were very much of that mindset, the general much less so. He openly discussed torture with diplomats, bragged about the use of violence by SAVAK, and almost from the start set the agency heading into its morass. He did few favors for himself in many conversations, badmouthing the Shah for his incompetence at every opportunity.

Bakhtiar was perhaps one of the most unsuitable choices to run a security agency. Corrupt, louche, egotistical, and violent, he ended up making SAVAK in his own image. There is no doubt the Shah enabled this in various ways, not least in the appointment of the boss. It was ultimately to come at a very high cost. Few things would do more damage to him than his own secret police.

The SAVAK boss fell from favor in 1961 when the new Kennedy administration pushed the Shah towards a more reformist line with the appointment as prime minister of Ali Amini, a liberal and respected former ambassador to Washington. Bakhtiar saw an opportunity to boost his power and foolishly approached the Americans, suggesting the possibility of a military coup to push the Shah back from wielding direct power. Rumors soon

THE VENUE

reached the Shah that his SAVAK chief had met with Kermit Roosevelt, a former CIA station chief in Tehran who was notorious as the hidden hand behind the 1953 coup. The Americans were not enthusiastic; the Kennedy administration was not keen on the Shah, but it had other, more important irons in its fire. The Shah was furious and exiled Bakhtiar to Europe.

From there, the general tried to ingratiate himself with everyone who might join him in ousting Mohammad Reza, including members of Tudeh, the party whose cadres he had enthusiastically rounded up and jailed just a few years earlier. He repeatedly tried to get the British to join him. Deeply embarrassed and anxious that the Shah might find out, they went to the emperor and reported on the general's activities. This only fueled the paranoia the Shah felt toward the United Kingdom. The Shah saw Bakhtiar's hand in many setbacks; he blamed him for protests in Germany during a state visit in 1967 and sacked the head of SAVAK in Europe for not doing enough to prevent the embarrassment.

By the end of the 1960s, Bakhtiar was in Iraq where he was plotting with many former enemies, allegedly including Khomeini, also in exile there. But his entourage was riddled with SAVAK informers. By one estimate, sixteen of his aides and assistants, cooks and typists were in the pay of Iranian intelligence. In 1970, Bakhtiar tried to persuade Saddam Hussein, then a rising force, to help him in a plot to kill the Shah during a visit to Turkey. Saddam, normally an enthusiastic murderer of political rivals, demurred, even though Iran had been involved in a coup attempt in January of that year. Bakhtiar's collusion with the Baathist government finally crossed a line. While on a hunting trip in August 1970, one of the SAVAK agents working as his driver shot him. The Shah could not have been happier.

* * *

THE SHAH'S PARTY

The Shah and SAVAK tended to get an easy ride from the American press until the mid-1970s, when their reputation became inescapable. It was precisely the relative openness of Iran, the ability of its people to travel, and indeed even the Shah's willingness to put himself in front of the media that created an environment in which he could be more easily scrutinized than many others. Among intellectual and leftist circles in the West, there was a deep-seated loathing of the Shah—his ostentation, his bejeweled wife, his oil wealth, and his supposed extravagance. The Saudi monarchy, more masculine, more tied to tradition and the desert, but also vastly more violent and repressive, never received the same level of bad press. Neither did the much more brutal republican regimes in Egypt, Syria and Iraq.

That SAVAK should accrue such excessive powers is not surprising given the situation in Iran. Not only did the Shah have anxieties at home but he was living in a dangerous neighborhood. New forces were blasting through the Middle East during the Cold War. Arab nationalism, tied to socialist and pro-Soviet political visions, was growing strongly in Egypt, Syria and Iraq. Militaries had taken inspiration from Gamal Abdel Al-Nasser's rise to power in 1952 and his abolition of Egypt's decrepit monarchy a year later. French and British failures in the Suez War in 1956, combined with their alliance with Israel, undermined the once-dominant colonial powers, and the United States and the Soviet Union became the leading external players in the fractious region.

SAVAK earned its reputation through its own brutality, but did it ever reach the scale and penetration suggested by so many opponents? It is unlikely. Most insiders estimate its full-time staff at around 5,000, far below the estimates provided by student groups and human rights organizations. What makes a secret police effective is its hidden reach, the sense that someone is always watching. Perhaps the most successful at this was the East

THE VENUE

German Stasi, which built on the reputation of the Nazi-era Gestapo, itself quite a small organization that created the image of omniscience. There was a heavy reliance on informants, many of them blackmailed, bullied or bribed into giving information, a great deal of which would be fraudulent or exaggerated. SAVAK never had the 90,000 permanent staff and 170,000 "collaborators" the Stasi used to control just sixteen million East Germans but behaved in a similar way by ensuring that no one ever felt safe from scrutiny.

How much control did SAVAK have over life in Iran? A cable from the United States Embassy in 1972 contained information from a local journalist about the corruption and excesses of SAVAK. It warned of the damage their unfettered power was having. Its increasingly indiscriminate violence against people who were often not even serious critics of the regime was undermining security and encouraging more people to join the opposition.

But a similar cable in 1976 dismisses the figures for political prisoners spread around by exiled groups, putting the number in the low hundreds. There were supposedly around 3,000 people in prison who might have fallen into the category. Still, many had committed some sort of criminal or violent act as the number of guerrilla attacks surged in the early 1970s. The Shah claimed, unreasonably, that there were no prisoners of conscience, but this was based on his view that being a member of Tudeh was illegal. In his mind, those imprisoned for their belief in communism were nothing more than common criminals.

By the end of his reign, the Shah was thoroughly disaffected with his security agency, suspicious that it was playing a role in his downfall. The former Central Bank Governor Khodadad Farmafarmaian saw the king shortly before the end and recalled him saying, in a shrill tone, that SAVAK "never knew anything at all." This was a profound change from the days in which he often intimated to ministers and others that his intelligence agencies provided him with an omniscient view of their activities, indeed of all the nation.

* * *

One of the founding narratives of the Revolution was the massive sacrifice in lives that it had taken to overthrow the Shah. The preamble to the 1979 Constitution speaks of the Revolution being "watered by the blood of 60,000 dead and 100,000 injured and disabled." The monarchy's willingness to shed the blood of its people stripped it of legitimacy. But how extensive was that violence? Emadeddin Baghi, a theologian, journalist, and human rights activist, pulled together all the documentation on deaths that he could access. He was commissioned by the official Martyrs' Foundation to examine the records and discovered that the death tolls under the Shah and during the Revolution were massively different from how they were portrayed. They were significantly lower, around 3,000 people, twenty times less than claimed by the authorities; they were almost all from Tehran rather than reflecting the national nature of the uprising as the government had always claimed; and they were very close to the figures put out at the time by the Shah's regime. It turns out that the Shah was not nearly as brutal as the Islamic government claimed. Between 1963 and the end of the Revolution in 1979, 3,164 people were killed fighting the government, according to the study. Of those, 2,781 died in the final year of the Shah's rule.

It is impossible to exonerate the Shah or SAVAK. Torture was used in Iran and there were too many political prisoners, of whom too many were executed. Each of the victims of the escalating brutality after 1971 had a life, a family, hopes for the future, people who mourned them. Those losses should never be minimized. The perception that SAVAK cultivated for itself in the last decade of the Shah's rule—that it was omniscient and relentlessly brutal—reflected some reality, but the legend grew

THE VENUE

far too large. The excesses of SAVAK de-legitimized the Shah in the eyes not just of Iranians but of the world. It also set a pattern for the abuses of the Islamic Republic, which have been on a much larger scale in every way and continue unabated.

The Islamic government built some of its legitimacy on the idea that the Shah had been uniquely violent, an idea supported by activists and politicians like Ted Kennedy. These ideas require some challenge. Baghi's research that showed this was far from the case was swiftly suppressed until he published it himself, beginning a new life of dissent against a government he had once supported. He has since spent many years in jail for his advocacy on human rights and his opposition to the death penalty. According to his studies, more than 10,000 people have been executed in Iran since 1979.

There is no doubt that loss of life has been considerable in the Islamic Republic. The grueling war against Iraq took probably somewhere around 200,000 lives: the numbers are not known exactly, but probably do not reach the figures of between 800,000 and one million that have often been cited. Immediately after the war, Iran claimed 650,000 dead while Iraq put its losses at 350,000. Both sides were exaggerating for effect: Baghdad needed to prove to the Gulf monarchies that funded its fight that it had held ground against Shia expansionism at great cost to itself. Iran needed to magnify its cult of martyrdom to justify the rule of the mullahs. One historian of the war put the death tolls at around 180,000 Iraqis and 600,000 Iranians, still shockingly high and up until then the deadliest conflict in recent Middle East history. About 85 per cent of the dead were soldiers, mostly young conscripts.

* * *

On 8 February 1971, nine young men stormed a police post in Siakhal, a mountain village 300 kilometers northwest of Tehran near the Caspian Sea. They were members of a group called the Organization of the Iranian People's Fadai Guerrillas, and their plan was to free two comrades who were being held there. As they entered the post, they killed three policemen but were unable to find the two prisoners, whom they feared would be tortured and might give up the location of hideouts in the area.

By the late 1960s, open political opposition to the Shah had mostly ground to a halt. SAVAK monitored political parties closely, and most leftist groups were so heavily infiltrated that many joked that their meetings consisted of government agents spying on each other. For some, their grim situation left only one option—armed action. The Fadai was founded in 1966, and after a sputtering start, including the arrest of several key figures and the departure of others to Lebanon to train with Palestinians, they began planning an insurgency. By September 1970, they had created a network of arms caches in the mountains north of Tehran. The aim was to carry out a series of attacks in the area that they believed would encourage the locals to rise up.

The Fadai found themselves divided from the start. This was a time of turmoil in leftist politics. Many were disillusioned with the Soviet Union and had turned towards Mao's China. Leftist guerrillas in Latin America, particularly Che Guevara, had roused young people around the world to a belief in violence. The foundational texts of revolution had emerged from Latin America: Che's *Guerrilla Warfare* and Carlos Marighella's *Minimanual of the Urban Guerrilla*. They were rapidly translated into Persian, a process that often stripped them of nuance and reduced them to a few simple precepts. One was stressing the importance of the revolutionary vanguard, known as the *foco* in Brazil, whose actions would spark the revolution. One side of the Fadai, inspired by the urban guerrillas in Latin America, believed they should start in the cities and build support from there. They saw the teeming slums of migrant workers as ripe for the picking. In fact, they were not; the religious right was already there and was increasingly winning them over. The other side, known somewhat inappropriately for Iran as "The Jungle Group", felt they should start with "armed propaganda" in the countryside to bring peasant farmers on board. Attacking the exploitative state where it was vulnerable would encourage them to take up arms. Like so many violent acts by untrained young militants in those days, the operation achieved little. The locals were not roused to revolt against the regime. In fact, they supported the police in arresting the guerrilla band and even enthusiastically tortured some of their captives before SAVAK got to them.

The Siakhal raid went spectacularly wrong in myriad ways. Accounts are confused and it is doubtful if anyone can now say exactly what happened, but it seems a member of the group managed to shoot and wound another who was trying to rescue him from the gendarmes. The Fadai stole some weapons from the police, one of the aims of the raid, but when they got them back to their minibus, it would not start. They ended up having to push the vehicle, surrounded by curious villagers they held off with their weapons. Finally, they managed to drive a short distance to pick up two colleagues. The minibus again broke down, and so they set off on foot into the hills.

Both sides in this bizarre confrontation were somewhat hapless. After earlier arresting one of the guerrilla group, SAVAK knew of the impending attack, but either did not warn the police in Siakhal or they ignored what they were told. The scuffle in the first moments of the attack, in which one guerrilla wounded a comrade, threw off the Fadai's plans; they failed to set explosives to blow up the post, nor did they attack a Forest Guard HQ as intended. They also left behind the ammunition for the weapons they had stolen and a pile of propaganda pamphlets they planned to distribute as part of their efforts to stir the locals into action. The small band was now stuck in the Gilan mountains in the middle of a winter night.

THE SHAH'S PARTY

This failed raid on a remote police post of no great consequence set alight a sputtering trail of gunpowder that would end in the explosions of 1978. Urban guerrilla warfare was in the air around the world in the early 1970s, a dark legacy of the *evenements* of 1968, and SAVAK was waiting for it. In November 1970, four men and a woman attacked the car of American Ambassador Douglas MacArthur Jr as he was returning home after a dinner with the Minister of the Court. The ambassador, his wife and driver all escaped unhurt, but SAVAK was alerted to the possibility that this new form of political violence might take hold.

The response to Siakhal was swift and furious, far out of proportion to the attack. Within days, hundreds of soldiers, some of them special forces, helped by local guides and police, were out searching for the Fadai. The authorities knew that one of the band was injured and they would be hiking through heavy snow on empty stomachs. It was only a matter of time. A long time, it turned out.

Buzzed by helicopters and battling through the mountains, the group found that many of their food stores had been ransacked by curious shepherds. They sheltered where they could in mountain huts, empty during the winter. Walking one day and resting the next, they were still at large after nine days when they finally found an untouched stash of supplies. At some point, they split into two groups, with one deciding in their hunger to ask some villagers for food and shelter. To their surprise, the locals refused them help, saying they had no food, and the menfolk were away, so they could not allow outsiders into their homes. They moved on to the next village, where one family did offer them support. But as they ate, villagers gathered at the house, eventually subduing the guerrillas after a brief fight. The rural poor, supposedly key to the coming revolution, disarmed them, tied them up, and beat them. By 18 February, four of the original nine-man group were in custody.

THE VENUE

The other five exchanged fire with approaching soldiers but managed to evade capture by hiding in a cave. As they struggled over the mountains, they encountered more patrols; finally, two were killed at a checkpoint on 21 February, nearly two weeks after the original attack. The next two were arrested, leaving only one still free or alive. He was finally nabbed on 27 February, just 16 kilometers from Siakhal.

During those nineteen days, five enlisted men and a civilian had died. Two officers, five corporals and three civilians were injured. The Shah was incredulous that a band of poorly prepared city kids had led his forces on a chase across the mountains for nearly three weeks. He dismissed the events as "a most vulgar, trivial, insane and suicidal act" by "ignorant people, manipulated by foreigners and influenced by a couple of movies." It was the sort of dismissive and rather petulant remark he made when completely furious about some government failure.

The guerrillas had set out to free their comrades, but they also had other aims. Most importantly, to show the Iranian people that resistance was alive. They also wanted to alert the country that the days of peaceful opposition were over. Like a growing number, they believed that peaceful actions were pointless in the face of state violence and that the performance of guerrilla action was a vital way to rouse the masses to revolution. They were the new vanguard of change, springing up across the world.

The Fadai were the influencers of their day, becoming heroes to many on university campuses, where dissent was growing. Disillusioned by the political torpor of the 1960s and inspired by a global array of guerrilla and protest movements—all very different but converging around the radical chic of the time—they were hugely successful at implanting themselves in the public consciousness. Their deployment of writing, poetry, and the theatrics of urban guerrilla attacks created a narrative that took hold among the young.

THE SHAH'S PARTY

Siakhal was a failed, minor attack that ended up having an outsized influence. Photographs of the Fadai were on the front pages of newspapers. The photographs were obviously obtained from families or universities, and all have an odd formality about them. The clean-shaven, handsome young men in suits and ties look as far from our idea of shaggy 1970s urban guerrillas as it is possible to get. This should have sent a message. Many young Iranians saw themselves in those images. The attack might have been a failure by most measures, but they also showed people that it was possible to stand up to the Shah.

The Shah's response was indicative of the shift in his mindset and the erosion of public support. The attack at Siakhal had been a failure for the guerrillas but the Shah turned it into a political victory for them. This small band of urban, middle-class revolutionaries had utterly misread the possibility of support among the peasants. Instead, villagers had beaten them and handed them over to the authorities. No mass uprising followed their actions but the massive over-reaction from the Shah did lead to political consequences that the revolutionaries had never imagined. Their executions after hasty military trials in April 1971, the arrest of more than 1,000 students and the increasing brutality of SAVAK made it ever clearer to many that there could be no compromise with the regime and that only violence would end its rule.

* * *

On the day the guests started to arrive, several explosions occurred in an attempt by the Fadai to knock out power supplies by blowing up transmission lines. Some damage was done to the foundations, but none of the towers collapsed, and power remained on. In a later raid on a Fadai safe house, SAVAK discovered an array of documents with details of cars driven by members of the court and other as well as home addresses for security officials.

THE VENUE

The threat of attacks during the event put everyone on edge. Several world leaders doubtless considered this in their decisions not to attend the party. To protect the event, the Shah's generals and secret police launched what was one of the largest security operations ever in Iran. One French chef working at the event complained that his pass had been checked more than forty times in a single day. Nomads who lived in the area were moved on, and the road from Shiraz was closed to all except official traffic. The rings of security ended up keeping almost everyone away from the celebrations and making them seem even more remote from the people.

Today, we are used to the idea of mammoth efforts to keep leaders safe and away from protestors. The costs of providing protection for the G7 meetings have grown immensely since the 1999 Battle of Seattle disrupted a World Trade Organization ministerial meeting. The security costs alone in 2021 for the G7 in Cornwall were at least £75 million. Entire areas of the southern British county were sealed off, the town where leaders met was barricaded with 3-meter-high fences, and more than 6,500 police were brought in to guard the event. Police officers cruised off the beach on jet skis while ubiquitous helicopters buzzed overhead. In 2018, Canada spent nearly twice as much protecting G7 leaders in Quebec.

Nowadays the G7 summit is invariably held in some remote resort that can be entirely cut off from the outside world. Persepolis was similar. Several concentric rings of security were put in place, starting dozens of kilometers from Persepolis and ending with extremely tight security around the tent city. Such were the efforts by the Iranians that they warranted a mention in the Presidential Daily Briefing provided to Nixon by the Central Intelligence Agency.

> The government is taking extraordinary precautions against possible terrorist actions during the two-week-long celebrations commemo-

THE SHAH'S PARTY

rating the 2,500th anniversary of the Persian monarchy beginning on Monday. The broad publicity to be given to the festivities provides an opportunity for dissident elements to advertise their cause by seeking to embarrass the government with assassinations or kidnappings. To counter this threat, the government has put all military and police on 24-hour alert, posted guards at key installations throughout the country, and stepped up patrols of the Iraqi border area. Suspected troublemakers have already been arrested.

There have already been some terrorist acts, including an unsuccessful attempt to kidnap Prince Shahram, the Shah's nephew. Police last week fought a running gun battle in Tehran with a group described as Maoist guerrillas. Unidentified groups around the country have for weeks been defacing statues of the Shah. Government security forces appear able to prevent large-scale disruptions.

A new unit bringing together the police, the army and SAVAK had been set up to ensure there would be no repeat of Siakhal. Inside the tent city, plain-clothed SAVAK officers lurked on every corner, adding to the somewhat strained atmosphere. Further out, soldiers stood guard, lining the road all the way to Shiraz. An estimate 800 people were taken into preventative detention.

Protests had been building since 1970 when students gathered in response to increases in bus fares. But terrorists, believed by many to have been supported by Iraq, had little effect with their ineffectual attempt to kidnap Prince Shahram, the son of the Shah's sister, from a street in Tehran being foiled. The government denied rumors of the attack, while also claiming that an explosion near the parliament building in Tehran that injured several people had been caused by a gas leak. "No heads of state were put off by the letter of protest sent them by the Ayatollah Khomeini, the major religious opponent of the regime, now exiled ..." wrote a British diplomat. Neither the Soviet Union nor China, both keen to improve relations with the Shah, had used their normal propaganda channels or surrogates to speak out against the party.

4

THE GUESTS

Is it not passing brave, to be a King, and ride in triumph through Persepolis?

Christopher Marlowe, *Tamburlaine*

12 October 1971

The first flight due into Shiraz was a Chinese government jet carrying the delegation from Beijing for the first-ever high-level visit to Iran by an official from the People's Republic. It never arrived.

A month before the party, a similar Trident jet had crashed in Mongolia. On board was Lin Biao, the minister of defense, and his family. Lin was the third of the Ten Marshals who had led the Communist People's Liberation Army to victory in 1949. He had marched his forces into Beijing, capturing the city and ending the civil war. Even with his prominence, he later had a relatively modest career until he was tapped to manage Mao's personality cult during the Cultural Revolution. In 1966, he was appointed vice chairman of the Chinese Communist Party and was named Mao's successor.

THE SHAH'S PARTY

Being Mao's deputy was never a comfortable fit. Lin, an anxious and sickly man who seemed to suffer from neurasthenia and hypochondria, was far from the picture of an iron-willed revolutionary general. But even during the turmoil of the Cultural Revolution, he managed to stay in favor with Mao and the swirl of ambitious and murderous people around him, including the chairman's wife Jiang Qing. He was behind the "Learn from Lei Feng" propaganda campaign that lionized a martyred soldier who was selflessly devoted to Mao and the Communist Party. Lei Feng, who was almost certainly fictitious, had spent his time washing the socks and emptying the chamber pots of other soldiers, all while singing the praises of Mao.

In the early morning of 13 September 1971, according to the official version, Lin and his family tried to flee China. He had been plotting the assassination of Mao and planned to set up a rival power base. After first starting out south towards Guangzhou, the plane turned and headed west to Russia. Over Mongolia, it ran out of fuel and crashed, killing all aboard. None of this story is certain, except the final crash. Lin may have been fleeing ahead of a purge or might have fallen victim to his own devastating paranoia. Despite his lofty positions, he had never seemed desperate for power, often turning down promotions due to his health and skipping meetings for months on end as he tried to avoid the traps set by Mao and his courtiers during the most perilous of times for the Chinese leadership.

His death set off a massive purge of senior officers. Within a month, a thousand people had been jailed. The PLA, which had been spared the worst ravages of the Cultural Revolution, was now thrown back into the turmoil of revolutionary politics. After a moment of calm, China was turbulent again. It was just how Mao liked it.

Amid all of this, Mao's trusty factotum, Premier Zhou Enlai, was busy organizing the re-emergence of China onto the diplo-

THE GUESTS

matic stage. During the Cultural Revolution, ambassadors had been recalled and punished, the norms of diplomacy overturned, and most efforts focused on aiding revolutions and distributing Mao's Little Red Book. A billion copies of the selection of Mao's writings were printed, possibly making it the most distributed book after the Bible.

Iran and China had not enjoyed close relations. The Shah loathed communism and was dismayed by Chinese society. "Like ants!" he murmured in horror. The Chinese had also been meddling in the Gulf, supporting an insurgency in Oman that created anxieties for Tehran. Iranian students abroad, often dismayed by the Stalinist associations of the Tudeh Party and its retreat in the face of the Shah's repression, had turned to Maoism in increasing numbers, raising the specter that it might emerge in Iran. In the mid-1960s, the secret police SAVAK had told the Shah that the Chinese might have been behind an assassination attempt that they believed had been organized by Maoist Iranian students in the United Kingdom.

China did not see Iran as a natural friend, but Beijing was emerging from its long isolation and was open to those it had enthusiastically denounced up until then. The autocrats in Beijing liked other autocrats, particularly if they could make neat arrangements with them that suited their transactional view of geopolitics. It was always easier to deal with a single figure in charge.

Mao and the Shah shared a common concern: Moscow. The Imperial Monarchy and the Maoist autocracy both saw enough in this mutual concern to find a way to reopen relations. In April 1971, Princess Ashraf traveled to Beijing on what was billed as a personal trip, but she met both Mao and Zhou. The Princess was as far from the ideal Maoist woman as could be imagined. Always dressed in French couture and expensive jewels, she was relentless in getting what she wanted.

THE SHAH'S PARTY

Another sister, Princess Fatema, visited just two weeks later. Soon, ambassadors from the countries were meeting in Islamabad and in August 1971, Iran and China established diplomatic relations. Moscow's increasing influence in Iraq and Yemen raised fears in Iran that the country might find itself surrounded. For Beijing, any enemy of their enemy was now a friend. The Shah's ambitions to be a regional power as the British pulled out of the Persian Gulf also required at least tacit agreements from various diplomatic heavyweights that they would not assert themselves there.

An invitation was sent to China for its head of state to attend. Soong Ching-ling, the widow of Sun Yat-Sen and the sister-in-law of the Nationalist leader Chiang Kai-Shek, was officially head of state, a position she shared with Dong Biwu, one of the founders of the Communist Party. They had taken over from Liu Shaoqi, who had been purged in the Cultural Revolution. The acting co-presidents declined, doubtless wary at the risks involved in attending such an event. They were almost certainly mindful of the treatment of Liu's widow, Wang Guangmei, an educated and cosmopolitan first lady of China who had joined him on many state visits abroad before the Cultural Revolution. On a trip to Indonesia, she had worn an elegant dress and a pearl necklace to an official banquet. It caught the resentful notice of Mao's wife, the former actor Jiang Qing. In 1967, Red Guards forced Wang to dress up in a tight traditional *qipao* dress and don a necklace of ping pong balls in a show of her bourgeois, counter-revolutionary attitude. She would spend twelve years in prison, many of them in isolation. She did not learn of her husband's death in a similar cell until years afterwards.

Given the constant turmoil in the highest ranks of the Chinese leadership, attending a luxurious party with European royalty and an array of other undesirables would not have featured on anyone's priorities in Beijing in 1971. But someone had

THE GUESTS

to go. The man chosen was Kuo Mojo, the vice chairman of the Standing Committee of the National People's Congress. (Kuo's name is more often transliterated today as Guo Moruo).

Kuo was a senior communist intellectual who was just emerging from a brutal purge during the Cultural Revolution. A longtime friend of Mao and the head of the Chinese Academy of Sciences, he had been forced in 1967 to admit that he had not understood his leader's works sufficiently and had written books that deserved to be burned. But Mao obviously had a soft spot for him and had him restored to his posts. A medical doctor by training, an archaeologist, historian, and poet by profession, he was given a role in rebuilding relations with the outside world. Simon Leys, the coruscating and brilliant Belgian sinologist, described him as "a pillar of China's cultural establishment who has been showered with countless official titles and honors, but his ruthless opportunism and shameless sycophancy have earned him the universal contempt of all Chinese intellectuals."

Emissaries like Kuo were sent out to renew contacts that had shrunk to such a degree that at one point China's only ambassador abroad was its envoy in Cairo. All other missions were headed by chargés d'affaires after the ambassadors were recalled for re-education at the hands of the Red Guards.

But Kuo, then 80, never made it to Persepolis. He conveniently fell ill on a flight from Beijing and his plane was diverted to Sichuan, where he was given medical treatment. His place was taken by the new Chinese chargé d'affaires in Tehran and the Chinese ambassador to Pakistan Zhang Tong. The pair were photographed in their Mao jackets, smiling nervously as they wandered around the tent city. Mixing with such an array of former and current enemies must have been nerve-wracking, particularly given the tumult at home that meant the slightest gesture might be misinterpreted.

* * *

THE SHAH'S PARTY

At the Congress of Vienna in 1815, the large salon where the delegates gathered had four entrances so officials from Britain, Russia, Prussia, and Austria could all enter at the same time. The chaotic protocol of an event with so many rulers. More than 200 states and princely houses were represented at the Congress that reordered Europe after the Napoleonic wars, as well as delegates from cities, abbeys and even publishers (there to demand a copyright law). The potential for snubs and resentment was great and so a new system was adopted that was based on seniority—time in office or on the throne—rather than power, a much more subjective condition.

The same rules applied at the party more than a century and a half later. Emperors came first, followed by kings. Next were crown princes and those representing monarchs, and then presidents, prime ministers, and so on down to those who were not representing a state. Haile Selassie had been on the Ethiopian throne for nearly forty-one years, including his exile in England during the Italian occupation of his country. He was the guest of honor, to be accompanied at meals by the Empress of Iran. But even the rigorous application of Vienna protocol, with help from the British Foreign Office, did not prevent the usual mutterings of discontent.

Ensuring that there was a decent turn out had turned into an obsession for the Shah and his court. The right to develop copper deposits in the eastern province of Kerman was dangled in front of the French and British if their heads of state would attend. The Dutch ambassador was warned of a sharp decline in relations unless he produced Queen Juliana. The German ambassador flew back to Bonn to get President Gustav Heinemann to RSVP positively.

The guest whose presence would have pleased the Shah the most was Richard Nixon, an old friend from when the king had welcomed the then vice president to Tehran with full pomp and

THE GUESTS

ceremony. It was decided even before Nixon received the formal invitation that he would not attend. Security anxieties and the demands of his time in 1971 meant he was never likely to go to what he would have regarded as an essentially empty event with the potential for diplomatic pitfalls. He was not known for his fondness for parties or international events. This was in the days before leaders spent much of their time on a seemingly endless circuit of huge multilateral summits. On top of this was the difficult presence of Soviet officials. Summitry at this time was something done between Washington and Moscow after much preparation. If Nixon met senior Soviet officials and came away with nothing, he risked looking weak or ineffectual. Vice President Spiro Agnew would attend. Vice presidents existed for exactly this type of event.

Protocol mattered in Iran. Unlike many royals, the Shah had impeccable manners, particularly with guests. But there was always some snickering about the occasional bouts of pomposity. As Queen Elizabeth II once said of a minor Austrian aristocrat, Princess Michael of Kent, marrying into her family, she "sounds a bit too grand for us." Similar jibes were made about the Pahlavis among diplomats and courtiers who dealt with their demands. Quite a few more secure monarchs were put off by the grandiosity, particularly by the lesser members of the clan. The titles collected by Mohammad Reza also came across as somewhat ridiculous. King of Kings sounds perhaps more pompous than it originally was when it really meant *primus inter pares* among the many tribal leaders of Persia. Shadow of God was just immodest. Light of the Aryans was a recent invention and had been granted to the Shah by parliament in 1965. It was a title that was always regarded with some embarrassment by Europeans, given that the word Aryan is indelibly tainted by association with the Nazis and their racial war on the world. It is a linguistic rather than racial term and is associated with those who spoke Aryan languages of South Asia and Iran.

THE SHAH'S PARTY

The Shah was quite restrained compared with many other monarchs. Among the titles of the last Ottoman Sultan, Ahmed Hamid II, were Lord of the Two Continents and the Two Seas, Sultan of Sultans, Commander of the Faithful and Guardian of the Two Holy Cities. The late twentieth century saw something of an explosion of new titles. Hafez Al-Assad of Syria styled himself "The Eternal Leader," while Kwame Nkrumah of Ghana added "The Redeemer" and "Messiah of Africa." Ugandan dictator Idi Amin favored "King of Scotland" but for more informal occasions would settle on "His Excellency President for Life Field Marshal Al-hadji Doctor Idi Amin Dada, VC, DSO, MC, Lord of all the Beasts of the Earth and Fishes of the Sea, Conqueror of the British Empire in all of Africa and Uganda in Particular." Next door in his benighted former French colony, former Sergeant Jean-Bedel Bokassa preferred just a simple Bokassa Le Premier, Emperor of the Central African Empire.

Generalissimo proliferated at one time although it has gone out of favor, perhaps too associated with Mussolini and the final image of him dangling upside down from a garage forecourt roof in Milan. Father of the Nation was popular with new countries emerging from colonialism. Ho Chi Minh stuck with a simple and modest "Uncle" and favored pictures of himself playing with children on the steps of his modest home. Stalin liked a similar look and appellation. Haile Selassie's titles might have been given a gloss of legitimacy by the age of his dynasty, but they were still extravagant: "Conquering Lion of the Tribe of Judah, King of Kings and Elect of God". His regnal name itself meant "Power of the Trinity." He had been born Tafari Makkonen.

Kim Il-Sung, in the early 1970s consolidating his supremacy over North Korea with an extravagant cult of personality, beats the lot: Party Center; Superior Person; Dear Leader; Respected Leader; Wise Leader; Brilliant Leader; Unique Leader; Dear Leader Who is a Perfect Incarnation of the Appearance that a

THE GUESTS

Leader Should Have; Guiding Sun Ray; Sun of Socialism, World Leader of the 20th Century; Glorious General Who Descended from Heaven; Eternal General Secretary of the Party and so on and on. People who study this issue have identified fifty-five different ways he was addressed in newspapers and official documents. He kept his titles after his death as president for eternity.

Titles matter. One of Khomeini's most skillful political moves before he came to power in 1979 was to quietly assume the title Imam, or rather when his followers started using it for him, he did not demur. Many Iranians are Twelver Shia and believe that the Twelfth Imam will return to earth to vanquish all wrongs and restore humanity to a state of perfection. Imam is a title reserved for him, not for mere ayatollahs, but Khomeini was slow to correct anyone, as he was when people started seeing his image on the moon or on loaves of flat bread. It was a clever ruse to allow his people to be swept away by his near divine status.

13 October 1971

Behind the scenes, there was chaos. Even as the event began, the guest list had not been finalized, and nobody was sure who was coming. Staff had been drafted to help with service from the royal palaces and from the Badrutt's Palace Hotel in St. Moritz and other luxury hotels the Shah favored in Europe. But the operations were complicated, not least because far more guests than expected had turned up, resulting in some shuffling of accommodation.

Maximilien, Cardinal von Furstenberg, the envoy of Pope Paul VI, was moved to a hotel in Shiraz and was promptly locked in his room until a handyman could be found to remove the faulty doorknob. The Belgian cardinal was a long-standing papal nuncio and Prefect of the Congregation for the Eastern Churches, which covered Iran. But on learning that his low ranking under

THE SHAH'S PARTY

the Vienna Protocol meant he did not warrant a tent, he threw a tantrum. The president of Germany canceled late in the day due to an eye operation, sending the head of the Bundestag, Kai-Uwe von Hassel, in his place. He, too, was banished to a hotel when an Afghan princess took precedence and commandeered his tent, taking his demotion no better than the cardinal had. As the senior Chinese official had not arrived due to a convenient diplomatic illness, the cardinal was finally given his tent.

In Shiraz, in the dormitories of the city's university, were hundreds of journalists, who were mostly kept away from Persepolis but were fed a constant stream of details about the opulence of the Shah's hospitality. They too were muttering about their accommodation and its distance from the action. Many had been unable to get passes for the tent city and resented being kept away from what they imagined was the excitement there. In fact, most of those who arrived were sleeping off their jetlag or touring the ruins.

* * *

The first of the motley collection of heads of state or their representatives to arrive was Imelda Marcos, first lady of the Philippines. Like the other guests, she was met at Shiraz Airport by the Shah's brother Abdul Reza and driven to Persepolis. Motorcades of black Cadillacs and eggplant-colored Mercedes 280-CEs sped along the new roads, which the National Iranian Oil Company had lined with flaming torches. Surrounding each limousine were four Jeeps packed with armed troops.

On arrival at Persepolis, Imelda and her 15-year-old daughter Maria Imelda, known as Imee, were greeted at a brief ceremony by the Shah and Shahbanou. Hundreds of Imperial Guards stood at attention to be reviewed by the Philippines first lady as a military band played the national anthems. As representative of a head of state, she was accorded the full rituals. Officials from

THE GUESTS

Liberia, South Korea and Swaziland, all mere members of governments, did not warrant the Imperial welcome.

Imelda and Imee were driven off to their tent. Footage of them wandering the empty encampment shows the pair surrounded by nervous Iranian army officers. Imee curtsied to everyone, presumably fearing a breach in protocol. As is so often the case in the world of royalty and political leaders there was a shortage of easy conversation. Everyone looks unsure as to what is supposed to be happening.

As they wandered somewhat aimlessly past the fountains, security guards scurried to re-arrange themselves out of camera shot. Along with her personal camera crew, Imelda had brought along an official suite of ladies-in-waiting and aides-de-camp and had also smuggled another guest into her tent. Cristina Ford, the Italian wife of Henry Ford II, had been allocated a hotel room in Shiraz but Imelda asked if she could stay amidst the luminaries in the camp. Empress Farah gave her permission. Imee was doubtless banished to the maid's room.

Ford and Marcos had become close friends. She was the wife of the motor heir who had emerged from middle class Italy to become a fixture of the global jet set while also professing to be nothing more than a simple housewife. She had told *LIFE* magazine just a few months before the party that she no longer "understands these butterflies who go out every night." A TV dinner and an early night were more her style.

A documentary made for consumption in the Philippines shows Marcos in an array of the puffy-sleeved traditional dresses known as *ternos*. At the banquet, Imee dressed as an Arabian princess with a gauzy veil and a glittering white dress, more *I Dream of Jeannie* than correct attire for Iran, but perhaps forgivable on a teenager. They toured the ruins carrying frilly parasols against the desert sun while being followed by yet more nervous military officers. Meanwhile in the film, the narrator struggles with the names of wines and words like caparisoned. The film gives a sense of the scale of the tent city and the ruins: it was undeniably spectacular. Otherwise, this is an Imelda-centered film: Imelda standing around awkwardly takes up most of the twenty minutes.

In 1986, Marcos would later flee an uprising by the Filipino people, just one of many of the Shah's guests who would be overthrown by popular revolts. In 2022, her son was elected president of the country.

> *Spiro T. Agnew, who was forced to resign as the 39th Vice President of the United States in 1973 when he pleaded no contest to a charge of income-tax evasion, died yesterday in Berlin, Md. He was 77 years old. John Ullrich, the owner of Ullrich Funeral Home in Berlin, Md., said Mr. Agnew died at Atlantic General Hospital in Berlin. A spokeswoman for Atlantic General Hospital would provide no details about his death.*
>
> *The New York Times*, 18 September 1996

Spiro Agnew found himself low in the protocol rankings at Persepolis but nevertheless he was allowed one privilege that only the Shah enjoyed. He was given permission to make the trip from Shiraz airport by helicopter as the Secret Service was worried by the 70-kilometer journey by car. He arrived and retreated to his tent as his attentive bodyguards, some of the fort-one agents who guarded the vice president on the trip, stood watch outside.

The Agnews were tired and decided to rest in their rooms. Along with his wife Judy, Agnew had flown into Ankara just days before at the start of a tour of Turkey, Iran and Greece. Nixon had other priorities so Agnew was sent off to second and third tier countries as well as doing the regular vice-presidential round of foreign funerals and inaugurations. But even moving the Vice President was a complicated exercise involving a presidential 707 with the call sign Air Force Two, and a large retinue of officials.

THE GUESTS

His instructions for meeting the Shah were limited; they were expected to have only fifteen minutes together, and the conversation was likely to be dominated by the Shah's desire for more weapons. If asked about the aerial refueling planes that the Shah was pressing for, Agnew was to say the administration was studying the issue. Nixon and Kissinger were eager to sell the Shah whatever he wanted but Congress and the Defense Department bureaucracy were hesitant, knowing that there was no limit to what he wanted to buy with his new oil money. Going back to Eisenhower, the Shah always asked for more arms, while successive United States governments always urged him to spend more on domestic issues. The Shah always resisted this idea, insisting that Iranians wanted to fight for their country even if defeat and occupation were the inevitable result of a Soviet invasion. The withdrawal of the British from East of Suez had given him new reasons for arms. He saw Iran as the new regional policeman, even extending its reach out into the Indian Ocean to counter growing Soviet influence there.

Otherwise, the main issue on the agenda was the worsening tension between Pakistan and India. Washington wanted the Shah to calm General Yahya Khan, the military ruler of Pakistan, and lower the temperature despite "continuing Indian troublemaking." The tone of Kissinger's memo shows where the sympathies of the administration lay. Kissinger knew what was going on. In 1970, Bengali nationalists had won elections, meaning they would come to power in the geographically divided state created by the partition of British India in 1947. In April 1971, the Pakistani military had launched Operation Searchlight, a collaboration with Bengali Islamist militias to carry out a genocide against nationalists, intellectuals, secularists and everyone else who opposed the government in Islamabad and wished to see independence. Such was the level of brutality, including mass rapes, that ten million refugees fled into India, prompting Indira

THE SHAH'S PARTY

Gandhi to respond by arming supporters of independence. The civil war soon became an international conflict.

India was officially non-aligned but leaned towards Moscow. Pakistan was heavily dependent on support and arms from the United States. It was also close to China and Yahya had acted as a go-between to set up meetings between Kissinger and top Chinese officials that led to a rapprochement. Nixon had announced in July 1971 that he would visit China the next year, a massive and shocking change to United States policy that would become the most enduring legacy of his presidency. He was keen to avoid the inevitable war brewing between India and Pakistan but at the same time was pushing hard against India. He despised Indira Gandhi, referring to her in taped conversations in the White House in luridly misogynist and racist terms. Indian women were the most unattractive people on earth and Indians in general were "sexless and pathetic," Nixon harrumphed. What India needed, he continued, was a mass famine. Kissinger, ever the sycophant, muttered agreement. He shared the president's loathing of Gandhi and her friendship with Moscow. They were eager to protect the Pakistanis despite their genocide in Bangladesh to ensure his access to China continued.

India formally entered the war on 3 December 1971 after Pakistan launched Operation Genghis Khan in which their United States-supplied jets carried out pre-emptive attacks against Indian Air Force bases, hoping to wipe out their air superiority in the way the Israelis had in the Six Day War. It was a terrible error on Yahya Khan's part; the general, by then dissolute and incompetent, spent much of the war drunk and pursuing women. It ended just thirteen days later with the unconditional surrender of Pakistani forces in Dhaka. A new nation was born, the Cold War got a few degrees colder with New Delhi signing a Treaty of Friendship with Moscow, and a United States administration found itself complicit in the murder of more than a million people.

* * *

The Nixon presidency was a new opportunity for the Shah. Finally, the occupant of the Oval Office liked him and found him a credible ruler rather than barely disguising their view of him as a tin pot dictator. Republicans generally liked the Shah; Democrats always struggled to keep up the necessary friendship with a man who wore uniforms and dark glasses too often and whose family was so openly corrupt. The Saudi royal family at least kept their obscene consumption behind high walls.

A report from the Embassy in Tehran, written just before the party, portrayed the Shah as a relatively benign figure, dragging his country into the modern era. But it also warned, quite presciently, of "soft spots" in the Iranian situation. The Shah was isolated, and information rarely reached him. "Even foreign ambassadors cringe before the Shah's responses to official presentations that displease him." His isolation was only likely to get worse, it noted. "The chances that he will fail to comprehend the intensity of, say, a political protest movement are likely to grow. Hence, so will the chances for miscalculation in how to deal with it."

The relationship had never been easy, with World War II and the 1953 coup gradually expanding the view that Washington had acquired too much power in Iran. People on both sides tended to think the United States had far more power to influence events there than it ever had. Iranians across the spectrum have spent far too much time and energy worrying about what the Americans—and the British—were up to rather than looking more closely at the dynamics of their own society. A malign cloud of suspicion and enmity hangs over the country, and it is far denser than in most nations; the paranoid style in Iranian politics likes a story, and Americans nearly always provided the best plots.

The Shah's relationship with U.S. presidents had always been touchy. When Roosevelt visited Tehran in November 1943 for his conference with Stalin and Churchill, he did not meet the young Shah at his palace, as diplomatic protocol demanded. Instead, he made him come to the American Legation. Relations with Truman were little better, although as the Cold War began, the United States recognized the necessity of supporting the Shah to prevent the Soviet Union from seeking to topple him. Eisenhower at least visited the country. He spent six hours in Tehran while on a jaunt around the world.

John Kennedy was a skeptic. The president thought the Shah demanded too much military aid and did too little to improve the lives of his people. The administration was barely focused on Iran, busy as it was with Cuba, Berlin, Indochina, and a torrent of domestic issues, many involving segregation in the South. Kennedy saw Mohammad Reza as rigid and authoritarian; there was clearly no warmth. Kennedy had also pushed the Shah to appoint a United States favorite, Ali Amini, as prime minister, even though the monarch preferred other, more amenable, politicians. Amini, who had served as ambassador in Washington and was both a known quantity and a liberal, served just over a year from 1961, never earning the trust of the Shah due to his pro-American views. In 1962, the Shah replaced him with his friend Asadollah Alam.

Lyndon Johnson, caught up with Vietnam and the Great Society reforms, never spent much time thinking about Iran. The Shah made the usual rounds of official visits and spent his time appealing for more weapons and more aid, with moderate results. The Iranian economy was growing, and United States businesses were starting to pay attention, but even though the country was on the frontline when it came to the Soviet Union, it received little attention in Washington.

THE GUESTS

That was to change when Richard Nixon became president in 1969. Assessments of the Shah had changed significantly since he was last in government and the two men had formed a bond when Nixon was out of office. The views of American diplomats had changed:

> The Shah is confused, frustrated, suspicious, proud, and stubborn, a young man who lives in the shadow of his father. His fears, questionings, and indecisiveness are permanent instabilities of character. Yet, he has great personal courage, many Western ideals, and a sincere, though often wavering, desire to raise and preserve his country.
>
> *(United States Embassy, Tehran 1951)*

> He (the Shah) is completely self-assured and is confident that he is leading the country in the right direction. He is also well-informed, and his ability to keep abreast of developments around the world is remarkable. He has an agile mind, sees the point quickly, and gets right to the heart of the issue.
>
> *(United States Embassy, Tehran 1970)*

The Shah and Nixon were made for each other. Both were awkward men, although Mohammad Reza did have perfect manners, unlike the sour and often ungracious American. Both had a sense of themselves as visionaries, above the concerns of little men, given to the broad strategic perspective rather than the petty details. They both enjoyed their monologues, the *tour d'horizon* of global politics and the idea that they existed on the rarified plane of the century's great leaders. Both admired Charles de Gaulle for often standing alone on the world stage, completely assured that his ideas were best for his country and everyone else. Like all such grand men, they abhorred their own bureaucracies, preferring to work around them whenever possible. The bold gesture was their signature move: the personal breakthrough, the

THE SHAH'S PARTY

direct confrontation. They also loathed the Democratic Party establishment in Washington, particularly the Kennedy family. Both spent much more time than they would admit hating people. Nixon was to write several glowing descriptions of the Shah in his memoirs, describing him as showing signs of strength as far back as 1953, when most people still saw a skinny man-child with little sense of himself.

Nixon is as much to blame as anyone for the grandiosity that gripped the regime from the early 1970s and contributed enormously to its failures. The Shah became the embodiment of the Nixon Doctrine, the idea elaborated in the wake of the failures in Vietnam that the United States would not be the world's policeman but would support its allies with arms and financing. For Nixon, the Shah was someone who had stuck by him in the wilderness years, treating him as a statesman when most people saw him as a bitter old has-been, the angry man of the "you won't have Nixon to kick around anymore" press conference in 1962 after his defeat for the governorship of California.

In 1967, Nixon visited Tehran, and the Shah presented to him a vision of the Gulf under threat from Soviet proxies in Egypt and Iraq. Moscow was determined to control the supply of oil from the region and would steadily try to subvert any government that stood in their way. The threat of communism loomed heavily over the Shah; the "red threat" had long been his biggest menace. In fact, the Soviets were wary of confrontation in the region and spent much of their time restraining radical Baathists in Damascus and Baghdad. They did not see a regional war as in their interests nor did they much want a confrontation with the United States. But during the Cold War, it was very easy for both the Shah and Nixon to convince themselves that the Middle East needed a massive build-up of arms, with Iran taking the lead.

Until Nixon, the Washington consensus had been that the Shah did not need so many weapons. His army was sufficient to deter aggression from most of his neighbors. Arming him excessively would only raise anxieties among the Arab nations in the Gulf, and Washington generally wanted to maintain a balance there. Pumping in weapons would only encourage the Soviets to do the same, raising the temperature in a highly inflammable part of the world.

Nixon had been in office 1,226 days before Air Force One finally landed in Tehran. Each one of those days had grated on Mohammad Reza. The Shah had hoped Nixon would join the celebration at Persepolis, but it was never likely. Nixon wanted to get down to business when he traveled and rarely did much beyond official meetings. He was also focused on the Soviet Union and China. By the time he got to Iran, he had already visited twenty-three countries, several twice. The telegrams from the ambassadors became increasingly desperate as the Shah started making pointed remarks. When asked by a visiting senator when he could next be expected in Washington, Mohammad Reza stonily responded that he had made many trips to the United States capital and "it was perhaps time for someone from over there to visit Iran."

In 1972, Nixon flew into Tehran and signed an agreement with the Shah that allowed him to buy any United States weapons system short of nuclear arms. The "blank check" would have a dramatic effect on the economy and on regional security as the Shah went on an unmatched spending spree. Coming just before the oil crisis sent prices soaring and money piling up in the Shah's treasury, the move was profoundly ill-conceived. But several factors came together at once: the British announcement that they were ending all military engagements in the Gulf from the end of 1971 made the Shah determined to take their place. In the U.S., the Six-Day War and the expansion of Soviet engagement with Syria and Iraq, made the Middle East a greater strategic focus.

THE SHAH'S PARTY

At the same time, arms purchases ramped up because of Vietnam were starting to decline; weapons manufacturers were pushing for new markets. Nixon was following a pattern that had already been set under Johnson. Although Johnson had little time for the Shah, he had allowed a gradual increase in arms purchases to keep him on side. By the time he left office in 1969, Iran was the biggest purchaser of weapons from the United States.

Nixon opened the floodgates. Between July and November 1972, the Shah ordered $3.5 billion of weapons. It was more than the entire annual bill for military aid to all United States allies put together. Up until his fall, he would spend billions more each year on weapons. When the Revolutionary Government came in, it would cancel nearly $10 billion of deals, including 160 F-16 jets, AWACS planes, submarines, and more than 13,000 missiles of various types.

The arms build-up certainly had a logic. The radicalism of the late 1960s and early 1970s was pressing up against Iran, most notably in Iraq but also elsewhere across the region. The regime in Syria moved closer to the Soviets. In 1968, the People's Democratic Republic of Yemen was established, earning the sobriquet the "Cuba of the Middle East." A leftist rebellion in Oman was threatening the rule of the Sultan there; the Shah sent forces to help put down the Chinese-supported guerrilla movement. Leftist opposition was bubbling up constantly in Turkey and Afghanistan. This was all tied together by the student movements rising up around the world and by covert support from the Soviet Union. The Cold War and the unsettled moment in the region called for a strengthening of military control and a tightening of the Shah's grip on society.

The impact of all this was devastating. The Shah became consumed with the grandiosity of Iran's future as a power not just in the Gulf but beyond in the Indian Ocean. He saw himself as a key player, almost on the level of the United States, in

THE GUESTS

securing the region against the Soviet threat. But Iran had almost no capacity to integrate these weapons into its armed forces, the leadership of which was constantly depleted by the Shah's appointment of toadies and supplicants rather than the most effective officers. He did head off a possible coup and did not meet the fate of so many of his fellow monarchs in the Middle East, but at the same time, he ensured his military would never be as effective as he wished and ultimately would not keep him in power.

> *Queen Elizabeth II, the UK's longest-serving monarch, has died at Balmoral aged 96, after reigning for 70 years. She died peacefully on Thursday afternoon at her Scottish estate, where she had spent much of the summer.*
>
> BBC, 8 September 2022

Despite his suspicions of the British, one of the guests he most hoped would join the party was Queen Elizabeth II. The Shah knew her well. He had made two state visits to the United Kingdom, and she came to Iran in 1961. There was not a great amount of warmth between the two royal families, although both covered the *froideur* with good manners and generosity. A year before the event, a debate started among senior civil servants about the advisability of the Queen attending. The Permanent Under-Secretary—the senior civil servant—at the Foreign Office, Denis Greenhill, recommended against it. "The ceremonies, lasting three days and possibly more, and taking place in Tehran and Persepolis, in the presence of a motley collection of heads of state or, more likely, their representatives, are likely to be arduous, disorganized and possibly undignified and insecure."

Embarrassingly, Queen Elizabeth was planning on making a state visit to Turkey at nearly the same moment and so her lack of availability had come with the sting that she would be right next door soon afterwards. Just after he took up his post as

THE SHAH'S PARTY

British ambassador, Peter Ramsbotham was summoned to Niavaran Palace and asked about the Queen's attendance. He found himself in an awkward bind. Queen Elizabeth did not attend this sort of "jamboree," as he later put it. When she went somewhere, she was the center of attention. She rarely attended large public events with other rulers. Ramsbotham could not find an easy way to explain this to the Shah.

If she could not come, the Shah insisted that Britain send her heir, Prince Charles. That was not possible either, as he was serving in the Royal Navy and was reluctant to interrupt his military service. This was mystifying to the Shah, who did not understand why he could not take some leave. Finally, Mohammad Reza grudgingly accepted a visit by Prince Philip and Princess Anne, father and daughter known for their rather churlish demeanors and propensity for gaffes. They would be among the lowest-ranked royals in attendance, far below the salt in protocol terms.

There was more to the resistance to the visit than reluctance to let the Queen attend a somewhat uncontrolled event. When the decision was made, the Shah was still raising difficulties over islands in the middle of the Gulf that were claimed by both Iran and the newly created United Arab Emirates, then a British protectorate of tiny sheikhdoms. The huge cultural and religious divide between Persians and Arabs was coming to the fore—it would endure over the next few decades as a major fissure across the region and the wider world. Shortly after the festivities ended, Iranian forces grabbed the three islands in the Strait of Hormuz, precipitating rage across the Arab world and a subtle shift in attention away from Iran and towards Saddam Hussein's Iraq.

The British government was trying to keep the Shah on their side without encouraging him to bully the states on the southern shore of the Persian Gulf. While they hoped he would step up to maintain security, they were also desperate to sell him anything they could as Britain's industrial position in the world rapidly drained away. Alam noted in his diary in 1972 that they were now "so forlorn that nothing interests them these days except commerce and arms deals." Britain was a constant source of irritation for the Shah, who was never as Anglophile as Alam. The satirical magazine *Private Eye* taunted him as the "Shit of Iran", the press wrote about the excesses of his family and regime, and student groups pressed for boycotts. Even the generally balanced *Financial Times* caused upset ahead of the party by mixing up the Iranian currency and the dollar and publishing a story that massively overstated the cost of the illuminations that decorated Tehran. Worst of all was the BBC Persian Service, long a source of deep resentment since it had helped undermine his father's rule in the 1940s.

The Shah was too important a regional player and a client for British business to be ignored. To ease the sting of her absence, he was invited to spend Ascot week at Windsor with the British monarch. This lengthy house party was a personal favorite for the Queen, who loved both racing and staying at Windsor for what was known as the Easter Court. Entertaining the ponderous Iranian monarch cannot have been a thrill for her, as this was usually a week for family and friends. She found him slightly difficult, always talking too much about dry governmental issues, even when off duty. Ramsbotham attended at Windsor, reminiscing later that the Queen was a dutiful host to the Shah, even rushing around to find a stallion for him to ride. Iranian men made it a matter of honor not to be seen on a mare or gelding. The only stallion available went by the name of Cossack, an unfortunate reminder of the lowly origins of the Pahlavis.

The visit to Windsor looked in doubt at one moment when the Shah had a tantrum at Mehrabad Airport in Tehran before his departure. He rehearsed his usual set of grievances against the BBC and the media in general, asking the British ambassador why it was worth visiting London when he was treated with such disrespect there. He was also aggrieved that the British were not taking a tough enough line against Iraq and the leader of Abu Dhabi, who was cozying up to Baghdad. His deeper anxiety was Soviet penetration into the Gulf, a perennial source of concern. The British were increasingly worried about the Shah's security in Britain, urging him to drive to the races at Ascot in a bullet-proof car rather than the traditional carriage ride. He refused, insisting on the transport always used by the British royals. His mood apparently improved during two days at the races with Queen Elizabeth and a trip to inspect military equipment. A courtier later told the British ambassador that the Shah had enjoyed everything except the fact that he had lost money at Ascot, whereas his Master of Ceremonies won £220.

* * *

Inevitably even the Shah's gifts of two ponies and an Arab stallion to Prince Philip and Princess Anne caused problems for the British Embassy after the party. The Princess had admired an expensive 2-year-old stallion while touring the Imperial Stables, declaring, "What a beautiful beast!" The Shah immediately gave it to her. And so began a lengthy chain of diplomatic cables back and forth between London and Tehran. A ban had been imposed on imports of horses from the Middle East because of a disease called African horse sickness. Diplomats discussed ways to quietly quarantine the stallion and the polo ponies to avoid offending the Shah by refusing his gifts. Various options were considered. Might they be left in Iran and cared for by the Imperial Stables? It might cause offence to the Shah but maybe it could be suggested that members of the British royal family would ride them on future visits, an idea that might soften the blow.

The exchanges grew somewhat tetchy after the head of the Royal Mews in London, Lieutenant Colonel John Miller, sug-

THE GUESTS

gested that the ponies might be sent to Spain where they would be looked after by the Marquess of Douro, while the horse should be left in Iran for Princess Anne to ride on her visits. A scribbled note on one of the cables noted that it made the embassy's efforts to find a solution "look pretty silly." "It is difficult to keep tabs on Royal whims," the author of the comments noted, something that would meet with a sigh of recognition among Iranian diplomats.

> *The French President Georges Pompidou died today, the president's office announced.*
>
> *The announcement said the 62-year-old president died at 0130 hrs.*
>
> *A few hours earlier, the president's office announced that Mr. Pompidou had cancelled all appointments because of an unstated illness.*
>
> The Associated Press, 3 April 1974

In August 1971, French President Georges Pompidou finally accepted his invitation to join the Shah at Persepolis. This was not much of a surprise given the close relations between France and Iran. The Shah was a great admirer of Charles de Gaulle, Pompidou's predecessor and mentor. He saw himself as a similar figure, the embodiment of his state and the greatest protector of its interests. They shared a grandiosity and a willingness to play off allies against each other. Both were demanding and proud, vain and somewhat lonely figures who had followers rather than friends.

In January, the French were still dithering over whether Pompidou would attend. When Alam complained about the delay in RSVPing, reminding the French ambassador that the Shah dutifully turned up in Paris whenever de Gaulle had held some major event, the envoy was scathing about his government: "Don't make the mistake of comparing the present lot with de Gaulle; they are quite in another league. A bunch of cringing politicians without any international standing. Even so, I shall go to France and see what can be done."

It turned out that no decision was going to be forthcoming any time soon whatever the ambassador did. Pompidou had *la gloire de la France* to uphold, and it was not clear that this could be done if he was going to be ranked way below a series of third-rate royalty and tin-pot Eastern European dictators. Having only been in office since 1969, he would have been well below many far less prominent leaders. This prompted a spiky series of responses from the Shah, whose profound Francophilia did not survive being disrespected by the French. He had got used to the lavish treatment they laid on whenever he visited Paris: they tended to extend the fullest state protocol even when he was on an unofficial visit or just stopping over. They also provided him with discreet medical care and other services.

As with so many members of the Persian elite, France was the European country the Shah most identified with. He spoke the language having been raised by a French governess and educated at school in francophone Switzerland. He was surrounded by French-educated staff and military officers trained at St Cyr. His wife had gone to a French girl's school in Tehran and then to university in Paris. Almost everything brought in for the party had come from Paris, seen then, as now, as the place for all forms of luxury. Bed linens, porcelain, wine and most of the food had been brought in from thirty French companies. Even the tents and landscaping came from France.

It was a relief in August when finally, Pompidou sent word that he was coming. His protocol chief even arranged a visit to Iran to organize his tour. This is when it all started to go wrong. It was clear that he was dissatisfied with the level of protocol he would be accorded. Word was sent to the Shah that the president was sadly too busy to attend.

In a subtle jibe at France, the Empress mentioned in her autobiography that the French were upset by their relatively low

THE GUESTS

ranking in terms of protocol. It had been much reported that President Pompidou had declined to attend and sent his honeymooning prime minister in his place. "Perhaps that is what upset them." She wrote. "At Eisenhower's funeral, for example, General de Gaulle sat, in all humility, in the place protocol assigned him." Resentment had run high at Pompidou's absence. The Shah went out of his way to ignore the newly married Prime Minister Jacques Chaban-Delmas throughout the event.

* * *

Despite his irritation at the French, the Shah was to make an odd decision in the coming years. After coming across a lump in the middle of his chest while holidaying on Kish Island, he summoned his doctor, Abdul Karim Ayadi. There was some concern that it was a swollen lymph node, and his doctor arranged for an expert to fly in from Paris. Normally, the Shah saw the expensive and discreet Doctor Karl Fellinger in Vienna or his doctors in Zurich during his winter holidays. There is some suggestion that a swollen lymph node had been biopsied, and lymphoma diagnosed as early as 1971. The secrecy around the Shah's health and his determination to keep his ailments secret means that much remains murky about his illness and its treatment.

From mid 1974, he was under regular observation by the French physician Georges Flandrin, who would fly in secretly and see the Shah at various safe houses around Tehran. Even the Shahbanou was not told about his illness, and there is some debate over whether even the Shah himself knew the seriousness of the disease, as his doctors avoided the dread word cancer and told him he had Waldenstrom's Syndrome. They even ensured that his bottles of pills were mislabeled in case he worked out for what he was being treated. British Foreign Secretary David Owen, a medical doctor by training, would later write of the Shah's illness, saying neither he nor his American counterparts had any idea of his diagnosis with lymphoma. It seems that his

THE SHAH'S PARTY

illness really did remain known only to a tiny number of people: four in Iran, including the Shah, and three doctors in France, two of whom had a history of very private treatment of prominent patients. Owen says that had he known, he is certain that the U.S. and European friends of Iran would have pressed the Shah for a democratic transition in 1977, before he lost control. It is hard to know if that was the case; there were certainly rumors of his illness throughout the mid-1970s, although this is a common enough occurrence for the powerful. Even if they did know, by that stage, they may have been unwilling to challenge the rich, grandiose, and very prickly Shah of that time.

It would later emerge that Georges Pompidou had throughout his presidency been suffering from Waldenstrom's Syndrome as well, experiencing bouts of ill health that meant he often delegated foreign travel to others. His sudden death in 1974 came as a surprise to most people; he, too, had kept his illness a secret. His widow would later deny the rare cancer killed him, blaming his death on blood poisoning from hemorrhoids.

* * *

On Dec. 25, 1989, the trial of Nicolae Ceaușescu and Elena Ceaușescu was held before an extraordinary military tribunal. The charges were: 1. Genocide. More than 60,000 victims. 2. Undermining of the state power through organization of armed actions against the people and the state power. 3. Destruction of public property through destruction and damaging of buildings and numerous explosions in cities, etc. 4. The undermining of the national economy. 5. The attempt to flee the country by taking advantage of more than $1 billion deposited in foreign banks. For these crimes against the Romanian people and Romania, the culprits Nicolae Ceaușescu and Elena Ceaușescu were condemned to death and the confiscation of their wealth. The sentence was definitive and was carried out.

Bucharest Radio, 25 December 1989.

THE GUESTS

Nicolae Ceaușescu had reason to be faintly disappointed by the sparse crowds lining the road as he drove from Shiraz Airport to Persepolis. The Romanian leader had just returned from state visits to China and North Korea, where tens of thousands of cheering people had been arrayed along every road he traveled. He had come back inspired by the displays of adoration organized by his hosts, particularly the mass games put on for him in Pyongyang. The crowds of North Koreans dancing, waving ribbons, and holding up cards that formed into enormous images must have thrilled his heart. Romanian newsreels showed residents of Pyongyang bouncing with joy at the sight of the diminutive Nicolae and his dowdy wife, Elena. Nobody staged an enthusiastic welcome quite like Kim Il-Sung. Even the parade at Persepolis was probably a disappointment with its relatively modest scale and its lack of an adoring crowd.

Ceaușescu was always something of an oddball, even among Eastern European leaders, and 1971 was the year in which he became odder yet. A dutiful Stalinist as a young man, he was among the only leaders in the Warsaw Pact who continued to deify the Soviet tyrant after 1956, while mixing a heavy dose of nationalism and an even larger measure of a personality cult into his communism. After the crushing of revolts in Hungary in 1956 and in Czechoslovakia in 1968, his comrades across the region were well aware of the Brezhnev Doctrine: stick to Moscow's line or face Soviet tanks on your lawn. But Romania had always tried to dance out of the bear hug, striking an autonomous pose, even as it relied massively on the Soviet Union for subsidies and trade.

Bucharest was known as one of the more open capitals in Eastern Europe. There was a rock music radio station—with limits. "Back in the USSR" by the Beatles was not played. There were exhibitions of American artists such as the previously reviled abstract expressionist Jackson Pollock. There was a Pepsi bottling plant. Literary journals featured a range of Western intellectuals and even exiled Romanians.

This all came to an end in 1971 with the visit to China and North Korea. Transcripts of his comments to a Central Committee meeting after his trip show how enormously impressed he was with both countries, particularly with the way the people came out to greet him. "I think we have to learn something from this, since everything was in good order ... all of their cultural activity (ballet, theatre) was set on revolutionary bases. They said: 'We do not want any bourgeois concept to get in here.'"

Ceaușescu thrilled to the orderly rows of housing and offices in Pyongyang, the innumerable monuments to Kim Il-Sung and the apparent discipline of North Koreans. The city had been levelled by American bombing during the Korean War, giving Kim the chance to remodel it in the image of the new Korea. By the late 1960s, Kim had established himself as the unchallenged paramount leader with all potential opponents purged. Any dissent, indeed, any failure to join in the prescribed worship of the leader, could result in three generations of family members being sent to a prison camp. Only the most loyal were allowed to live in Pyongyang, where heavily subsidized living standards were high for the time.

And so started a cultural revolution in Romania that would only end with Ceaușescu and his wife being shot dead by a firing squad after a perfunctory trial on Christmas Day 1989. Romania had gone from being one of the most open countries in the region to the most totalitarian, with the government in control of every aspect of the lives of its people, and Ceaușescu and his wife at the center of a cult of personality.

Kim Il-Sung was clearly the inspiration, along with Mao and Stalin. Cults of personality of the twentieth century have some similarities: often a young peasant boy made good against the odds; early heroism and struggles to overcome evil opponents; a lack of education but a huge knowledge and intelligence; time in prison or the wilderness that is overcome through strength of will; and an emergence not as the choice of the people but as the necessary leader for the moment. If there is a mentor or guide, he is now well in the past and inferior to the current leader in many unspoken ways. The cult relies on the creation of an aura of magnificence surrounding the leader, who professes modesty in public but maintains a security system that ensures maximum obedience and adulation. The slightest slip can land you in jail.

Ceaușescu followed the model closely. Born into a peasant family in 1918, he was an unprepossessing child of little note. He was later mentored by Gheorghe Gheorghiu-Dej, the communist politician favored by the Red Army, which had invaded the country in 1944. As Ceaușescu climbed the ranks, he first appeared to be somewhat liberal, allowing a loosening in many areas once he headed the party after 1965. The totalitarianism for which he was known emerged in the 1970s: culture was to center around the nation and the idea of harking back to the imagined past of the Dacian state. This band of tough warriors had created a highly centralized and militarized state to hold off the advances of the Roman Empire. It was as advanced as the Greeks; indeed, Romanians had often done such things ahead of others, a sign of their intrinsic superiority, according to the regime. Ceaușescu was not just part of the Communist Pantheon of Marx, Engels, and Lenin but also part of a historic chain of great Romanian leaders, including the Dacian kings Burebista and Decebalus.

Known by then as the *Conducator*, a Romanian word close to *Il Duce* or the *Fuhrer*, Ceaușescu moved away from any recognizable form of communism to one that blended Western-funded industrialization, egregious biopolitics, and a North Korean-style cult. His mostly uneducated wife was endlessly praised for her mastery of science, accruing honorary doctorates on their many foreign trips. Western states enjoyed trying to peel him away

THE SHAH'S PARTY

from the Soviet Bloc by hosting lavish state visits. While staying at Buckingham Palace, Queen Elizabeth made him a Knight Grand Cross of the Order of the Bath. He responded by stealing palace ashtrays. Driving through London in an open carriage with the Queen, he looks astonished to find himself there, waving delightedly at the bemused spectators.

Western powers tried to encourage his Tito-like independence from Moscow but his positions only occasionally rattled the Politburo there. They understood what many credulous journalists and politicians in the West did not. Despite the Pepsi plant and the state visits, Ceaușescu was to the core a Stalinist. He craved the same dominance over the party system, the same security system, the same obsession with heavy industry, whatever the cost, the same cult of personality, but with some Romanian characteristics. The communist party had always been something of a bit player before it was installed in power by the Red Army. None of the leaders had any heroic history as revolutionaries or partisans against Nazi rule. Their legitimacy was always fragile; Ceaușescu manufactured a heroic past by comparing himself with figures who had lived nearly two millennia earlier.

The Shah was playing a similar game. He toed the line when it came to friendships with the Eastern Bloc, engaging enough to keep Washington wary but not excessively dissatisfied. From the late 1960s, he stepped up energy sales to countries like Romania, an oil producer itself. Bucharest sold its own refined products to Europe at higher prices than the crude it bought from the Shah to power its heavy industries. In Iran, the crude and natural gas were exchanged for factory equipment: the Soviets built a steel mill, and other countries contributed what they could as the Shah's plans to build an industrial state grew more ambitious.

The performance of independence from Moscow by Ceaușescu allowed him to get away with running one of the worst dictator-

THE GUESTS

ships in Eastern Europe. Not only did Romanians endure poverty, intrusion into the most intimate aspects of their lives, and a dismal pretense of worshipping their mediocre leaders throughout the 1970s and 1980s, but their grandiosity also ruined the once-beautiful city of Bucharest. Enamored of the vast avenues and massive buildings of Pyongyang, Ceaușescu wanted to start with a blank slate too, so that he could build a capital worthy of a great socialist state. He left behind one of the world's largest ever buildings, a pharaonic monstrosity built on land carved out of the old city center.

* * *

The revolution began in the western university town of Timisoara where a protestant pastor stood up against efforts to evict him from his church. His parishioners protested and the police shot them. The ripple of discontent built from there. On 21 December 1989, Ceaușescu addressed a crowd that had been bused in to show he retained the support of the people. About two minutes into one of Ceaușescu's litanies of his own great achievements, the crowd started to jeer. A chant of "Timisoara" began, led by workers from a power plant. A startled Ceaușescu raised his hand to silence the crowd. They did not obey, and the revolution swelled in front of his eyes. State television quickly cut the live broadcast and replaced it with patriotic songs, but it was too late. The whole country had seen the very moment when a dictator lost power.

The Ceaușescus fled the next day as protesters broke into the building, hustled across the rooftop by their Securitate bodyguards. Their overloaded helicopter had to land just outside the capital, from where they commandeered a passing car. The driver took them to a nearby technical college, where the director locked them in an office. They were arrested shortly afterwards and taken into military custody. On 22 December, after the apparent suicide of the minister of defense, the army had turned against them, and it was all over. A trial lasting just two hours followed. They were shot in the courtyard by three commandos on Christmas Day. Ceaușescu is said to have sung the *Internationale* as he was executed.

Christmas celebrations had been banned up to that point. It was the first time in years that people enjoyed the festival. Ceaușescu had left behind a broken country. Thousands of children were in state orphanages, living in unimaginably awful conditions. The number of dead in the revolution was closer to 1,000 than the 60,000 he was accused of killing. There was no genocide, but there was nearly half a century of Stalinist policies that diminished the lives of Romanians in thousands of ways. It was a time of fear and poverty. Their welfare was never his priority. His policy of paying off foreign debt had left the population wracked with malnutrition and illness. Romania started its new democratic era in the worst state of any Eastern European country.

* * *

It is impossible to know if the Ceaușescus enjoyed their time at Persepolis. Given their taste for luxury and foreign visits, they probably did, even if it did not match the scale of the welcomes they had just received in Pyongyang and Beijing. A record of the conversation with the Shah is held in the Romanian archives. It was a platitudinous and wooden exchange about Middle East peace, with both men expressing banal hopes that Israel and Egypt could find a way to improve their relations. Apart from meetings with the Shah and Tito, they only emerged from their tent for meals. They did not have much experience mixing with royalty, but it was something they came to enjoy, even in the odd manner of the paranoid and insecure people they both were. It is not known if they helped themselves to anything from their tent.

THE GUESTS

To the working class, all the working people and citizens, and all the nations and nationalities of the Socialist Federal Republic of Yugoslavia:

Comrade Tito has died.

On May 4th, 1980, at 15:05 in Ljubljana, the great heart of the President of our Socialist Yugoslavia, the President of the Presidency of Yugoslavia, the President of the League of Communists of Yugoslavia, Marshal of Yugoslavia, and the Commander-in-chief of the Yugoslav armed forces, Josip Broz Tito, has stopped beating.

Great sorrow and pain are shaking up the working class, nations and nationalities of our country, every citizen, worker, soldier, war veteran, farmer, intellectual, every creator, pioneer and youth, and every girl and mother.

Statement from the Central Committee of the League of Communists of Yugoslavia. *4 May, 1980.*

One of the disappointments for the Shah was how few truly historic or important figures attended the party. Second-string officials from the United States, the Soviet Union, France, and elsewhere led their delegations, not the true centers of power. The United Kingdom sent second tier royalty. Haile Selassie, one of the longest reigning monarchs, was a catch, but otherwise the royals were either dull Belgians or not even monarchs. An obscure prince from Thailand; some interchangeable Gulf sheikhs; a deposed king from Greece; a Prince of Spain who had not yet acceded to the throne. No wonder the Shah's face had ticked with fury when the RSVPs came in.

Apart from Haile Selassie, the only historic figures were Léopold Senghor and Tito, the dictator of Yugoslavia. The leader of Yugoslavia's resistance to Nazi occupation had shaped a nation out of the wreckage of World War II all while standing up to Stalin as the Soviet leader imposed his will across his new satellites in Eastern Europe. But his legacy turned to ashes when his country fell apart after his death, crumbling into one of the worst conflicts in Europe in decades.

THE SHAH'S PARTY

His wife, Jovanka Broz, cut a fine figure with a towering bouffant of impossibly black hair. She cut through crowds like a battleship in silk and fur, entirely comfortable, it seemed, with the collected royalty and jet set. Broz had joined the Yugoslav partisans aged 17, eventually ending up as part of the staff around Tito who were to ensure his comfort and safety. She ended up as his personal secretary in 1946, staying so close to him that she aroused the jealousy and suspicion of other staff. Sometime in the early 1950s, she married the boss.

She became quite the global figure as Tito was feted around the world as the exemplar of the independent communist. At home, she played a diminished role in his life as he neared the end, being pushed aside for the last few years. He would die in 1980 after being treated by Michael DeBakey, the Texan celebrity surgeon who was also involved in the mismanaged medical care that the Shah endured as he wandered in exile.

Tito was much in demand. He knew many of the guests well, as he traveled often, and those in the West were keen to ingratiate themselves with a communist who had stayed out of the Soviet orbit, much as they were with Ceaușescu. Tito was one of the many figures at the party who might have uttered the words *"Après moi, le deluge,"* the doom-laden phrase attributed variously to Louis XIV or his mistress Madame de Pompadour. Not long after his death, Yugoslavia fell apart. Hundreds of thousands would die in the war that followed.

> *A spokesman of the PMAC today announced the death in bed of former Emperor Haile Selassie. He died as a result of illness. It is to be recalled that the former emperor had been hospitalized under the care of Dr. Asrat Weldeyes in collaboration with foreign doctors. At that time a successful operation was performed. Since then, however his health had deteriorated.*
>
> Radio Ethiopia. 28 August 1975

THE GUESTS

Haile Selassie almost found himself overshadowed by his pet chihuahua at Persepolis. Cheecheebee, one in a long line of royal favorites, romped around the tents sporting a diamond collar and a mean temperament. Cheecheebee followed the emperor everywhere, snapping at anyone unwise enough to try to pet him. Dogs played an important role in the court of the Lion of Judah. A previous favorite, another tiny, bulging-eyed male chihuahua named Lulu, was known for singling out any official who might be less than loyal to the emperor. If she touched the foot of an official while they stood around the king, he knew they were not to be trusted. At Persepolis, officials eager to discuss Haile Selassie's recent meetings with Mao and Zhou Enlai had to run the gauntlet of the yapping Cheecheebee to enter the emperor's tent. In quieter moments, the chihuahua dozed next to the 79-year-old monarch on a checked couch in his tent as visitors came and went.

In his book *King of Kings*, written after the overthrow of Haile Selassie, Ryszard Kapuściński wrote of Lulu pissing on the feet of court officials while a palace servant scurried around wiping up. None of them was allowed to move as the dog did its circuit. The story supposedly came from the man whose job it was to mop up after the dog. Like so many stories in his books, it is almost certainly made up, perhaps tittle-tattle that the Polish writer heard at expatriate dinner parties. Even his biographer does not believe it is true.

Ras Tafari, as Haile Selassie was known before he ascended the throne, ruled Ethiopia for fifty-eight years as regent and then emperor, becoming one of the most famous Africans around the world, admired for resisting colonialism and inspiring the beliefs of Rastafarianism. He was the longest serving monarch to appear at the festivities and had a growing friendship with the Shah as they bonded as fellow emperors ruling over ancient lands. Haile Selassie's monarchy supposedly extended back 3,500 years to the

THE SHAH'S PARTY

Queen of Sheba, known, like Cyrus the Great, for her appearance in the Bible. He was supposedly the 225th monarch of the House of David, descended from the child of Solomon and the Queen of Sheba.

By 1971, Haile Selassie was ruling an increasingly restive empire. Much like Iran, discontent was bubbling under the surface, and he was at a loss as to how to control it. The two rulers had much in common. Both led independent states that had not fully succumbed to colonialism, but both had also seen their nations invaded: Ethiopia by Mussolini's Italy in 1936 and Iran by Britain and the Soviet Union in 1941. Both claimed ties to ancient histories and aspired to be regional powers. Both had been modernizing forces in their societies but saw this as a top-down process by which they would drag their often-unwilling people into the twentieth century. Both saw themselves as the source of all progress in their countries. Within a decade of the party, both nations would see the end of their monarchies and be plunged into years of violence and war.

In the 1960s, it was the specter of Gamal Abdel Al-Nasser in Egypt that brought Iran and Ethiopia together, a subject explored by the historian Robert Steele. The rash of leftist republican regimes that overthrew monarchs across the Middle East were a direct threat to the Shah. Nasser was part of the so-called Casablanca Bloc of African states, many of which had a radical agenda of merging nations to form a powerful African counterweight to the colonial powers. The Ghanaian leader Kwame Nkrumah spoke of erasing the colonial borders across the continent and joining up as one pan-African state. A rival group known as the Monrovia Bloc preferred a more modest program of political union among defined nation-states. In 1960, Haile Selassie's own Imperial Bodyguard attempted to replace him with his son, describing their action as an effort to end the country's backwardness. The Shah was immediately supportive in the aftermath, wanting to avoid the fall of yet another monarch.

THE GUESTS

Although not part of any radical movement of the time, Haile Selassie was still deeply respected across Africa for his resistance to colonialism and for the wars he had fought against the Italians. In 1963, he organized a conference in Addis Ababa that led to the founding of the Organization of African Unity, the forerunner of today's African Union. His capital was now the center of diplomatic and international activity on the continent and, therefore, a key place for Iran to build a growing web of connections.

Ironically, it was the rise in oil prices in the early 1970s, led substantially by the Shah, that was to drive the political upheavals that led to the overthrow of Haile Selassie. In 1973, the country was hit by a famine that killed at least 100,000 people in Tigray and Wollo, the latest in a series of such events caused in part by the feudal landholding system that had never been reformed.

In 1974, a slow-moving coup led by the sinister and seemingly anonymous "Derg" or "Committee" took power. The oil crisis had left the country unable to afford food or energy imports. A series of mutinies in the armed forces shook the establishment. Belated reforms in many areas were introduced, but it was far too late; as Alexis de Tocqueville had noted, the most dangerous time for any government is when it tries to change. Power quickly moved from the palace to the coup leaders, who were backed by the Soviet Union.

Eventually as the Derg gained control, Haile Selassie was removed from office and finally arrested, driven off from his palace in the back seat of a VW Beetle. Most of the imperial family, including the crown prince, fled to London. Haile Selassie died in August 1975, officially after prostate surgery, but quite possibly from asphyxiation with ether. He was buried under the floorboards of a palace toilet, where his remains were discovered in 1992. Haile Selassie was finally interred at Addis Ababa's Trinity Cathedral in 2000. The purges and civil war after the emperor's overthrow led to as many as two million deaths, many of them from famines caused by war, forced relocations and other state policies.

> Leopold Sedar Senghor, an African statesman and poet who led Senegal to independence in 1960 and became the West African nation's first president, died at his home in France on Thursday. He was 95. President Abdoulaye Wade announced the death in Senegal's capital, Dakar. He did not give the cause of death. Senghor reportedly suffered from heart trouble and spent three days in a hospital last week.
>
> Associated Press, 21 December 2001

The odd juxtaposition of guests was a sign of how skillfully the Shah had developed Iran's relations around the world. Marshal Tito, the only Eastern European leader to stand up to Stalin, stayed near Nikolai Podgorny, the stolid apparatchik who served as head of state of the Soviet Union. Amid the fountains and wilting trees of the star-shaped city, Imelda Marcos and Cristina Ford might have encountered Mao-suited Chinese diplomats or the Australian Governor-General Paul Hasluck, an acerbic politician and writer. Doubtless, the Indian president V. V. Giri took care to avoid his Pakistani counterpart, General Yahya Khan; tensions would build to war by the end of the year. While most of the European royal guests, many linked by marriage or blood, must have enjoyed the relaxed opportunities to mix, there may have been some strained efforts to miss each other. Did the distinctly "former" status of King Constantine of Greece undermine his standing among other monarchs? Did Constantine and Juan Carlos of Spain, impecunious brothers-in-law known as notorious freeloaders, hit up the Shah for money, as they often would during the 1970s, as they cultivated much richer royal families in the Middle East? At a time of deep geopolitical divides, many leaders did not want to be photographed sharing a joke with a rival. It is not recorded, for example, if South African President

THE GUESTS

Jacobus "Jim" Fouché and the Senegalese leader Léopold Senghor met during their days at Persepolis.

The two men could hardly be more different. Fouché was a farmer and politician, born in the Boer Republic of the Orange Free State in 1898. A former defense minister, he was elected to the mostly ceremonial post in 1968 and served as president of the apartheid state until 1975. From then, he seems to disappear with little trace. The Shah had invited him, despite the risks of associating with the racist government in South Africa, as he was eager to build contacts with potential allies that were also concerned about security in the Indian Ocean. Senghor was a poet, a philosopher, a founder of the *Negritude* movement, and the first president of Senegal, a figure mentioned in the same breath as the key leaders of independence movements across Africa, and a writer whose works are influential to this day.

Senghor started his career as a professor at universities in Tours and Paris. During World War II he was captured by the Germans and spent more than two years in prison camps, narrowly escaping execution. At the end of the war, he began a political career, pressing for French citizenship for Africans and the inclusion of colonies in a global French federalist state. This approach was unusual in that most political figures from Africa wanted to be free of colonialism. He eventually changed his position and was elected president of Senegal on its independence in 1960.

He avoided many of the pitfalls of post-colonial Africa, tending towards an Africanized form of socialism rather than the harder line pro-Soviet Marxism that took hold in many countries. But he did sink into the authoritarianism that plagued so many nations in that time. By 1962 he had outlawed all other political parties, positioning himself, much like the Shah, as both the essential political and cultural figure of his time. He would rule Senegal until the end of his fifth term in 1980.

His legacy in Senegal is mixed but his place as a poet and thinker endured through his promotion of *Negritude*, the idea that Africans needed to develop their own modern culture rather than take on Western and colonial attitudes. But *Negritude* promoted African culture within a framework of connections to France; leaders such as Senghor did not disavow their colonial history. Nevertheless, he ended up as a strange relic of the transition away from colonialism. He remained remote from his compatriots, always speaking French rather than Wolof. His preference for close links with France was attributed to his opposition to the more nationalist forces among trade unionists and students; France helped him stay in power and kept him relevant around the world. The special relationship between French power and wealth and francophone Senegalese ensured that he remained on top. He would even be elected to the Académie française, the most elite gathering in Paris. He was the first African to be accorded the honor. After stepping down from the presidency, he returned to France, spending his declining years at his country house in Normandy.

The relationship between the Shah and Senghor was burgeoning in the 1970s when Iran was keen to promote its relationship with Africa. In 1976, on a visit to Senegal, the Empress laid a foundation stone for a new city to be built with Iranian money. As recounted by the historian Robert Steele, the new settlement of Keur Farah Pahlavi was to have a refinery that would use Iranian crude while shipping out phosphates for fertilizer. It was to be designed by the Israeli-Canadian architect Moshe Safdie, who laid out a plan for a new city protected from the wild Atlantic by a large area of dunes.

It was an unusual move for Iran and a sign of changing priorities in the 1970s when the Shah saw himself as more than a regional figure and wanted a diplomacy that spanned the world. Several advisors, notably Shafa, had been urging him for some time to pay more attention to Africa to broaden Iranian links. In May 1971, Iran established diplomatic relations with Senegal and opened an embassy.

THE GUESTS

Haile Selassie and Senghor were probably the most palatable Africans for the Shah. Senghor shared his elitism and Francophilia; Haile Selassie was a fellow emperor. Senghor saw it the same way, telling a newly appointed ambassador that the relationship "expresses itself, essentially, in the dialogue between *Iranité* and *Négritude*, which must be an essential contribution to the dialogue of cultures, which we have been organizing for several years from either side." Beyond the cultural links, there was significant investment in Keur Farah Pahlavi. The project was abandoned in 1979 shortly after the Revolution. Although gaining access to fertilizer in exchange for oil might still have made economic sense, the project was too closely associated with the Pahlavis to continue.

> *Former Soviet President Nikolai Podgorny, who rose to power as a member of the three-man troika that ousted Nikita Khrushchev, has died, Soviet sources said today. He was 79. There was no immediate announcement but an official at the presidium of the Soviet legislature, which Podgorny once headed as chief of state, said Podgorny died Monday night.*
>
> United Press International, 12 January 1983

Russia always looms there right next to Iran; a threat, an opportunity, a challenge. It had, over the centuries, had its eyes on Iran's territory, conquering vast swathes of what had been part of the country and incorporating it into the Russian Empire and then the Soviet Union. Throughout the Shah's reign it was something of a frenemy; a useful counterpoint to the United States when the Shah wanted to gain some concession, but also a persistent worry given its ever-expanding role in the Arab world. Almost his entire reign was shaped by the logic of the Cold War with all its efforts to contain the attempts of Moscow to change the power arrangements of the Middle East. While the Shah toyed with the Russians to gain access to resources, he also bitterly resented their support for Iraq, Syria, Egypt, and others in the region that always raised the concern he was being surrounded by hostile forces.

Moscow felt a similar mix of resentment and desire for influence. The banning of the communist Tudeh Party in 1949 and the signing of the Baghdad Treaty in 1955, which led to the CENTO military alliance, left the Soviets concerned that Iran was now firmly aligned against them. American listening stations were positioned right on their frontier, while spy planes flew almost daily from bases there in what was called Operation Dark Gene. Along with Turkey and Pakistan, there was an array of nations opposed to the Soviet Union along what the Politburo often saw as the country's soft underbelly. Around 10 per cent of the Soviet population was Muslim, and the now-independent countries of the Caucasus and Central Asia were never as well-integrated into the system as Moscow would have liked. Mutual suspicions and anxieties were profound.

The Soviet Union swung between an eagerness to embrace the Shah, perhaps to lure him away from his close relations with the West, and efforts to undermine him, mainly through the sad and ineffectual Tudeh Party. The positions were self-defeating; the closer Moscow moved to Tehran, the weaker and more demoralized were the Tudeh leaders, mostly in exile in Eastern Europe. In the 1960s, the Shah had successfully embraced Eastern Europe and opened growing economic links with the region.

Representing Moscow at the party was Nikolai Podgorny, a Communist Party apparatchik born to a working-class family in Ukraine who had risen steadily up the ladder from an engineering job in a sugar factory to become Chairman of the Presidium of the Supreme Soviet and thus the head of state. Once at the summit of Soviet power, his influence steadily ebbed away, particularly after 1968 when Brezhnev consolidated his position as the head of the Party. By the early 1970s, Podgorny was clinging

THE GUESTS

to his increasingly precarious position; he ranked third in the communist hierarchy, but as head of state, he was top in terms of diplomatic protocol. This had rankled Brezhnev, who was not accorded full state honors when he traveled abroad; the pair were bitter rivals when it came to using foreign travel to promote themselves at home.

The party was an appealing chance for Podgorny to mix with his fellow heads of state and to meet several key Eastern Bloc figures in a risk-free environment in which he would not be attacked back at home. As with many other leaders, there were some potentially difficult encounters to be avoided. Relations with China were so bad that the neighbors had narrowly avoided a major conflagration after a border war in the late 1960s. Pakistan was another foe, as was South Africa. Many of Russia's allies in the region, such as Iraq, were either represented at a low level or had not been invited. The fact that the United States was represented only by the vice president gave Podgorny a moment to shine as head of state. The whisky flowed freely in Podgorny's tent as he entertained supplicants from around the world.

At home, Podgorny enjoyed a less prominent position. Brezhnev had emerged as the dominant force after some back and forth in the 1960s, when the head of state had been a more moderate figure in the leadership, urging the expansion of the Party and a focus on providing more consumer goods to a population living with a stagnating economy. The aftermath of Stalin's rule and Khrushchev's overturning of his cult of personality had left what seemed like a group of faceless apparatchiks running the country. Still, the competition among elites was intense.

* * *

The Shah had been in a wary dance with Moscow since he was raised to the throne during the British-Soviet occupation of his country. He first met Stalin when the Soviet leader attended the Tehran conference in 1943 with Roosevelt and Churchill. Stalin had better manners than his Western counterparts, visiting the Iranian head of state in his palace, as protocol dictated. In July 1946, Princess Ashraf met for more than two hours with Stalin, lamenting the weakness of her brother, warning the Soviets that he was in no position to carry out much-needed reforms, and urging them to pull back their troops from Iran. A record of the conversation was taken by the Soviets, which records Stalin pushing back on Ashraf's claims that her brother was powerless and beset by corrupt, incompetent politicians. "Comrade Stalin says that we are well-inclined to Iran and the Shah," the note says. "We don't eat people and don't plan to eat Iran. Tsarist Russia intended to seize Iran, but the Soviet Union is not Tsarist Russia." Stalin was clearly quite taken by Ashraf, the first foreign royal he is believed to have received. It is doubtful, however, that the Shah was much reassured.

This was the Shah at a low point in his relations with Moscow, his sister pushing the idea that he was too weak and beset with problems to make any headway against his nation's many challenges. Stalin did withdraw his troops, preoccupied as he was with establishing dominance in Eastern Europe. As the Shah's position strengthened at home, so did his determination to play the Soviets off against the U.S., maintaining cordial ties to extract weapons and aid from Washington. But deep within him lay a constant nagging fear that the Soviets were steadily surrounding Iran and intended at some stage to seize its oil and its access to the Gulf. There is no doubt that Moscow had ambitions across the Middle East but their relations with allies were never easy. While Arab leaders liked Soviet weaponry and aid, they were nearly always hesitant to do Moscow's bidding.

In 1956, the Shah had pledged to Khrushchev that he would not allow foreign bases in Iran. It was a step towards a foreign policy that was less entirely aligned with that of the United States. He was moving from being a U.S. client towards something approaching a partnership. Neutrality did not appeal to him; he often mentioned that Iran had been neutral in 1941 when Britain and the Soviet Union occupied it and that its posture had provided no security. He wanted to be close to Washington but never experience the high-handed disregard he had felt in the early years of his reign. In 1958, he learned that Washington had not informed him when one of his generals had asked for help in plotting a coup; his response was to move forward with the policy of détente with Moscow that he started during a visit there just after Khrushchev's speech denouncing Stalin.

Relations remained slightly tetchy even during a series of high-level visits but Moscow remained a useful tool for the Shah in leveraging money and arms out of Washington. It was something of a high-wire act, though: get too close to the Soviets and he would put his security at risk.

5

THE GIFT

As the guests entered their tents, they would have found a small wooden presentation case. Inside was a clay object, roughly the size of a child's rugby ball. It was marked by a deep crack and covered with a dense, scratchy script, like the footprints of birds from a distant past. Each guest had received a replica of an object that has become a key emblem of Iranian nationalism. It has taken on meaning far beyond what it is—a message left in a Babylonian temple at the time of Cyrus the Great.

The replicas were smaller than the actual Cylinder, an unassuming pale clay object about 22 centimeters long that resides in the British Museum. In the 130 years since the Cyrus Cylinder was discovered in Babylon, it has taken on an extraordinary array of meanings, connecting the ancient world to the identity of Iranians today, unlike anything else. It is now a national emblem, embraced alike by Islamists in Tehran and pro-royalist Iranian-Americans in Los Angeles.

Almost utilitarian with its lack of ornamentation, it carries a weight of history far beyond its appearance and slightly battered state. It starts with an early manifestation of an Iran-Iraq war in

THE SHAH'S PARTY

539 BCE. Belshazzar, King of Babylon, had taken Jerusalem and sacked the Temple of Solomon. Back in his capital, he held a feast at which, according to the Bible story, a hand appeared and wrote on a wall in Hebrew that he had been found wanting and his kingdom was to be handed over to the Medes and the Persians. That night the forces of Cyrus took Babylon, ending the torment of the Jews and changing their history forever.

The Cylinder records the moment of Cyrus's victory and supposedly tells the world of his momentous decision to allow the captive people of Babylon, notably the Jews, to go free and to recover the objects that were stolen from them, including all the precious objects taken from the Temple in Jerusalem. This marked the start of the first great empire and model of imperial rule that recognized the diversity of languages, religions and cultures that could co-exist under one ruler. Expanded by his successors, the empire eventually stretched from modern-day Libya to Afghanistan, home to many hundreds of different peoples who were mostly allowed to continue with their lives and customs if they acknowledged the power of the Persians and paid sufficient tribute.

"The things we make have one characteristic: they usually last longer than we do," wrote Neil McGregor, the former director of the British Museum. "We have one life; they have many lives and in each of those lives—at different times and different places—they may mean many different things." By the ninteenth century, Babylon had become a huge lure for European archaeologists. They were obsessed with the idea of verifying events in the Bible by locating places and objects that appeared in the Old Testament. Up until then, the only mention of the sacking of the Temple in Jerusalem and of the enslavement of the Jews was in the Bible. In 1879, an expedition from the British Museum discovered and deciphered the Cylinder, and, for the first time, there was proof of the Biblical story from another source.

THE GIFT

The Cylinder offers wobbly evidence at best for Cyrus's actions because it was written not by Persians but by the priests of Marduk, the God of Babylon, who is said to have handed the land over to Cyrus. For the Jews, it had, of course, been Jehovah who had handed over the city. And what was the Cylinder? It may well have been a standard object put in all temples in Babylon as a religious press release to welcome a new ruler. Rather than having some deep significance, it was probably a quotidian object used by Mardukian priests to signal their obedience to a new king and to display that ruler's magnanimity in allowing the temples to remain open.

Almost any meaning can be slotted into the words on the Cylinder. As it was discovered and first interpreted around the time that Jews in Europe were embracing Zionism, it became an important symbol of the desire of the diaspora to return to a new homeland. George V, King of England at the time of the Balfour Declaration in 1919, which declared the intention to create a Jewish state, and Cyrus were often portrayed as two heroes of Zionism. Israel's first president, David Ben-Gurion, lavished praise on Cyrus due to the biblical stories about the liberation of Jews from Babylon.

The Cylinder would gain another currency later in the twentieth century when it was adopted by Iran as a symbol of the ancient nature of its monarch and the just rule of Persian emperors. Not only was this one of the earliest documents from the reign of Cyrus, who brought the empire together, but it was a statement of the ancient worthiness of Persian rulers and their dedication to human rights, ideas the Shah wished to attach to his own reign.

In fact, the Cylinder says nothing about human rights, words not much mentioned anywhere before the 1940s. It starts off with references to Nabonidus, the father of Belshazzar and Cyrus's predecessor as ruler of Babylon, and then goes on to lament failings in his treatment of the local religion. Nabonidus makes blasphemous offerings, he lacks awe for the god Marduk and interrupts the worship of others. Appalled by this behavior, Marduk looks around for a just leader in the region and spots Cyrus. He causes him to conquer the Medes, then the dominant group in what is now Iran, and then orders him to take Babylon. Cyrus arrives in the city triumphant and immediately returns various religious objects to their correct temples. Lands are at peace and Cyrus carries out a major renovation of the neglected temples, providing elaborate new decorations.

Nowhere on the Cylinder is there any mention of anyone in exile being allowed to return home. There is nothing on the Jews or any people other than Babylonians. It is all about the city and its shrines; Cyrus frees the people from forced labor and repairs their temples. It says nothing about Cyrus's own religious preferences, something underlined in another cylinder found in the remains of the city of Ur, in which the Persian king makes much the same claims about reconstructing the moon temple there.

Historians believe the Cylinder, which was probably buried in the wall of a building in the manner of a foundation stone, was a way for the Persian conqueror to establish himself in a line of Babylonian rulers. The city likely enjoyed various protections from taxes and other burdens as the home of the shrine of Marduk. Nabonidus may have violated these privileges and Cyrus restored them to show his dedication to the people. The text of the Cylinder has many echoes in others and suggests the claims were part of a standard package of propaganda for all new rulers. Each claimed a long ancestry, said they had gathered up scattered people, and praised themselves for rebuilding neglected shrines. Far from being about human rights or the return of Jews to Jerusalem, the Cylinder is an attempt by Cyrus to legitimize his conquest by appealing to priests, a powerful group in Babylon who had clashed for many years with Nabonidus over his attempts to reform religion.

THE GIFT

While the priests, whose power was restored by Cyrus, may have rejoiced and praised his name, not all Babylonians were as welcoming. There were rebellions against Persian rule in 522 BCE, 521 BCE, 484 BCE, and 482 BCE. The first two even attempted to restore the heirs of Nabonidus to the throne. It is a stretch to claim that the Cylinder showed the true feelings of the people of Babylon.

Expanding the claims of the Cylinder to propose a whole new way of ruling, with tolerance for all the people of the empire, does not bear much examination either. Xerxes would later sack Babylon and remove the Marduk statue from the shrine, probably destroying it. Cambyses would conquer Egypt, returning power to some shrines where he had support and destroying others. It was all a matter of expediency. Darius protected the workers of the sacred grove of Apollo but demolished other Ionian Greek temples in areas that revolted against him. Human rights or religious freedoms as we conceive them today were never part of the discussion.

* * *

This association of the Cylinder with human rights is, at minimum, an anachronism. Rather like so much of the public relations output of the Pahlavi era, the subject of human rights was there to add luster to royal rule but was observed mostly in the breach. Just as the cylinder arrived on loan from the British Museum in 1971 for what was its first ever trip to Iran, a campaign was underway against leftist guerrillas that led to some of the worst abuses of the Shah's reign. The Cylinder captured the Pahlavi vision of the State and the Emperor as a leader who handed down rights to his subjects. They were not seen as intrinsic to the individual but as something that his people enjoyed because the Shah granted them.

After 1979, anything associated with the monarchy was deemed unacceptable, and interest in the Cylinder waned. But theocracy inevitably had to be tempered with the nationalism that lies at the heart of Iranian identity. In 2010, the Cylinder returned to Iran to an exhibition opened with some fanfare by then-President Mahmoud Ahmadinejad, the populist former mayor of Tehran who turned to such nationalist symbols in his struggles with the religious establishment. Ironically, given that the Cylinder is supposed to speak of human rights and be linked to the liberation of the Jews in Babylon, Ahmadinejad was one of the foremost Iranian opponents of the existence of Israel.

The return of the Cylinder to Iran for a second time in 2010 sparked debate about the nature of Iranian identity and the way in which the freedoms supposedly captured in the document are lived in a society that has seen decades of violence and suppression. The freedom of religion supposedly captured in the document and in the Iranian Constitution is severely curtailed. We have little sense of what those freedoms meant when the Cylinder was made. Was there any clear difference between religion and other aspects of life? Could one have been a Babylonian worshipping their own god outside of their own territory? Was it truly a statement of reality, or was it wishful thinking—Babylonian priestly pleading to be left alone by Cyrus? We do know that the empire allowed a degree of tolerance but how much is unclear and what sort of restrictions existed are also unknown. McGregor rather over-eagerly described the Cylinder as "one of the great expressions of a long-held human aspiration," presumably to be free of religious persecution.

During its visit to Tehran in 2010, a giant replica of the Cylinder was part of a ceremony involving various people dressed in the clothing of Cyrus's time, all rather reminiscent of the parade at Persepolis in 1971. Alongside was a young man in a military uniform, waving a national flag. It is known in Persian as the Charter of Cyrus, showing how wedded Iranians have become to the interpretation of the script as laying down rights.

THE GIFT

When it did go on display in Tehran, the event was portrayed as a homecoming, although its only time in Iran had been back in 1971. This is, after all, an object made by the Babylonians, inscribed in Akkadian script with the concerns of priests whose religion was far removed from the faith of ancient Persians.

Like the Mona Lisa, the Cylinder is so over-analyzed that almost all the contradictory theories of its origins and original meaning are left worthless. Its meaning is determined by whatever you ascribe to it. For McGregor, it stands alongside the United States Constitution as an "historic statement of how a disparate polity may be humanely governed." But just like the U.S. constitution, the Cylinder is subject to endless debate about the intentions of its creators. Should it stand as what was written centuries ago, or should its meaning be interpreted for our times? The Cylinder was not a constitution or even a statement of intent. It was a song of praise for a new absolute ruler, written in uncertain times of conquest and containing the hopes of a people rather more than the reality of their treatment.

The Jews of Babylon, in exile since Nebuchadnezzar forced them from Jerusalem in 586 BCE, had a strong interest in getting on the right side of Cyrus. We do not have much idea of what his religion was—there is nothing much in any texts that point to one thing or another. There is not much to suggest that he was interested in imposing whatever he believed in on others, although this should not necessarily be seen as an example of tolerance but rather simply pragmatism. The Persian Empire was more about money than ideology. The lack of information has meant that everyone, from Jews to Persians to Indian Muslims could project their ideas on to Cyrus. The Jewish God claims credit for Cyrus's success—as had the Babylonian Marduk, and Cyrus claimed descent from Saul, the first Hebrew king. So, both Babylonians and the city's Jews had reasons to support Cyrus.

THE SHAH'S PARTY

The journey from a relatively obscure object in the British Museum to something that would attract hundreds of thousands of visitors in Tehran was circuitous. At some point, the cultural machinery of the Pahlavis, with its obsession with Cyrus, latched onto the object and decided to promote its text as the first ever statement of human rights. Not only is this now almost universally accepted by Iranians—despite the lack of evidence—but Iran managed to convince many in the international world of this. A replica sits in a case outside the United Nations Security Council in New York alongside other gifts from unsavory regimes trying to gloss over their histories.

Tours of the Cylinder in both Iran and the United States were accompanied by rock band-style merchandising. In the manner of a medieval relic, it could draw huge crowds. More than thirty new books on Cyrus—none of them containing much in the way of new material as so few sources are available—came out in just a few years. Almost everything imaginable was embellished with the Cylinder's image to appeal to nationalist audiences in both Iran and among the diaspora. The British Museum, of course, got a piece of the action. Its replica, life-size, unlike the one given to the guests at Persepolis, retails for £2,000.

* * *

The loan of the Cylinder in 1971 nearly ended up causing a diplomatic incident. A curator from the British Museum accompanied the Cylinder to Tehran where it was displayed in the museum beneath the Shahyad Arch, opened on the last day of the party. This was done without consulting the embassy, possibly because the ambassador, who was concerned that once it was in Iran, it might never leave again, would have advised against it. The Cylinder was due back in London for its starring role in an exhibition called "Royal Persia," organized to celebrate the anniversary. Concerns emerged that it might not make it back to London.

THE GIFT

The ambassador had to warn Prince Philip, who was leading the British delegation to the party, that the Shah might request the Cylinder be given to Iran. Prudently, during the opening ceremony for the museum under the new monument, the prince avoided the Shah, who was busy with other guests.

A rather eclectic group of politicians and others had been invited to the party from London, including the former Labour Party Attorney General and Nuremburg prosecutor Lord Shawcross. It seems that they were lobbied by the Iranians to ask for the Cylinder to be given to Iran or presented on permanent loan. After returning to London, Shawcross and the MP Sir Clive Bossom wrote to Prime Minister Edward Heath to ask that the British Museum donate the Cylinder. They were rebuffed; the museum was not allowed by law to give away objects in its collection, and any permanent loan would open the door to requests from myriad governments around the world wanting back their treasures, many of them acquired by much more dubious means than the Cylinder.

6

THE HOST

Most of the guests knew their host. The Shah traveled often, ensuring that he was always heard in centers of power around the world. He clearly enjoyed being Shah when that meant flag-waving crowds and state dinners. By 1971, the great and the good had started to court him more assiduously, putting Tehran, and soon St. Moritz, on their itineraries. Western economies were on increasingly shaky ground. The post-war economic miracle had grit in the gears with low productivity, ever-higher wage demands, and competition from the emerging tigers in Asia. Energy use was high per dollar of GDP produced; cars were large and thirsty. Everyone was after Iran's oil, markets, or petrodollars. The 1970s would be the decade of the oil crisis, with the Shah one of the main players pushing for ever higher prices.

The Polish writer Czeslaw Milosz wrote: "All biographies are obviously false.... not excluding my own. Biographies are like shells; they don't tell you much about the mollusk that lived in them." They were useful, he believed, only because "they allow one to more or less recreate the era in which a given life was lived." Mohammad Reza Pahlavi is much biographied, but almost all these books offer just caricatures. He is either a terrible despot or the unmatched savior of the Iranian people. However, his life spans the three decades following World War II, from decolonization to the revolutionary era that emerged in the late 1960s.

After 1979, biographers struggled not to write as though every act signaled the coming end of his regime; the dark foreshadowing of Khomeini looms in every scene, although few saw the signs at the time. Before his overthrow, biographies had tended towards hagiography. The Indian journalist R.K. Karanjia, a Parsi from Mumbai, conducted many interviews with the Shah and produced a fawning series of books that give a sense of what the Iranian monarch wanted to put out into the world. Even then there are some unintentional revelations: the pomposity, the sexism, his shuddering horror at emerging youth culture.

There are many books by associates, some of them, such as the Minister of the Court Asadollah Alam's diaries, are even quite revealing, but they are all accompanied by the loudest possible sound of axes being ground and reputations being restored or polished. Government papers from his time are controlled by the Islamic government and have been published in a highly selective manner. Nobody fully knows what documentation would become available to historians if power ever changed in Tehran. Without more of the records, the history will always be sketchy.

Historians now shy away from the history of "Great Men" around which their work was once constructed. Their world is one of theory, micro-histories and statistics. They do have a point. Great Men have always been the focus, to an excessive degree, in Iran. Four men dominate the history of twentieth-century Iran: Reza Shah, Mohammad Reza Pahlavi, Mossadegh, and Khomeini. Of course, many other Iranians shaped the century, but they tend to fall away in most accounts, leaving just these four with their weaknesses, desires, prejudices, bitterness, and resentments. Making sense of them is still something of an

THE HOST

industry as biographers toil away, often using the same material, chasing after tiny amounts of new grist for their mills. However, in a society that has put so much emphasis on a handful of all-powerful leaders, to the detriment of the people, it is impossible to ignore these men.

Diplomatic materials from other states provide some useful information particularly as ambassadors often dealt directly with the Shah. But they also come with a set of shortcomings. The Shah's suspicion of foreigners ran deep; he might have been polyglot and cosmopolitan, but he had stored up as many resentments and fears as the average Iranian. He tended to be scrupulously polite to visiting foreigners but rarely gave much away, sometimes coming across as aloof and wary.

Histories of the years between 1925 and 1979 focus on the ambitions and excesses of the Pahlavi monarchs as well as the brief periods of more open rule that interrupted this era. Their efforts undeniably changed Iran in many ways. But there are always many histories to be told: resistance to the Pahlavis was a constant; tribes rebelled; civil servants dragged their feet; ambitious men looked enviously at the throne. The Shahs' powers were often curtailed in various ways; their ambitions always exceeded their reach given that often they could not even control those working directly under them. What one historian called the Shah's "muscle-bound version of self-confidence about science and technological progress" was the public face of a regime that was determined to beat all neighbors in the race for development, even trying to surpass the European states where it sent so many to be educated.

* * *

Biographies of the Shah tend to focus on certain set pieces: becoming crown prince at the age of six, leaving for school in Switzerland as a young teenager, and being appointed Shah just before his twenty-second birthday, as his father was sent into exile. His sister Ashraf makes brief appearances: she is twice the man but, sadly for her father, a woman, and therefore condemned to irrelevance, while the weaker twin is pushed into the spotlight. There were two major assassination attempts and a brief exile in Rome before the overthrow of Mossadegh in 1953 with the help of the British and Americans. As the Shah matured and consolidated his power, the set pieces become more grandiose: images of him crowning himself, the self-conscious family shots, state visits and banquets. A life boiled down to pictures of a man looking at things: models, maps, planes, tanks, his children.

There is no shortage of hagiographies and like all such books they are notable only for their dullness. This Shah is a visionary, a modernizer, a man who wakes each day energized by a desire to help his people. He is modest and kind to Iranians, who spontaneously adorn him with the title of "Light of the Aryans." He walks among his people without a care for his own security, only for their welfare. When there are setbacks, such as the failure of his first two marriages, he suffers in silent dignity, always thinking only of his duty. He is pragmatic and wants to bring the best of what is on offer around the world to Iran.

There was a rash of such books in the 1970s, mostly commissioned by the court or proposed by opportunistic writers. The British politician and military historian Lord Chalfont tested the patience of the Iranian ambassador to London in the 1970s by proposing yet another worshipful study of the Pahlavis, with the focus on the Shah's twin sister Princess Ashraf. Parviz Radji diplomatically danced away from the subject, recalling the plethora of books produced for the fiftieth anniversary of the dynasty in 1975. Radji, who had worked with Ashraf and was widely rumored to have been her lover, told her that while a biography might highlight her courage and loyalty at such challenging moments as the coup against Mossadegh, it might be taken as

THE HOST

pointing to the lack of such attributes in so many others, in other words, in the Shah himself. The wily and wise ambassador knew that hagiographies simply embarrass everyone involved. He spent much of his time in London preventing yet more of them.

The other side of the Manichean approaches to the Shah's life includes books such as *Crowned Cannibals* by Reza Baraheni, a poet and literary critic who spent much of his life in jail or exile. A regular writer for the *New York Review of Books*, Baraheni was a fixture in anti-Pahlavi circles and after the Revolution tried to endear himself to an unimpressed Khomeini. The book pictures Tehran under the Shah as a swirling vortex of orgies and corruption: the title itself suggests some of its excesses. Hundreds of thousands of people were imprisoned. Thousands were slaughtered in the streets or disappeared. Iranians die in their millions. Caligula had nothing on the Pahlavi court as described by Baraheni.

The tone of *Crowned Cannibals* is one of relentless hyperbole, along with some tabloid techniques of insinuating gossip into the narrative while denying responsibility for it. It is riddled with clear falsehoods: people located in places they could never have been; descriptions of events that so obviously did not happen; a kaleidoscope of excess all described in a tone of near-insane fury at the Shah and those around him. It sold well at a time when the Shah was widely hated, but seems callous in the face of what was to come after his fall, none of which needed exaggeration for people to understand its full horror. It fits nicely alongside so many of the biographies in its extremes. Writing about the Shah will inflame one group or another. To examine the comments on any online article or YouTube clip of the Shah to this day is to see the polarization of Iranian life play out again and again in extremes of worship and derision.

* * *

THE SHAH'S PARTY

Writing after the death in 2016 of the Shah's sister, Ashraf the Iranian-American academic Hamid Dabashi wrote of the impossibility now of biography of the Pahlavis. They had, in his view, become fictional characters to serve the needs of readers. Ashraf was either a saint or Lady Macbeth. She had become something like a demonic figure from the *Shahnameh*, Ferdowsi's epic poem. The bright white or pitch-black shading of Iranian life meant that little could be done except write fiction.

This seems to be an idea the Polish journalist Ryszard Kapuściński took to heart in his book *Shah of Shahs*. Written in 1982 and published in English in 1985, it is likely the most widely read biography of the monarch. It was a huge hit in literary circles in the United States, where Kapuściński was also a darling of the *New York Review of Books*. A reviewer praised Kapuściński for not just showing the Pahlavis as actors in their own drama but for the way the writer "climbs on the stage himself, picks up the props to examine them, tapping the scenery and then turning to address a soliloquy to the audience." Iran, wrote another reviewer, was "like his Ethiopia, a region of the mind." The telltale word there is "his", the proprietorial ownership of a country, achieved after just a brief visit. Ownership that required no knowledge of history, no effort to talk to people, and no commitment to actual reporting.

Kapuściński insisted on his authenticity as a journalist while deriding all others as clichés of privilege and remove. He famously claimed to have been sentenced to death four times and to have witnessed twenty-seven revolutions, although he never said which ones, and his biographer was unable to confirm the count. His was a world of actual experience among the people. He was not just hanging out by the pools of five-star hotels, talking to diplomats. He was on the street, absorbing the essence of revolution, breathing deeply that heady mix of sweat, smoke, and cordite.

THE HOST

Except he was not. He arrived in Iran after the fall of the Shah and wrote a book that seemed to be cobbled together from seemingly random, and often suspiciously unlikely, conversations. Nothing is sourced or verified. There is no reporting in any real sense. It is fragmented and vaporous. Anecdote, even the wispiest story, becomes fact or allegory. *Shah of Shahs* is structured around a handful of images that Kapuściński claims to be perusing in a hotel room amidst the aftermath of the revolution.

Photographs often do not show what we think. The image of the Shah as a child standing next to his father is interpreted as a tiny, frightened child, always trying to live up to his father's image. The relationship was always much more complex than that. Reza Shah was a tough autocrat, but he seems to have had quite a soft side with his children. He surely wanted his crown prince to be well-educated, westernized, and comfortable with the modern world. However, he was also, by all accounts, a caring father to his children, not a bully or a despot. If anything, the Shah's mother might have been the stricter parent. The other images represent nothing except the moment in which they are taken. They are grossly over-determined in the reading that Kapuściński gives them, a single thread from which he weaves an elaborate fictional tapestry. Another biography, by the French journalist Gerard Villiers, features a portrait of Reza Shah and three of his children, including his heir, looking relaxed in a flower-filled garden. Taken by Henri Cartier-Bresson, it shows none of the menace or fear that Kapuściński suggests.

How much can you make up before you should acknowledge that you are writing fiction? Even the gushing reviewers cannot help themselves in nodding towards the character of his writing, with even his friend Salman Rushdie challenging him on some of his anecdotes while marveling at his style as a writer. Which brings us to another key problem with Kapuściński. He was writing for a state-controlled news agency from a communist country

THE SHAH'S PARTY

where the deeply repressive ruling party, of which he was an honored member, controlled all the media.

Kapuściński's biographer was forced to wrestle with this problem. How did he travel the world at a time when almost no Poles got to leave the country unless he was a favored apparatchik? And if he was a communist propagandist, why is he taken seriously as a non-fiction writer? No *Pravda* correspondent is so honored. The standard line is that his writings are allegories of life in Poland. He is writing not about Haile Selassie but Edward Gierek, First Secretary of the Polish United Workers' Party in the 1970s; he describes life under the Shah of Iran but alludes to the Poland ruled by General Wojciech Jaruzelski, the last Communist president. When he points the finger at suffocating dictatorships and the dusty repression of imperial courts, he is throwing shade on the United Workers' Party. But if that is the case, then they cannot be taken as serious works about either Haile Selassie or Mohammad Reza. If an Iranian had gone to cover the Solidarity movement in Gdansk and written it up as an opaque allegory of industrial relations in the Islamic Republic would any critic have been quite as effusive in their praise?

As far as biography goes, it is a failure. The Shah is just another despot, the same as all the other despots Kapuściński encountered at those twenty-sevem revolutions. *Shah of Shahs* is a curiously dated book. Kapuściński had not visited Iran when it was ruled by the Shah, but he portrays it much as Poland must have been in the 1960s. It was never like Eastern Europe under communism. SAVAK at its very worst never came close to the panopticon reach of the East German Stasi or the Polish secret police, known as the SB. Iran had an exuberant cultural scene, most of which steered clear of direct criticism of the monarchy; however, there was nothing like the soul-deadening official social realism of Poland. Kapuściński is given a photograph of people waiting at a bus stop, supposedly taken by a SAVAK agent (It is

THE HOST

hard not to allow an eyebrow to rise in skepticism at this point—why would such a person admit in the aftermath of the Revolution that he worked for SAVAK, never mind give the Polish journalist what would seem like a banal photograph?). The photograph supposedly portrays Iranians waiting in silence, fearful that any one of those standing near them could report them for any complaint. One of them apparently is a SAVAK agent, listening in. An old man with a bad heart complains to the others of the heavy, oppressive air at that time of the year. The SAVAK agent, reading this as an allusion to the nature of the regime, marches the old man off to prison. It is a lot to glean from a blurry photograph, which even the author admits resembles people waiting at a bus stop anywhere in the world.

There was fear in Iran. It worsened after 1971. But SAVAK never had the total reach that Kapuściński claimed. Iranians traveled freely, if they could afford it. Poles only got to leave the country if they were privileged party members like Kapuściński. They could live where they wanted; there were no passes to be acquired if one wanted to move from one's home. They worshipped freely and could visit shrines in Iraq and Saudi Arabia on pilgrimages. Jews, Christians, and Bahais lived under the Shah mostly unthreatened, and Islamist groups operated underground with surprisingly little attention given the enduring focus on left-wing dissent. Religious studies classes proliferated, as did other forms of political activity, none of which were ever witnessed or recorded by the Polish writer. The Shah of *The Shah of Shahs* is a fairy tale character, a stock Oriental despot, seen from very far away. In 2001, Kapuściński gave an interview to a British newspaper. "We have too many fables," he said. "Too much make-believe. Journalists must deepen their anthropological and cultural knowledge and explain the context of events. They must read."

THE SHAH'S PARTY

15 October 1971

As the sun came up behind the ruins of Persepolis, the tent city stirred. Prince Reza, the 10-year-old heir to the Peacock Throne, busied himself driving around in a golf cart, delivering breakfast to his parents' guests. The vast machinery assembled to cater for the party came alive; dozens of young French chefs worked away to prepare for the banquet. An army of soldiers camped nearby had grown out their beards so they could look the part of ancient Persian warriors; dozens of smartly uniformed officers waited to guide guests to their seats for the parade. Persepolis had not seen this much life since the hard partying Alexander burned it to the ground.

The morning was spent on informal diplomacy with many guests trying to see Haile Selassie to discuss his recent meetings with Mao Zedong. Marshal Tito welcomed the leaders of Romania, Finland, and Czechoslovakia to his tent, perhaps to discuss their shared concerns about the Soviet Union. The Ethiopian Emperor also dropped by the Yugoslav leader's tent but refused to answer questions about his China trip. Indeed, the public exchanges were as banal as possible. Spiro Agnew spent the morning on the phone in his tent; his spokesman refused to say to whom he was speaking. Apparently, he was suffering from an upset stomach. Nurses were seen rushing back and forth to the tent while the press were kept at a distance.

No event under the Shah would be complete without a military review. At the party, the emphasis was on connecting emerging Iranian power to Persian history. The parade would begin with the Achaemenid period and extend through the centuries to emphasize the ancient nature of Iranian power. Ancient trumpets sounded for the first time in centuries as 3,000 soldiers with elaborate costumes marched past the stand. They were followed by ranks of cavalry, chariots, and even ships on wheeled

THE HOST

floats, although Persia had never been known as a great naval power. Eventually, members of the contemporary armed forces goose-stepped past, looking precise and formidable.

None of this was a message much enjoyed by the visitors from the other side of the Persian Gulf. The southern shore of this sea was edged with former British protectorates that were emerging into independence. Bahrain became independent in August 1971, followed by Qatar a month later. The Trucial States merged to form the United Arab Emirates in December of that year.

Kuwait and Bahrain had significant Shia populations that their Sunni rulers had long regarded with suspicion. In July 1970, British commandos had defeated the Baloch guards around the palace of the Sultan of Oman and installed his Sandhurst-educated son Qaboos on the throne. Just a few months later, Qaboos was at the party alongside the top royals from Abu Dhabi, Kuwait, and Bahrain, all of them shakily emerging into worlds of power and wealth as the oil started flowing. Qaboos was to embrace the Shah, becoming reliant on him to defeat the Chinese-supported communist Dhofar Rebellion that had plagued his nation from the early 1960s until 1976.

For the Shah, this was all an opportunity. The party was his coming-out event, aimed to "establish Iran anew in Western perceptions." It was not just aimed at the West, but also the Arab world, ranging from the hostile pro-Soviet states such as Iraq and Syria to existing allies such as Egypt and Jordan. Not only was the Shah trying to connect his own people to the grandeur of their past, but he also wished to impress on his neighbors that he was the emerging force in their unsettled region.

Guests were bused towards a vast stand set up before the Persepolis Platform to view the military parade. Even here, no expense was spared; the furniture had been provided by Maison Jansen in Paris. The Perspex and gilt tables and chairs used for the audience still fetch considerable sums on antique auction sites. The seventy senior guests sat in a single line, the sun shining directly into their eyes.

The parade began with men costumed in the armor and uniforms of the Achaemenid dynasty, progressing through the ages to the present, and linking together the 2,500 years of dynastic rule in Persia. Of course, this rule had seen vast dislocations and disruptions, including Greek, Arab, and Mongol invasions; it had never enjoyed the seamless continuity the Shah wanted to suggest.

A guide to the event was published in several languages, providing background information on the different uniforms worn throughout the ages. This had been the subject of much study by Iranian historians and archaeologists, who examined the various representations of kings, warriors, and soldiers that appeared on everything from stone reliefs to silver chalices. The parade was dismissed as an overblown Cecil B. DeMille production, but it had been based on some serious scholarship about the uniforms, armor, weapons, and machinery of war. The signal to the region was clear: Iran had been fighting for a long time, and its military power would rise again.

It had taken decades to develop the parade of soldiers that passed by in two hours, the crowd shielding their eyes from the sun. The committee that organized it met 340 times in the 1960s and an additional 105 times in the years immediately preceding the event, illustrating the vast amount of work that had gone into it. Art historians, archaeologists, and the curator of the Military Museum in Tehran all participated in the elaborate recreations of armor, weapons, and musical instruments. It had taken twelve years to research, design, and make the clothing.

The martial emphasis was unsurprising, even if it had little historical connection to Persepolis, a site that was most likely used by Achaemenid monarchs to celebrate the lunar new year and the arrival of spring rather than to highlight their military prowess. The city was not even well fortified; it would fall to Alexander without a fight. The Shah loved military equipment, spending billions on his army to make it among the most powerful in the region. Although this raised a whole array of concerns, most Western suppliers were eager to encourage his shopping binges even as they distorted the economy and flooded the country with foreign military experts. To this day, the Middle East sustains the global arms industry; it is replete with undemocratic countries plagued by deep anxieties and multiple, overlapping security forces, all of which require extensive armaments. The money being spent in the 1970s was astonishing; it would only grow in subsequent decades.

The replicas of siege machines and other equipment that Persian soldiers had once used to build their vast empire rather belied the notion that this was somehow a benign and kindly conquest. The Persian Empire, like all empires that followed, had been based on violence and military might, although the Shah attempted to downplay this in his speech at the event. Quoting Darius the Great, he said: "I love truth and abhor evil. I do not wish the strong to oppress the weak in my kingdom. I do not wish one to cause loss to another out of wickedness."

The guests went off to enjoy a Persian buffet and traditional music and dance. The press studiously ignored this celebration of culinary and other arts from across the country, continuing their riff on the excesses of the event. An informal evening of Persian food and entertainment did not fit the narrative of grandiosity and foreign excess that the international media had decided was central to the party.

* * *

Biography nearly always puts too much explanatory weight on childhood. The dead hand of Freud lies heavily on the keyboard as authors search for meaning in whatever form of abuse, neglect, or excess might have blighted the subject's early years. For the Shah, perhaps the most critical moment was stepping onto a steamer bound for Baku, leaving his country and family behind for the next six years. Of course, he did not leave alone. The Minister of the Court, who managed the affairs of the imperial family, accompanied him on the trip. He spent his time in Switzerland with an entourage that included a guardian, a physician, and a Persian language teacher, lest his mother tongue fade too much. His friend, Hussein Fardust, was to accompany him, becoming one of the Shah's few close companions and one of several mysterious figures in his life.

The first stop was to move in with a law professor in the town of Vennes, just outside Lausanne. He did not settle well. There were fights with an Egyptian boy and rough tackles on the soccer field. The 12-year-old still expected the deference he was accustomed to at home; this did not win him friends in Switzerland. After a year, he would be asked to leave his school. He moved on to Le Rosey, the elite boarding school located in Rolle, for most of the year, and to the ski resort of Gstaad in the winter term. It seems he understood that, despite the entourage, he would be expected to fit in at Le Rosey, which was then favored by wealthy Americans living abroad, European aristocrats shedding unwanted stepchildren, and various royals—exiled or otherwise—who sought a neutral venue to educate their heirs.

The primary source for Mohammad Reza's time in school is a much-cited article that appeared in *The New Yorker* magazine in 1949. It tells the story of the crown prince getting into a scrap on his first day at school and losing badly. He then graciously shakes hands with the boy and becomes one of the class. Written by a fellow former pupil long after the events, a fleeting encounter is loaded with meaning in almost every biography of the Shah.

The demanding behavior of an uncertain 13-year-old on his first day at boarding school is offset by what the young prince would later write in the school magazine, extolling the sense of community and equality among these, admittedly very privileged, students. He seems like a happy teenager, reasonably well-adjusted, and with a passion for sports, which would remain with him throughout his life. He was fluent in French and English, although his mother tongue became slightly uncertain, a trait that was inevitably held against him at home; he was fluent but never eloquent in Persian.

By the time he returned to Iran, he had hardly seen his family except for brief visits to Switzerland by his mother and twin sister. But he had grown up surrounded by young men of his own age and an entourage of Persians who kept him at least somewhat grounded in his own culture. He wrote of how well students who did not return home during the school holidays were treated. A British vice consul in Berne visited Le Rosey to assess the crown prince and wrote that he was popular, intelligent, and egalitarian.

The British report is one of the first to mention Ernest Perron, the son of a gardener-handyman at Le Rosey, who was to become a near-constant companion of the Shah for the next twenty years, even moving to Tehran. He was a decade older than Mohammad Reza, gay, effete, and very Catholic. Thin and frail, he limped and was obsessed with the occult. His passions were reading palms and analyzing handwriting. He was, in short, the most unlikely companion for a sporty, confident, heterosexual Muslim crown prince.

But was the Shah confident? Abbas Milani is the most thoughtful analyst of this friendship, seeing how its interpretation has been constantly used to undermine the Shah. Was Perron the Shah's *selfobject*, the person who bolstered his confidence by offering up some distorted mirror? John Kennedy had a similar lifelong friend in Lem Billings, another lonely gay man who offered a limitless supply of worship, love, and always-available company, perhaps shoring up the ego in moments of vulnerability that could only be revealed in the most private moments with a subservient figure.

After the Revolution, the new regime published a scurrilous book called *Ernest Perron: The Husband of the Shah of Iran*. It was as short on evidence as most of the attacks on the monarch. Indeed, there is no proof at all that the Shah was gay. But he was clearly homosocial; he liked sex with women and the company of men, and he wanted these men to be loyal, dependent, and to focus their lives entirely on him. Perron's survival at court was possibly because he reminded the Shah of something he was not allowed to admit at home: that he had been very happy at Le Rosey, living something close to a normal life. As Milani wrote, "it was politically untenable for him to admit to the fact that he loved life away from the court, the country, and the cares of the state." His sister also gave the game away in her autobiography, describing her twin as healthier, happier, and less rough around the edges after his time in Switzerland.

The many tales of the Shah's unhappy childhood illustrate the perils of biography. All childhoods have moments of anxiety as people find their place in the world, learn to navigate societies and families filled with friends and foes, and sometimes people who are both. What is clear is that he grew up with an attentive father who was perhaps more doting than might have been expected. The childhood of Prince Philip, the husband of Queen Elizabeth II and just a few years younger than the Shah, was far more grim: exiled as a baby from Greece, fleeing the country asleep in an orange crate; a mother with severe mental illnesses who became an Greek Orthodox nun; a penniless father who spent his time in a state of down-at-heel torpor in Monaco with his mistress; sisters married to Nazis, one of whom died with her children in a plane crash and then, on top of all that, education at Gordonstoun, a veritable Scottish gulag compared to the *dou-*

THE HOST

ceur of life at Le Rosey. And despite this litany of woe, very little of his childhood attaches to any weaknesses he might have shown as a member of a royal family.

If biography presents problems, autobiography is even more slippery and uncertain. The Shah produced three of them: they were ghost-written and intended to bolster his political position or to try to secure his place in history, a desperate and largely pompous effort to give his legacy some shape as it slipped through his fingers in exile. He had every reason to play up the isolation and sadness of his time at Le Rosey, both to buttress his patriotism and love of both family and nation, but also to signal that he had always, and would always, suffer nobly for his people.

His marriages were portrayed similarly: there was no love in the first dynastic link-up with the Egyptian monarchy through his marriage to Princess Fawzia, then part of a much more respectable line than the Pahlavis. There was love but no children in the second marriage to the impetuous half-German Soraya, an intelligent woman of startling beauty, who stirred up life at court before spending her life in an indolent exile in Europe. Perron was probably the closest witness to the Shah's first two marriages: the limping jester seen disappearing down the palace corridor, just avoiding being caught listening at the door. Soraya loathed "the diabolic Swiss" and tried to have him banned from the palace in 1951. In 1954, he fell out of favor with the Shah after a botched attempt to negotiate a new oil deal with the British. He left Iran, dying in Switzerland in 1961.

* * *

Of all the ideas that have persisted about the Shah, one of the most durable has been about the extreme brutality and repression of his regime. There is no doubt that there was violence during his thirty-eight years on the throne. Some of that violence was inflicted on entirely innocent people, some of it was even indiscriminate, and all of it is regrettable. The stain on the Pahlavi dynasty seems to be irremovable; the 2012 Hollywood film *Argo* begins with a prologue that includes a sharp comment on the violence of the regime and the decadence of the Pahlavis.

The emergence of the Shah on the world stage coincided with the rise of a new force in global affairs, one that focused on human rights. Although the United Nations had responded to the crimes of World War II by enshrining these rights in a universal declaration in 1948, they had not captured the popular imagination or been adopted by political leaders. South Africa's violent policy of apartheid, the Vietnam War, the horrors of Biafra, and the social uprisings of 1968 all aided the emergence of a new public awareness of rights and their protections. It was no longer enough in many Western countries to be anti-communist to get a pass when it came to how you treated your people.

Martin Ennals was one of the founders of Amnesty International. During his time as secretary-general, the organization exploded in importance and size, driving the growth of what is today a web of organizations that monitor and report on abuses. Amnesty International moved human rights from a marginal subject into the mainstream with enormous success; indeed, few organizations have raised the profile of an issue and maintained it for so long.

Amnesty began with a focus on what it called "prisoners of conscience," non-violent people who were jailed for their political views. Its founding legend was told by Peter Berenson, a British lawyer, who said he was reading a newspaper on the London Underground when he saw an article about two Portuguese students at the University of Coimbra who were jailed for raising a toast to freedom. Nobody has ever found this article so it is unclear if the inspiration came from this, but Berenson believed that by bringing together people who were outraged by such cases, they could put pressure on governments to free prisoners.

THE HOST

By the early 1970s, Amnesty had expanded its remit to cover torture and unfair trials, as well as extending its reach around the world. Under the leadership of Ennals, the organization paid particular attention to Iran, a subject that was raising tensions in the United Kingdom due to concerns among Labour politicians about London's close relationship with Tehran. British officials were loath to press the Shah on human rights; it was their role to keep his wallet open to buy their exports, particularly of arms. The Shah was notoriously sensitive to slights, and he kept a keen and wary eye on the British, with ambassadors to London obliged to monitor the press closely for any information about him. He would never accept that the media in the United Kingdom was free to say what it liked, always believing the government directed it.

The emphasis in the 1960s and 1970s tended to be on rightwing governments rather than those on the left. The focus thus swung towards the Shah much more than, say, the nominally socialist Assad family in Syria. Pinochet and the other generals in Latin America, all dark glasses and gold braid, were a more accessible and compelling story than the mysterious Khmers Rouges in the jungles of Indochina or the communist government in Hanoi. Not only were figures like the Shah so obviously, cartoonishly villainous, but they were embraced by unfortunate figures such as Richard Nixon and British Prime Minister Edward Heath. They made perfect targets.

Human rights organizations defend themselves against charges of bias by saying they focus on the individual and that all countries must be held to the standards of the Universal Declaration of Human Rights. Of course, they also make a multitude of decisions about language, evidence, where they spend their time and money and what emphasis they put on certain countries. Often this is determined by funding: there may be more money for coverage of a certain country or issue. Amnesty International

THE SHAH'S PARTY

funds itself mostly from small donors, so it faces less financial pressure; however, it still needs to maintain a public base by tackling issues that meet popular interests and expectations. They also end up focusing on those places where it is possible to get information. Extremely closed countries—back then, notably North Korea and Albania, but really the entire Eastern Bloc—managed to avoid much attention as nobody could gain access.

Iran was the best possible target: it had genuine human rights problems; it had a media-savvy, Western-based, English-speaking opposition, centered around Iranian student groups in the West but also including appealing poets and artists; and it had witnesses with compelling stories to tell. The Shah was skilled at making himself look terrible, from the excesses of Persepolis to his peevish interviews with correspondents while lolling by a fireplace in St. Moritz. Jacking up global oil prices brought him to the attention of the masses; he became personally to blame for the hours-long wait to buy petrol; for crushing unemployment, for three-day work weeks and strikes. The Saudi royals were smart to send out Sheikh Yamani, their non-royal oil minister, to face the baying crowds. The Shah's prickly lack of charm made him easy to goad; the Western media went from the generally sycophantic world of *TIME* and *Newsweek* in the 1960s to adopting a sharper edge.

Ennals became extremely influential on Iran, not least because his brother was a Labour minister and himself a high-profile campaigner on human rights. His comment that Iran had the worst human rights record in the world took hold in every assessment of the Shah's rule; it was the human rights equivalent of the myth that Empress Farah bathed in deer milk.

The 1970s were a time in which Vietnam held hundreds of thousands in re-education camps; China was going through the Cultural Revolution with its entire population cast into a dark abyss of political chaos; and Brezhnev's Soviet Union was locking up its dissidents in psychiatric hospitals. Argentina's generals were starting their project of disappearing 40,000 people, many of them tortured and thrown alive from planes into the River Plate. In Cambodia, millions were being worked to death in one of the worst genocides of the twentieth century. Kim Il-Sung ran an extensive network of gulags in North Korea for hundreds of thousands of people who deviated even slightly from his ideology and Indonesia's military dictator Suharto began the slaughter and starvation of half a million people in East Timor. In Haiti, Baby Doc Duvalier had just inherited his father's dictatorship; thousands more would die from his regime's brutality until his overthrow fifteen years later. Mengistu Haile Mariam would overthrow Haile Selassie in 1974 and begin a period of violence and deprivation that would leave some two million Ethiopians dead. Chile under General Augusto Pinochet saw thousands murdered, tens of thousands tortured, and hundreds of thousands exiled. Neither left nor right regimes had a monopoly on murdering and abusing their own people.

A report from Amnesty in 1976, read into the Congressional Record during hearings on human rights in Iran, said that they did not know the number of political prisoners but believed it to be in the thousands. It then quoted exile groups as putting the figure somewhere between 20,000 and 100,000. This figure was then taken up by these very groups and given the Amnesty stamp of approval, although the organization itself had not used this figure. From then on, the figure of 100,000 political prisoners was regularly published even though this number came out of thin air. It persists; there is a vastly exaggerated sense of the abuses under the Shah's regime.

Nobody writing at that time questioned this figure, although to their credit, Amnesty included a comment from the Shah that around 3,000 people had been held for "terrorist" activities. There had been violence by both the leftist and the Islamist urban guerrilla groups that emerged in the late 1960s, and some legitimate detentions. When asked about torture in Iran, the Shah tended to come back with evasive accusations about the West and their use of psychological methods to extract information.

What is striking about the Amnesty report is that the numbers in it are modest: they identify one person who was tortured to death, they say that eighteen people tried by military tribunals were executed, nine people were killed "while trying to escape" prison—this is the one set of extra-judicial killings known to have occurred at that time. Two French lawyers who investigated the case found the government's version risible, and it was. The men were killed because a SAVAK agent had been shot by a leftist guerrilla whom the intelligence agency believed was connected to the group. SAVAK officers took the men from Evin prison and murdered them in retaliation.

The Amnesty report was fair about what was happening, and the numbers are borne out by subsequent research on imprisonment, torture, and extra-judicial killings under the Shah. They happened, causing immeasurable pain to the victims and their families, they had a disastrous impact on his image around the world, and they contributed to the hatred of the Shah that boiled up. But they were never on the scale that the opposition made out.

Reza Baraheni, who had served time in jail in Iran before leaving for Canada, became an influential voice speaking out against the Shah. He waged an intense campaign, testifying before Congressional committees in the United States. He charged that the Shah had executed tens of thousands, more than 300,000 people had been imprisoned at various times, and 1,500 more were being picked up every month. The figures were, to say the least, exaggerated and were never supported by evidence. The circular effect of reporting took hold: they had been mentioned in congressional testimony. They were picked up by journalists whose reports were used to justify the figures among the opposition. The real figures are not knowable now but may have been as few as one per cent of those cited by people such as Bahreni.

> Every schoolteacher of some experience will tell you that in some villages schoolchildren are taken out to graze the grass for their lunch. In many villages, people still exchange their daughters for a cow because they can milk a cow and till land with it which they can hardly do with their daughters,

Bahreni wrote. One wonders to what degree those listening to Bahreni took him at his word or saw in him a tendency for hyperbole.

Labour MPs and Democratic members of Congress took up the case against the Shah with enthusiasm. He had always rubbed the Democratic establishment in Washington the wrong way: he was too close to Republicans, too friendly with Nixon and Kissinger and too complicit in the oil crisis of 1973. The Kennedy family had long taken against the Shah, perhaps seeing in his parvenu ways something of their own family. The same brothers, whose Great Gatsby carelessness had led to numerous tragedies, felt that the Shah was a brutal figure who needed to be instructed on how to run his country. Edward Kennedy turned on his rival Jimmy Carter during the 1979 Democratic primary campaign, when the Shah had entered the United States for medical treatment. "The Shah," he said, "had the reins of power and ran one of the most violent regimes in the history of mankind—in the form of terrorism and the basic and fundamental violations of human rights, in the most cruel circumstances, to his own people."

* * *

There were several periods of intense political violence or conflict under Mohammad Reza. In the Azerbaijan crisis of 1946, in which pro-Soviet Iranians with the backing of Moscow tried to create a breakaway republic, some 2,000 people are believed to have died. Following Mossadegh's ouster, it is estimated that approximately 4,000 people were arrested, most of whom were members of the Tudeh Party. Of these, some fifty were executed, and another fifteen are thought to have died under torture. Another fifty or so are believed to have died in the street fighting. Another round of both arrests and killings occurred after the uprising in June 1963. While Khomeini put the number killed at 15,000, there is no evidence for it being much more than the 320 recorded in police files. Some might have been buried privately, or their bodies not taken to hospitals. After 1971, political violence worsened, and Amnesty put the number executed for political crimes at 300 up until 1979. Around 3,000 died in violence during the Revolution. In the thirty-eight years of Mohammad Reza's rule, around 6,000 people are believed to have died in political violence or conflict.

For the sake of comparison, in France from 1941 to 1979, civilian deaths that can be linked to government action or policies included about 75,000 Jews deported by the Vichy government who died in German camps. Some 125,000–400,000 died in the First Indochina War. In Algeria, somewhere between half a million and 1.5 million Algerians died along with around 6,000 French civilians. In the Bemileke War in French Cameroon, there were believed to be somewhere between 60,000 and 75,000 civilian deaths. As many as 300 Algerians may have died in central Paris, many of them drowning in the Seine, when the police put down protests in 1961. With the end of most of its empire, deaths because of the French state diminished, but killings still occurred during various interventions in Africa. It is still easy to reach a very conservative toll of around 600,000 civilians dying because of the actions of the French state during the same period that the Shah ruled Iran. The figure might be as high as two million.

Did the Shah really "run one of the most violent regimes in the history of mankind," in the words of Senator Edward

THE HOST

Kennedy? While the notion of comparison can be dismissed as "whataboutism," it is perhaps important to remember the extent of violence perpetrated by states around the world, even in a country like France, which sees itself as the originator of the concept of human rights.

> The Shah was a survivalist of considerable skill—he was actually one of the longest-reigning monarchs of the twentieth century, which is perhaps why his fall remains a subject of inquiry. The vast majority of his peers who came to power after World War II fell long before him—Nkrumah, Sukarno, Farouk, Faisal, Ben Bella, Batista, and Trujillo had all gone.
>
> Oriana Fallaci

Persepolis was not quite "peak Shah," but it was close. The economic success of the 1960s had been immense. Millions of Iranians had climbed up ladders of wealth and education. Tens of thousands had traveled overseas or even within their own country for the first time. New roads, railways, planes, and cars changed the mental geography of millions of people. Movies, television, radio, and literacy reached across a land that, under the Qajars, had remained stubbornly resistant to progress. There were gaps, and some deep tensions, but the propagandists of state television did not have to look far to see progress: new buildings, new ideas, new images. The representation of modernity as men in lab coats wearing safety goggles was universal and powerful in the 1960s and the following decade.

There was a build-up to Persepolis in terms of the Shah's increasing authoritarianism and association of himself with the country. In 1966, a new history of the Pahlavi dynasty recorded in microscopic detail all the feats the two kings had accomplished in just forty-one years. The coronation in 1967 blended European-invented tradition with some local flourishes. It was all a long way from any previous dynasty with its mix of modernity

THE SHAH'S PARTY

(Farah was the first woman to be crowned as Empress) and pretend pageantry (fake eighteenth-century Austrian carriages purchased new for the occasion). But the event was not played up for international attention beyond the inevitable coverage in *LIFE* and the European photo magazines.

It did, however, set in motion a series of events that would shape the 1970s in Iran. It was around the time of the coronation that the comparisons between the Shah and Cyrus the Great surfaced. Both Mohammad Reza and Cyrus were portrayed as heroic kings who rescued Iran from backwardness, promoted its global role, and cared for their beloved people. The myth of Cyrus as a munificent proponent of human rights had been around for centuries, drawing on Greek histories, as there is little direct evidence from his time. It established a set of beliefs about Cyrus that are still accepted by many, perhaps most, Iranians to this day. Persian-language Facebook and social media are filled with people who police a set of beliefs about Cyrus and other early Persian kings, promulgated first and with most enthusiasm by the developers of Pahlavism.

A warning sign of the troubles to come was the proliferation of statues of the Shah. Underground Tudeh publications mocked the absurdity of claims that the world was "studying and imitating what has been achieved through the Shah's genius." An article from the party's *Mardom* newspaper reminded readers that all dictators think they are essential and irreplaceable, but most end up as footnotes in history. Of course, the Communist Party of Iran, Tudeh, had been uncritical, even worshipful, of Stalin, so its version of history should be taken with a grain of salt. Still, the view increasingly aligned with many in a growing middle class who were tiring of the Shah's self-promotion.

The jet-setting glamour of winters in St. Moritz and parties on Kish Island were easy to contrast with the squalor of south Tehran or the poverty of rural Iran. His family's corruption and

THE HOST

the arrogance of his court combined with the sinister control of SAVAK and the reliance on the United States at a particularly dark time in the Cold War. Mohammad Reza's lack of personal warmth, his distance, his rigidity meant he was never able to relate to people; his one effort was to strive for magnificence; his only speech was to sing his own praises; his lack of trust, indeed his fear, of his own people was too obvious.

At the same time, many other monarchs, particularly those in Europe, were cultivating images that placed them closer to their people. Queen Elizabeth had a documentary made about her in 1968 that "let light in on the magic," something many advisors warned her not to do. The royal family turned out to be studiously dull, their greatest pleasure rainy picnics on windswept Scottish hillsides. The Dutch had already become bicycling royals. Even the King of Thailand, an aloof and unsmiling Buddhist with vast wealth and a distaste for democracy, mixed with farmers and trekked in shirt sleeves through the remote highlands of his land.

The late 1960s were a moment in which the cult of personality, discredited after the death of Stalin in 1953, developed a new lease on life. From North Korea to Egypt, from Mao to Ceaușescu to the King of Thailand, the memories of the Soviet leader's excesses faded, and rulers of every political stripe began the process of ensuring that their image was everywhere. In Iran, this meant that the Shah and Shahbanou were featured on the front of every newspaper, at the top of every television news bulletin, on every stamp, and on the walls of every government office. But it has always been a hard act to carry off; it requires the enforcement of a high level of obedience in a population.

That came through SAVAK. Although the name struck fear into the hearts of many, it was never entirely effective at stemming opposition. Nor was the Shah good at the retail side of maintaining a cult of personality. Kim Il-Sung was a brutal dictator but also a masterful politician, almost like an old-style

THE SHAH'S PARTY

American ward boss. He traveled relentlessly, offering "on-the-spot guidance" to soldiers, farmers, and factory workers while also doling out benefits to keep the elites sweet. Anywhere you visit in North Korea has a memorial to a visit by Kim, usually a stone block or panel with his signature and the date of his tour, as well as photographs of him with people, in which he appears cheerful and engaged. The crowds around him appear not simply deferential or afraid but genuinely excited and joyful. One would have to be skeptical about these images, but it does seem that there was some connection, although with a cult of personality on this scale, how can we ever know? Images of the Shah never show that level of joy among his people. They often exhibit some fear, considerable groveling deference, and occasionally awkwardness.

Ultimately, his mix of shyness, resentment, arrogance, and insecurity caused him to undercut his own position. The vacillations are visible in his manner: sometimes diffident, with eyes lowered, and at other times filled with the off-putting bravado—most on show, it seems, when he was interviewed by women and questioned about his views on women. We know from Asadollah Alam's diaries that the uncertainties were always there when he was on ground where he did not feel confident. He was master of any discussion of military hardware, knowledge developed through hours of reading weaponry catalogues, or of oil prices. Still, he knew little about the real concerns of Iranians beyond sharing the national obsession with rainfall and drought. He knew that he was surrounded by sycophants, particularly his weak prime minister. He sometimes abhorred this, but he did not enjoy the company of men who might have stood up to him.

* * *

Although the Shah was portrayed in the 1970s as a leader of almost unmatched brutality, he was an amateur compared with many of his contemporaries. His enemies were not executed and mostly did not die in prison cells. Mossadegh lived under house arrest in internal exile in Ahmadabad, Khomeini was sent into exile in Turkey and then Iraq. Ali Amini, Zahedi, and others who fell from favor were given sinecures of various types. One powerful enemy, General Bakhtiar, was assassinated in Iraq. Still, he had aligned himself with the regime there, an act of outrageous treason that might have provoked any Iranian to violence.

The Shah allowed a variety of less-than-supportive figures not just to continue living but to maintain a foothold in political life. Arsanjani, the agriculture minister who managed land reform in the 1960s, could carry through on his plans and take considerable credit, all the while speaking out against feudalism and steadily undercutting the Shah. Other figures became ambassadors or were allowed to move into business. Many in the court intervened to save friends from SAVAK. The Queen and those in her entourage regularly spoke up on behalf of artists, filmmakers, and others, creating tensions with the Shah, who occasionally accused his wife of harboring those who opposed him. Some regarded his willingness to tolerate some dissent as weakness: Alam urged a harder line against all opposition but was frequently overruled. The Shah was constantly irritated by his family, by foreign dignitaries, by his ministers and others, but he rarely confronted them; this inability to make some of the difficult choices seems to have worsened in his last years as illness and its accompanying depression took hold.

> *Kings alone know the riddles of their kingdom;*
> *O Hafez, you are a beggarly loner; hold your peace!*
>
> Hafez

Many people other than the Shah have been blamed for his downfall. His sister, Ashraf, became an emblem of the corruption and excess of the times; her children were notorious for their sleazy behavior, and she for her ruthless hauteur. A twin who had all the attributes her brother lacked, she was the tiny, fierce, and relentless yin to his yang. Her life, when it ended in 2016 after ninety-six years, was reduced in her obituaries to a few emblematic events: an assassination attempt in 1977 when the Rolls Royce in which she was being driven was raked with gunfire in Juan-les-Pins on the Cote d'Azur; a supposed bribe of a fur coat and an envelope of cash that led her to return to Iran to support her brother after the coup in 1953; a dressing down she once gave the notoriously indecisive Shah in front of foreign diplomats. She reveled in the name "The Black Panther," given to her by French journalists who tracked her activities in the South of France. An obituary described her as a "mink-clad sybarite." In fact, she preferred to wear her much more precious sable coat, a gift from Stalin.

These stories, and indeed her own two biographies, feel incomplete. What frustrations lay beneath the surface of a woman who might have possessed more leadership qualities than her twin, yet was often blamed for her part in his downfall. Although she held no official position beyond heading the Iranian Women's Association and some United Nations sinecures, she saw herself as a significant political leader. A British government file about a planned visit to London in 1976 reveals a series of relentless demands her office made for protocol upgrades. Letters went back and forth for months over who would be present to meet her at the airport and whether the Prime Minister would offer her lunch. The British Embassy in Tehran knew not to upset the princess with a protocol slip-up.

Ashraf's involvement in various forms of criminality was frequently alleged. *Le Monde* wrote of her near arrest when at Geneva's Cointrin Airport, one of her suitcases was found to contain several kilograms of heroin. She sued the newspaper for half a million francs, but the court only awarded her 1,000 francs in damages, suggesting that perhaps there was some truth to the

THE HOST

report. French customs officials caught her smuggling 800,000 francs into the country, while she had only declared 10,000. A former head of SAVAK in the United States wrote of her urging him to "hire a few negroes" to get rid of some demonstrators who had sprayed her car with shaving foam to protest her appointment to the UN Human Rights Commission in New York. He demurred but was repeatedly pressed by her to do something to avenge her humiliation.

A 1971 State Department report described Ashraf as a polarizing figure due to her "vivid personality," her entourage of handsome men, and her close association with the Shah. While more sophisticated circles in Tehran discounted much of the talk of orgies and excess, many young people saw in her everything that was supposedly wrong with the regime: its corruption, favoritism, and excesses. There was, of course, no small measure of both sexism and displacement in this. It was easier and less perilous to attack Ashraf than her brother.

The finger of blame has often also been pointed at Asadollah Alam. The Minister of the Court was one of the Shah's few friends, but, like his sister, he was said to have led him astray, ignored corruption, particularly within the royal family, and paid too little attention to the growing disillusionment of the Iranian people as the excesses of the 1970s came up against the harshness of modern urban life. Like Ashraf, Alam was Francophile, urbane, with a taste for the same call girls sent from Paris by Madame Claude and shared among the Shah, his court minister, and his doctor, all of whom were to die within years of each other.

Alam also failed to control corruption, mainly due to his own shortcomings in this area. According to the diplomat Amir Aslan Afshar, Alam almost certainly diverted at least $800,000 from the budget to promote the party in the United States and was involved in the diversion of funds related to the construction of grain silos. Pahlavi elites seemed not to see corruption as a problem, although studies from the time showed that young people were increasingly dismayed by it. By the 1970s, the country was awash with money; indeed, it had more than it could have spent without worsening the inflation and other economic obstacles it faced through the decade. Today, it would have been encouraged to stash the money in a sovereign wealth fund to avoid the problems that come with a large oil sector. The oil curse—an overvalued currency, a collapse in domestic production, inflation, obscene corruption, and flaccid human development—afflicted not just Iran but almost all oil-producing states in the 1970s. Nigeria, Venezuela, Indonesia, and Saudi Arabia were all perhaps even more corrupt than Iran back then; elites looted those states with impunity, just as the elites of the Islamic Revolution and their families have looted Iran since 1979.

The fifty or so princes and princesses who made up the Pahlavi clan were certainly more avaricious, self-indulgent, and poorly behaved than the Shah ever was himself. He failed to rein them in, finding it hard to control his family and generally preferring to avoid confrontation. Their near-constant engagement in all manner of corruption was toxic because it was so widely known and discussed. The blame tended to go directly onto the Imperial couple themselves; why did they do so little to control their families? When the family overstepped an invisible line, he had Alam chastise them, a mostly ineffectual strategy when none of them saw what they were doing as wrong.

The Shah's position was bound to leave him with a sense of entitlement and self-importance, but he also suffered from a fatal lack of connection to his people. A semi-mystical view of the world and a belief in an almost divine right of kings was only slightly leavened in private by an ironic or knowing edge. His interviews are almost painful to read, as they are so pompous and unwilling to acknowledge anyone but himself. A lifetime of tiny humiliations, and indeed some major ones, had created a tense

THE HOST

knot of nerve endings balled up inside him. Anxiety overlaid a paranoid manner that was far from uncommon in a society that ran on rumors and gossip. Diplomats found it almost impossible to get him to take their word for anything, such was his constant belief that he was being undermined by a conspiracy of foreigners. Of course, the Anglo-American conspiracies of his younger days were bound to raise endless questions about the motives of politicians in London and Washington. Unsurprisingly, one of the few leaders ever to like the Shah was Richard Nixon. The two shared many characteristics, not least a fear that everyone, secretly or not so secretly, looked down on them. They also shared a deep hatred of the Kennedy family.

One of the most revealing moments for the Shah was the interview with the Italian journalist Oriana Fallaci. She broke almost every taboo in her interview with the Shah: she asked if he was as sad as he appeared, was it lonely at the top and was he planning on taking a second wife. "A stupid, vile, disgusting libel," he harrumphed in response to the rumors that had spread when an over-enthusiastic mistress told people they were in love and were to marry. A longer response laid out the rules for taking more than one wife, saying a secret marriage would have violated them.

> Hmm... all I can say is that women, when they are in power, are crueler than men. Much more cruel. Much more bloodthirsty. I'm quoting facts not opinions. You're heartless when you are rulers. Think of Caterina de'Medici. Catherine of Russia, Elizabeth I of England, not to mention your Lucrezia Borgia with her poisons and intrigues. You're schemers, you're evil. Everyone one of you.

Barbara Walters, the American television personality who was close to the Pahlavi regime, willingly accepting their gifts and hospitality, returned to a similar subject when she interviewed the Shah and Farah Diba together in 1977. She asked the Shah if women and men were equal. His hesitant, rambling answer—essentially no, but there were some exceptional women—left his wife's eyes brimming with tears.

Even paranoiacs have enemies, and the Shah certainly did have genuine foes. As with Nixon, a favorite focus of hatred was the media, although he was also keen to speak to the world when he could. He loathed *Le Monde*. The BBC Persian Service was still seen as a tool of British imperialism, as it had been when it broadcast tirades against his father before his ouster. By the 1970s, it had lost much of its influence but was still accorded outlandish powers to shape opinion in Iran, becoming a daily subject of rants at his court minister.

For a man of his position, the Shah was unfailingly polite to staff and servants, although he complained relentlessly about everyone's inadequacies to others. He rarely raised his voice, but he seemed to bristle in the company of journalists, often falling into the traps laid by the likes of Fallaci, whose journalistic shtick was to get people to say something ridiculous about themselves. Henry Kissinger famously told her he saw himself as "the cowboy who leads the wagon train by riding ahead alone on his horse." The juxtaposition of that image with the dumpy academic with his rumbling German accent was tragically comic. The Secretary of State later wrote that it was "the single most disastrous conversation I have ever had with any member of the press."

Comedy never mixes well with power. In 1971, the Censorship Bureau in Tehran closed the satirical newspaper *Tawfiq* that had been founded in 1923, near the start of the Pahlavi era. Depending on the politics of the moment and what was allowed, it veered between a more literary bent and a more critical and political line. From 1941, it was edited by the founder's son, Mohammad-Ali Tawfiq, and his three cousins, known as the Tawfiq Brothers. The relative political openness following the abdication of Reza Shah created the space, and a banned magazine, *Omid*, provided many of the writers and cartoonists who flourished at *Tawfiq*.

The editors and proprietor often spent time in jail, when officials were irritated by the cartoons or mockery of members of the Majlis. At one time the paper appeared to align with Tudeh policies but when Mossadegh came to power, it became more nationalist in tone and was often quite critical of the Shah. The paper accommodated a variety of political views, although it was not supportive of the Shah. A series of articles criticizing the monarch in 1953 earned the proprietor a stint in internal exile on Kharg Island, then a sweaty backwater, and the paper was closed for four years. His house and the paper's offices were also burned to the ground.

By the time it was revived, it had a narrower scope in which to operate, and the three Tawfiq brothers, by then all government officials, went on to run their own magazine, although this would eventually bear the Tawfiq name. Each edition came with a line that it supported no political party, although writers invented the satirical Party of Donkeys. Its manifesto included the ideas: "Donkeys of Iran and the World Unite! Create a world in which donkeys can live in comfort. Support the creation of a Bank of Hay. Oppose and end all donkey-like despotism. Create an atmosphere in which every donkey can freely bray."

Cartoons were a central part of the newspaper, although they often resulted in bans. Those editions that escaped censorship sold 30,000 copies or three times that for some special editions; these were astonishing numbers for the time. Editors knew there was one subject that could not be touched, and they generally steered clear of it: the Imperial family. The newspaper was closed on the orders of Prime Minister Hoveyda in 1971 at a time when he was supporting a rival magazine to undermine *Tawfiq*. Rumors abounded about what had prompted the closure. One suggestion was that the Shah was upset by a cartoon that showed Iran as a ghostly cemetery. Asadollah Alam suggested in his diaries that the newspaper was linked to the Soviet Union, an unlikely charge at that time. A time of grandiosity did not allow for the corrosive power of humor.

* * *

Talking to Fallaci in 1973, the Shah started with a provocation.

> I believe I have a task to carry out, a mission, and I intend to perform it to the end without renouncing my throne. One cannot foretell the future obviously, but I am persuaded that the monarchy in Iran will last longer than your regimes. Or maybe I should say that your regimes won't last and mine will.

He went on to delve into his mystical side, much to the surprise of the Italian journalist. Asked about loneliness at the top, he replied: "I'm not entirely alone, because a force others can't perceive accompanies me. My mystical force. Moreover, I receive messages. I have lived with God beside me since I was five years old. Since that is, God sent me these visions." These words might have emerged from the mouth of Khomeini, although the Imam preferred others to notice his closeness to God and promote his holiness on his behalf, rather than pointing it out himself. The interview went downhill after his admission of religious visions. He went on to attack women, democracy, priests, left-wingers, the Western press, Iraq, Arabs, and on and on. The last line is just a statement from Fallaci: "You frighten me, Your Majesty."

This was one of many anti-Western tirades that generally reflected the Shah's delusions that his country was on an unending rise and was soon to become the Japan of the Middle East, with a similarly disciplined, cohesive population and a distinctly non-Western identity. But this was not simply irritation at not always being accorded the respect he wanted; Persepolis had shown he could attract at least a few A-listers. Nixon had visited, and the much-despised British had been reduced to begging him

THE HOST

to buy tanks and Concordes. Valéry Giscard d'Estaing hovered outside his hotel rooms in St. Moritz and Zurich; Kissinger and Nixon begged him not to raise oil prices while offering him his pick of weapon systems. His anger at the West was rooted in something else: a fear of democracy, of accountability, and of transparency, as well as challenges to his supreme power. He saw in those societies a spiritual emptiness that would not allow a man to declare himself a divinely guided monarch nor impose his vision on a country that needed to be dragged into modernity.

Often Mohammad Reza faced cameras or reporters with a preternatural calm, happily discussing arcane matters of oil policy in great detail. At other times, he would launch off into an angry series of dubious assertions: Western democracies were on the brink of failure; oil would run out in a short time and should only be used for petrochemicals; Iran was more progressive in its policies than Sweden as they had not nationalized their forests; Iran would shortly catch up with Japan as an industrial power; communists were a threat. Well, Iranian communists were a threat; others in the Soviet Union could be traded with when necessary or played off against the capitalist West. In the Shah's mind, Iran enjoyed "true socialism" as factories were owned by workers, land had been distributed to farmers, and people voted for village councils. There were familiar laments about the threats of feminism, students, and clerics. Iraq was seen as a constant menace—which it genuinely was, given the expansionist, violent delusions of Saddam Hussein—while the other Arab countries were dismissed as irrelevant, particularly the backward Saudis. These monologues were entirely self-oriented and ungenerous. He never mentioned any other Iranians, pointing to anyone else who might have delivered achievements. Nobody else mattered, not even his wife.

It lost him friends, unnecessarily. Western diplomats would grow skeptical, in part because of his paranoia and dismissal of

THE SHAH'S PARTY

countries that were allies. But as pointless as some of these jeremiads seemed, they served a purpose in the Pahlavi state, alongside hundreds of other actions that promoted two key ideas: democracy was weak and unsuitable for Iran, and that there was something special deep in the soul of Iranians that could only be nurtured by a monarchy. Constitutional democracy was an alienating system captured by demagogues and corrupt businesses. It did not feed the soul. Only a nation led by a monarchy under God would work for Iran.

This system resulted in all power stemming from the Shah; access to him was key to any person, and no independent power centers were allowed to thrive for long. Becoming the tallest flower in the Shah's garden put any official at risk of being cut down. This worked well enough in the early days of his absolute power after 1953, but gradually became untenable as the country and its economy became much more complex. Corruption raged out of control; professional managerial experience was often scorned in favor of connections, and officials were regularly undercut. Chronic intrigue was the result as officials dedicated more time to managing their rivalries than implementing public policy. Disillusionment among the emerging technocratic class ran deep when they realized that merit would only play a limited role in any advancement. Likewise, students who saw few prospects ahead of them because they lacked connections saw little reason to stick to their studies.

Khomeini's views on how to run the country were not that different. You might just replace "Monarch" with "Mullah." His theory of *Velayat e-faqih*, essentially rule by the clerics, was rejected by the mainstream of religious teachers and lawyers. Most theologians believed that religion and politics did not mix well: their ideology very much followed the line that politics was a separate worldly realm. *Velayat e-faqih* was a new view of how the world should work, essentially conjured up during his exile with some intellectual backing from several people who combined left-wing revolutionary views with religion. Khomeini would never acknowledge their contribution: his inspiration was divine. But they played a vital role in creating the conditions for his rule.

The Shah, fluent in French and English, educated in Switzerland, at home with foreigners and knowledgeable about geopolitics, a lover of technology, was at heart both a mystic and a nationalist. "I believe in God. And this is why I believe I have a divine command to do what I am doing. This and the special relationship between the Persian people and their king, that makes it a very special relationship that maybe some other people cannot understand."

His court, picking up on these views, promoted intellectuals who were both anti-Western and anti-modern. The sociologist and historian Ali Mirsepassi has written on how these intellectuals, embedded in the court, royal think tanks, universities, and newspapers, promoted the ideas that the Shah clearly felt lay at the heart of his rule. Western democracy was corrupt and unsuitable for Iranians, and anyway, it was in a process of collapse. Communism simply equaled a form of Soviet colonialism. It also lacked any soul and did not fit with the way Iranians saw the world. Iran would carve its own way. The king was divinely chosen and therefore had no need to share power.

This justification for Pahlavism also involved bludgeoning the idea of constitutional rule, which ended with the coup against Mossadegh. It was always an intellectual house of cards, the Pahlavis straining for legitimacy on the basis that only they could both modernize Iran and somehow still represent its traditional soul. It brought forth an array of tensions: Iran had to be a single Persian-speaking state, not an array of different ethnic groups; it had to be focused on the single figure of the Shah, without the diversion of any charismatic politicians; it needed a mighty army, while also making sure that army never hid within its ranks a Napoleon or Nasser; it needed a focus on some essential notion of what it meant to be an Iranian while launching the country through an extraordinarily rapid encounter with modernity; it needed to hold fast to Shiism while denying the clergy much of a say in life; it had to balance a cultural myth anchored in the village while undergoing one of the most rapid urbanizations of any society. This list could go on.

Velayat e-faqih literally means the Guardianship of the Faithful, and it was initially applied to those in society who were particularly vulnerable: widows, orphans, and people with disabilities. Those who could not care for themselves were put under clerical guardianship. Khomeini took this and applied it—in a very new way—to the entire country, as if an entire people were incapable of ruling themselves. He first put the idea down on paper in 1970. In short, God intended Islamic law to be implemented. The people who knew Islamic law best were religious scholars; therefore, they should be in charge until the Twelfth Imam returned to rule. But his marshalling of evidence was highly selective. Only one of the twelve Imams had risen up against the Caliphs. The other eleven had remained quiet and in the case of the final Imam gone into hiding rather than directly take on a bad ruler. But the example chosen fitted his vision of religious rule and the appointment of himself as Supreme Leader.

Khomeini had undergone an evolution on this idea during his exile. He had been a constitutionalist, even a supporter of monarchy, as long as the Shah reigned and did not rule. He had mostly followed the view that there could be no legitimate government during the occultation of the Twelfth Imam. So, the clergy should remain obedient to whomever was in power. But exile brought forward a change in his views; Islam could not be protected under monarchs, and Islamic jurists must occupy the pinnacle of power. Even in this, he wavered. Before

THE HOST

the Revolution, he said he believed in a progressive constitutional government as long as the Shah was gone; almost immediately, when he returned to Iran, he instituted a constitutional form of *Velayat e-faqih* that put him at the apex of political and religious power. On his deathbed, he said he did not think that his successor needed similar religious qualifications but should still rule unfettered.

Both the Shah and Khomeini had a rather slippery sense of ideology. The Shah dismissed one-party states as the conceit of dictators before abolishing all political parties except his own King's Party. Khomeini portrayed himself as a unifying figure in favor of justice and human rights ahead of the Revolution, only to wage a brutal campaign against anyone who opposed him. For both, ideology was something that could be adapted to suit the situation as long as you held power.

It is this idea that would betray the Shah. His promotion of the idea of an essential Iranian—Shia, mystical, in thrall to authority, alert to the misleading temptations of the West, anchored in the rural past—was similar to the reductive, imaginary vision that Khomeini promoted. The Shah's anti-Western views, encouraged in so many ways during the 1970s, also laid the groundwork for the chants of "Death to America," which remain a ritualistic, content-free mantra in Iran. In recent years, it has often been replaced with chants against clerical rule.

Two key ideas fermented amid the rapid changes of the 1970s. Westoxification, the idea coined by the writer Jalal Al-e Ahmad, suggested that Iranian elites were poisoned by their unthinking adoration of all things Western. Pastoral modernity, the imagining of the country as an unchanging utopia of harmony, cohesion, traditional culture, and solidarity, also emerged as a key idea in the decade before the Revolution. In the 1970s, everything from novels to films to the way the royal family acted aimed to portray the countryside as the antidote to everything harmful about modernity in cities. It was telling that most of those promoting pastoralism had almost no experience of rural life apart from picnicking or skiing there.

Even the events at Persepolis were connected to this. Their mastermind, Shafa, was key to the direction the court took in the 1970s in trying to connect to the past. From the odd attempt at forging a mystical connection with the ancient past, through the Shah's pledge to Cyrus at his tomb, to the march past of ancient soldiers, the aim was to tap into what was imagined to be the core nature of Iran, stretching back unchanged over thousands of years and now embodied in the Shah.

It was all contradictory in so many ways, as the mixing of political, religious, and nationalist thought often is. The Shah was unabashed in his belief that he owed his throne to divine intervention (rather than the machinations of the British and American secret services). Yet, he was entirely secular in his behavior. Khomeini was profoundly religious and abstemious in all ways, and yet far more skilled in the secular world of politics in a manner that many more senior religious figures in the country abhorred. They turned out to be two sides of the same coin, profoundly anti-democratic figures who toyed with religion to legitimize authoritarian rule.

> Saith Darius the king: Ahuramazda, the greatest of the Gods—he created me; he made me king; he bestowed upon me this kingdom, great, possessed of good horses, possessed of good men.
>
> An inscription on a tablet celebrating the construction of a palace by Darius, the fourth king of the dynasty.

Was it his thin voice, quavering with emotion, that undermined the moment? Or in retrospect, the emptiness of this gesture? Claiming descent from this unknown man in such an obvious manner may have been what made this ceremony so unsatisfying. When Mohammad Reza stepped off the helicopter at the tomb of Cyrus at Pasargadae, his short pledge to the founder of the Persian Empire rippled outwards. But the effects of this speech were not quite what had been planned.

The Shah descended from the sky, as he always did, in one of his elegant pale blue helicopters. Just forty-five minutes later, the "Ceremony for the Glorification of Cyrus" was over, and the Shah's helicopters were in the air again. After laying a wreath at the tomb, saluting Cyrus with a 101-gun salute and the singing of the Imperial hymn, the Shah gave a short speech. He was not a great orator; in the documentary made of the party, Orson Welles speaks over him in more impressively stentorian tones.

A tear had fallen down the Shah's cheek as he stood in front of the stark tomb in the desert. It was, Asadollah Alam later remarked, one of the rare occasions in which this controlled man had shown some emotion. At that moment, the Shah, born the son of a barely educated army sergeant but crowned King of Kings and named Light of the Aryans, felt a profound connection to a man who had died 2,500 years before.

The idea of a connection is absurd on the face of it. But in the past fifty years, Middle East nations have all strived to find links to their very distant past. Saddam Hussein spent lavishly on archaeology and a kitsch rebuilding of Babylon. Egyptians now have a massive billion-dollar museum that is the largest in the world dedicated to a single culture. The Gulf nations and even Saudi Arabia are all spending lavishly on museums and tourism, looking to a past that was once scorned as being disconnected from Islam.

Despite the Islamic Republic's efforts in its early days to downplay archaeology and history, the subjects remained very much alive in Iran. When the Hollywood movie *300* was released in 2007, there was a furious reaction against its depiction of the Battle of Thermopylae at which 300 Spartan warriors fought the powerful Persian army commanded by Xerxes I so that the remainder of the Greek forces could escape. Javad Shamaqdari, a filmmaker and deputy culture minister under President Mahmoud Ahmadinejad, accused the movie of "plundering Iran's historic past and insulting this civilization." *300*, based on a graphic novel aimed at teenage boys and featuring a posse of musclebound Spartans, was nothing but "psychological warfare" against Iran, he complained.

Iranian bloggers rose as one to defend an empire that had ended more than 2,000 years ago. The movie seemed to enrage the Iranian communities in Canada and the United States most, perhaps because they could actually see *300*, unlike people in Iran. The Iranian-American comedian Maz Jobhani saw how this ancient history had become part of the performance of being Persian outside Iran. In his stand-up show, he portrayed an angry contributor to a list-server ranting about how no Spartan was going to take him down. Chest puffed and a scowl on his face, he confronted people on Sunset Boulevard in Los Angeles, asking them if they were Spartans.

Iranians were genuinely incensed about the depiction of their army in what was just a comic book entertainment of no historical value. The response from outside Iran had much to do with the ideas about identity that have grown up within the diaspora, ideas that owe much to the Pahlavi dynasty's promotion of the ancient world. Even within Iran, the Achaemenids, so long out of political fashion under the Islamic regime, had come back to the fore as Ahmadinejad sought to bolster his flagging support.

The past in Iran was not just another country; it was almost another world. Life under Cyrus was utterly removed from how people lived in 1971. Cyrus lived from around 600 to 530 BCE. Herodotus, the great classical historian who shaped our views of the ancient world, was born half a century later. Xenophon, a Greek mercenary who fought in Persia and wrote the adulatory *Cyropaedia*, was born a century after Cyrus died. They cobbled together what they heard, passed on in oral cultures that always enjoyed a good story.

THE HOST

Cyrus was from Persis, an area known as Fars today, and he was the son and grandson of local kings. Although he may have founded an empire, he started as little more than a tribal chief. Persis was under the control of the more powerful Medean kingdom. Overthrowing them—and then merging his history into that of Medea by claiming descent from their king—was the first in a series of steps he took towards taking control of territory that would eventually extend from the Nile in Egypt to the Indus in what is now Pakistan. It was the first great empire, and it set the model for ruling such an extensive and diverse area.

Cyrus controlled his empire through satraps, governors who were empowered to run their domains. They mostly left the local people to their own devices as long as they were obedient and paid their taxes. But this was not a world of any gentleness or tolerance. It was force of arms that maintained Persian power. Totting up the death tolls recorded in Greek histories of Cyrus' rule put the number killed at more than 100,000. We do not know the total population with much accuracy at the time, but some studies suggest that the Achaemenid Empire, at its peak, controlled as many as 35 million people, approximately a quarter of the world's population. We do know that the empire constantly expanded and contracted as parts of it rebelled and were later brought back under Persian control through war. Rebellions were a near-constant problem with some areas, like Egypt, spending decades outside the control of the Persian kings before coming back into the fold through re-conquest.

The Achaemenids themselves made no bones about this, although they also tried to present their rule as a battle of good against evil, truth against lies. An inscription at Persepolis above a relief of Darius being carried on a sedan chair by representatives of the subject races says it all: "If you shall now think, how many lands does King Darius hold? Then look at the sculptures of those who bear the throne, then you shall know ... the spear of a Persian man has gone far.... A Persian man has delivered battle far from Persia." They may not have enforced a cultural or linguistic uniformity across their empire, but they did demand obedience and taxes.

We do not know if Cyrus himself wove the myths that grew up around him, or whether they were developed later; however, his life incorporated several stories that are common to many cultures. He was said to have been cast out as a boy and spent his childhood unrecognized as a prince, a familiar story when it comes to the founding of a new dynasty. The royal boy initially denied his heritage to prove himself, as without royal status, it lends a veneer of meritocracy to the process.

* * *

The official program at Pasargadae told everyone what the message from the Shah was to be:

> Twenty five centuries ago, in a world where ruling was based on threats, terror and fear, and where the conquerors beliefs were imposed on the conquered, the Iranian Empire was founded by Cyrus the Great on the highest human principles of mutual understanding among nations and religious freedom. The moral and spiritual life of my people has been based on these principles.

It was a fantastical assertion. As is the case in all countries, popular Iranian understanding of history came from myths, poems, and a jumble of childhood tales as well as the very recent set of histories pulled together as part of the Pahlavi exercise in promoting an ideology to support the monarchy. Much as children in Britain learn about King Alfred burning the cakes and Canute showing he could not turn back the waves, Iranians believed that the ancient king Jamshid, a hero of Ferdowsi's poem, the *Shahnameh*, lived at Persepolis and had been the founder of the nation many hundreds of years before Cyrus.

THE HOST

Cyrus drifted out of focus during much of the history of Iran. Under the Sassanids, he was known as one of many Achaemenid monarchs but not seen as having any great significance. Sassanian history provided the background for the *Shahnameh* and the general understanding of history for the next 900 or so years. Cyrus does not appear in the poem although it seems that some of his deeds are ascribed to others.

He lacked several important attributes, as far as many were concerned. Most importantly, perhaps, was his absence from the *Shahnameh*, which held a central place in Iranian historiography and storytelling. He also did not appear in other Iranian sources: what we know of Cyrus comes from the Bible and from Greek sources. Otherwise, there is only some information from archaeology, a discipline that emerged only after the Pahlavis came to power. Cyrus was not a Muslim, obviously, and it was in the history since the conversion of the country to Islam that many Iranians located much of their identity.

Over the years, though, there had been some rather desperate efforts to anchor Cyrus in the history of Islam. The thinking was that if he was mentioned in the Bible, where he is described as a messiah, or "anointed one," for his role in freeing the Jews from their Babylonian exile, then perhaps he was also mentioned in the Koran. In nineteenth-century India, a movement emerged to create what they saw as a more modern vision of Islam in response to colonial contact. One of those who led this movement was Sir Sayyed Ahmed Khan, an aristocrat who became a judge employed by the British East India Company. He was a passionate believer in improving the lot of his co-religionists. He set up schools and colleges, encouraged the use of Urdu as a language for all Muslims, and was among the first to suggest that India be partitioned to protect the minority. He was hugely influential on Muslim leaders in British India in the twentieth century, including Mohammad Ali Jinnah, the Muslim League leader and founder of Pakistan.

THE SHAH'S PARTY

Eager to find a place for Cyrus in Islamic history, twentieth-century historians turned to India and the work of Sir Sayyed, who had written several commentaries on the Koran. He was keen to link Islamic tradition to what had gone before and claimed that the description of a mysterious character in the Koran—Dul Qarnayn, or "Two Horned"—was Darius, the successor to Cyrus and the creator of Persepolis, where a statue existed that had two horns. Various Indian researchers were eager to connect India and Iran to prove that monotheism predated the Koran and that Cyrus was the figure in the Holy Book. This served the aim of connecting distant, and often excluded, India and Iran much more closely to the origins of Islam on the Arabian Peninsula.

This idea was taken up by Abul Kalam Azad, India's first education minister after independence and a theologian who was also eager to link his country firmly to Islam, as well as to establish the ancient origins of monotheism. Earlier notions that Cyrus appears in the Koran never attracted much attention: historians had been trying to identify the figure of Two Horns for centuries with many settling on Alexander. That did not fit so well with the demands of Pahlavi nationalism. Each of the Muslim guests was given a copy of a work that explained how Cyrus was mentioned in the Koran.

Such was the political importance of Cyrus, and the intrusion of the state into such matters, that in the early 1970s, an academic who was translating Azad's work into Persian was approached by SAVAK. An agent had heard that the translator was going to publish a version that claimed that Cyrus's mother was Jewish and that his first language was Hebrew. There is no evidence to support this, but the mere fact that the possible publication aroused concern in the secret police illustrates how seriously the state was taking Cyrus ahead of the party. There were correct ways to think about Cyrus and some very incorrect ways that were not going to be tolerated.

THE HOST

The author of the study went on to say that the glories of Cyrus's rule, celebrated at Persepolis, were the reasons why the Aryan people of Iran were able to live in such peace and stability compared to others, particularly the Arabs. And thus were encapsulated so many of the ideological issues being reinforced by the events: Iranians are the heirs of a great empire, were the first to rule fairly and have been ruled fairly by kings ever since, and are not Arabs. Squeezing Cyrus into the Koran also helped bridge the gap between contemporary Iran and the ancient empire with which the Pahlavis were so keen to associate themselves.

* * *

After the Revolution, a new Cyrus emerged. Commentaries on the Koran were purged of any suggestion that Cyrus was mentioned, and he was displaced from his position as the man who had established the Persian throne. Rather than the first king, he went back to being just another in a long line. Commentaries suggested his prominence was part of a Jewish conspiracy and that the identification of him as being mentioned in the Koran was unreliable. It almost certainly was. Archaeologists today dismiss the idea that the winged figure on the tomb of Cyrus represents him. It does not fit with the tradition of tombs at the time.

Sadegh Khalkhali, a religious judge notorious for his ruthless violence, set the negative tone of Cyrus for the ten years after the Revolution with his accusations of homosexuality. Still, by the time Akbar Hashemi Rafsanjani became president in 1989, a more pragmatic and nationalist view was in vogue. Khomeini was dead, and with him the notion of a broad Islamic *ummah* taking priority over the nation. Dhul-Qarnayn was once again said to be Cyrus; the number of books published on the Achaemenids grew massively, and once again, it was acceptable to anchor the origins of Iran with Cyrus.

THE SHAH'S PARTY

President Mohammad Khatami, a moderate cleric elected in 1997, took a further step, visiting Persepolis as president in 2001 and authoring a book that attempted to reconcile Iran's ancient history with its Islamic present. "Khatami is the follower of Cyrus, leading Iran in times of great crisis and despair, in light of the American efforts to take control of the region. By electing Khatami, the youth have expressed their desire to return to past glories."

His successor after 2005, the populist Ahmadinejad, also took up the idea of linking himself to Persepolis, associating himself with the past in almost as obvious a way as the Shah. The Pahlavi vision of history had finally won. Iranian identity involved both religion and nationalism; neither would suffice on their own.

* * *

Despite the glitter of the coronation and the party, the Shah was relatively modest when it came to his cult of personality, although it worsened in the 1970s. The toadies surrounding the Syrian dictator Assad declared him, among many things, "the country's premier pharmacist" and said he "knew all things about all subjects." During Saddam Hussein's thirty-five years near to or at the top of the Iraqi state, he fabricated a cult that drew extensively on the country's ancient Mesopotamian history, much as the Shah had drawn on the Achaemenids. This reached a peak during the Iran-Iraq war in the 1980s when both Saddam and Khomeini placed themselves at the center of cults at a time of immense tension. Saddam's focus was on connecting history to himself and his cult of personality through archaeology. In what must be a unique situation, archaeologists were the first officials to be received by Saddam after he appointed himself president. Their budgets grew massively throughout the 1980s as they wove together imaginary links between ancient Mesopotamia and the modern pan-Arab fantasies of the Baath Party. Millions were poured into an effort to rebuild Babylon. "Yesterday Nebuchadnezzar, Today Saddam" was the slogan of a celebration of the first anniversary of the invasion of Iran.

In 1975, the Shah, who frequently denigrated the idea of democracy, declared a one-party state. He abolished the existing sham parties, which were led by different personalities but shared an ideology of total obedience to the emperor. They were known as the "Yes and the Yes Sir Parties." He then established the single Rastakhiz, or Renaissance party, in their place. The idea may have come from Gholamreza Afkhani, an American-educated professor of political science and an advisor to the Queen. The two existing parties had little real following, of course because they were powerless empty vessels. Afkhani suggested that a single party headed by the Shah might lead to greater political participation. In this, he was correct, although not in the way he imagined he would be.

The Shah had often been known to dismiss the idea of a one-party state as bordering on fascism. It was also too close to the communism he abhorred, so why he went along with this step is still something of a mystery. He was facing ever tougher economic and political times, but this decision did nothing to resolve the problems that were bubbling up. After more than a decade of double-digit economic growth, the economy began to falter. Oil revenues were down from their peak, inflation was rising, and the surge in spending at the beginning of the 1970s had encountered dozens of bottlenecks, from a shortage of port capacity to a lack of skilled workers. A strong currency, inflation, and price stabilization efforts had wounded much of the domestic economy, and growing consumption was increasingly dependent on imports. Managing the economy was hindered by the fact that ministries tended to fake many of the figures to please the Shah. Nobody even knew with any accuracy how many people lived in Iran. The court, often blind to anything except its will to change the country, became ever more removed from what was going on outside north Tehran.

As inflation soared, the Shah cranked up public spending, pouring fuel on the raging fire. Bazaaris felt the heat of it when they tried to raise prices and were punished, sometimes on the spot, by police enforcing price rules to limit inflation. With prices kept artificially low, production in some areas, such as food, slowed, and shortages worsened. Student volunteers from the Rastakhiz Party were hired as enforcers, further antagonizing the traders, who were being devastated by inflation.

Even though democratic institutions and parties had been obliterated since 1953, the Shah felt the hot breath of dissent on his neck as economic problems worsened. SAVAK tried to reassure him that, in fact, he had widespread support across the country, but he felt growing pressure. In an interview with an oral history project after the Revolution, one senior official of the time summed up what many felt.

> On the day the Shah announced the creation of Rastakhiz ... It was obvious to me that this was the last effort by him, similar to final efforts of a person in the process of being drowned. In order to save himself he was grabbing on anything nearby. Until then, there were dim hopes for the return of democracy and the establishment of some kind of popular political system in Iran. Rastakhiz destroyed all hopes.

* * *

Mohamed Reza Pahlavi, the bloodsucker of the century, has died at last.

Mohammad Reza Pahlavi "King of Kings and the Pharaoh of his time" died. Behold how history repeats itself. The treacherous Shah dies next to the tomb of the ancient Egyptian Pharaohs and in the asylum of Sadat in disgrace, misery, and vagrancy in the same state of despair in which the Pharaoh and his army were thrown in the sea.

THE HOST

How admonitory is history. Listen to the words of God when he says: Today we deliver you from the sea so that you may become a symbol for future generations and indeed the majority of people are heedless to our communications.

Upon the orders of God, Pharaoh's body was thrown out of the sea so that it may serve as a lesson to future generations and a symbol of Satan and all that was satanic. How well the bodies of Pharaohs lying along the Nile are expressive of oppression, exploitation and despotism, coupled with imperial pomp and glory. And today the body of Mohammad Reza can serve as a good lesson for generations to come.

It would be better to bring him back to this country to serve as a symbol of years of torture, exploitation and oppression and to keep alive memories of numerous martyrdoms and torments so that we may not forget the significance of our glorious Revolution and as a tribute and respect for the blood of our martyrs, we may bury our discords with the body of the Pharaoh of our time as the martyrs are looking forward to the final victory of the Islamic Revolution of Iran. Those who ignore the divine words of God are none but the Pharaohs of our time like Carter, Sadat, Begin and Saddam Hussein (president of Iraq) who do not seem to take a lesson from such dark dooms.

Radio Tehran. 27 July 1980.

7

THE HOSTESS

Iranians find their identity in poems, so wrote Farah Diba. "There is not a peasant, buried in his hamlet, far from any school, who cannot recite a poem by Hafez or Saadi," Indeed, to this day, taxi drivers in Shiraz play tapes or radio broadcasts of poetry as they drive the crowded streets of the city that was home to these greats of Persian literature.

It was a love of the arts that defined Farah. She was studying architecture in Paris when the Shah's daughter and sisters spotted her as a potential queen. She became his third wife in 1959 and played the part to perfection. An heir was rapidly delivered, and she became a sensation not just for her beauty, but for her warmth and dignity. She was the most potent star in a royal family that mostly lacked the common touch.

In her autobiography, Farah tried to identify the heart of the national soul. Persians loved poetry; were hospitable, sometimes to an extreme; and they lived at the crossroads of the world's cultures. They were also brigands, divided into heavily armed tribes that could bear a deep grudge. All true, to a point, but Persian identity had been so limited under the Pahlavis, at home and abroad, by state control, by scrutiny of everything from dress to speech to education. From the 1920s onwards, Turkey and Iran, insecure empires with far more diversity than their leaders cared to recognize, were even more forceful than colonial governments in creating homogenous modern "new men."

Dressed in suits and fedoras, these new men lived in apartments with unveiled wives, read newspapers, worked in offices, traveled by bus, and went to the cinema. They aspired to education for their children, preferably abroad in English, French or German. They admired railways and industry and embraced their new identities with full-throated support for the Turkish nationalist leader, Ataturk, or Reza Shah. Except, of course, when they did not, for perhaps an enduring aspect of the Persian soul that Farah neglected to mention was a longing to be free, to fight against controls, and to experience something of the democracy that had been enshrined in the 1906 constitution.

Many people in the countryside, even those who had known little schooling, would know the lines from Hafez:

> *For we have not come here to take prisoners,*
> *Or to confine our wondrous spirits*
> *But to experience ever and ever more deeply*
> *our divine courage, freedom, and light!*

* * *

While empress, Farah was publicly enthusiastic about the celebrations. The anniversary was a "not-to-be-missed opportunity of making known the Iran of yesterday and the Iran of today, of showing the world the greatness of its past and the immense possibilities of its future." The party had come out of a "wonderful team spirit" she wrote, before admitting her own, perhaps more honest view that Iranians could often be excessively individualistic.

THE HOSTESS

Underneath her words of praise for the occasion, there were tremors of anxiety. "There were already criticisms, unfortunately concerning minor points of detail. The essence of the occasion had not been seized, and I told myself that it was perhaps partly my fault, that I could not have explained it clearly enough." She admits she was not at her best, taking pills to sleep and then different drugs to get her through the long days. "I followed all the ceremonies like someone suffering from amnesia, seeing almost nothing."

Farah revealed the degree to which she had absorbed the monarchical view of the world from the top down. People needed events explained to them, and if they did not understand, she was willing to admit that perhaps she had fallen short in her explanations. The problem was in the implementation, not in allowing a palace committee to design a national celebration that barely involved any of the public.

But there were always human touches with the Empress. She showed her well-regarded grace and kindness; a French chef had brought a cake for her birthday from Paris, but an icing crown on the top had broken at the last minute. The baker was in floods of tears. The Queen, burdened by a myriad stresses at such an event, took the time to comfort him.

After the tour of the site, the guests enjoyed an informal buffet of Iranian food, followed by fireworks, which Farah worried might upset security officers, fearing it to be some sort of attack. The buffalo, horses, and camels that were to appear in the parade might bolt, causing chaos. The display went on interminably, with guests kept up until 4.30 in the morning on a chilly night. "By the end, exhaustion was almost total," reported the British Ambassador. "A major-general in charge of the military parade passed half away through the plate glass door of the Hotel Darius at Persepolis while at the back a surfeited sheikh was found half drowned in the swimming pool."

THE SHAH'S PARTY

The last section of her chapter was defensive: the costs of Persepolis had not even been close to the inflated figures in the press, and many of those who attended had done so at their own expense in order to be part of the events.

> Of all the tasks that fell to me in the preparation for the festivities, coping with (the press) was the most difficult and depressing, for just as I had predicted, a wave of acerbic criticisms about expenditures on luxuries slowly arose from the West. The journalists got on this hobbyhorse and rode it again and again. What kind of monarchy is dressed by Lanvin and eats at Maxim's when its people still sometimes lack food and schools? ... A final fireworks display was held on this occasion, and, in the last group photo, I can clearly be seen giving a sigh of relief".

Part of the problem was that no news was bad news for the media. They were excluded from many events and then forced to go to those of no interest. The absence of any real story left them with little to do but report the gossip and badmouth the hosts. The Empress knew the damage had been done. She would have liked everything to have been made in Iran, but it had proved impossible because of the late start in the arrangements. She would have liked more people to have seen the involvement of many Iranians and not just focused on the visiting royals. Schools were built, roads paved, and electricity pylons raised. All of that passed by unnoticed while the media focused on the array of false eyelashes and wigs available.

* * *

Long after she left Iran, the Empress remained a popular figure in Europe, especially in Germany. But the left in Germany had not always taken to her, especially after the student Benno Ohnesorg was killed by a West Berlin police officer, later revealed to be an East German Stasi agent, at a protest against the Shah and the Empress. In 1967, just before that state visit, a young

THE HOSTESS

Iranian activist had published a book that would become hugely influential in shaping views among the left.

Bahman Nirumand, author of the *Modell eines Entwicklungslandes oder Die Diktatur der Freien Welt* ("Persia, a model of a developing nation or the dictatorship of the Free World" or in English, "Iran: The New Imperialism in Action"), was a formative influence on the emerging '68 generation. The author was from a prosperous family of civil servants and had grown up from his early teens in Berlin, where his father was Iranian consul general. Educated at universities across Germany, he returned home to teach in 1960. There, he established a Marxist organization, fleeing back to Germany one step ahead of SAVAK in 1965.

The book tells a now familiar story of dynastic rule and decay, foreign exploitation and the emergence of new forms of domination as Iran struggled under Russia, Britain and then the United States. The book gives an account of the overthrow of Mossadegh and the iniquities imposed on Iran by oil companies and others. However, in the mid-1960s, it was a revelation to many who had previously accepted the post-war settlement in Germany, with its assumptions about the righteousness of American power, the benefits of NATO membership, and the threat posed by the Soviet Union.

His work got a significant boost in May 1967 when the influential columnist Ulrike Meinhof, a star of the German left before becoming a central figure in the Baader-Meinhof Gang, wrote an "Open Letter to Farah" in which she quoted extensively from Nirumand's book. Meinhof contrasted the Empress's descriptions of her country in an article in the *Neue Revue* magazine with supposed facts about disease and torture in Iran.

When Farah wrote that "like most Persians" she summered on the Caspian Sea, Meinhof responded:

> 'Like most Persians.' Isn't that a bit of an exaggeration? In Balochistan and Mehran, 'most Persians'—80 percent of them—suf-

fer from hereditary syphilis. And 'most Persians' are peasants with an annual income of less than 100 dollars. And most Persian women see every second child die—fifty of every one hundred children die from starvation, poverty and disease. And do the children who spend 14 hours a day knotting carpets, do they, most of them, travel to the Persian Riviera on the Caspian Sea for the summer?

Meinhof's rebuttal of Farah's admittedly infelicitous words is a masterpiece of deception. Data for syphilis transmission in rural Iran in the 1960s are hard to find. Still, a study of more than two million blood samples in 1974 found the incidence of syphilis antibodies at 0.3 per cent. Nowhere on earth has seen hereditary rates of 80 per cent, although in the 1950s in Iran, a form of syphilis infection known as *bejel* was found among the rural poor. Infant mortality can be hard to measure in a society like Iran in the 1960s but it was around 15 per cent and declined sharply after 1964. It was not even close to 50 per cent.

She went on to chide the Empress for saying she was "starving for" Persian deserts when living in Paris as a student. People in Iran were eating straw soaked in water, Meinhof asserted, without pausing to question this unlikely diet. The future urban guerrilla, then a leading radical chic figure in Hamburg, told the 28-year-old that she could expect to live just two more years, as 30 was the life expectancy of Iranians. Again, a highly dubious assertion that also shows a misunderstanding of life expectancy data. In fact, in 1967, life expectancy was about 50 in Iran, lower than the 70 in Europe then, but almost entirely because far too many children died young, particularly in rural areas. It was certainly not 30, and anyone who lived past the age of five could expect to live a normal lifespan.

Meinhof went on for several pages of tendentious figures, none of which showed any context or knowledge about a country that she had never visited. The "facts" are drawn from Nirumand's book, which adopts the same conceit, juxtaposing the life and words of the Imperial family against the realities of a poor country. But the irony is that Nirumand and Meinhof had far less knowledge of the hardships of life in Iran than Farah did. She had traveled the country, admittedly mostly in the bubble of security and freshly painted rooms in which all royals exist, but she also saw for herself the many social projects she sponsored. Due to the policies laid down in the 1960s and 1970s, including universal education and healthcare, Iran was to develop at a faster pace than most countries. By 2003, child mortality was down to about 2.6 per cent of live births. Life expectancy had climbed by around 20 years. Syphilis was almost unknown. These improvements were the result of policies put in place decades earlier.

The method here is one of guilting the reader. Meinhof berates not just Farah but everyone who has blindly believed Imperial PR, on which the Shah had spent millions of dollars. "I don't know if there are people who can sleep well at night and are not ashamed after reading" Niramund's book, she wrote. While affecting shock that anyone might believe Farah's puff piece, she is entirely credulous about Niramund's assertions. She cites him as saying that only 514,480 peasants know how to read, never pausing to question the spurious accuracy of that figure. Twenty per cent of Iranians are heroin addicts; the Shah stole two billion dollars in aid money just after the 1953 coup, there are 60,000 secret service agents, and on and on in a torrent of misleading factoids. It might not have been true, but it felt true to the German left, and that was what mattered.

Meinhof tapped into a feeling that would only grow; everything the Iranian government said about itself was a sham, just feel-good propaganda that hid an ever more gruesome reality. And that the Imperial family, particularly Farah, were complicit in misleading everyone about the true nature of Iran: the failed land reforms; the torture; the grinding poverty at the bottom and the appalling excess at the top. The message would only spread and its impact deepen.

THE SHAH'S PARTY

Niramund's book could not have come at a better time to build opposition to the Shah in Europe. It caught an emerging mood of resentment and historical reassessment that would erupt in the 1968 movement. Various threads came together: the Frankfurt Auschwitz trials of Nazis in the 1960s exposed more of the horrors of their rule; a recession in 1966 bit deeply in a country that had become used to a never-ending economic miracle; opposition to the war in Vietnam was growing in influence and students were developing an increasing awareness of conditions of poverty and abuse of power around the world.

* * *

In the library at the Niavaran Palace in Tehran is a polished bronze sculpture by the artist Parviz Tanavoli. Commissioned by the Empress in 1971, it is a representation of the Persian word *heech*, meaning "nothing." It is a swirl of calligraphy, an idea that curves elegantly and lightly into the air despite its metal heft. Tanavoli, one of the Saqqa-Kana School that emerged in the 1960s out of the Tehran College of Decorative Arts, was often inspired by Shia motifs, talismans, and objects such as locks, gates, and even kitchen implements. In the late 1950s, Tanavoli had become obsessed with religious posters and the street art of Shiism: the images of mourning, saints, and the promise of rebirth. His works mix the readymade objects of Duchamp with Pop Art and the everyday imagery of religion alongside the lightness of Sufi poetry, especially the words of Rumi:

> *Existence is all nothing and*
> *All beings nothing ...*
> *After you die*
> *Do you know what shall be?*
> *There shall be love and kindness*
> *The remainder, nothing*

THE HOSTESS

After the sculpture was delivered to the Niavaran Palace, Tanavoli was summoned to explain it. The suspicion was that it was a musing on the rule of the emperor. Tanavoli rushed to write a statement explaining that it was to do with the artist's inner self, not a commentary on the Pahlavis. After the Revolution, his *Heech* sculptures, a "logo for emptiness" in the words of the curator Fereshteh Daftari, would come under attack from a Revolutionary critic as "decadent imperialist art."

Farah, exiled for more than half her life, reviled by some but probably admired quietly by far more, was emerging in the 1970s as a vital force in the arts in Iran, a person who opened space for creativity. *Heech* is a complex image and a difficult idea; Tanavoli's sculpture, a beautiful, rising life force emerging from nothing, was both modern and traditional, grounded in Iranian culture but contemporary, both beautiful and perhaps slyly critical. It came as much from Tanavoli's mastery of Persian folk art as from his education in modernism in Milan. Farah was an early fan of the artist, showing something of her significant prescience as a collector. His work now sells for millions of dollars, and versions of *Heech* have been shown in the Metropolitan Museum in New York and the British Museum in London. Tanavoli's work is emblematic of the contemporary culture that emerged under the Pahlavis: modernism fused with local motifs, calligraphy, and craft to produce something new, yet not without subtle criticisms of the times. The art of the 1960s and 70s was not an act of mimicry but an engagement with tradition and modernity that was complex and nuanced. The occidentalism of the time that reduced all aspects of Western life to the decadent was as simplistic, as tired and as irrelevant as the orientalist views of Iran that persisted in some quarters.

Niavaran Palace, designed by the prolific architects Mohsen Faraghi and Abdol-Aziz Farmanfarmaian, set the tone of modernity that the Queen admired. Completed in 1967 and subsequently expanded over the next decade, the palace is surprisingly modest; it would barely qualify as the staff quarters for today's Middle Eastern potentates or Russian oligarchs. It looks more like the residence of an American ambassador than that of an emperor. It was built to live in; there are some large entertaining spaces, but it also features modestly scaled rooms for everyday life. There are still Disney stickers on the walls of the children's bathroom. Even its only grand space, a reception area with a large louvered roof that opens to the cool air of the North Tehran hills, is relatively modest; it is a place for large family gatherings rather than vast state occasions. You can imagine people playing cards here. It is not a room for coronations.

Just after the departure of the Shah and Shahbanou in January 1979, foreign journalists were taken on tours of Niavaran to show them that it had not been stripped of its contents. Many expressed surprise at its relative modesty. As doleful servants manned their posts, journalists wandered the empty rooms, writing of the odd mix of luxury (a collection of first-rate art, including works by Modigliani, Calder, and Giacometti) and the mundane (a statuette of Abraham Lincoln inscribed "Presented by Mayor William C. Telford, Springfield, Illinois").

Rumors had abounded about how the Shah lived. He was said to have kept a fully armed Harrier jump jet on his back lawn, ready to defend the palace. Iran never bought those planes, so this was clearly not true. People also believed the palace must have been stripped of its precious objects, but the mostly modest furnishings were left behind. Apart from a few artworks and some Persian antiquities purchased by the Queen, many of the objects were gifts, such as a Gobelins tapestry from Charles de Gaulle. After the fall, the palace was still filled with mundane signs of family life: the empress's makeup and French hairspray on a dressing table; a stuffed, fluffy spaniel and a chipped wooden figure on a toy chest in the family's living room.

* * *

THE HOSTESS

At Art Basel in 2007, the Iranian-born dealer Tony Shafrazi was offering a triptych of portraits by Andy Warhol for an estimated price of $7 million. The images of the Shah, of the Empress, and of Princess Ashraf were brightly colored screen prints, the sort rattled off by the dozen by Warhol in the 1970s at a fixed price of $25,000. These were the ubiquitous society portraits of that age: actors, designers, socialites, and royalty lined up to have a few Polaroids taken by the artist. These were then turned into screen prints, and a few daubs of color on the lips and eyes created the signature look. "All my portraits have to be the same size, so they'll all fit together and make one big painting called Portraits of Society," Warhol told his amanuensis Bob Colacello. "That's a good idea, isn't it? Maybe the Metropolitan Museum would want it someday."

The portraits offer a surprisingly informal view of the three royals. The Shah is shown in a high-collared uniform against a pale blue background. His expression is confident and amused; a slight smile touches his lips. The Shahbanou is posed with her neck extended forward against a pink background. A similar tone marks her lips and eyes. The image is informal, she looks jet-setting and glamorous, an habitué of Studio 54 rather than the Empress of Iran.

The most startling image is that of Princess Ashraf. Her head is thrown back, her lips are a deep red, and her jewelry is colored a bright blue. It is the most informal of the three. The Princess appears girlish, flirtatious, and light-hearted. It is hard to square this carefree image with a woman who was known as the most challenging and most demanding member of the squabbling family.

Warhol had met the Shah and the Shahbanou at a state dinner at the White House. Colacello later recalled it was a rare moment in which the artist wore his black tuxedo pants, pulling them on over the jeans he usually wore with a formal jacket.

THE SHAH'S PARTY

When he came back to the hotel ... he said 'Oh, the Empress was so sweet, and she was so beautiful. The Shah was very cool to me, he was not that friendly.' After dinner, the Shahbanou had followed him from room to room. He said he was running from the Green Room to the Red Room, to the Blue Room; he said he was so afraid she was going to ask him to dance. Later, years later, the Empress told me 'No! I just wanted to have a conversation with him about his art!'

Warhol saw the Pahlavis less as royalty and more as members of a global jet set that he was eager to meet and exploit. The portraits were a collision of Iranian money and Warholian greed. They were part of his enormously lucrative series of society portraits in the 1970s—the images of the likes of Liza Minnelli, Carolina Herrera, and Diane von Furstenberg, and dozens of others. They were not part of the series of screen prints, ranging from Mao to Elvis to Marilyn Monroe to the mourning Jackie Kennedy, that were the icons of the 1960s, but rather something driven by the ever more acquisitive artist and his desire for money.

The initial deal was for a portrait of the Shahbanou. The Polaroids were taken on a 1976 visit to Tehran organized by a member of the prominent Farmanfarmaian family and Fereydoon Hoveyda—the ambassador to the United Nations and brother of the Shah's long-serving prime minister. Warhol had not much enjoyed the visit, complaining at length about the heat and spending most of his time hiding out in the Royal Tehran Hilton, eating caviar in his room. Colacello said the artist did not much like to contaminate his pop vision of the world with history or local art when he traveled. "He liked to go to fancy restaurants, and he wanted to make money. He basically considered them business trips, and the idea was to sell as much art as possible. So, most of our time was spent with rich collectors."

The Polaroids of Princess Ashraf were taken at a dinner at the Iranian Mission in New York. Warhol had met her first at her Manhattan home, side-by-side townhouses on Beekman Place by

THE HOSTESS

the East River. In 1976, he had attended a party at which all the Iranian royal women were wearing the same Yves Saint Laurent dress in different colors. He had been impressed by the wealth, telling Colacello that each of the dresses would have cost at least $10,000. His eyes had lit up. They were the perfect clients for his portraits, and what better way to develop the market than through commissions from the Imperial family?

The portrait of the Shah was not based on a Polaroid, like those of the Shahbanou and Princess Ashraf. Instead, and to Warhol's regret, he was provided with several official portraits. He selected one that showed the Shah with a slight smile. Fereydoon Hoveyda's wife, Gisela, urged him to go light on the color on the lips and eyes—it was clear there was some anxiety that the portrait would end up, like so many of the series, portraying the Shah as a luridly made-up drag queen. Warhol reassured the ambassador and his wife that the portrait would represent a "modern monarch."

While Warhol enjoyed the money—he earned a slightly discounted $180,000 from the Shahbanou's commission for the nine editions—what he really wanted was a gift from the Queen of golden imperial caviar, the rarest type. No one could have captured the excess of that moment better than Warhol. The fact that so many Iranians were part of the jet set excess of those years is encapsulated in that triptych on sale in Basel. The three Pahlavis, immortalized at great cost by the society portraitist of their time. Unsurprisingly, Warhol did not earn plaudits from all quarters. *The Village Voice* dubbed him "fascist chic's recording angel."

* * *

We can never know how popular Farah was when her husband ruled Iran, nor can we do much more than guess at how people see her today. In a somewhat mistimed hagiography published in

THE SHAH'S PARTY

1978, the British journalist Lesley Blanch wrote: "To her people, the Shahbanou has attained the status of some kind of living goddess. I do not exaggerate." More recently, a very unscientific sampling from conversations across Iran suggests she evokes some nostalgia for what seemed like easier times. She is seen as kind and cultured, genuinely concerned about the people and their welfare. Khomeini and his followers spewed much bile at her in the wake of the Revolution, urging her to kill her ill husband to redeem herself for her supposed crimes.

An endless amount of invective has been levelled at her: she was nothing but an extravagant dilettante who wasted millions on art while people starved. Or she was the kinder, gentler false front for a terrible regime. Like all lives endlessly put through a media wringer, the story is complicated. Her power ebbed and flowed, but she probably never entirely commanded any situation. She had to be decorous, disciplined, a beautiful jewel, but one that never outshone the Shah himself. She did her duty in providing an heir, something that the Shah's previous wives had conspicuously failed to do. An inability to have children ended the Shah's marriage to Queen Soraya, the one woman he was said to have loved above all others. Farah leavened the Shah's awkwardness through family life, culture and decency, something that earned her both love and resentment from him. She would later suffer searing tragedies as her children struggled with exile. Two of them would die by their own hands.

There can be no doubt she played an essential role in the development of cultural life in Iran during the 1960s and 1970s: the low point for her was probably the Persepolis celebrations, but there were highs, including a wealth of new museums and an enduring respect for the cultural life of a diverse and fascinating civilization. She opened doors and pushed projects forward rather than having the ideas herself, but she was smart enough to surround herself with intelligent people and help their projects emerge from a muddy and resistant bureaucracy. She elevated

THE HOSTESS

women in a way that has endured despite the inequities of the Islamic regime. Her role in public and intellectual life has been endlessly scorned even though she did much to highlight positive aspects of Iranian life.

The myths endure. She spent millions on jewels and was said to have bathed daily in deer's milk. This was a common belief in villages in Iran although deer are not much milked anywhere, except some reindeer in the Arctic. Her life was often quite modest outside the demands of ceremonial occasions. She was photographed as often in casual clothes and a headscarf visiting remote villages as she was in full regalia attending a banquet. Most of the jewels were in the state collection, amassed by the Qajar dynasty decades before. They remain in the Central Bank's Museum in Tehran.

All this appears regularly in the anti-Shah diatribes of the emerging guerrilla movements of the early 1970s. The Mojahedin-e Khalq, a strange Islamist cult that persists to this day, albeit in exile, issued a statement in early 1973 urging its followers to be abstemious and not fear the torture that might await them in prison. The MEK, which evolved from leftist revolutionaries to a bizarre cult-like organization in opposition to the Islamic Republic, saw the world as divided into two types of people: "On the one hand stands the person who holds huge celebrations, goes skiing in Switzerland, buys million-dollar skin coats, or bathes in milk, regardless of how people live in slums in hunger and cold and poverty." On the other side stood the true fighters:

> Had they not won in the battle against their own rebellious selves or satanic temptations, these fighters could have instead built palaces of injustice over the bones of the masses or committed abominations in cabarets every night, just as these vile and beastly criminals, that is the security forces, do.

* * *

THE SHAH'S PARTY

Farah became empress and a global figure at the age of just 21. At the time, she was a student in Paris, the child of a widowed mother who had depended on wealthier relatives to raise an upper-middle-class daughter in Tehran. Francophile, polyglot, intellectually curious, while perhaps not a great intellect, her marriage seems to have been arranged by Princess Farnaz, the Shah's daughter from his first marriage. In a matter of weeks, she went from being a young woman with bohemian sympathies, if not practices, to a soon-to-be queen who stayed in a suite at the Hotel Crillon in Paris while buying her trousseau at Dior. She handled the transition with aplomb, becoming a byword for beauty, glamour, and a subtle intelligence while remaining a modest and demure figure.

She also survived her husband's family and entourage. She even managed to endear herself to her mother-in-law, no friend to the Shah's previous wives. Her sisters-in-law were dedicated practitioners of divide and rule within the court. Farah was no match for them. She endured much. Her husband's courtiers procured for him, ensuring a steady flow of blondes from Paris or amenable women in the nightclub of the Badrutt's Palace Hotel in St. Moritz. All of this was public knowledge, endlessly gossiped about in Tehran and around the world. Rumors often swirled around that the Shah had taken a second wife; he was often asked about this in interviews. None of it can have been easy, even for an empress insulated from many travails.

It was clear from early on that she would never be a perfect fit with the Pahlavis. Courtiers were there to serve her husband, not her. She was mostly kept in the dark about important issues and only emerged as a force after she had done her dynastic duty and produced her two sons, the heir and the spare. Her husband's top officials—the court minister notably—patronized her and lied to her face; their priority was the power and appetites of her husband and very rarely to deliver what she wanted. There was a

THE HOSTESS

grueling medieval aspect to it all; women who married into monarchies or ruling families rarely survived to enjoy the experience unless they were particularly passive.

All of this came at a cost. She complained often about dealing with a hostile international media, one that scorned her cultural efforts and tied her to the worst that was going on in the country. She forgets how positive much of the coverage was. James Morris, the British writer later known as Jan Morris, wrote of her in *Vogue* in 1969:

> She has youth, exceptional warmth, persistence, organizational abilities and a practical intelligence ... Ringed by protocol, beset by the staggering problems of a great ancient country hurtling late into the twentieth century, Empress Farah is beautiful, thoughtful, aware, wanting in hubris but not in humor or courage; in fact, a queen for these days.

Apart from a few encounters with the likes of Sally Quinn, the *Washington Post* columnist, who portrayed her as weary and complaining, she generally got a good press. Quinn's article, headlined "Being the Empress of Iran Isn't Easy," caught her at a low moment, clearly exhausted by the preparations for the party and stressed by the emerging criticism that it was too Western and too extravagant. She smoked a steady stream of Winston cigarettes and complained about how difficult it was to give her children a normal upbringing in a world of groveling servants and overly attentive bodyguards.

Most interviewers were touched by her modesty, saddened by the occasional humiliations she endured at her husband's hands, and impressed by her intelligence. Was it all a cynical charade, aimed at putting a positive spin on a dark regime? It is hard to be that dark, given what seemed to be a genuine dedication to advancing the cause of Iranian women. But it all came from a certain place; the necessity of going along with her husband's deepening autocracy in the late 1960s and 1970s. Inevitably, she

THE SHAH'S PARTY

became part of the endless debates about what it means to be Iranian: the modernizing logic of the Shah's rule was in many ways undermined by his determination to be the center of all power and activity in his kingdom. Farah's agenda for tempering the headlong rush to development with social work and arts, particularly traditional handicrafts, which had once made up a significant part of the economy, complicated the image somewhat. Her intellectual court, as well as that of other members of the royal family, including the Shah, muddied the waters of modernization in a way that opened the door to the ideas of Westoxification and the rejection of a more liberal worldview. The repression that followed the Revolution drew on many ideas that had been bubbling away for some time, even in the palaces of Tehran.

* * *

The company she kept says much about her. In the mid-1960s, after the birth of her first three children, Farah settled into a new role as cultural arbiter and political figure. Her emergence as a champion of women's rights, local cultures, and global high art came as part of the White Revolution: modernization meant women were to have a place in the public sphere, and as empress, Farah would lead the way. In 1967, she was not only the first woman to attend the coronation of a Shah, but she was also crowned Empress herself. This had never been part of royal life: although some women were powerful at court, they operated far behind the scenes, whereas Farah was a fully public figure. As she built up her position, those around her flourished in the sort of influential cultural positions that shaped the public vision of Pahlavism in a way that failed to secure the legitimacy of the regime. As the project failed and increasing challenges arose, so did repression.

In the somewhat fevered imaginings common in the Iranian diaspora, there have always been mixed feelings about the Queen.

THE HOSTESS

Did she somehow promote the downfall through her generally more liberal attitudes in the 1970s? Did those around her have an agenda to push a conservative country too far towards a Western view of the world? Was she somehow a crypto-leftist too heavily influenced by her associates? The top suspect in terms of influence was the Queen's cousin Reza Qotbi, who rode the family connection to become the head of the state broadcaster and one of the most influential cultural figures in the country.

Qotbi was among her closest relatives, almost like a brother to her, and would ultimately become her closest advisor, occasionally prompting rifts with her husband. His early engagements with politics were not on the left but with an ultra-nationalist movement that fought with communists in the streets. After an education in electrical engineering in France, he returned to Iran to find himself related to one of its most important people. He was appointed to set up a new national broadcaster with the clear aim of supporting the Shah's White Revolution and promoting the emerging ideology of Pahlavism.

This proved a challenge for him. Not only had he befriended and hired many free-thinking figures from the left to work on the new TV and radio channels, but his proximity to the court also gave him space and protection from SAVAK, which he used to promote a more open vision of the country. Farah has often written of her complete devotion to the Shah's policies, but as her power at court grew alongside her interest in cultural and social issues, so did tensions over what freedoms to allow.

Qotbi became something of an internal opposition force, lining up against Alam and others who had more severe ideas of how to run a state. The new view of television did not always mesh with the ideas of court traditionalists: they insisted on the dreary recitations of the royal family's activities, which always topped the news. Qotbi wanted to replace these with something approaching real stories. His more intellectual approach to broadcasting drew

THE SHAH'S PARTY

in many acclaimed artists and filmmakers. However, their output was not always popular with the public, which enjoyed trashy TV and *filmfarsi*, the local answer to Bollywood.

Qotbi, youthful, energetic, intelligent, and driven, brought all the country's television channels under one roof and hired some of the best and brightest. Those who had run into trouble with SAVAK knew that the TV was one of the few government offices that might employ them. In 1971, radio was brought under the same roof and Qotbi controlled media that was by then reaching a growing share of the population. But the Palace was ramping up the Shah's cult of personality just at the time when Qotbi was pushing the boundaries of what could be shown on television. It was not long before Mohammad Reza started to see the state broadcaster as a nest of communist subversives.

In 1967, Qotbi, under the patronage of the Shahbanou, launched the Shiraz Arts Festival, a gathering of international performers from around the world that was something of a forerunner of the large international festivals popular today. It broke much new ground, bringing together drama, music from avant-garde composers, and dancing from local performers. It was a heady mix of world music and dance alongside performances from the likes of Russian ballet corps and the world's best orchestras. Shiraz led to the creation of pieces that were unique to their place and time. *Orghast*, a massive work of experimental drama, combined Iranian writers Arby Ovanessian and Mahin Tajadod with the director Peter Brook and the poet Ted Hughes. It was performed by actors from eight countries. The experimental playwright Robert Wilson would put on *Ka Mountain*, a collaboration with Iranians in which performers covered several hillsides in a work that lasted 168 hours, a whole week. In 1974, the French choreographer Maurice Béjart produced a ballet called *Golestan*, based on the works of the poet Saadi and set to traditional music from Balochistan.

THE HOSTESS

Hamid Darwish and others who have written about intellectual life in Iran during the twentieth century have demonstrated how a vibrant cosmopolitan world persisted under the Shah and, in many ways, was encouraged by the court. The Shiraz Arts Festival exposed many people to leading figures in music, theater, film, and literature, acting as "a means of oxygenation and a necessary aid to enhancing and transforming the cultural sphere," in the words of the curator and writer Vali Mahlouji. It is, unfortunately, better remembered now for the mostly manufactured outrage caused by a play, *Pig, Child, Fire*, written and performed by the dissident Hungarian Squat Theatre Company.

For some, the involvement of the court led them to turn their backs on the festival, but it has recently been re-evaluated, as have many other actions of the Pahlavi establishment. It began the year of the coronation when Farah took on a more prominent public role than any queen had before. The festival began by focusing on Iranian traditions, but also featured musicians and others from around the world for ten days at the end of August. By the time it ended a decade later, as the rumbles of revolution could be heard, it had become one of the most recognized and dynamic arts festivals anywhere. It was groundbreaking in its mix of modern and traditional, East and West. It was way ahead of its time; few then recognized the importance of breaking down colonial barriers or the vital role of culture in diversifying an economy or positioning a country. The media coverage, almost all of it favorable, was transformative for Iran and all entirely undone by the bleak intolerance of the Islamic Republic.

For some, the festival became an emblem of "Westoxification" and the sinful embrace of un-Islamic values. It was also rejected as somehow un-Iranian, although nothing could be further from the truth. The festival always featured Iranian music and theater, even leading a revival in the passion plays that celebrated the life of the martyr Ali, the son-in-law of the Prophet Muhammad.

THE SHAH'S PARTY

These plays, *ta'ziyeh*, had been banned by Reza Shah in the 1930s as being emblematic of the dark, obscurantist side of Shi'ism as well as channeling the oppositional potential of the faith. They persisted in villages where authorities tended to ignore them; they were so much a part of life. The festival presented them as something traditional rather than revolutionary, but they were enormously popular, with 70,000 people attending performances in 1977 of a seven-act *ta'ziyeh*. The revival of this dramatic form in the 1970s, alongside the re-emergence of many Shia performances of mourning, death, and resistance, was part of the contradictory actions of the court. On one hand it was trying to reduce the role of mullahs in political life, on the other it was embracing radical Shia spiritualism, even giving it a prominent international stage. It would open the door to many troubles.

8

GHOSTS AT THE BANQUET

On 18 August 1953, a BOAC flight landed in Rome, and into a jostling crowd of journalists stepped the Shah and his then-wife, Queen Soraya. Both were wearing dark glasses, but they failed to hide the strain on their faces as officials cleared a path for them. The Queen, aged just 21, cast her head down as she faced a barrage of flashbulbs. Only her darkly made-up lips stand out in the photographs. Mohammad Reza, gaunt and dressed in a boxy, double-breasted gray suit too large for his frame, stares uncertainly into the camera, his eyes just visible through his dark lenses.

Five days before, the Shah had fled his residence on the Caspian Sea and flown to Baghdad after failing to remove the nationalist Prime Minister Mohammad Mossadegh. After a brief and anxious stay in the Iraqi capital, he had decided to go on to Rome. The press coverage of a couple whose glamour was undeniable was unflattering. The Rome correspondent of Britain's *Daily Mail* wrote, "As the Shah talked to me today, his face was ash-grey and he appeared to need a shave." The description of his "beautiful Queen" suggested the speed of their departure from Iran. "She wore a cheap-looking brown silk dress and seemed on

THE SHAH'S PARTY

the verge of tears. Her red crocodile handbag did not match her dress. She had no hat, and her hair was disheveled."

Their panicked departure had begun at the royal retreat in Kelardasht on 13 August when, hearing by radio that his attempt to dismiss Prime Minister Mossadegh had failed, the Shah ordered his plane readied. He was shocked by events in Tehran and the resistance to the removal of Mossadegh. He now realized that, like his father, he might live out his life in exile.

Tensions had been building for years between Mossadegh, who had nationalized the oil industry, and the British and Americans. A number of factors came together: the enormous importance of oil in the security thinking of the West, as well as the end of colonialism and the emergence of the United States as the Western superpower. Washington had several fundamental concerns at this time: it aimed to exclude the Russians from influencing Iran, gently usher Britain out of the country, and ensure the Shah was bound as tightly as possible to America.

Britain had dominated the petroleum sector since the beginning of the century, paying Iran a pittance, failing to honor agreements to train its nationals, and even treating them as third-class citizens in their own country. Winston Churchill, prime minister again in 1953 after a post-war interlude in opposition, had been involved in some of the early decisions to ensure British naval supremacy through control of fuel and was adamant that the Anglo-Iranian Oil Company would not lose its pre-eminent position.

Churchill's contempt for Mossadegh was limitless, perhaps because the men were similarly self-dramatizing figures, prone to depression and sulking while in the political wilderness but still maintaining an intense hold on their followers and compatriots. Both liked to work in bed in their pajamas, and both skillfully deployed their eccentricities and humor against their friends and enemies alike. The British leader ordered plans drawn up to remove the prime minister, failing to understand, or perhaps care, that Mossadegh was one of the few democratic and legitimate figures in Iranian politics.

The British economy was still in its post-World War II doldrums. The country was bankrupt, shedding colonies and influence at a humiliating speed. One of the few crown jewels that remained was Anglo-Iranian, a monopoly that maintained a deep and increasingly outdated colonial mindset at a time of emerging nationalism. Even U.S. officials were embarrassed by Anglo-Iranian and the British government's unbending support for the company, but Washington had a different set of anxieties about Mossadegh. They feared his democratic coalition would open up space for the Tudeh Party, the Soviet-backed communists. It would be a catastrophe if Iran were to tip into Moscow's orbit. In an early version of the domino theory that would lead America astray in Indochina, analysts in Washington believed that if Iran fell to Soviet influence, the rest of the Middle East would soon follow.

Mossadegh had no intention of allowing the Tudeh into power, nor would he tolerate the exploitative arrangement with the British. But his options were limited. Backing down with a deal that expanded royalty payments but left the oil in British hands would undermine his support, but throwing the British out would mean the entire industry, including the world's largest oil refinery at Abadan, would grind to a halt. Neither side was willing to blink.

At the center of Mossadegh's appeal was his fight with Anglo-Iranian. The oil industry in Iran had grown up on the back of appallingly exploitative agreements reached when the Qajar dynasty was at its weakest and most dissolute. No democratic Iranian leader could allow this system of exploitation to continue. Anglo-Iranian was run by the British, or more specifically, the type of British person who gave the country a bad name. Imperviously imperial, it treated even educated Iranian engineers as second-class citizens and ran its own independent fiefdom in Abadan, home to the country's vital oil refinery. In 1901, the Qajars signed an agreement with William Knox D'Arcy, often described as a British adventurer with all the undertones of crookedness that the term implies, allowing him to search for oil. Knox went on to transform himself into a vastly wealthy oil baron. A decision by Winston Churchill, then First Lord of the Admiralty, to buy a "golden share" would change Anglo-Iranian relations forever. Churchill knew that a ship could travel one and a half times as far on a ton of oil than coal. He also knew that oil takes very few people to produce and move, unlike coal, with its vast unionized workforces and their socialist tendencies. Oil was a cornerstone of both imperialism and continued aristocratic rule.

What happened in August 1953 remains contentious; the United States has acknowledged its role in the coup that removed the elected government of Iran and set it on the path to decades of dictatorship. But U.S. involvement in some of the mechanics of the coup may be overstated; it fed into the paranoid streak in Iranian politics. In a country buffeted by the great powers and lacking a free media, it was easy for rumors to circulate, and to this day, all sides of every dispute are quick to blame foreigners for any setback. U.S. documents declassified recently suggest that the CIA might have been claiming too much credit for what they saw as a win for the West.

The Shah would describe his flight as a cunning ploy to rouse his people against Mossadegh. There was no mention of the anxieties he clearly felt, fleeing into exile with no money and no support. Soraya, divorced and exiled soon after the episode, would write of those days in much less certain terms. The Shah told her he had no money stashed abroad and that he would struggle to support his extended family. He said he wanted to buy a farm so that they would be able to feed their children. Even covering their immediate expenses was a problem. They had arrived with no cash, and none was forthcoming from the embassy, which even tried to deny the Shah the keys to a sports car Soraya had left there.

Mossadegh had spent many decades in the wilderness before his election to the Iranian parliament in 1944. During that time, he nurtured some deep grievances against the Pahlavis and the British, particularly over their control of the oil industry. His long period outside politics had a complicated impact. On one hand, he had not been compromised by taking government jobs under Reza Shah. On the other, he had not developed the skills of compromise and negotiation that are essential for anyone who leads a coalition and wants to stay in power. For Mossadegh, it was all or nothing, and his demands were backed by an excoriating rhetorical style that often allowed others little room for maneuver.

Mossadegh decided to take on the Shah and Britain at the same time. He did this with just the support of the National Front, a coalition made up of eminent figures but one that lacked form or discipline. He did not enjoy any solid backing in the parliament, in the bazaars, or among businesses. The Tudeh party offered only the most lukewarm support. He appealed over them to the people, unleashing the forces of populism and the mob. Once released, they were ultimately exploited more effectively by the United States, Britain, and the right-wing royalists who loathed the prime minister.

Confronting all his enemies at once without building an effective coalition was an error. Direct attacks on his opponents were a mistake. Taking to his bed was not always a successful political approach, but nevertheless, he did it often. The Shah, however, made a great mistake in the way in which Mossadegh was removed. Ultimately, having the United States return him to his throne less than a decade after the British had placed him there meant he would always suffer from more than a whiff of illegitimacy.

* * *

Mussy Duck. Winston Churchill's nickname for Mossadegh betrayed much more about the British prime minister's racism and schoolboy sense of humor than it did about his Iranian opposite number. Mossadegh would be both ridiculed and worshiped throughout his long life; admired for his principled stands, his forbearance in opposition, and yet scorned by some for his chaotic, emotional approach to politics. He would become one of those figures who embody an idea. He was also a screen onto which many Iranians projected their political desires. Neither the ridicule nor the obeisance says much about him. His legacies were perhaps few in a real sense: there were no great building projects, either political or real, no ideology, no great popular movement or political party. But somehow, he haunted the reign of Mohammad Reza every single day, sapping the Shah's legitimacy, standing silently behind the throne mouthing the story of what might have been.

By 1971, Mossadegh had been dead for more than four years and had been off the political scene since being sent into internal exile at his rural home in 1953. But he silently followed the Shah wherever he went, undermining the story of a great monarchy and a Great Civilization. The British historian Ali Ansari, one of the preeminent contemporary writers on Iranian politics and nationalism, described Mossadegh as the best example of Hegel's dictum that political genius is the identification of an individual with a principle. Mossadegh's principle was a democratic Iran standing up to colonial bullies.

His career mostly took place in the third act of a long and complicated life. An aristocrat whose mother was a Qajar princess and whose father was minister of finance, he was first elected to parliament at the age of 24 but was too young to take his seat. He left parliament in 1925 when his old rival, Reza Shah, was appointed Shah. He later rejoined the Majlis after Reza Shah's exile, rising to be prime minister in 1951, a period when the young Shah's power was at its nadir.

Mossadegh, shaped by the 1906 move towards constitutionalism, was opposed to monarchy despite his own aristocratic roots, and he had an adept sense of the new political times. He was clearly difficult, devious, and exhausting to those who preferred linear narratives and coherent plans. For the British, he was the very embodiment of the unreliable Persian. For many today, his fall is an emblem of American interference, Exhibit A for those pointing out pernicious CIA meddling around the world. For many Iranians, he is a symbol of democracy, resistance, and courage.

Mossadegh was that essential figure of his time in Iran, one of many extraordinary people who came out of the post-colonial moment. This was the era of Nehru, Sukarno, Tito, Mao, Ho Chi Minh, Nkrumah, Senghor, and Nyerere. They would transform their nations, defeat superpowers, slaughter millions, and implant themselves in the consciousness of their homelands in a way that is almost impossible to imagine anyone doing today. Mossadegh did not survive nearly as long politically and never achieved as much, for good or ill, as the others in the Bandung Generation, but he certainly wormed his way into the brains of Iranians.

That niggling remembrance, that hope, that sense of being in control of one's own destiny, that idea of national dignity would sap the self-confidence of Mohammad Reza over the long years of his rule. Mossadegh's central accusation against the Shah and his father—that they were foreign-backed interlopers—would never disappear. Instead, the steady drip of his name and his ideas formed stalagmites of resentment.

THE SHAH'S PARTY

The language used by the British about Mossadegh was telling. A 1951 article in *The World Today*, a journal of the Royal Institute for International Affairs—better known as Chatham House today—described the crisis as being driven by the character of Persians and the failure of an aristocracy to care for its people. If Anglo-Iranian had a fault, it was that it did not tell its story of generosity and fairness well enough, unlike the equivalent American corporation in Saudi Arabia.

> To take the Persian character first: this has many points in its favor. It is renowned for its excellent manners and its quick wit. But these virtues are offset by some less agreeable features. One of these is a lack of moral courage; another is an infinite capacity for envy; a third is a belief, amounting to conceit, in a Persian's capacity to perform any task, however technical or difficult.

The anonymous author wrote.

> Once Dr Moussadek had started proclaiming nationalization would cure all ills and that 'the nation's disasters lie solely in the existence of the Oil Company' and once [prime minister] Razmara had been murdered, nobody had the courage to be anything less than equally dogmatic and extreme.

The article ignored the grievous imbalances in the 1901 Agreement and the revised relationship that Anglo-Iranian had signed with Reza Shah in 1933. Iran was entitled to a percentage of Anglo-Iranian's profits, but how those were determined was never clear. The company never published any consolidated accounts and did not include any money generated by its global activities outside Iran, even though these were all funded by Iranian oil. It sold oil to the British navy at below cost and paid vastly more in taxes to the Exchequer in London than it did in royalties to the government in Tehran. Anglo-Iranian saw its revenues grow at an astonishing pace through the 1930s and 1940s. Iran remained as poor as ever.

GHOSTS AT THE BANQUET

British control of Iran's oil was illegitimate in the eyes of almost all Iranians, and those who had brought this about would forever be tainted by it. World leaders might be lining up to bow to Mohammad Reza at his great fete, but he could never escape the ghost of Mossadegh, who had challenged the culture of theft, colonial domination, and unfairness of the Anglo-Iranian agreement. No amount of paternalistic improvements to the welfare of workers, carefully documented in company public relations films, could change the fundamentally crooked nature of the deals Anglo-Iranian had signed.

Oil and the confrontation with Anglo-Iranian was key for Mossadegh, but what he wanted above all was to ensure that the Shah never held real power. Here he failed. The Shah went from being a slightly fragile and ineffectual young man to an absolute monarch because of foreign interference, Mossadegh's misjudgments, and the military.

For those in the coalition that Mossadegh pulled together during his brief time in power, the aim was to resist dictatorship, but the movement tipped into anti-colonialism and even xenophobia in a way that has always haunted Iranian nationalism. A dark landscape of real foreign interventions drew in fantasies of total control from outside, causing democrats to lose focus on the real threat—dictatorship at home—and focus instead on these ghosts. Although many Iranians have positioned the prime minister at the head of a pantheon of democratic heroes, there are always doubts. His alliance with Tudeh in retrospect does not seem like such a threat to the welfare of a nation, but they were a Stalinist party in a country that had endured much Russian, and then Soviet, meddling. His politics of chaos and the street, his populism—which later finds echoes in that of Khomeini—were all dangers to the establishment.

Mossadegh's rule and his overthrow still spark immense debate. Everything in his life was pored over: Did he try to evade

THE SHAH'S PARTY

age requirements to get into parliament? What was the nature of his neurological condition that disrupted his education in Europe? Was he epileptic or a manic depressive, prone to energetic bursts of grandiosity and also sudden weeping jags? Was he a freemason? Had he joined an autocratic Shah in trying to overturn the constitution? It was all grist for his many enemies, but the endless debates kept his memory alive.

Much of Mossadegh's time under Reza Shah was spent in internal exile, a time of silence and isolation. Somewhat out of the blue, he was arrested in 1940 but freed soon afterwards. By 1941, as Iran was dragged into the war, he was held again, only freed after the intervention of then Crown Prince Mohammad Reza. Ernest Perron, the mysterious friend the prince had met while at school in Switzerland, was a patient of Mossadegh's doctor son and interceded on his behalf. Shortly afterwards, the Crown Prince became Shah and, in 1944, Mossadegh was back in the Majlis. The Shah offered him the job of prime minister, but he turned it down, possibly before he was blocked by the British anyway. British officials described him as "touchy and nationalistic" and as a "demagogue and a windbag." Something about him played into the prejudices of the British; he was almost universally loathed by them and particularly by the influential official and academic Ann Lambton, who advised the Foreign Office to undermine the prime minister in every way they could.

In 1949, Mossadegh had formed the National Front, and by 1951, he was the prime minister with a mission to get the British out of the country. After a battle in the Majlis, he was finally able to pass a law nationalizing the Anglo-Iranian Oil Company. Almost immediately, the British decided they had to be rid of him. In 1952, Mossadegh clashed with the Shah over control of the military and resigned. Two weeks later, he was back in power, riding a wave of popular anger at the Shah. But the fact that members of the Tudeh Party had played a role in his return to office would fire up American opposition and ultimately lead to his removal. The United States government, generally reluctant to promote British colonial interests, was much more concerned about Iran tipping into Moscow's sphere of influence.

Being in opposition was always easier for Mossadegh. He found himself facing some of the greatest challenges with his allies, particularly those who had brought out their followers onto the streets to support his re-appointment as premier. His alliance with conservative religious figures broke down over his reluctance to appoint them to key positions. Other, less political religious supporters were irritated by his refusal to go after the community of Baha'is, a religious minority. Plans to get rid of the Majlis met with opposition.

A new administration had just come into office in Washington, and it was more concerned with pushing back against communist expansion than encouraging the emerging forces of democracy and self-determination. With Eisenhower, British complaints met with less skepticism, and plans were developed to remove the Iranian premier.

There are real disagreements to be had over Mossadegh. Was he a great democrat? No, he had a tendency to high-handed rule, and for much of his time in office, he ruled by decree. He had some unsavory allies as well, including both Tudeh and the murderous Fedaiyan-e Islam. But he was more legitimate than many others and had stood up to autocrats more often than most. Was his removal by the Shah legitimate? No, but it was probably legal given that the Shah had the power to remove prime ministers. Was he a man of the people? Absolutely not, although he was a populist willing to say and do a great many things that look manipulative. Did he have a vision for Iran? Not much beyond the 1906 Constitution and ownership of their own oil, but those were significant ideas in themselves. His

THE SHAH'S PARTY

overthrow became the Shah's greatest sin for the Iranian people. It would be a stain on him for most of his reign. He would always be America's man, in thrall to foreigners, less a patriot than the man he removed.

In 1952, *TIME*, possibly at the peak of its global influence, named Mossadegh its Man of the Year and described him as Iran's George Washington. This must have infuriated the Shah. In the Manichean manner of so much in Iran, Mossadegh is either worshipped or loathed, seen as the great savior of Iran whose determination to reclaim the country's resources was principled and noble or as a buffoonish egomaniac whose undercutting of the Shah ultimately led to the Revolution.

Populist proto-tyrant or true democrat barely matters, he shaped not just most of the reign of the Shah but its historic interpretation. It is impossible to think of the Shah without Mossadegh, without those photographs with Queen Soraya in Rome, a young, weak monarch in exile, fleeing from an elderly man who spent most of his days in bed. The Shah's restoration at the hands of the army, the British, and the Americans would mean he would be seen through a lens of weakness for his entire life.

Mossadegh died in 1967 after a long period of house arrest. He was not allowed to be buried, as he requested, with those who died in the 1951 uprising that returned him to office. He was instead interred at his home in the country. On the anniversary of his death, shortly after the Revolution in 1979, two million people are said to have visited his grave, the first time Iranians had been allowed to pay their respects.

* * *

Apart from the soldiers guarding the site and a smattering of young royals such as the 21-year-old Princess Anne, few young people came to the party. Outside of those in the Shah's family, young people featured little in his daily life, although he was obsessed with the behavior of students. More than half the population was under 24 in 1971. Like most developing countries, Iran's demographic profile was very young as child mortality had declined sharply while the birth rate remained high. Traditional veneration for elders was breaking down, particularly among the urban young. They were much more literate than their elders, more likely to have been educated or traveled abroad, and more willing to challenge authority.

A team of diplomats in the U.S. Embassy set out in 1971 to examine the attitudes of young Iranians. Given the paucity of studies and the lack of polling in those days, the short paper offers a rare look at this demographic. Its focus is mainly on relatively well-educated and prosperous young people in cities, particularly Tehran, as they were seen as more likely to have attitudes that would affect U.S. interests in the future. While betraying many of the prejudices of the State Department—then as now, a very white, middle-class, and rather narrow-minded institution—the report opens up a world to which few were paying attention.

The report left no doubt that young people in cities were disillusioned by the Shah's rule. They often held contradictory ideas about him, seeing him both as someone who cared for Iran and also used his position to enrich himself. Ambivalence and apathy characterized their views of him. They wanted him to reign, not rule, and they wanted him to bring his family under control. Corruption in the Imperial family aroused some ire. Princess Ashraf, the Shah's twin, inspired particular opprobrium. "Because of her vivid personality, special closeness to the Shah and the large number of young men in her intimate circle, rumors, and speculation about her, almost always unfavorable and in spicy detail, are constantly in circulation among young Iranians." There was a strong sense that she embarrassed Iran abroad.

THE SHAH'S PARTY

Other members of the extensive imperial family were seen as parasites, dominating emerging businesses only because of their position; only two of the Shah's brothers, Gholam Reza and Abdul Reza, commanded any popular respect.

Young people viewed the government with cynicism; ministers simply took orders from above. Prime Minister Hoveyda was the subject of much caustic commentary in two humor magazines, *Tawfiq* and *Karikatur*, despite his efforts to defang them. These were allowed to target politicians for mockery as long as they avoided three subjects: the royal family, SAVAK, and the military. Instead, they focused on politicians. Hoveyda was seen as a toadying and almost irrelevant figure. What mattered in Iranian political life was the Shah.

Few young Iranians were able to articulate what changes they wanted to see. Preventing the public emergence of any vision for the future other than that presented by the Shah would prove to be a terrible error. Even in 1971, when the Shah was near the peak of his power and the U.S. Embassy was no hotbed of radical analysis, it was seen that young people wanted change. Young people wanted more democracy, more openness, more freedom, even if they were unsure of how this transition would be managed or what the end result would look like.

Communism seemed to hold little appeal—although it should be said that American diplomats were unlikely to find anyone openly professing communism to them at that time. The American mission also had a tendency to avoid opposition figures for fear of upsetting the Shah. Many of those on the left had moved away from the Tudeh Party, which was described as having "a minuscule membership, the majority of whom are probably Government intelligence officials who have infiltrated the party." Some students, particularly those in Western Europe, were drawn to Maoism, the burgeoning ideology at the time, despite the horrors of the Cultural Revolution, but the driving force of their politics was more opposition to the Shah's unlimited power than anything else.

What many young people wanted was a change that might benefit themselves: a less closed and corrupt system that allowed them to rise up the ladders of business or government service. Government and business were seen as heavily rigged in favor of the connected. The rumblings of discontent had been there for some time, but various factors were making it more of a problem. The population was growing, meaning there were larger numbers of young people each year who needed jobs and wanted a better education. Education had improved markedly, but that had mostly raised expectations that were not being met.

Alongside this discontent was a growing opposition to the United States. Iranian nationalism was increasingly focused on a dislike of the United States as a world power. U.S. involvement in Vietnam had inexorably damaged the democratic image of America in Iran, as it had the world over. There was a deepening cynicism about the U.S. and its domestic and international policies, the paper warned. Nixon was deeply disliked by the young at home and abroad.

Young men were still profoundly shaped by a patriarchal and patrilineal traditional society, and these ideas remained deeply embedded despite efforts to raise the position of women. Men still wanted to marry a virgin and for her to stay at home. Family ties drove the rationale for almost all social and economic decisions, promoting the short-term opportunism that hampered Iranian development. Family was how you found a job, got ahead, stayed ahead. Family dominated almost all decisions.

Religion was undergoing a reawakening, particularly on campuses where an Islamic viewpoint was a permissible way to set oneself against the Shah. "It is necessary to emphasize that this growth of interest is on a small scale and affects an extremely limited percentage of the student body," the report said. "It is

THE SHAH'S PARTY

interesting, however, as an indication of one of the possible paths of reaction against Westernization and modernization can take in the Iranian society."

What the report missed, with its focus on the upper- and middle-class young people that the embassy staff could easily reach, was a problem that has plagued Iran for decades. The large cohort of 15 to 29-year-olds placed enormous demands on the economy to provide opportunities. Young people leave school or university and enter "waithood," a period before full adulthood in which they have few prospects for jobs and cannot afford marriage. Poorer countries had few opportunities, while the energy-rich nations suffered from the oil curse, which stifled the development of economies and people. Employment, housing, and marriage—the three markers of adulthood—would elude them. Most lacked much in the way of autonomy, skills, or networks, the factors that might determine happiness in a job. Waithood has plagued the Middle East for decades and has become an even bigger issue today in Iran than in the 1970s, with increasing numbers of people delaying marriage or never marrying. More than a million Iranian women over 40 have never been married.

Then, as now, personal status counts for much in Iran. To be seen as someone with class and moral character was important, not just for the individual but for the family. Going against family rules is still often seen as putting the standing of the entire family at risk. But in the 1970s, conformity was breaking down amid the frustrations about the low quality of university education, the few opportunities for expression, and the political torpor under the Shah. Most young people regarded the White Revolution as something of a bust, ignoring the evident changes that had occurred while pushing to the fore the many lapses. Stories of corrupt local officials stealing the money for schools, bathhouses, and other public facilities abounded. The young people who joined the Shah's Literacy Corps often found their idealism challenged by local officials who demanded payments for everything they tried to do. Nothing breeds cynicism quite like encountering the reality of a deeply corrupt system.

* * *

It is impossible to compress the lives being led by millions of young Iranians in the early 1970s into any summary. Much depended on background, wealth, politics, and education. For the burgeoning *jeunesse dorée* in Tehran, there were nights on the dance floors of La Boheme, La Chiminee, or Cave Argent. New hotels across the city had international restaurants, dance clubs, and swimming pools. People were moving into ever larger houses in North Tehran and traveling more; Paris, Beirut, and London were all increasingly accessible. Consumption had come to Iran and was filtering down to the emerging middle classes.

Variety, the U.S. entertainment newspaper, listed some of the entertainment in Tehran in December 1971 in its "Chatter" column, alongside events in London and Paris. An Indian circus had played to more than 100,000 people. The Empress had published a children's book. Anne Lambton, author of the *Mancatcher's Manual*, had presented a fashion show at the Royal Tehran Hilton, backed by a pop group called Masters of Mediocrity. The Casino Ab Ali Supper Club was featuring the Piero Georgetti Combo, the Winnie Hovler Dancers, French chanteuse Corrine, the Russian Siberian Boys, and "Yank thrush Barbara Lewis." Googoosh, the sultry singing star of the time, and indeed for decades afterwards, was playing at The Miami, alongside exotic Lebanese dancer Lina Shouki, renowned for having mastered both Persian and Arab forms of belly dancing.

The *American Women's Club Handbook for Tehran*, also published in 1971, presents an almost idyllic picture of life in the capital, with its array of cultural events, museums, shopping, as

THE SHAH'S PARTY

well as places to hike and picnic. Often, these publications give a window into the sort of anxieties expatriates and local elites have about the societies around them. Apart from a few good-humored complaints about the traffic, the AWC felt no need to offer any warnings to foreigners. Tehran by the 1970s was an increasingly cosmopolitan and comfortable city where foreigners felt at ease.

Of course, this existence was out of reach for the vast majority and would remain so. Many young people, particularly men, were leaving their villages for jobs in the city. There, they would find new opportunities, choices, and stresses. Tehran had more than a hundred cinemas, many of them showing the ever-growing output of what was known as *filmfarsi*, B movies that drew on an array of traditional sources and western models. The movies offered the same escapism as they do the world over: tough guys caught in impossible situations; romance across the barriers of class and wealth; working-class heroes taking down the corrupt and powerful. While it was much mocked for its clumsy continuity and incoherent plotting, *filmfarsi* was hugely popular, with more than one release a week in the early 1970s. Cinemas were cheap and available to all.

Such was the demand that theaters shared the film reels to maximize viewings. A big movie of the time illustrated both the popularity of film and of this genre. *Reza the Biker* followed the life of a man employed to take reels of film between cinemas so that a single set could be projected at the same time. The movie, which turns on an unlikely plot of two lookalike men who swap lives, won the prize for best movie in 1970.

Youth culture, movies, and music all reflected an undercurrent of dissent coming together on campuses and in cafes, an inevitable confluence of trends brought back from abroad by the more than 40,000 students outside the country, as well as a growing sense of despair at the heavy hand of the security forces on campus. Social life may have been opening up, but politics felt as constrained as ever. The press trotted out the same line, dictated from on high, while the realities of rapid growth and incomplete reforms—known as the White Revolution—were starting to become more visible. Iran was now importing a million tons of wheat a year to make up for declining yields. Far from liberating farmers to grow more, land reforms had become a confused mess, pushing ever more people to the cities.

In May 1971, students focused on the upcoming anniversary party and its costs. Demonstrations at the University of Tehran had included banners saying, "The White Revolution is a hoax" and "Down with the 2,500th anniversary." Students demanded the release of colleagues arrested by the secret police, SAVAK. Running battles between the police and students broke out at the Polytechnic when students came out in sympathy for their colleagues at the University. More than 400 students were arrested, and dozens of faculty threatened to resign unless the police left campuses.

Student unrest had been brewing since 1968, when students were inspired by the global uprising that rocked campuses. Education had expanded at an extraordinary rate throughout the 1960s: the number of students in high schools and at universities tripled in a decade. There was a shortage of qualified teachers. The University of Tehran had 500 faculty for 17,000 students, but had managed to become encumbered with 4,000 administrators. High schools averaged one teacher for every forty-five students. Students were ground down by bureaucracy and the indolence of many staff. It was hardly surprising they were angry.

Even though the quality of universities was generally low, competition to get in was ferocious. In 1970, 64,000 people had taken the exams for 9,000 places. Often, it would take years of repeating the concours for people to gain entrance. Once they graduated, students found themselves in a difficult job market.

THE SHAH'S PARTY

Although there was a desperate need for skilled engineers and other professionals, few people were sufficiently qualified. Many ended up in jobs that failed to make the best of their education. Three-quarters of agricultural engineers were in administrative jobs. Those returning from education abroad often found themselves frustrated by the clogged bureaucracy and the challenges of pushing through change. Fazlollah Reza, a brilliant US-educated engineer and polymath who had taught at McGill and MIT, was lured back to head Arymehr University of Industry; he lasted only a year.

Frustrations with education and job opportunities coincided with social anxieties as well. Students were rapidly becoming vastly better educated than their parents, and they were also delaying marriage; the average age of marriage increased significantly during this time. One of the few doctors addressing the worsening state of mental health at this time was Professor Saheboz-Zamani, head of the Tehran Department of Public Health section dealing with these issues. He warned that outlets for sex were decreasing for men. Traditionally, theological students had visited "concubines" in a quiet, yet tolerated, manner. Now, young people were not only delaying marriage but also had few opportunities for sex before their weddings. Meanwhile, sexuality was increasingly obvious in movies, on the American television channels that broadcast in Tehran, and in an ever-growing number of publications. Even the Shah recognized this as a problem, discussing the issue of sexual frustration in a traditional society undergoing change with a visiting delegation of British MPs.

The behavior of young people has always stirred their elders into a state of anxiety, often without cause. Iran under the Shah saw a regular series of moral panics. The government tried a number of responses that followed the usual patterns: youth clubs, a minister to tend to their welfare, and sharp swings between bribery and repression. The Empress even gave a speech criticizing some of this window dressing. But the major problem was a lack of any political voice, and that was not something the Shah was willing to change. The lack of outlets for political expression meant that people turned to underground sources of information and action. Maoism was more popular than ever on campus. Not all opposition took the form of leftist idealism. The Hosseiniyeh Ershad became increasingly popular for its lecture series by increasingly conservative religious figures. A British Embassy assessment of youth problems written in 1971 identified this as a danger. "There has been a series of extremely popular lectures on monarchy and religion given by a young university teacher and attended by the intelligentsia; the clear but unexpressed moral of these lectures was that the monarchy must be destroyed for religion to become free."

* * *

The vast expansion of education in Iran during the Shah's rule created many of the conditions that would undermine him. His vision was for a well-qualified, technocratic, middle-class society, but he sent his people off to be educated at a time of turmoil in European and American education. The growth in university studies in Iran during the Pahlavi era was immense, even though the environment in universities was sometimes stifling and the quality of education was often poor. The Shah, as he did in so many areas of life, wanted change and modernization, but then undermined the very institutions that might have promoted his aims. Even the new Pahlavi University in Shiraz, modelled on American lines and supported with considerable funding, offered a rigid, controlling environment where critical thinking, particularly about the state or politics, was not encouraged.

In 1811, Crown Prince Abbas Mirza sent two men to study in England. Five more followed a few years later to study medicine and engineering. But it was France that became the preferred destination for Persian students in the nineteenth century. Many of those who spent time in Paris witnessed the political upheavals in the country across those decades, but more than that, they were profoundly influenced by the modernizing forces at work there. In 1910, the Majlis passed a law, funding scholarships for thirty students a year to go abroad. Half of them were to study education, and many of those became involved in starting up universities in Iran. By 1928, a hundred students were going to Europe each year on government scholarships, and many others went with their own funds.

Under Mohammad Reza, the number of students expanded significantly. In 1946, there were about 2,000 Iranians studying abroad and 6,000 in Iran. By 1960, those figures were 20,000 abroad and the same number at home. Just a decade after that, tens of thousands were abroad, and about 120,000 students were at university in Iran. In 1978, on the eve of the Revolution, around 70,000 Iranians were abroad at college. Iran represented just 1 per cent of the world's population, but 8 per cent of the students studying outside their own country.

That dramatic growth created an environment in which political activism exploded. Given the limitations on speech, assembly, and education within Iran, for many, going abroad was the first time they had been encouraged to think critically about their government and education. Although students abroad were a key part of dissent, their association was more or less the only functioning organized opposition to the government during the most repressive moments of the 1970s

The government encouraged many Iranians to seek their education abroad, and this built on a trend in educated circles for some time. The elites were remarkably cosmopolitan, seeking knowledge in a range of countries in the West and elsewhere. Many Iranians had been educated in Lebanon, India, Turkey, and across Europe and the United States. From the nineteenth century onwards, an increasingly international intellectual culture would shape much of the political thinking in Iran. Almost all the prominent political writers, and many political leaders, from the last days of the Qajar dynasty onwards would be educated abroad or spend many influential years of their lives outside of Iran. The diversity within Iran means that, in many ways, it is a country that overflows its borders: it is filled with Turkish, Arabic, and Azeri speakers, as well as Balochs, people of African descent, Georgians, Armenians, Jews, and others. Iranian cities, for much of the twentieth century, were highly diverse, and within those cultures, there were numerous connections to others around the world.

The Shah, to his credit, was open to this diversity; after all, he shared the polyglot, cosmopolitan world view of many. He hired religious minorities in his court and government, and, with a few tragic exceptions, prevented the persecution of minorities that had occasionally ruptured Iranian life for centuries.

But as was so often the case, he gave with one hand and took with the other. The expansion of education and the openness to the world came with a close-minded, stagnant view of institutions and their autonomy. Universities, often incubators of trouble for dictators, were kept on a short leash, particularly as they were a location of much resistance to his rule. His government co-opted many of the newly educated and occasionally radicalized, but put them into dead-end jobs where they were undermined by the corrupt and connected. Advancement to the highest levels more often than not depended on connections at court.

The very same cosmopolitanism that the Shah clearly understood to be necessary to his vision of a modern country would ultimately be a major cause of his problems and eventually lead to his removal from power. Even those who led the religious resurgence in Iran, such as the influential writers Ali Shariati and Jalal Al-e Ahmad, emerged from an international milieu in

THE SHAH'S PARTY

which they had been enabled to think more freely outside the fences that the Pahlavi bureaucracy tried to erect around political activism at home.

* * *

> I recall a cable coming in from the Embassy in May 1978, which identified Khomeini, who figured in the troubles but wasn't revered yet as the leader of the stature he later acquired. That the Embassy had to identify him in a cable to the Washington audience tells you something about how much we knew about Iranian internal politics and Khomeini's role in it.

So wrote Henry Precht, a State Department desk officer who was well aware of how little Washington knew of Iranian politics at that time. A year later, Washington would initiate a decades-long effort to comprehend one of its most significant foreign policy catastrophes of the twentieth century. At the heart of the failure was their inability to predict Khomeini's rise to power. Westerners could never get a grip on Khomeini. In part, he was not well known, and his works were not widely read. Many got him horribly wrong. Richard Falk, a Princeton professor writing in *Foreign Policy* magazine in 1979, trilled that Khomeini's entourage were deeply concerned about human rights and were "committed to a struggle against all forms of oppression."

Populists tend to come to power to the astonishment of the establishment. Hitler was not taken seriously until it was too late; neither were Mussolini nor Donald Trump. Many Iranians would later propagate the view that Khomeini was a product of British and United States intelligence—the rationales are, as is so often the case in conspiracy theories, rather tortured and lacking in internal coherence. For many in Iran, the mere fact of his ascendancy was so astonishing that it could only have happened as a result of malign interference by a major power.

GHOSTS AT THE BANQUET

Khomeini seems less of a mystery in a world of aggressive populism. He was never a fundamentalist in that he did not urge a return to the original text or a change in the Shia view that religious followers should look to a "source of emulation" for guidance. He was an innovator in Shia theology, shattering a long-held consensus and opening up taboo subjects. Although his vision of the world was wrapped in theology, some of it simplistic and questioned by other religious scholars, his language was that of a rabble-rouser. The Shah was tailor-made to be an enemy. His aloofness, part shyness, part cultivated posture as the lonely monarch bearing the entire burden of his nation, made it challenging to tackle a figure like Khomeini, who was quick to insult and disparage. Khomeini made his own truth in the manner of populists: his speeches and declarations are filled with factually incorrect statements, indeed, outright lies that he must have known to be false. He relentlessly embellished embarrassing facts to make them even worse. He had a masterful ability to find a weakness and exploit it.

There is a sense that Khomeini was stubbornly doctrinaire, but his success so late in life seems to have stemmed from a wily pragmatism and an unerring ability to outmaneuver others. His politics had always been based on conspiracies, something that tapped into a deep vein of thought among Iranians. They were victims of numerous foreign machinations in the nineteenth and twentieth centuries, which made even the most bizarre conspiracies more credible in the minds of many. And as a nation of storytellers, there was always something compelling about a narrative that took flight.

As the Shah's inability to read his own country worsened in the 1970s, Khomeini seemed to develop an astonishing capacity not just to see where it was heading but to shape the direction. Once in power, he was remarkable in his ability to divert attention from his own failures, effortlessly creating a new outrage to move people away from some grave mistake or to undermine an opponent. The crisis around the American Embassy hostage taking in 1979 undermined a government he saw as too liberal and allowed him to reassert his authority. The war with Iraq provided excuses for brutal purges. The fatwa against the British writer Salman Rushdie for his book *The Satanic Verses* was an effort to divert Iranians from the terrible human losses of the war and a deepening economic malaise. Condemning Rushdie to hell overstepped the powers of a cleric, even an ayatollah, but Khomeini frequently crossed the lines of what was acceptable.

Several groups have amassed political power over the past 150 years, but they can be broadly categorized into a short list: monarchists, nationalists, mullahs, and the left. At various times, the latter three pushed for concessions from the first. In the mid-nineteenth century, they united to prevent the monarchy from granting concessions to a British businessman. They came together again to create the constitutional movement in the early twentieth century. Nationalists tended to dominate, keeping the religious right and the leftists within the movement but distant from power. That ended in 1979, when they were all finally outflanked by Khomeini.

Khomeini's tactics look somewhat similar when viewed from this decade. He made the Shah the intense focus of his hatred. No falsehood was too great. He lied all the time and never sought to correct anything. Likewise, he whipped people into a frenzy of hatred about Jews, Bahais and other minorities, an established trick of populists. Everyone bad in his mind was Jewish or had joined a global Jewish conspiracy. It was a promise of a new rule under which only he could remake the system in a way that benefited the ordinary man. Everything else was what would come to be known as "fake news."

He was skilled at making use of the latest communications as a way to skirt controls on the media and clever in driving home a few central points. Far from being an accomplished scholar, he exaggerated his expertise, much to the consternation of other, more moderate ayatollahs, all of whom tended to play by the rules and maintain their hierarchies and religious decorum. Khomeini swept past them all and into power. The unlucky ones ended up dead.

As with most populists, Khomeini failed to deliver on his promises. The economy crashed, and war erupted with Iraq. Human rights abuses rose to a level not seen since the Mongol invasions. His former allies were decimated in one way or another—exiled or murdered—only those who could prove their ideological purity survived in the climate of Islamic populism.

How did this glowering figure, seemingly from some dark past, rise and oust a man as urbane and sophisticated as the Shah? Khomeini was, in reality, a very modern figure; he possessed the qualities that appeal to many who are drawn to charisma. He was cunning, ascetic, innovative, dishonest, and utterly without scruples. He provided people in crisis with a sense of belonging and community, and that charisma extended far beyond Iran's boundaries. He was much more than a national figure.

Khomeini came to dominate the political swirl after the fall of the Shah by virtue of his certainty. He simply said the Shah had to go and denied him any possibility of legitimacy. The populist leader demands obedience and conformity; he asserts his power in that way. His was a radical mysticism, based on the millenarian thought of the Shia faith but also grounded in his unflagging personal belief that he would lead the emergence of a new order in Iran.

* * *

It is tempting to interweave the lives of the Shah and Khomeini. It is thought that they might have met twice: once when Khomeini was part of a delegation requesting clemency for the

THE SHAH'S PARTY

assassin of a prime minister, and once when Ayatollah Borujerdi sent him to raise money to restore the golden-domed shrine of Fatima Masumeh, the daughter and sister of Imams, in Qom. The Shah paid little attention to the members of the delegation, a snub that might have burned the intense man. The Shah gave little heed to him later as well. He was simply part of the black conspiracy. The government paid the religious establishment subsidies to be quiet and obedient, and it mostly was. The exception was Khomeini, and he was in exile.

When he was young, Khomeini had apprenticed himself to Abdolkarim Haeri, one of the teachers in Qom who had accumulated a significant number of followers but would live a life of extreme abstemiousness, a manner that Khomeini would adopt himself. Asceticism and self-denial are successful ways to draw attention to oneself, no matter that there is a profound difference between the lives of the truly poor and those who cosplay deprivation. Khomeini was ostentatiously ascetic, rather like Mahatma Gandhi, never succumbing to temptation. He lived on a diet of yoghurt and bread, often spent days in a near trance in complete isolation, and worked hard to appear as though he cared nothing for power.

While studying theology in the 1920s, Khomeini met many people who had fled the Soviet Union after its occupation of the Caucasus. Refugees told of the repression of Muslims by the Bolsheviks, with some seeing it as a Jewish plot to create a world government and destroy Islam. The virulent strain of anti-Semitism that was one of his leitmotifs may have been born here, but there are other possibilities. Anti-Semitism ran through Iranian society, going back many centuries. Pogroms and forced conversions had occurred throughout history, one of the worst in Shiraz in 1910, when the city's 6,000 Jews were dispossessed and twelve people were killed.

The future cleric grew up in a time of occupation by the Russians, British, and Turks during World War I and the steady decline of the dying Qajar dynasty. Maybe this shaped some of his views on Islamic government, but those most likely emerged at a much later date. His mentor Haeri tended to avoid entanglements in politics and was strictly of the quietist Shia school. The religious establishment was generally in support of the monarchy; indeed, they were behind Reza Shah's decision to become Shah rather than declaring a republic as his idol, Kemal Ataturk, had done in neighboring Turkey. Although Reza Shah held the *ulema* in some contempt and did much to introduce a secular state, they remained mostly supportive of a monarchy as a buffer against communism, which was always seen as the greater threat to their way of life.

After Haeri's death, Khomeini apprenticed himself to Ayatollah Borujerdi, who also mostly steered clear of politics. Borujerdi had access to the Shah, with whom he negotiated a truce between clerics and the palace. His main role, though, had been to stabilize the religious establishment, anchoring it to the Pahlavi regime rather than positioning it in opposition. Khomeini was close to this paragon of conservatism and quietist religion, serving as his personal secretary for many years. It seems an inexplicable relationship given the aggressive politics that the younger man would later adopt in violation of all his teacher's principles.

Khomeini emerged as an opponent of the Shah in the early 1960s at a time when the *ulema* were moving closer to more critical political engagement. The White Revolution was challenging their interests and many of their ideas. It stripped them of some of their financial independence, although the money from their land holdings was made up in expanded donations from the bazaaris, particularly in the 1970s when the Shah's punitive economic policies aroused anger in this group.

Khomeini was a master of crafting a powerful political image for himself, a skill essential for a populist leader. People must know exactly where you stand and who you are in the clearest terms. He was unswerving in his public presentation of himself as stern and pious. Asked in 1979 what he felt returning home from exile after sixteen years, he answered: "Nothing." He never wavered when it came to his image, although he would often dissemble and deceive about his intentions. He had a limited number of messages, all expressed in simple language: The Shah must go. Jews threaten Islam. Death to America.

One of the most revealing portraits of Khomeini comes from an unlikely source, the wife of the head of SAVAK. When Khomeini was arrested in 1963, he was held at a SAVAK villa, where he was regularly visited by Hassan Pakravan. The general in charge of the secret police told his wife that Khomeini was charismatic and very courteous. The two men discussed religion, philosophy and history but what struck Pakravan, a polyglot intellectual with a rich knowledge of French literature and Persian poetry, were the wide lacunae in the ayatollah's knowledge. "His ignorance in history and philosophy is quite something. He said that America had oppressed Iran for the last 25 centuries. He's very, very, very ignorant."

In 1963, Pakravan had pleaded with the Shah for clemency for Khomeini. Rather than being executed, the Ayatollah was sent into exile. There was no such plea for Pakravan when he was arrested in February 1979. He was executed on 11 April of that year, almost certainly on Khomeini's orders. The next day, his face, contorted in death, was shown on the front page of newspapers.

Khomeini may have been ignorant, but he was also very clever. Bazaaris were a significant force and vital allies for any religious figure. Traders funded clerics, built madrasas, and paid for students, without whom no religious figure could build a true following. Khomeini repaid their loyalty by insisting on protecting private property and highlighting threats to their welfare. In the 1960s, he accused the Shah of trying to hand over the economy to the Americans. In 1971, in his attack on the Persepolis party, he railed that the Shah was forcing businessmen to contribute to the wasteful celebrations. His opposition to the White Revolution was mostly based on his misogynistic opposition to allowing women greater access to the public sphere, but he threw in enough on the losses faced by businesses to win their support.

Many bazaaris lost out in the emerging consumer economy that was developing in the 1960s and then took off during the oil boom. Economic control shifted away from them to those who could obtain either manufacturing or import licenses, in other words, those with connections to the palace or the bureaucracy. Khomeini sought a more open system, often declaring that Islam supported private property and free enterprise, although he rarely demonstrated a profound understanding of economics. "Islam differs sharply from communism," he said. "Whereas the former respects private property, the latter supports the sharing of all things, including wives and homosexuals."

Khomeini's Iran is what comes from populism. It has delivered little in the way of improved living standards for its people, but it has kept Iran in a state of turmoil for more than four decades. Populism demands the constant creation of enemies. Although Khomeini came to power promising a chicken in every pot and an end to the corruption and inequality that marred the Pahlavi years, he mostly delivered poverty. The immediate aftermath of the Revolution saw an economic collapse and the concentration of wealth in the hands of a new elite. Sanctions provided a convenient excuse for the economic mismanagement and rapacious theft that afflicts Iran.

The legacy of all this is a country in which many people, even among those who remain conservative and religious, hate the government. Many others have lost all interest in religion, seeing it all as just another cynical and corrupt exercise in power. Iranians are among the few people anywhere in the Muslim world who are eager to tell you that they are atheists. Anyone who is conspicuously foreign in Iran is likely to meet many people who are keen to express their hatred of the government. In Tehran, almost any encounter is likely to move rapidly to how corrupt the elites are, the vile behavior of the various security forces, and the absurdity of government policies. The country boils with rage at the clerics and their rule.

* * *

The British diplomat who noticed in 1971 that a young lecturer was drawing crowds in Tehran with his sulphurous denunciations of the monarchy was very prescient. The man in question was Ali Shariati, a French-educated sociologist who would emerge as one of the foremost intellectual inspirations of a revolution he did not live to see. Shariati was ascetic, suspicious, contemptuous of indulgence, a dour, somewhat sad man who spent years in France in joyless isolation from all that country had to offer.

By 1971, he had emerged at the center of a new movement, helping to create a revolutionary Islam that would shake the world. As is the case with so many figures in modern Iranian history, nobody has yet settled on a clear sense of who he was: an Islamic Martin Luther who pushed a religious establishment into radical change; a naïve utopian whose ideas were taken to extremes by his unhinged followers; a SAVAK provocateur used to undermine the traditional left; an intellectual borrower whose ideas were empty and dangerous. It is not impossible that he was all of the above.

Shariati was unusual for his blending of Marxist ideas of class with the idea that equality and justice were core values of Islam, particularly Shiism. Islam in its earliest days had been about overthrowing unjust leaders and demanding equality in a highly stratified society. Now it was also about ending colonialism and the forces of Western corruption that had kept Iran down. Marx,

Fanon, and the Prophet Muhammad came together in his thinking, with Islam holding the upper hand.

He was from a lower-middle-class family in Khorasan. His father was a semi-qualified religious teacher who never completed the full training necessary to become a cleric but did accumulate a large library of religious books. His father taught what he saw as a form of Shiism that was compatible with modernity, rejecting both soulless Marxism and the ossified theology of establishment clerics. Shariati would eventually take these ideas and run with them. Although generally an inattentive, lonely, and uninspired student, he absorbed his father's library, becoming a religious autodidact, something that later fueled his iconoclasm and originality compared with the hidebound products of Islamic schools.

He would find inspiration in the life of Abu Dharr al-Ghifari, a companion of the Prophet, who is often described as the first "Islamic socialist." Abu Dharr was one of the first converts to Islam, a supporter of the Prophet Muhammad's son-in-law Ali, and an opponent of the Umayyad Caliphate. He called for an egalitarian faith that erased all vestiges of class and tribe. This was an Islam of equality, fraternity, justice, and liberation, all of which appealed enormously to Shariati's idealism and his impatience with the quietist Shia establishment. Although after the Revolution, the clerics would try to reposition themselves as eternal opponents of unjust rulers, they had often been complicit in the heavy-handed misrule of successive Iranian dynasties.

His political coming of age coincided with the National Front government in the early 1950s. His first major work took on the idea that Islam could provide an alternative to both the West and the Soviet Union. This was an idea he had lifted without attribution from the author Abolqassem Shakibnia. It was an early example of a habit of appropriating ideas and passing them off as his own. Islam offered a spiritual path between the materialism of both communism and capitalism, an appealing idea in the midst of the hardening Cold War. Iran was caught between the two, with even the Shah sometimes straining at the pressure this put the country under. Pahlavi ideas of modernization had not significantly reduced economic exploitation, instead it had shuffled the problems around. Landowners kept control of sharecroppers by reassigning them as farm laborers. Farmers who moved to the city ended up in factories or construction sites with even less autonomy and income. Even the middle classes were caught on the escalator of expectations: that house, that car, that school always seemed to be just out of reach.

A spiritual hunger was growing in the country, as evidenced by the growing popularity not just of Shariati but of a range of clergy who were offering a critical approach to modern life. The secularization policies put in place by Reza Shah had certainly diminished the power of the clergy: they lost control of education and courts; they had to prove their credentials in order to wear religious garb; and their financial support was diminished. But Iranians went on worshipping, often at home. Clerics traveled house to house, advising, teaching, and moralizing in the private realm, particularly among women. Pushing religion partway underground had just made it more appealing. By the 1970s, messages could be spread in new ways: cassette tapes and pungent Roneo Vickers mimeostats may seem primitive today, but they were a breakthrough then. Being able to listen to sermons in a country with a high level of illiteracy was important, but it also drove home the emotional and personal aspects of teaching. On the background of these tapes could be heard the lamentations of followers, the far echoes of martyrdom in a faith obsessed with it.

His father had instilled in him an early fervor for religion and politics, including a deep skepticism about the monarchy. Shariati's hatred for the regime was deepened by eight months in prison in 1957. As the Shah was consolidating his power, anyone associated with the National Front government that had been removed in 1953 was liable to be jailed on the slightest pretext. Guards shaved his head and beat him. It was an awakening to the cruelty of the Pahlavi state. Surprisingly, his arrest did not hinder his advance up the educational ladder. As he had come top of his class in his master's degree, he was sent to France on a state scholarship to study for a doctorate.

Student opposition to the Shah started to emerge in the 1950s and 1960s when tens of thousands of Iranians went abroad to study, most funded by the government. This coincided with the Algerian independence movement, which had shaken French politics to its core. The hagiographies that describe Shariati's time in France portray him as part of this revolutionary struggle; jailed for his support of Algerian independence, teaching Franz Fanon about Islam, working alongside the likes of Sartre. It is all hugely overstated, although he did correspond with Fanon, who remained skeptical that Islam, with its deep schisms and its long history of passivity in the face of power, would help the cause of liberation.

France itself was re-emerging after its humiliation in World War II; it was an exuberant society, lost in itself and its style. It was also an emerging technological power, with a nuclear *force de frappe*, and a new Gaullist confidence. It was amnesiac, or trying to be, emerging out of defeat by Germany and the loss of colonies in Indochina and Algeria. There was a profound darkness below the shimmering beauty of Paris. In 1961, hundreds of supporters of the Algerian National Liberation Front were beaten and then drowned in the Seine after a march. The police action was headed by Maurice Papon, the *prefect de police*, who would much later be convicted of crimes against humanity as a Vichy collaborator.

Shariati was something of a wearisome scold in France. He was homesick and, when not studying, spent his time lamenting all the fun that others were having. "Inventions are only conducted in the field of dance, cabaret, wine and gambling houses," he wrote. "Research is limited to the variety of ways and kinds of copulation among the different people of the world, fashion, eroticism and the means and ways of looking after tourists and rich Americans and Orientals." He wrote home that he liked his view over the Montparnasse cemetery "because it is the only pure, uncorrupted and soulful corner in this city of wine, lust and money." Like many of those who shaped the future of political Islam, his worldview was shaped by an imaginary of Western decadence; Sayyad Qutb, the Egyptian radical whose work underpinned much Sunni extremism, had refined his dislike of the West during his time as a student in the tiny Colorado town of Greeley, a place hardly known for its decadence or debauchery.

Surprisingly, given his glum demeanor, Shariati was passionate about his country's poets, many of whom express a joyful, sybaritic side of life. The spirituality of Rumi and others sustained him during his lonely years, as he struggled to master French by translating complex works of philosophy and sociology. While often expressing hostility towards France, he also recognized, with some pain, that he enjoyed many freedoms there that were missing in Iran. The French security forces had their hands full with the Algerian conflict; they had no interest in Iranian students. He had discovered a world that was not hemmed in by stodgy clerics on one side and a powerful state on the other. In 1964, he completed a PhD in Persian literature and returned home. Almost immediately, he was jailed again but managed to be freed after several prominent academics intervened on his behalf. Appointed to the history faculty at the University of Mashhad, he became a compelling teacher, developing his ideas about Islam and its role in addressing social justice. This was not a message the university authorities wanted to hear, and he was dismissed in 1968.

GHOSTS AT THE BANQUET

By the start of the 1970s, a growing circle of religious scholars and secular philosophers was following Shariati. He had become a star lecturer even as he offended almost all sides of the many divides in Iranian life. The religious were outraged by his novel interpretations of Shia thinking and his evident contempt for the clerical hierarchy. Socialists were perturbed by his intense spirituality and devotion, which seemed like a throwback to the obscurantism of religion. But both sides were shaped by his views. They would eventually be distorted, rewritten, banned, promoted and exaggerated but to many, they were at the heart of this dramatic change in Iranian society. Even Khomeini was certainly influenced, although he never acknowledged being shaped by anyone.

Many Iranians were engaged in strenuous discussions about their relationship with the West, with Marxism and its various factions, with religion and with the future of governance. There was almost no consensus on anything except that almost all wanted to see the Shah go or at least step back to a constitutional role. Shariati saw his work as part of a never-ending discussion of core human interests, an instinctual ideology around fairness, justice and an end to exploitation. He wanted to bring together the ideologies—Marxism, Existentialism and humanism—to reach a perfected, dynamic and populist form of Islam. The alternative was a static, repressive religion; in his view institutionalized faiths were disguised and reactionary forms of polytheism, one of the worst insults that could be thrown around in Islamist circles.

In August 1970, he laid out one of his key ideas, one that would be adopted by many others, mostly without attribution. Monotheistic religions were revolutionary by their very nature. He explained this by suggesting that there was a key aspect to believing in a single God; it meant the belief in a single humanity, unified and equal regardless of race or position. There was no source of authority except for God and therefore man should not accept any form of human subjugation. Polytheistic religions with their hierarchies of Gods were simply a way for ruling elites to convince the masses that their lowly position was a pre-determined fate that they should accept. In his view, the idea of caste was central to polytheism.

Where his ideas became truly controversial, angering many in the religious hierarchy and leading to the sidelining of his vision under Khomeini, was the suggestion that the traditional Shia clergy were polytheists. Most of the rituals of Shiism were a corruption of Islam, he complained, and the clergy were just tools of those in power. Their embrace of the status quo—the quietist position known as *intizar*, or "waiting"—undermined their claim to be Muslims.

Apparently lacking sufficient enemies, a week later he took on intellectuals. Western intellectuals reflected the problems of their own societies but those in the developing world, including Iran, were influenced by the West and therefore presented a distorted image. While anti-clerical intellectuals in the West had freed their minds and created an environment of openness and scientific advances, similar moves in countries like Iran simply removed the last barrier to colonialism and exploitation. Islam might be flawed in Iran but Westernized anti-clericism was not the answer. Even those who had taken on the idea of "Westoxification," a term coined by the writer Jalal Al-e Ahmad, were excoriated. Reading a few articles by Fanon and Césaire did not qualify you to comment on religion in Iran, he told the crowd. He also took shots at the relationship between the mullahs and their financial supporters among the bazaaris. This relationship, he warned, kept Shiism in its box, limiting its revolutionary potential.

"Do you know what is the source of misery for Islam?" Shariati asked.

GHOSTS AT THE BANQUET

> It is the formation of, and the dependency of the religion on, the [petit-bourgeoisie] class, establishing [as they have,] a connection between the seminary and the bazaar. Should Islam be able one day to get rid of this dirty connection, it will, forever, assume the leadership of humanity; and should this relation continue, Islam has been lost forever.

Inevitably, few of the clergy, intellectuals or bazaaris were happy about these criticisms. The intellectual establishment dismissed him as insufficiently committed to Marxism but the clerics were much more annoyed. A plan emerged to purge him from the school where he had been lecturing. Shariati had many strikes against him: he had no formal religious training; the contents of his lectures stretched the boundaries of what was acceptable in polite religious society; and members of his family were said not to be Muslims in good standing.

Many strands of thought were developing in Iran in the late 1960s. Some, like Shariati and Al-e Ahmad, were reaching towards a somewhat nebulous definition of Iranian identity anchored in a revolutionary reworking of Shiism and a rejection of most Western ideas. Modernity—industry, bureaucracy, mass entertainment, individuality, freedom of action—created intense challenges: around the world, capitalism was being portrayed as empty, ruthless and lacking in nourishment for the soul. The capitalist West was "the harshest, most savage, most selfish, most dishonest, oppressive society one could possibly imagine," according to the French historian Michel Foucault. Many Iranian intellectuals were nodding in agreement having drunk deep from the thinking of Martin Heidegger and other anti-Enlightenment philosophers.

Although the state spent large sums promoting Pahlavism, with its focus on the Shah, monarchy and Iran's dynastic history, it did not gain much purchase. Many were disillusioned by the overthrow of Mossadegh and others felt stifled in a country where newspapers just trotted out the same pabulum about the royal family and the endless optimistic progress of the Shah-People Revolution. Although the state promoted certain intellectual strains, they were contradictory and half-hearted. The Shah spoke of modernization and overtaking the West; he embraced technology but scorned the open societies that produced it. Television showed royal activities and Western movies, but it rarely engaged in any development of national identity. If anything, it heightened the gap many felt between their lives and the Westernization that was proceeding apace.

In the early 1970s, with the political space closing further as the Shah launched his campaigns against left-wing urban guerrillas, religion became that much more appealing, particularly when blended with criticism of a westernizing, modernizing society that was advancing sometimes at warp speed and sometimes at the pace of an overburdened mule. As preparations were underway for the Persepolis events, Shariati began a series of lectures at the Hosseiniyeh Ershad. It was a contentious time at the school and several key religious intellectuals clearly loathed Shariati. But he was a magnetic draw, and the series of lectures he began on 9 April 1971 was a hit. They were open to the public as it was, according to Shariati, the intellectual's role to bridge the gap between them and the masses. Attendees were hardly the masses; they were the increasingly disillusioned middle classes of Tehran looking for spiritual and intellectual succor at a time of worsening repression and widening economic divisions.

The lectures covered a great sweep of world religions, but they focused on one key element: religion as a driver of revolutionary change. Protestants and Buddhists had challenged the orthodoxies of moribund religious establishments, shaking off the corruption and torpor of organized religion to become forces of liberation. Shiism could do the same; it had become a polytheist faith with its saints and shrines. It needed to return to a pure monotheistic, revolutionary form that challenged power and searched for justice. Explaining how religions became polytheistic, he said that when priests gained power, they became a class for themselves and were only interested in themselves thus joining the ruling elite. They were part of the political, economic and religious repression of the masses. If Islam was not engaged in freeing people from repression, it had just become one of many infidelities out there. Clergy who resisted leading their followers to enlightenment were part of a massive system of exploitation.

SAVAK kept a watch on the likes of Shariati but did little to prevent him speaking or writing. Hosseiniyeh Ershad, the venue for his most important lectures, functioned without too much intrusion as SAVAK saw it as an escape valve for some of the pressures that were building up. This light touch has always raised the suspicion that Shariati was deliberately cultivated by the security agency in order to divert young people away from Marxism to a less aggressive, more religiously-inflected form of political action. Shariati's biographer Ali Rahnema has reconstituted the history from SAVAK documents: they show a delicate dance between the academic and the security force.

Shariati spoke in a looping, evasive manner during his many encounters with SAVAK officers, who pressed him to renounce Marxism in more forthright language. The approach illustrated some of the divisions within the Pahlavi state: parts of SAVAK felt that it was better to support Islamic activities as a bulwark against communism, confident that the clergy would stick to their historic role as defenders of tradition against left-wing revolution. Others felt a rising, and prescient, fear that the language of martyrdom, resistance and opposition to the regime used by Shariati and others was starting to represent a threat. That view was mostly pushed aside. It was possible for everyone to find something they liked in Shariati's lectures: he was opposed to capitalism, repression and the dusty religious establishment but he also rejected the materialism and atheism of conventional Marxism. These hybrid views allowed the creation of the coalition that would come together to overthrow the Shah; it also created the environment for the repression to follow.

Shariati did not live to see the Revolution that he helped bring about. He died of a heart attack in a drab apartment in Brighton, England, where he had gone into exile in May 1977. He lived in the United Kingdom only for a month before his death. In the decades since, his death aged just 43 has been blamed on SAVAK. No evidence for this has ever surfaced.

* * *

> An inmate visits the library at Evin Prison and asks for books to read; the librarian says, "We don't have any books, but we do have all the authors."

The most famous group of buildings in Iran remains something of a mystery. Surrounded by high walls and backed up into the steep slopes of the Alborz Hills, there is no clear view of the complex. The buildings are clustered together such that even in satellite images it is hard to grasp the layout. A dense array of metal roofs, some small courtyards, and haphazard parking. On Google Maps, the buildings are described as the prosecutor's office, another as a hospital, and one is simply labeled as a government office. The largest, set slightly apart from the others, is called Unit 209.

There are many descriptions of the Evin House of Detention, but it is still difficult to make sense of the 43 hectares of hell. It is not some transparent Benthamite Panopticon but an invisible maze. In 1979, just after the Revolution, V.S. Naipaul stayed in the former Hyatt Hotel overlooking Evin but had not known it was a prison.

GHOSTS AT THE BANQUET

I was amazed that, though I had looked at it for many days, I had seen it merely as part of the view and hadn't wondered about it: a monstrous concrete hangar of a building, sand-colored, rising above the green of the poplars and chinars. Over the next two or three days, the plan of the prison and the prison grounds became clearer, detail by detail ... the prison was so extensive, such a large part of northern Tehran, that it took a long time to read.

In 2001, Golmohammad Rahati, a filmmaker and journalist wrote of the prison where he spent time:

> When Evin is pointed out to the curious visitor, all he or she can make out are dark brown, arid hills along the Alborz mountains, with one slope separated from its surroundings by a fence. Only from certain rooftops, like that of the "Freedom Hotel" (Hotel Azadi) towering over the Evin neighborhood, can one see a handful of buildings belonging to the prison complex. A large part of the prison, however, blends neatly into nature, being built underground, beneath the hills. I cannot think of another landmark that is as elegantly less-is-more and as imposing at the same time. By merging with Tehran's stately mountainous surroundings, Evin gains an aura of inevitability. It comes with the city.

The illegibility of the complex is not helped by the fact that those who have written about it spent much of their time in those underground facilities, held in dark cells, or blindfolded as they were moved around. What many experienced was the squalor of their surroundings, the grimy, thin blankets, stinking latrines, paint marked with a scratched palimpsest of the pain and isolation of previous occupants. The only occasional sense of the outside world was a glimpse of sycamores through a high, barred window or the laughter that blew across from a nearby restaurant garden.

Mostly, there was noise. Harsh voices behind a door, a scream from far down a long corridor. "Pain-saturated cries filled the air around me," wrote Marina Nerat, author of a memoir of her time in the prison. "Heavy, deep, and desperate, they got into my skin, spreading into every cell of my body. The poor man was being torn apart. The world became a slab of lead sitting on my chest." Nerat could hear a man being whipped, followed by a scream and a moment of silence.

The message in these sounds was clear. You are next. But the use of sounds went beyond that dread. Sound has long been a weapon in prison, a way to disorient and confuse, to strip away layers of sanity and to break a person. Acousmatic noises are those that do not have a visible source; they put the listener into an uncertain place, and they are a significant source of anxiety for prisoners. Nerat, a Christian of part-Russian descent, arrested on trumped-up charges aged just 16, found herself suffering physical pain from the sounds she heard. She wrote: "I had never seen the inside of Evin. It had been a black nightmare of angry voices, lashes, screams, firing guns, and the whisper of rubber slipper brushing against linoleum and stone floors."

Ramin Jahanbegloo, an internationally renowned philosopher and writer, heard bird song as he was led blindfolded down a corridor in Evin in 2006. A guard told him that prisoners kept them in their cells to drown out the screams of people being tortured. He wrote of the smell of prison, "a five-day sweat," but also found he had to read assiduously at night to escape from the "frightening silence." When he first arrived in Evin, he would hear his own labored breathing and "as if coming from a great distance, the sound of a man moaning." He had been imprisoned for supposedly trying to launch a counter-revolution against the Islamic government. Finding life in Iran difficult, he had taken a job in New Delhi and was arrested after coming home for a holiday.

The canaries that Jahanbegloo heard were an effort by prisoners to regain control of the sounds of prison life. Noise in prisons is a constant source of stress, and in some cases, prisoners have been found to suffer deafness as a result. In Evin, the constant use of blindfolds and the soundscape of torture and degradation was part of the way to strip humanity from inmates going back to its early years in the 1970s. Disorientation through sound amplified vulnerability. A favorite tool of torture at the time was a chair with a built-in metal helmet, known as the Apollo due to its resemblance to the space suits used by astronauts. When the victim was tortured, usually with electricity, their screams would be caught and amplified by the metal helmet.

There were, for a long time, unsurprisingly, few photographs to help us make sense of the prison. In 2003 an Iranian-born Canadian journalist took some photographs of a demonstration outside the prison gates. Two weeks later, her body was handed back to her family. She had been beaten, tortured, and raped. Her eardrums were ruptured, her nose broken, and her body was covered with lash marks. Given the reality of reporting on the prison, it is remarkable that so many images have emerged in recent years, through hackers, leaks, and even in some cases official sources trying to challenge accusations of abuses.

Being deprived of sight, particularly when being moved between rooms or being tortured, means that many writers inevitably concentrate on sound, smell, and touch in their recollections. The smell of the torture chambers and the torturers themselves is a common thread: sweat, bad breath, the proximity of other pungent humans. The sounds of others being tortured were commonplace; in the case of Evin, this seems to have been real sounds rather than the recordings that were used in many countries to intimidate and undermine.

Perhaps the most terrifying sound was that of executions, described by Hengameh Haj Hassan, a nurse jailed in Evin in 1981: "In Unit 209, every day about 6.00 pm, at dinner time, we heard an enormous and deafening noise, like a lorry shedding a heavy load of metal ... It was the discharge of tens of firearms being fired at once on our friends." Loud noises can produce

THE SHAH'S PARTY

hyperacusis, a sensitivity to sound that results in physical pain and mental trauma. Accounts of the traumatic nature of sound in Evin are all from survivors; we do not know of the many who were executed, died from poor health, or were driven to suicide in part by the relentless, terrifying noise.

Some newer parts of the prison were designed to minimize sound transmission and heighten the sense of isolation. Many prisoners described cells located deep underground. One said he would only occasionally hear the call to prayer, sounding from far away. Otherwise, there was no noise. Silence is as disorienting as noise to those in isolation. Solitary confinement has proved to be a form of torture in itself, weakening resistance and shattering mental well-being. Unit 209 is where the solitary cells are in Evin. They have slightly better conditions than other areas of the prison, with toilets and washing facilities in the cells. Still, the isolation was ferocious and soul-crushing, according to the many accounts of life there. "White torture" was the term used by detainees to describe the way that silence was used to push them closer to the confessions the authorities wanted. Videotapes of people admitting their crimes against the Revolution would not just reinforce the state's power but discredit people; there was no martyrdom or suggestion of bravery for those who recanted in public.

Evin was designed in 1971 for SAVAK as a modern facility for holding prisoners in better conditions than in the city's squalid jails, many dating from the Qajar era. As is so often the case, architecture and the idea of reform and modernity were fused. As is also so often the case, the design eventually became a way for violence to be inflicted on the imprisoned, for them to be broken by their conditions, by fear, by isolation, and by sound.

Prisoners were once dumped in dungeons, below ground and out of sight. With modernity came the idea of the Panopticon and the constant surveillance of prisoners who never knew when they were being watched. Alongside bureaucratic regimes of punishment, they had to moderate their own behavior, living in a constant state of fear of all-seeing and all-powerful guards. Modern technologies of cameras and microphones extended this in prisons; every move could be seen. In 2021, this was turned on the authorities at Evin when hackers tapped into the surveillance feeds and then released footage of abuses carried out by guards. The surveillers became the surveilled, never knowing when their behavior would be displayed for all.

* * *

The point of torture is to extend fear far outside the prison. When those who survive are released, they go home as different people, silent, damaged, and living warnings to others. The power of Evin is in the ghosts that slip out into society. Evin has become one of the most emblematic prisons in the world, up there with the Bastille, the Lubyanka of the Soviet Union, and Abu Ghraib in Iraq.

"Since I left Evin, I have not been able to sleep without sleeping pills. It is terrible. The loneliness never leaves you, long after you are 'free.' Every door that is closed on you affects you," wrote the satirist Ebrahim Nabavi.

> They get what they want without having to hit you. They know enough about you to control the information that you get: they can make you believe that the president has resigned, that they have your wife, that someone you trust has told them lies about you. You begin to break. And once you break, they have control.

Nabavi, who had been a government official in the Islamic Republic but eventually went into exile in the United States, made a satirical video in which he confesses to increasingly absurd "crimes" against the government as well as affairs with Marilyn Monroe and former French First Lady Carla Bruni. The comedian and author took his own life in August 2025.

THE SHAH'S PARTY

As is so often the case with deeply abusive prisons, it was designed to be a modern, humane place, but, like so many aspects of the Shah's rule, it went wrong soon after the emergence of urban terrorist groups in 1971. It was taken over by SAVAK after opening, and in the following years, it went from being a prison aimed at improving conditions to being notorious for its brutality. That would only get worse over the years after the Revolution as the new regime became ever more abusive.

From academic works to reports by human rights organizations, there is a vast catalogue of writing on the depravity of a jail designed to torment and to destroy, and one where conditions have steadily gotten worse. We do not know the names of all the victims, but in the past five decades, thousands of people have suffered within its walls. Those who have spoken out or written about their experiences tell of the same torture, deprivation of food and health care, and life in crowded, dirty conditions. They tell of solidarity but also informers and the perpetual uncertainty they created. These are stories of courage, terrible fear, and desperation.

* * *

The Shah's plane took off from Mehrabad Airport on 16 January 1979. A few hours later, at dawn the next day, a crowd stormed Evin. The buoyant, cheering group raced through the buildings, peering into empty cells, taking in the still cooking pots of rice on the kitchen stoves, and climbing to the rooftop. Throwing open the prison doors is always an iconic moment in a revolution. In fact, most prisoners had already been freed, just as they had when the Bastille was stormed, but that did not dampen the enthusiasm of the crowd.

Later that day, on a bright and cold afternoon, Ayatollah Mahmoud Taleghani, one of the leaders of the Revolution and a former inmate at Evin, visited with his daughter and announced that the jail would be turned into a museum. Less than a month later, on 13 February, the prison gates closed again. A few weeks later, a new cohort of prisoners arrived.

The most influential and enduring construction project in Iran in 1971 was not the tent city at Persepolis or any of the vast number of schools built to celebrate the 2,500th anniversary, but the construction of Evin Prison. The state purchased a large private garden in the scenic village of Evin, high in the Alborz foothills in northern Tehran. It had once belonged to Ziaeddin Tabatabaei, who had served as prime minister in the 1920s. The leafy and cool grounds of this aristocratic home were an idyllic place in one of the most prized areas on the edge of the city. It was to be a prison for pre-trial detention with a relaxed regime. It was to be a model for reform of the penal system, clean and uncrowded, a sign of the modernity sweeping across the country.

Prisons are a window into the soul of a state. The gulag was the defining idea of the Soviet Union. To know Nazi Germany, you only have to know of the concentration camps. Those are extremes, but the state of a society is visible in its jails and how it treats its prisoners. Cruelty and reform have often gone side by side; the paternalistic side of society comes out in full force at times, before swinging back to repression. Iran's history of prisons reveals much about the society the Shah was trying to manage; during his rule, the country shifted from being relatively open to profoundly authoritarian.

Evin is among the most common setting for books about Iran outside of Persepolis. Unlike the ruins, it is hardly seen. There are very few photographs of it beyond its gate with the large sign saying Evin House of Detention. A handful of pictures taken inside show women sitting on bunk beds, hiding their faces, while others show drab exercise yards. The photographer Gilles Peress took a famous image known as "Savak Agents On Trial at Evin Prison." Two men in sharp suits hold the bridges of their noses so as to shield their faces from the camera. Behind them are photographs of mostly young men, in the wide lapels and collars of those days: the victims. The photos were family mementoes, taken in studios in smart suits with freshly barbered hair and moustaches. They all seem to have bright eyes, full of promise.

Evin was one of the projects that exposed the tensions at the heart of Pahlavi rule. It was designed and built as a modernizing project, aimed at improving prison conditions for those awaiting trial. But it coincided with a retreat from modernity and the reintroduction on a large scale of torture. It would house most of the key religious and political figures who opposed the Shah. It would then become one of the most notorious sites of the Islamic Republic, a place of deep injustice to this day. Ironically, it was built by business associates of Mohammad Barzagan, a political prisoner under the Shah and the first prime minister after the Revolution.

Now Evin is surrounded by the sprawl of Tehran, hidden from those driving by on the Yadegar-e Eman freeway by a metal barricade and surrounded by a high white wall. Just nearby is a neighborhood of popular restaurants, some of them with gardens. They are said to be popular with the guards who work in the prison.

Evin was built to house just 320 people in conditions that were supposed to be vastly superior to those of the ancient jails still in use. But under both the Shah and the Islamic Republic, the prison population grew massively. By the end of the Shah's rule, it had been expanded to contain 1,500 prisoners. As well as the cells, there was an interrogation unit, a courtroom, and an execution yard.

Cells designed for one are now shared by up to eight prisoners. Satellite images show three exercise yards, but otherwise the space is now grimly packed with buildings, with none of the once lush garden remaining. A photograph by the French Magnum photographer Jean Gaumy, taken in 1986, shows a vast workshop with several hundred men working at sewing machines, each raising a fist as they chanted Islamic slogans. In 2025, Israeli jets bombed the prison, killing prisoners, guards, and civilians visiting their families. Among the buildings hit was Unit 209, where several people being held for their political views were killed. The Iranian government said eighty people had died in the attack, half of them prisoners.

* * *

As Evin was being built, torture was returning to Iran. As societies modernize, they tend to move away from physical torture to more refined means of punishment. Abuse in the town square is replaced by incarceration behind high walls. For about forty years up until then, the physical abuse of people by the state had significantly reduced.

In the 1930s, Reza Shah's regime was fairly confident in itself. It was riding a wave of modernization, confident in its position that it was liberating people from backward practices and bringing them into a world modelled on European modernity. He did not like communists and put some in prison, but they were not tortured and did not have to make confessions. The aim was to stymie the activities of rival political groups by cutting them off from their leaders. As is so often the case, there was a creeping authoritarianism afoot. Membership in a banned party became a crime, punishable by up to ten years in solitary confinement. Espionage charges were added to those of being a communist, signaling not just treason but support from foreigners. It would set some of the patterns of abuse by judicial authorities for the next century.

Being a leftist was linked inevitably not just to treason against the monarchy but to the Soviet Union. The emergence of Iranian nationalism was partly a result of this opposition. The first great enemy was the country that loomed so dangerously just a few hours from the capital: the vast, turbulent, and unknowable Russian Empire, which included Azeris and others with family and other links across the border. Those who opposed the triumvirate of God, King, and Homeland were traitors. A new category of enemy. Not all enemies were communists; a group of fascist officers was arrested in the 1930s, including one who had translated Hitler's *Mein Kampf* into Persian.

When Reza Shah was forced to abdicate in 1941, prison conditions relaxed. Many political prisoners were released, torture abated, and fewer people were jailed for political crimes. The Ministry of Justice took control, and while it did not punish many of those who had been responsible for torture under Reza Shah, it also did not campaign against political opponents. The joint British-Soviet condominium over Iran had little interest in politics except for crushing any support for Nazi Germany. Its main interest was logistics, using the country to transport Western materiel to the Soviet Union.

Another burst of repression came with the collapse of the pro-Soviet Azeri state that Moscow had confected in a large chunk of Iran. It is not known how many were executed at that time, but the numbers clearly ran into the dozens. The emergence of the democratic interlude led by Mohammad Mossadegh once again improved conditions, although the prime minister had his own record of repressive legislation. The 1952 Societal Security Law banned strikes in government offices, restricted assembly, and ended appeals of the death penalty. As is so often the case, once governments of any stripe have tried out the tools of repression, they like to keep them lying around just in case.

The fall of Mossadegh inevitably led to a new round of imprisonment. Once again, the focus was on the Tudeh Party. Torture ramped up, although it did not become as routine or as violent as it would in the future. It was a shock to the many members of the party caught up in the new wave of arrests. They saw torture as something that happened in fascist regimes, not something that was part of the rapidly modernizing country they saw around them. In the 1950s, about a dozen Tudeh members died in prison as a result of torture, mostly from blows to the head during interrogations. Party members were once again tried for being spies and for treason, although historians believe there were few contacts with the Soviet Union. Some Tudeh members, acting on their own volition, had carried out assassinations. They were to inspire some of the leftist violence of the 1970s, but they were not carrying out party orders, as Tudeh had banned members from violent acts.

There was a softening of the prison regime in the 1960s. Only about a dozen Tudeh prisoners remained in jail. There were no show trials and few arrests of opponents. Those who were in prison at this time did not report torture. One writer jailed in the 1960s described his time inside as almost as if he were living under the utopian communist regime he wanted to see across the whole country. Prisoners taught each other languages and other skills, gardened and studied, held political meetings, and enjoyed a range of other freedoms. It was probably the most lenient time in the twentieth century.

By the time of the Revolution, the regime in Evin had softened again, only to worsen dramatically across the 1980s. Many political prisoners had been freed under pressure, particularly from the United States under President Jimmy Carter. Leftist terrorism had been stifled; it never stood a chance anyway against a much more competent and powerful state. Nor did it attract a vast amount of popular support. International pressure on the Shah, much of it developed by the overseas student movement, had grown, and he could no longer condone torture in any way. But just as the repression lifted, the Revolution gained strength. The Shah had left it too late to change.

* * *

THE SHAH'S PARTY

Evin haunts those who were there. They come from all walks of life: this prison held Maoists and ayatollahs, courtiers and high school students, criminals and patriots. It was a place of unusual mixing and strange associations. Abbas Milani, jailed for his left-wing politics in the 1970s but later a sympathetic biographer of the Shah, spent time in Evin with Ayatollah Montazeri, Khomeini's closest colleague in Tehran and later his deputy in the Islamic Republic.

After 1971, SAVAK started to deploy torture as a way to extract not just information about guerrilla cells or arms caches but also to get opponents of the Shah to recant their positions. As challenges to his legitimacy grew, so did the demand for those willing to say they were wrong in opposing him. This would become another terrible legacy for the Shah, as it was taken up with much more enthusiasm under the Islamic Republic. Public confessions were key. Rather like the Spanish Inquisition, it was not enough to punish your opposition or to remove them from society; they were required to recant.

Under both the Shah and the Islamic Republic, recanting and denouncing former colleagues was also a way of creating rifts in the opposition. Reza Baraheni, the poet and writer, recanted in an interview broadcast on the radio and published in newspapers in 1973, 100 days after his release from prison. In his subsequent exile, he wrote about his torture in prison but never linked it to his own recantation; it was clearly a source of embarrassment and humiliation, as the expectation in the opposition was that you did the impossible and withstood the pain and abuse. Once you had admitted your errors on state radio, it was impossible to be trusted again.

The favored method of torture in Evin was bastinado, or beatings on the soles of the feet. It was unbearably painful but left few visible marks. Other methods were more elaborate, according to a study by the historian Ervand Abrahamian.

GHOSTS AT THE BANQUET

> Brute force was supplemented with the bastinado; sleep deprivation; extensive solitary confinement; glaring searchlights; standing in one place for hours on end; nail extractions; snakes (favored for use with women); electrical shocks with cattle prods, often into the rectum; cigarette burns; sitting on hot grills; acid dripped into nostrils; near-drownings; mock executions; and an electric chair with a large metal mask to muffle screams while amplifying them for the victim. This latter contraption was dubbed the Apollo—an allusion to the American space capsules. Prisoners were also humiliated by being raped, urinated on, and forced to stand naked.

Maryan Namzie, a political activist and committed secularist jailed in Evin in the 1980s, described being tortured with the bastinado.

> Again, the crack of the whip and lashes hit the soles of my feet one after another. With every hit, my body trembles like a leaf that has become captured in a whirlwind. It's as if it's not my body; I am engulfed in pain. I feel I am dying and I hope I will die quickly because this pain is intolerable. They will kill me, but I wish they had killed me before the torture. I don't know how long he beats me. I try to think of my memories—of Mojtaba, Ali, and the rest of my friends. But I cannot focus my thoughts. The pain doesn't allow me. They stop the lashings. I feel they are out of breath. They untie my hands and legs and tell me to stand up and leave the room. I sit on the bed. I see my feet. I don't believe they are mine. They are large and purple.

Prison literature has a long and ancient history. *The Consolation of Philosophy*, one of the most important works of early Christianity and perhaps the last classical work, was written in 523 CE when Boethius was in prison awaiting trial. Cervantes, Marco Polo, and Martin Luther all used their time inside to write. The Marquis de Sade produced most of his works during the eleven years he spent in prison. The Indonesian writer Pramoedya Ananta Toer wrote his masterful *Buru Quartet* while living on the prison island of the same name. Writing was often banned inside Evin, but nevertheless, Iranian writers have written dozens of memoirs about imprisonment in Evin.

Prison experiences are often similar, and these books reflect that. Whether in Evin under the Shah or under the Islamic government, the treatment only varied over time in its brutality. Heat, dirt, abuse, and prison friendships were the commonality, although in Evin, the authorities made ample use of informers to ensure that inmates regarded each other with constant suspicion. Under the Shah, the religious prisoners often kept themselves apart from the mostly left-wing political detainees and at one stage insisted on separate accommodation as communists fell into the same category as infidels and were unclean. Some barriers did come down. Abbas's friendship with Ayatollah Montazeri involved an exchange of lessons: English language teaching for lessons in Shia theology. Education by different students was common in the easier prison regime under the Shah. It became more challenging to communicate under the more brutal treatment the guards adopted under the Revolutionary Government.

Torture in Evin has been well-documented; the silences it created in families across the country have been extensively written about. People did not talk about Evin. Only when they left the country did Iranians discuss their experiences there. For many, it was a typical day at home when they heard the engine of a Mercedes ticking outside. Then the knock and the demand to accompany a member of SAVAK or, later, the Revolutionary Guards. And then a descent into a world of torture that has shamed Iranian governments now for fifty years.

Abrahamian surmised that torture, which was rarely used under Reza Shah and had diminished significantly up until the 1960s, made a comeback due to the challenges the Shah was facing in the early 1970s. It became a standard tool by which the state extracted confessions and ideological recantations. It was not enough to lock up supposed enemies. They had to confess their sins publicly, much like during the struggle sessions of the Cultural Revolution or the show trials under Stalin. Torture had become a way in which the state sought legitimacy. Its enemies had to speak publicly in its favor. Even their silence was robbed from them.

* * *

Just a few weeks after it was supposed to be closed by the new Revolutionary Government, Khomeini appointed Mohammad Kachouyi as the new warden, who had spent several years as a prisoner there in the early 1970s. For a while, a relatively benign regime prevailed in the prison, with more books permitted and lower levels of brutality. But as violence built up against the new government, the treatment of prisoners worsened. When the Mojahedin-e Khalq tried to overthrow the new government in 1981, violence was unleashed in a staggering way. Between June 1981 and June 1985, nearly 8,000 people would be executed. Kachouyi was assassinated in 1981 by the MEK, and the state prosecutor, Asadollah Ladjevardi, was appointed to the post. He moved his family into a house on the prison grounds. He implemented what he described as a reform regime that encouraged prisoners to study Islam and repent of their wrongdoings.

Around a quarter of those executed for being members of the MEK were teenagers still at school. For his astonishing crimes, Ladjevardi would come to be known as the Butcher of Evin. He was a short man with a flat face who had lost an eye in a bomb explosion in 1975. Conditions under his rule were more brutal than they had ever been under the Shah. He would be assassinated in 1998 at his tailor's shop in the Tehran bazaar by members of the Mojaheddin carrying Israeli-made Uzi machine guns.

In 2012, President Mahmoud Ahmadinejad was in the last year of his second term as president. He was by then an emblem

THE SHAH'S PARTY

in the West of everything that was wrong with the Iranian government. A populist whose very demeanor somehow signaled hostility and contempt for the rest of the world, he had riled many by denying the Holocaust, calling for Israel to be wiped out, and goading others in the Middle East. With his scruffy suits and scraggly beard, he looked just like what he was: one of the student activists from the early days of the Revolution who was responsible for taking hostages at the U.S. Embassy. He had risen from the working class of South Tehran to become mayor of the city and eventually president.

His annual trip to the United Nations General Assembly in New York was an opportunity for mischief-making. Still, that year, his attention was drawn to the arrest in Tehran of his press spokesman. Ali Akbar Javanfekr had been held for supposedly publishing an article on his website that was "offensive to public decency" and was sentenced to six months in Evin.

What was happening was a power struggle between Ahmadinejad, supposedly head of state and the government, and Ayatollah Khamenei, the actual power in the country, who had a veto over everything. Khamenei had supported Ahmadinejad during the 2009 Green Movement to protest the theft of the presidential election. However, the Ayatollah lost patience with the populist president and turned on him. He could not throw the president in jail, but could imprison his aides. Ahmadinejad demanded access to the prison but was denied. Word came back that Government officials were too busy dealing with the economic slump caused by mismanagement.

The little spat between rivals in the government illustrated the power that Evin still holds in Iran. Ahmedinejad wanted to embarrass hardliners by exposing the realities of the prison: it was a gruesome center for torture and abuse that was at the center of government policy. Not that human rights had been a vast concern of the populist president up until his colleague was jailed. However, his opponents at the top of the religious establishment would not let him play this game.

* * *

In 2015, the Mayor of Tehran, Mohammed Baqer Qalibaf, said he had permission to turn the prison into a public park, returning it to its garden state. Iranians took to social media to say it would "reek of blood" and hold memories of "the worst moments in life." The mayor said that he had won the consent of the authorities to close the prison. Three years later, it was still open.

The state had built a new prison south of the city on the road to Qom. Known as the Tehran Central Prison, it was believed to be the largest such facility in the Middle East. It was constructed with the intention of accommodating prisoners from Evin and other jails. Located in the middle of a desolate stretch of desert, it had few public transport links, making it difficult for families to visit or protest there, as they could do outside Evin. Just a few years after its construction in 2012, complaints were appearing in newspapers about the terrible conditions at the jail, which was already overcrowded, dirty, and lacking sufficient water. Prisoners endured a regime of sublime pettiness as well as brutality. Inmates were released in the evenings after the prison's storerooms had closed, and so they had to wait overnight outside the jail to collect their belongings.

* * *

A prison is more than architecture. Accounts of life in prison often focus on the walls, the doors, the windows, the light or lack of it. They share the images and vocabulary of writing about architecture. But in the accounts of Evin, the prison is first experienced often in glimpses through the gaps in a blindfold. The smells of the place—the cologne worn by a secret policeman, the scent of blood—dominate rather than the architecture itself; the procedures are there to isolate but also to give just a glimpse of the suffering to come.

For Nasrin Parvaz, a leftist labor activist arrested in 1981 as the Khomeini regime rounded up its former collaborators, the experiences of prison were all new:

> Some are stretched out with big and black feet that I have never seen before. Some of their feet have been bandaged, and blood is seeping through the bandages. I look at the walls and catch my breath horrified. The walls are bloodstained. First, I think they are dirty, but now I see there are bloody handprints. It seems that the prisoner leaned her hands on the wall in order to get up but couldn't because the bloody prints can be seen from one meter up the wall down to the floor.

The experience was based around insufficiency: not enough time to wash, not enough time in the fresh air, not enough food but mostly not enough space, the women lying in corridors, unconscious from torture or in the constant perilous state of half recovery, aided only by the other prisoners.

The emphasis of imprisonment under the Shah had been containment more than confession. People were locked up to prevent them from engaging in political acts that opposed Pahlavi rule. People were thrown together; indeed, in some ways, the coalition of diverse groups that brought him down was forged in Evin, where socialists and Tudeh party members mixed with religious leaders.

After the Revolution, imprisonment became a means to extract confessions. These were required by the state to validate its worldview, even when that was confused. Jason Rezaian, at one point in his imprisonment, confessed not to spying but to writing well-balanced and fair stories for *The Washington Post*. These stories might actually cause Americans to change their negative views of Iran. Through this, he warned his captors, Americans would find ways to infiltrate the Iranian state with moderates and undermine Islamic rule. The paranoid mind has a logic all its own, but this is a common idea expressed in dictatorships; it allows anyone, whether or not they oppose the state, to be accused of spying and other crimes.

In some ways, the Shah and the Ayatollah shared similar aims in their prison regimes: to isolate and contain, and to reform those with undesirable ideas. Both focused on the left: this was always the main enemy, despite the very limited hold it had on Iran. The looming presence of the Soviet Union to the north and the emergence of Baathism in neighboring Iraq and Syria created a sense of being surrounded for the Shah. Khomeini showed a similar fear of the left. When they started to contest the Revolution after 1980, the brutality of the religious regime was astonishing, far exceeding anything the Shah had ever inflicted on his people.

Mohammad Reza cannot be held responsible for the brutality of the Islamic regime. Still, he did, unfortunately, allow a pattern to be set, and it was institutions created under his rule—notably SAVAK and its prisons—that were ready-made tools for the massive repression that began after the Revolution.

9

THE BANQUET

14 OCTOBER 1971

The Menu

Oeufs de Cailles aux Perles
Mousse de Queues d'Ecrevisses
Selle d'agneau des grands plateaux farcie et rôtie dans son jus
Sorbet au vieux Champagne
Paon à l'Imperiale
Turban de Figues
Café Mokka

"Should I have served them bread and radishes?" the Shah responded when asked about the extravagance of the food served at his party. The menus, along with the tents, probably aroused more criticism than any other aspect of the event. Two big meals were planned at the party. A formal banquet at the end of the first full day, at which the guests of honor would sit at a long serpentine table in the dining tent that was the centerpiece of the campsite. On the third evening, a more informal buffet of Iranian food was offered. There was also room service for the tents, with Maxim's chefs offering to cook anything that guests desired.

THE SHAH'S PARTY

The kitchens, temporary set-ups just outside the camp area, had a mammoth task. Not only did they have to prepare the elaborate meals for the VIPs, but also for the large contingent of officials, bodyguards, and other hangers-on. Outside temperatures rose as high as 40 degrees centigrade. The young French kitchen staff stripped down to their underwear to cook, much to the shock of the local security guards.

As banquets go, the food was far less immodest than many similar events; indeed, it would hardly pass muster in a great many Michelin-starred restaurants today with their 24-course tasting menus. A mousse of langoustines, saddle of lamb, quail, a champagne sorbet, and a dessert of figs. It was certainly much less elaborate than most banquets from Edwardian England or the Qajar court.

The highlight was *Paon a l'Imperial*, 100 peacocks with their tail feathers spread, surrounded by cold roast quail served *en gelée*. The peacocks were taxidermied and used as centerpieces just for show. They were "attended by their court" of the smaller roast quail. Each of the peacocks had cost $100, according to Maxim's. Peacocks are eaten in some cultures—they can to this day be found in live poultry markets in Hispanic neighborhoods of New York, where they are sold as *pavo real*, or royal turkey. They are mostly young birds, bred and raised for the table, and no elaborate feathers are on display. Wild peacocks that have strutted their stuff are said to be stringy and tough; younger ones have the darker meat of game birds.

Producing such a meal in the middle of a desert in a location that had only recently been wired for electricity was a challenge. Not only had Maxim's been hired, but staff were pulled in from some of the most luxurious establishments in Europe, including the Badrutt's Palace Hotel in St. Moritz. Dante Franzetti was the manager of the King's Club, the oldest nightclub in Switzerland and the epicenter of *après-ski* for the jet set of the 1960s. Having organized parties for the wealthiest people in Europe, he was well-equipped to manage the extravaganza in Iran. "Everyone wanted to attend. I mean, everyone. As for my position, I was the only waiter in a tuxedo. All the others wore uniforms." These were custom-made in the pale blue of the Pahlavi court.

Relations between the Swiss waiters and the French crew from Maxim's were not easy. The Swiss had arrived first and established the way they liked to do things. Hugo Keusch, the head waiter from Badrutt's Palace, was held down by two of the Maxim's staff while a third punched him in the face. Another waiter then told Keusch that his mother was sick and he needed to return to Switzerland. He had reached Tehran before he discovered it was just a ruse to get rid of him.

* * *

As the Shah had addressed his people at Pasargadae, conjuring up the spirit of Cyrus the Great to link his reign to thousands of years of history, at the dinner, he would invoke a set of international values to promote Iran to the world. This was the Iran that had contributed to global history, whose glittering civilization was a gift to the planet.

> I take the present assembly of the great personages of the world at Persepolis, the historic birthplace of the Persian Empire, as a good omen, because I feel that in our gathering this evening, past history is linked with the realities of today. Naturally, such a bond of past and present, achieved by understanding and friendship, is to be taken as a good omen ...

The meal, subject to derisive commentary in the media for its luxury and Frenchness, would have been quite familiar in a way to the Achaemenids, who built Persepolis. Feasting in the ancient world was a central social and political act, a place to build alliances, establish hierarchies of power, and reward the loyal. Those who eat together are tied by bonds of friendship and mutual

THE SHAH'S PARTY

obligation. Food is personal, political, and rich in symbolism, hence the criticisms of those who felt this meal was overblown and alien to Persian culture.

Feasting for the Achaemenids established who was welcome at the table, and who was not, as well as who was served which foods and drinks in which ways. The performance of eating mapped out the hierarchical and centralizing nature of this new political system. Feasting on the vast scale of the ancient world was one of the main functions of the state: the records that have survived from Persepolis show how much attention was devoted to the organization of meals. None of this was quite on the scale of the Assyrians. In 879 BCE, King Ashurnasirpal II invited all his subjects to celebrate the renovation of the city of Nimrud. Some 70,000 people turned up and were fed for ten days.

Greek chroniclers made much of Achaemenid feasting. The king ate off elaborate dishes made from precious metals and stones. To use clay bowls was regarded as a form of punishment for courtiers who were out of favor. Some of the most beautiful artefacts that survive from that time are rhytons, or drinking cups, many made from gold and fashioned after lions, antelope, and horses. The Athenians captured many of these when they defeated the forces of Xerxes, and they were soon imitated across the region.

Greeks marveled at the contrast between their impecunious lives and the splendor of the Persians. Herodotus records that after the Battle of Plataea in 479 BCE, a victorious Spartan general was astonished at how the Persian king lived.

> It is said that Xerxes, on his retreat from Greece, left his tent with Mardonius. When Pausanias saw it ... he summoned Mardonius' bakers and cooks and told them to prepare a meal of the same sort as they were accustomed to preparing for their former master. The order was obeyed, and when Pausanias saw ... everything prepared for the feast with great magnificence, he could hardly believe his eyes

THE BANQUET

... and just for a joke ordered his own servants to get ready an ordinary Spartan dinner. The difference between the two meals was indeed remarkable ... Pausanias laughed ... saying "[behold] the folly of the Persians who, living in this style, came to Greece to rob us of our poverty.

A typical Spartan meal was known as black broth. It involved boiling pigs' feet and blood with vinegar. An ancient food critic spat it out on tasting it, while another commented, "Now I understand why Spartans do not fear death."

Ending his toast, the Shah told his guests that leaders had to ensure "love, peace, and cooperation for mankind" so that all people would "enjoy the full amenities of science and civilization." This was a modern ruler, determined to bring progress to his nation while honoring its past. The festival was, for the Shah, all "in honor of Iranian cultural heritage, which belongs to humanity as a whole. In fact, your host this evening is 'History' itself rather than ourselves." Haile Selassie would respond in a similar tone, emperor to emperor. "These celebrations show how to use history positively. Not for false glorification or idle self-congratulation but for new strength and revitalization."

And then the meal began. With caviar, of course.

* * *

Every delicate spoonful of caviar comes with a large serving of sadness. In spring, female sturgeon swim towards the warm waters of the Iranian coast of the Caspian Sea to lay their eggs. Some of the fish are as many as 300 years old and can weigh a ton or more. The species has been around since the Triassic Age, when all the modern continents were fused into one giant landmass, Pangaea. They were contemporaries of dinosaurs, living when the first tiny mammals evolved and long before there was any sign of their nemesis, humankind. Until the nineteenth century, various species of sturgeon were the dominant large fish in nearly all rivers across the Northern Hemisphere.

THE SHAH'S PARTY

The taste of their oily, salted eggs, which softly burst between the tongue and palate, has pushed wild sturgeon close to extinction, for until recently, there was no way to extract the eggs without killing the fish. They are bludgeoned to death on the decks of fishing boats, and the millions of eggs extracted for processing into caviar, a word that comes from the Persian term for "cake of strength." The process is not for the squeamish. Henry Kissinger was said to have gone green and woozy watching a fisherman slice open a giant beluga sturgeon in the heat of an Iranian summer.

The Shah did not eat caviar. He preferred a simple diet, and although the delicacy was always served at his banquets, he usually ate leeks or artichokes. Food did not move him in the way that sex did; he was not among those Iranians taking the Air France flight to Paris in time for dinner. He was slim all his life, eventually becoming shockingly gaunt when illness struck him in the 1970s. He tended to spend mealtimes tuning out his clamorous relatives and feeding titbits to his spoiled gray Great Dane, Beno. The dog, one of a varied pack living with the family, enraged the Queen by eating from the plates of guests. The Shah never noticed what he ate or where he sat, unlike many of his courtiers, who were obsessed beyond reason with *placement* and what they were served. But he was a generous host who had a free hand with Iran's most famous food, one as bound up with the country, its history, and its resentments, as oil.

Iranians have never eaten much caviar, and indeed they do not to this day. The sturgeon evolved long before scaly fish and, like other smooth fish such as sharks and dogfish, it was considered *haram* or unclean. Most of those who ate it in Iran were either non-practicing Muslims or of other faiths. It was a product for export, carefully graded from the finest large silver beluga eggs to the cheaper, packed caviar cake, treated with salt and drained over horse-hair mesh before being put into blue and silver tins.

THE BANQUET

Those living on the Caspian shore who did eat roe tended to prefer mullet eggs, eaten all over the world as bottarga. Sturgeon itself, known in Iran by its Turkish name *ozun borun*, was rarely eaten, although it was served *à la brochette* in an Armenian restaurant on Tehran's Ferdowsi Square.

For twenty-five years, Russia had controlled Iran's caviar, just as Britain controlled its oil. Russians had held the concession on the food since the Qajar monarchy doled out deals to keep its tottering finances from collapsing. In 1927, the Soviet Union, as desperate for cash as the Qajars, kidnapped the White Russian who still ran the concession. They then presented the government with a demand for a joint fishing company for the Caspian. Iranians could keep all the *halal* fish they caught, but would sell the Russians anything *haram*, including sturgeon.

It was a terrible deal for Iran, as all such deals were then. For giving up 100 tons of caviar a year and 4000 tons of sturgeon, Iran was paid $120,000, a fraction of the more than two million dollars it was worth at the time. The Soviets never let the government in Tehran look at the books or occupy what was supposed to be a rotating chairmanship of the joint company. Soviet imperialism was no less crooked than the British form.

That all ended in 1952, when Mossadegh summoned the Soviet ambassador to his residence in the middle of the night, the time he liked to hold meetings, and told him that the concession was ending. Given that Ambassador Ivan Sadchikov had cheered when Mossadegh nationalized the Anglo-Iranian Oil Company, he had to stifle his complaints. Iran once again controlled its own caviar. Mossadegh nationalized the caviar and sturgeon business, but almost all of its output still went to the Soviet Union.

Foreign friends of the Shah could expect one of the handsome tins to be delivered at Christmas or other festivals. Iranian embassies, particularly those in London, Paris, and Washington, were famous for their generosity with the eggs, laying out large spreads at the most quotidian receptions. The best caviar, that from the species *Huso huso*, or the beluga sturgeon, was known as Golden Imperial Caviar and had been reserved only for the Shah's palaces. Iranian Embassies were very much the place to be seen in the go-go years of the 1970s, drawing the scorn of the Australian art critic Robert Hughes, who wrote contemptuously of the social scene in New York: "Warhol and the *Interview* crowd at the tub of caviar in the consulates, like pigeons around a birdbath."

Come the Revolution, caviar presented a quandary to the new authorities. It was seen as a Western luxury item—most of it was sold abroad. If eating it was forbidden under religious law, so was trading in it. Shia were the most restrictive of all schools of Islam when it comes to eating seafood. They followed the injunction in Leviticus that only those fish with fins and scales could be eaten. The Koran explicitly bans the consumption of three things: pork, alcohol, and carrion. The rest is subject to interpretation. Under the Shah, enforcement of dietary rules was not a state matter. Alcohol was available, and *haram* forms of seafood were widely enjoyed. People decided for themselves whether they wanted to follow religious injunctions on what they ate. But rules are important to people: they signal membership in a group and commitment to that group. In the Islamic Republic, food would take on an outsized importance for the state.

Seafood has always been a problem for some Muslims, being both mostly *haram* and delicious. Shrimp are quite popular in Iran, eaten in a stew with coriander and fenugreek. They have been classified as both fish and birds under Shia law. One cleric decided that they were scaled fish because they wriggle inside their shell, which was a little like a scale. Others decided that they were sea locusts, and as locusts are classified as birds, they

THE BANQUET

could be eaten. Often, animals and fish were paired off by resemblance—so a fish that looked like a particular animal was also edible if the land animal could be eaten.

Sturgeon are known as dog fish in Persian, which would suggest that they would be banned on two grounds: not having many scales and resembling dogs. But sturgeon have some scales, and in Jewish law, caviar can be kosher if prepared under the supervision of a rabbi. Some dishes of fish eggs used roe from mullet, a halal fish, but others did eat sturgeon eggs, justifying it by saying that if the Prophet Muhammad had known how delicious they were, he surely would have allowed it.

Clerics had generally issued broad guidelines and then left it up to individuals what they ate, but after the Revolution, bureaucrats needed rules, and these were supposed to comply with Islamic thinking. So, in 1981, examples of the three main species of sturgeon were taken to Qom to be examined by a committee of clerics. Scales were found along the backs of the fish, and so they were determined to be suitable for consumption. The lucrative export industry could resume.

Inevitably, there was resistance. Traditionalists opposed the determination by experts that sturgeon were halal, and so it was referred to the Grand Ayatollah Mohammad-Reza Golpayegani, a conservative figure generally friendly to the new regime. He, too, said it should be determined by experts. The question of whether production could continue went right up to Khomeini, who, unusually for him, deferred to the experts as to whether sturgeons have scales. It seems that the small number they have near their tails was sufficient to have them declared fit for consumption. There was some pushback from traditionalists, so one of their number was drafted in to back up Khomeini's ruling.

Eventually, the ban was lifted, and the earlier, rather sudden shift from halal to haram was ascribed to a Soviet plot to deprive Iranians of a lucrative industry and a delicious food. The Revolu-

THE SHAH'S PARTY

tionary Guard newspaper justified the change as a way in which misunderstandings of the past were being overturned by the new religious government. The mullahs were simply lifting the veil of ignorance that had been imposed on Iran by outsiders.

> *Pain of love and drunkenness kills us, someday*
> *Only the beloved or wine can cure us*
>
> Hafez

Ancient Persians liked their wine. We know this both from the Persepolis Fortification Archive, essentially a collection of receipts and invoices found at the site, and Greek writers who took the time to mention it, often and mostly censoriously. Wine was enjoyable, but it made you soft, according to these Greeks, and there is a certain disdain in their accounts of excessive drinking. Heraclides of Cyme, author of a multi-volume *Persica* that is lost but some of which was passed down by Athenaeus, was unusual in offering a more positive view.

> For, more than any other people in the world, [the Persians] devote themselves to pleasure and luxury, and yet at the same time they are the noblest and the bravest of the barbarians. In fact, enjoyment of pleasure and luxury is the mark of free men; it liberates and elevates the spirit. Conversely, to live a life of hard labor is the mark of slaves and men of low birth.

The Fortification Archive lists rations of wine being given to horses, prized to the point of worship by the Achaemenids. Priests were provided from royal cellars with the best vintages, many of which came from afar. The priests drank it before reciting holy texts. The Lydians—people from what is today Western Turkey—are shown in the friezes of the *Apadana* stairway bringing tributes of wine and drinking bowls. Trade was rapid and sophisticated. Wines came from Armenia, Macedonia, and the Levant. Cupbearers were important officials with a considerable

THE BANQUET

knowledge of various vintages, the sommeliers of the age. Darius III was said to only drink wines that came from the slopes above Damascus. Several Greek writers commented on the sophistication of Persian palates.

The archive offers little sense of how wines tasted, even as it shows that people enjoyed them in large quantities: five liters a day for members of the royal family. From earlier texts in Mesopotamia, it seems wine of the time was mostly red, sweet, and often enhanced with spices, tree gums, and honey. Hittites left behind much more comprehensive records and accounts of their world than the Achaemenids, and from them we know of a complex and sophisticated wine culture, particularly among the rulers. Vineyards cost at least forty times the price of arable land, and there were severe penalties for letting animals trample vines.

Hittites, Assyrians, and Achaemenids all left evidence of elaborate feasting and table settings of astonishing beauty, particularly those involved with wine drinking. Vessels in the shape of animals seem to have been common to all these cultures, and by the time of the Achaemenids, metalsmiths were fashioning elaborate cups in gold and silver. Banquets were public and political displays of wealth and power; it was enormously important who was admitted, who ate where, and who served the king wine. Only the closest courtiers ever ate with the monarch, who otherwise sat apart. In the Museum of Iran is a gold rhyton, a 22-centimeter high wine cup in the shape of a winged lion, with some of the most detailed and sophisticated gold work ever found. Another slightly smaller lion rhyton dating from 500 BCE is in the Metropolitan Museum in New York. These eventually became popular across the Greek world, a Persian luxury that spread despite Greek anxieties that this way of life was somehow corrupting.

Jamshid, the legendary first king of the Persians and supposed founder of the civilization, was said to have also discovered wine,

THE SHAH'S PARTY

or rather, one of his maids did. He loved grapes and had some put away in jars so he could eat them out of season. The jars were labelled "poison" to keep out pilferers. Of course, the grapes fermented into wine. A maidservant, suffering from terrible headaches, decided to kill herself with the poison to end her misery and drank from one of the vessels. The sweet elixir cured her headache and made her feel relaxed and happy. She told the king, and the pleasures of the grape began.

The wines for the party were delivered four weeks early. The 410 cases needed to settle ahead of the banquet. Supplies were significant: a thousand bottles of champagne, including an old vintage to be served at dinner. A thousand bottles of Bordeaux and the same of Burgundy were put in a cellar built specially for wine storage. There was a cognac from 1860, but there were only twelve bottles for the 500 guests at the banquet. As the bottles were decanted, a waiter re-filled them with Courvoisier brandy and carried on serving.

Rudolf Pazeller, son of the chief concierge at the Badrutt's Palace Hotel in St. Moritz, joined the staff organizing the banquet, tasting the wine to ensure none of it had suffered too egregiously on its long journey from France to the Persian desert. "We also had to test the glasses. They were crystal, and their necks were ultra-thin, magnificent, wow! We tested by flicking our forefingers against them—and ping, a few hundred broke," he said.

The guests started off with Dom Pérignon 1959. The champagne served with dessert was a 1911 vintage from the same house, tinged pink with age, and according to Pazeller, not one bottle had gone bad, remarkable for a 60-year-old wine. The Château Lafite Rothschild 1945 that filled those glasses is hard to find today, certainly in the magnums that were poured in the huge blue tent. Bottles average around $3,000 today, magnums much more. This was the famous "Victory Vintage," marked with a V on the label, that came a year after the liberation of

THE BANQUET

France. The deep winter freeze limited the amount of grapes, and frosts persisted right up until May. But the summer was warm and dry; the grapes grew under drought conditions, meaning it was a small harvest with intense flavors. For many, 1945 was the best vintage ever for Château Lafite.

After the dignitaries had left, the soldiers clearing up the tent city were at a loss for what to do with the leftover wine. To the horror of the Swiss and French waiters, they smashed the bottles and let the wine soak into the sand.

14 October 1971

King Frederik IX of Denmark had been on the throne since 1947, which put him third behind Haile Selassie of Ethiopia and the Shah himself in order of precedence at the party. Arriving first at the Tent of Honor for the dinner, the 71-year-old monarch found himself at a loss for what to do. "Does anyone know where the hell I have to go?" he bellowed to nobody in particular. He was there with Queen Ingrid as well as his daughter Queen Anne-Marie of Greece and her deposed husband Constantine. A court flunky rapidly emerged from the blue velvet walls of the tent and quickly positioned the Danish monarch near the Shah and Shahbanou in the receiving line. Soon, a mass of royals were backing up outside the tent, bracing themselves against the winds that swept sand through the desert air, rattling the chandeliers that hung from the tented ceiling.

Weighed down by a heavy military great coat and a chestful of medals, the tiny Haile Selassie was almost carried through the tent by the Empress, who towered over him. On top of a significant hairdo sat a towering diamond tiara made by the New York jeweler Harry Winston from the Iranian royal collection of stones. The party was a chance to dig out the best jewels and orders—"battle dress" as Elizabeth II called it when decked out in her finery.

THE SHAH'S PARTY

The guests were arrayed along a vast table, shaped in a serpentine manner so that the guests could see others along its length. The Shah sat between Queen Ingrid of Denmark and Queen Fabiola of the Belgians. Empress Farah sat between Haile Selassie and King Frederick. The order of precedence placed the other guests in order of how long they had been on the throne, been heir to the throne, or been president of their country. Princess Anne, at that time a distant fourth in line to the British throne, sat on one of the smaller tables for thirteen guests. She sat at table six, facing the guests of honor and looking "noticeably unamused."

The party had not got off to a rollicking start. It was also the Shahbanou's thirty-third birthday, but it would have none of the relaxed fun of her party a year earlier, when the Minister of the Court Asadollah Alam had organized a desert retreat at his private estate in Birjand with camel rides, folk music, and a sumptuous birthday cake. That party had been something of a dress rehearsal down to food from Maxim's and a tented village. It had been a huge success with the Queen and her children dancing with local farmers around campfires.

There was also an ominous moment in which a weekly magazine published a report on the birthday party, noting the cost of the cake. This prompted a row between the Shah and the Queen, who had complained about the extravagance and was worried about how it would appear to the public. The Shah dismissed her complaints, saying she should not "kowtow to public opinion."

Unlike the exuberant birthday festivities, the party at Persepolis was all about protocol and formality, even if the service sometimes failed to live up to the expected standards. *The Los Angeles Times* reported that a waiter dropped a piece of bread on the tent floor, only to retrieve it and serve it to the Empress. Another spilled wine on Tito's jacket. Unperturbed, the Marshal wiped it off with a napkin.

THE BANQUET

Most of the guests sat stiffly for the first service, only relaxing as the wines came out. The Shah's court was known for its rather dour formality at these sorts of events, although he was much more relaxed in private. He was not a bicycling monarch in the manner of the Scandinavian royals, nor did the very freshly minted Pahlavi dynasty have the confidence of an ancient heritage that might have allowed it to set aside some protocol. Anyway, it would have been dangerous to have relaxed too much: the protocol rules of the Congress of Vienna had already put Pompidou's nose out of joint. Not carrying them out to the letter could easily have caused a diplomatic incident.

The guests may have been in a desert camp, but this was one where tiaras and decorations were worn to dinner, and nobody wanted to commit a faux pas. Barbara Walters, then a presenter on the NBC morning show *Today*, captured some of the fustiness of the event when she remarked loudly as the guests entered that the socialite Charlotte Ford, dressed in a white backless halter dress, was the only woman wearing a stylish gown.

If it were all a little starchy, that was hardly a surprise. Relations among many of the countries represented at the dinner were not good. Most of the Arab countries had frosty ties with Iran. They particularly resented the resurrection of memories of Cyrus, the great Persian empire builder who had conquered the forebears of the Arabs. But most of them came nevertheless, particularly the array of leaders from the new states that faced Iran across the Persian Gulf. The Shah had drawn the line at any Israeli representation as the countries did not have formal diplomatic ties despite their close security and economic relations. Israel had trained the secret police who were guarding the event, but they were not welcome to send a delegation, something that produced some miffed commentary in the Israeli press.

Personal and political differences were set aside for the event. Princess Anne's unsmiling demeanor—in fact, her usual manner in public, as with her mother, she suffered terribly from Hannoverian resting face—was remarked upon in several press reports. One suggested a possible reason: Crown Prince Carl-Gustaf of Sweden had recently said in an interview that he had no desire to marry her. Anne had felt the same way; the era of European dynastic marriages was over, but she must have bristled at this very public dismissal, nevertheless. Others must have felt the *longueurs* of the party and its rich food acutely. Queen Ingrid of Denmark had delayed ulcer surgery to attend the event and would be operated on as soon as she returned to Copenhagen.

14 October 1971

After the banquet, the guests were guided to a large stand filled with seats upholstered in the Imperial blue. Temperatures had plummeted, and so blankets were available, and many of the women dressed in fur wraps. Across the ruins, a *son-et-lumière* began, put together by a Belgian known for his wartime collaboration with the Nazis and his prolific production of biographies. Andre Castelot worked with Pierre Arnaud, the French writer of the *mise-en-scène* for the light show, and the Iranian composer Loris Tjecknavorian to produce an event that began with the founding of the ancient Persian capital and ended, somewhat inappropriately, with its destruction by Alexander.

Tjecknavorian, an Armenian-Iranian composer and conductor, had studied in Vienna under Carl Orff, composer of the famous "Carmina Burana", and then went on to a prominent international career, ultimately recording more than one hundred albums, including his score for the show at Persepolis. In the early 1970s, he was a paragon of how the Pahlavi state saw culture, composing operas based on the epic poem the *Shahnameh* that were played on traditional instruments. He was a prolific composer of film music, scoring more than forty movies, including hits for such stars as Googoosh.

THE BANQUET

Pierre Arnaud used lights to mimic the flames that had burned down the massive *Apadana*, the great columned reception hall roofed with ancient cedars of Lebanon that were decorated with gold and silver. Some guests may have known the story of the destruction of what was the greatest city of its time; it had been a popular subject for art, poetry, and even operas in the West, where the cult of Alexander had waxed and waned but is always alive.

Was this Alexander's greatest crime? Or was it justice, given that the Persian emperor Xerxes had burned down the Acropolis when he sacked Athens in 480 and 479 BCE? A great monument destroyed in revenge for the destruction of a great monument, which, in turn, had been destroyed in revenge for the destruction of the Persian city of Sardis? Only the Acropolis would rise again. Xerxes had offered the last Athenians in the city the chance to surrender; the Acropolis was only burned when they refused. The complex in Athens was rebuilt, incorporating memorials to the Persian destruction. Persepolis, burned on a whim it seems, and after it had been conquered, disappeared into the sands of the desert, becoming part of the mythology of ancient Persian kings until it was identified again after nearly two millennia.

* * *

As Alexander approached Persepolis down the royal road spanning Turkey and Iran, he would have come across a sprawling city in a fertile plain. Cut into the side of the mountains was the royal palace, a cluster of buildings on a huge platform. Enormous wooden-roofed buildings of a size unknown elsewhere at that time housed the reception halls. A treasury contained almost all the accumulated wealth of the Persian Empire.

It would take thousands of pack animals, some brought in from as far away as Babylon, to carry off the gold and silver from Persepolis. Plutarch put the number at 10,000 mules and 5,000 camels. An account by Diodorus of Sicily repeatedly mentions the great wealth and adds that the men were killed and the women enslaved. "It is an eternal rule the world over that when a city is taken, the citizens, their persons and all their property fall into the hands of the conquerors," wrote Xenophon. The very limited laws of war at the time applied mostly to preserving shrines, which were supposed to be *hors de combat*. Alexander did not even follow this rule.

The reasons why Alexander destroyed Persepolis remain obscure. Permenion, a general close to the king, urged him not to do it, saying he would be held in contempt if he were to destroy one of the greatest cities in the world. Some historians, perhaps inevitably, have blamed a woman. Thaïs was a concubine from Athens, a woman of some allure, highly cultured and skilled at singing and the recitation of poetry. She is believed to have encouraged the arson as revenge for the burning of the Acropolis. "What was most remarkable was that the sacrilege committed by Xerxes, king of the Persians, against the Acropolis of Athens was avenged by a single woman, a fellow-citizen of the victims, who, many years later, and, in sport, inflicted the same treatment on the Persians," wrote Diodorus.

Was all this just the result of a *komos*, a sort of drunken Greek conga line, that got out of control? Alexander was known for his drinking, something that was part of court life among the Macedonians. We do not know if Thaïs was truly responsible. Many of the early historians might have been writing her into a bigger role as she later became the powerful mistress of Ptolemy, the Macedonian general who emerged as pharaoh of Egypt. It certainly gave her a place in history. She appears in seventeenth-century Dutch tapestries, paintings by the eighteenth-century artist Joshua Reynolds, and in plays from ancient Greece up to the present day. She is one of only a handful of women described by Dante in his *Divine Comedy*. She is stranded in the circle

THE BANQUET

reserved for flatterers, standing up to her neck in a trench full of shit, representing all courtesans throughout history. It is a harsh judgment, for what would be the point of a courtesan who was shrewish and critical rather than a wily flatterer? She almost certainly worked hard for the money. The poet Dryden is more flattering, comparing her beauty and impact to Helen of Troy. Alexander, who saw himself as a continuation of the Homeric tradition, would have enjoyed the comparison.

Fire roared through the palaces. Their highly decorated wooden roofs made from cedars of Lebanon and walls lined with banners and decorations were all fuel for the flames. Ebony and teak were used for some of the decorations, and the halls were filled with gilded furniture, all of it highly flammable. Archaeologists working on the site in the 1930s would excavate a one-meter-deep layer of cedar ash. Everything else was gone. In the ashes of the Treasury, the huge meeting hall known as the *Apadana* and the other palace buildings, only semi-precious stones and tiny fragments of metal, believed to be decorative nails, have been found. There is no evidence of any of the treasure that Alexander looted from the city.

Historians have asked why Alexander burned the palace when he was trying to establish himself as a legitimate heir to Darius and ruler of the Achaemenids. Beyond the idea of revenge, it has been suggested that this was a defining last act for the peoples of Greece before their war took on a more self-interested tone. He wanted to mark himself out as the King of the East rather than the successor to the Persian Emperor, or to end any connection between the capital of the empire and the satraps that ruled its lands. Pretending to be a Persian king might have stretched the loyalties of his already rumbling Macedonians too far.

The destruction seems to have been accompanied by a surge of cruelty and vandalism on the part of Alexander's army. This was not unusual; it was something of a piratical mob and is

THE SHAH'S PARTY

remembered as such in later Persian accounts. They ransacked cities, enslaved tens of thousands of people, and shipped huge amounts of wealth back home to Macedonia. Most of the army were Alexander's compatriots; only a few thousand Greeks joined the supposedly united front of the Hellenic League. Far more Greeks fought on the side of the Persians than for Alexander. For a century or more, thousands of Greeks had moved to the Persian Empire, often in search of work. The inelastic economy of impoverished Greece and the frequent exiling of those who fell from grace meant that there had been a steady march of former leaders, mercenaries, farmers, artisans, and others towards the Persian empire.

Macedonia ran on a war economy that required constant new infusions of looted wealth to keep it going. It was an extravagant Ponzi scheme that required money to fund the wars that brought in new money, a constant cycle of wealth and poverty for the Macedonian rulers. When Philip was assassinated, he was launching a Pan-Hellenic crusade in Asia, supposedly to avenge the Persian invasion from decades earlier but also to fill his depleted coffers. On his death, Alexander is said to have lamented about the small amount of gold and large debts he had inherited. His overdraft was eight times the amount Philip had left behind in the Treasury.

What happened to the money taken from Persia? It is hard to tell. A certain amount got shipped back to Macedonia. Some was beaten into coin, but surprisingly little. Slaves were put to work in various places: the invasion had led to a massive shortage of labor back home in Macedonia; indeed, the loss of some 30,000 men to fighting in the East may have caused a demographic shock from which Alexander's kingdom never recovered.

*　*　*

In the flames of Persepolis, the Achaemenid Empire died, and Alexander earned his enduring reputation as conqueror and

THE BANQUET

destroyer. We know a significant amount about him because of the fascination that has endured since his short, tumultuous life. He was the first global celebrity. For Macedonians, Alexander was the greatest general and ruler of all time. For Persians, he was a brutal, callow youth whose wretched invasion must have caused no end of misery. Even Alexander himself may have had moments of regret. When he saw that the Tomb of Cyrus at Pasargadae had been damaged by his forces, he ordered it repaired.

Persian history absorbed Alexander, as it absorbed so many other people from its empire and its surrounding lands. He appears in the Zoroastrian text *Arda Viraf*. He invades Persia and destroys temples and religious texts.

> They say that, once upon a time, the pious Zartosht made the religion, which he had received, current in the world; and till the completion of 300 years, the religion was in purity, and men were without doubts. But afterward, the accursed evil spirit, the wicked one, in order to made men doubtful of this religion, instigated the accursed Alexander, the Roman, who was dwelling in Egypt, so that he came to the country of Iran with severe cruelty and war and devastation; he also slew the ruler of Iran, and destroyed the metropolis and empire, and made them desolate.

More than a millennium after he lived, Alexander featured in the *Shahnameh* as a half-Persian prince called Iskandar, a grandson of Philip who was born in Rome. Philip's daughter is married off to the Persian King Darab, one of several monarchs in the *Shahnameh* that do not correspond to any known ruler. The daughter, Nahid, suffers from bad breath, which proves a hindrance to the marriage, and she is sent back to her father. Pregnant, she gives birth to Iskandar, who is adopted by Philip. Meanwhile, Darab takes another wife who produces a son, Darius, setting up the inevitable confrontation between the half-brothers. Darius is wounded in battle and dies in Iskandar's arms while the new monarch vows to marry the Persian king's daughter and protect the Zoroastrian faith.

Unpicking history from this time is astonishingly difficult; the tiniest details still provoke endless arguments among academics. Even the contemporary historians who witnessed events have many axes to grind; each has his own Alexander. There is the man who inherits his father's debts and, in just a few years, is the richest man in history. There is the Alexander who rejects the timorous advice of his elders and betters and charges onwards. There is the Alexander who sleeps with Amazons, adopts Persian dress in honor of those he conquers, and is so courteous and so generous in victory that Darius, the vanquished Persian king, says he is happy to be beaten by such a man.

Is any of this true? Probably not, but who knows? What we know about Alexander comes to us mostly from fragments of histories that are included in the works of later writers. Even that was a complex process; historians of the ancient world did not cite earlier historians but took in echoes of themes and vocabulary from earlier works. In the case of Alexander, it is complicated by the highly propagandistic nature of the writing and the degree to which they were engaged in different aims. In some, they are venerating Alexander, linking him to Homer as a new Achilles, and are filled with slightly distorted images from the Trojan Wars, a thousand years before he lived. Others are influenced by later works and ideas: there is imagery that links some writing to Zoroastrianism. Were these later additions captured in oral traditions in Persia and then incorporated back into the works of Greeks and Romans?

The early historians were writing from Macedonian or Greek viewpoints. They were not the same. We tend to think of Greece as a unified Hellenic culture, but it was always fractious and divided. Sparta, for example, a highly militarized, austere society disliked by most of its neighbors, did not join the

THE BANQUET

Hellenic League to fight under Alexander. And throughout his time in the East, Alexander was constantly trying to hold the idea of pan-Hellenism together in the face of endless grievances from the bickering cities. But this war helped harden Greek identity, and later it would shape the way in which Europeans have seen Persia.

Although Alexander's achievements are extraordinary, they were mostly negative. He burned through the Persian Empire. It was broken up for parts: Ptolemy took over Egypt, establishing the dynasty that would eventually lead to Cleopatra and Roman rule. Sassanians took over what is now Syria and Iraq, also eventually coming under Roman rule. Other satraps became kings across the region. Even the Hellenic League, pulled together from fractious cities, did not last; it was breaking up even as Alexander was still fighting in Persia.

The successors were a credit to Alexander. These were men of substance, somewhat unlike their successful but perhaps overly flamboyant and reckless boy-king. While he destroyed, they mostly built, and their dynasties endured for some time, given the swash and backswash of conflict there. The region suffered from what today is called a war economy: with no great improvements in the technology of farming or energy, the only way to expand one's power and wealth was to seize land and people. It was a demographically strained time: labor was in short supply, and therefore it was worth conquering cities and enslaving their inhabitants.

Some historians have been taken with the idea of Alexander as an early proponent of creative destruction. He broke up the economically moribund Persian Empire and liberated its stored wealth, stirring up economic progress across the region. There is a widespread belief that the empire was already falling apart; distance and mountains had meant that all power had to be local and that satraps were now more interested in doing their own thing than following orders from the center.

THE SHAH'S PARTY

14 October 1971, Pacific Standard Time

Just as the guests were doing the rounds of their meetings or relaxing in their tents on the morning of 15 October in Persepolis, an explosion blasted through the Iranian Consulate at 3400 Washington Street in San Francisco. Parviz Adle, the consul, was out, but his wife and children were at home in the large corner house in Presidio Heights when explosives equivalent to 120 sticks of dynamite wrecked the garage, tore apart the consul's car, and set fire to the building. It was the most powerful bomb in California up to that time.

Glass from around fifty nearby buildings was scattered all over when the consul's wife and three children fled the building on bare feet. As the police hustled them away, a crowd of Iranian protestors from the Confederation of Iranian Students gathered, having seen news of the bomb on television, and chanted "Death to the Shah." The confederation denied responsibility for the bombing.

Moira Johnston, a Canadian woman living across the street, was lying in bed writing when the room went white, filled with plaster dust, flying glass, and tangled blinds. On the pillow next to her was a piece of glass a foot across that had narrowly missed her. She ran to the next-door bedroom to check on her 4-year-old son. He was unhurt but lying amidst piles of rubble and clouds of debris. Fearing more explosions, she barricaded her child in a cupboard, surrounding him with quilts. Her husband had just left the house to pick up a student who was staying with them; his car had been parked just outside the Consulate. The explosion bent neighboring trees and could be heard four miles away.

Writing a few weeks after the attack, which caused widespread damage to surrounding buildings, many of which were survivors of the city's 1906 earthquake, Johnston described the bombing as part of the worsening violence in the city.

THE BANQUET

> As a judge is yanked from his courtroom and shot outside a library we use regularly; as prisoners and guards kill each other in San Quentin across the Bay; as young Weathermen blow themselves and their basement bomb factory up two blocks from the Greenwich Village brownstone we had restored; as the Zodiac killer dumps a victim near our local tennis courts; as an Iranian immolates himself on our corner, I feel my own threshold of violence rising to the point where I am no longer shocked when the building across the street is blown up.

The Consul suggested he knew the names of those involved, suggesting they were Iranian dissidents. Student groups disavowed any connection to the attack on the consulate, the site of so many demonstrations that one neighbor tried to have the city declare the office a public nuisance.

Just before the bombing, the Iran Student Association headquarters in Washington was set alight in an arson attack that caused widespread damage. The first presumption was that the office was being used as a bomb factory, but the local police rejected this, suggesting instead that the fire had been set either by the Shah's security agency SAVAK or by a rival grouping of Arab students. No arrests were made in either bombing.

> Some of the brightest people in the country, some of them in important official posts and some in the government, would meet, and we would develop scenarios as to what might happen. Not one person, not one scenario turned out to be anywhere near the truth, near to reality, near to what actually took place when the Revolution came.
>
> Khodadad Farmanfarmaian, former government official

Just over a year before the Shah left Iran, President Carter spoke at the Niavaran Palace at a New Year's Eve dinner. "Because of the great leadership of the Shah, Iran is an island of stability in one of the more troubled areas of the world." Raising his glass to

THE SHAH'S PARTY

a leader whose virtues were a fairly new discovery for him, he added, "This is a great tribute to you, your majesty, and to your leadership and to the respect and the admiration and love which your people give to you." How could a figure who seemed so much the master of his domain, who projected such confidence and ambition, end up skulking off into his sad exile? And how could the Iranians have chosen such a bleak and uncompromising figure as Khomeini as their new leader?

Revolutions have always challenged easy comprehension. Regimes seem rock solid until suddenly they are not, and only in retrospect can we identify the weaknesses we did not see before. The sudden giddy moment when the dictator falls is incredibly exhilarating, even if the aftermath is a time of betrayal and disappointment. The surge through the palace gates, the joyful revelations of the leader's excesses. The private zoo with its bewildered, abandoned animals; the dozens of pairs of identical alligator shoes, more than anyone could wear in a lifetime; the gold AK-47; and the bad art. The mix of luxury and tawdriness enshrined in the presidential bedroom. Waving a flag from the tank, putting flowers in the rifles of the grinning teenage guards, the crowds in the streets as the harried entourage flees on a military cargo plane. But the elation is almost always short-lived. Youthful dissent often ends in the prison cell and the torture chamber, followed at best by exile in a gray Stockholm suburb or, more often, the shallow grave by the airport road.

Was it modernization that doomed the Shah? Did the rushed encounter with modernity—money, jobs, timekeeping, factories, migration, alienation, and all the other dislocations of an industrial society—ensure his fall? Did the opposition of the religious establishment to land reform and economic change create the conditions that undermined his legitimacy? The role of clerics in fomenting dissent and the ultimate victory of Khomeini's innovative brand of theocracy has challenged those who took the

THE BANQUET

strictly Marxist view of revolutions. If it was not just about class tensions, then what role did ideology and culture play? Why did the vast machinery of repression under the Shah fail to respond? What happened to SAVAK and the military? Did fractures in that establishment, itself challenged by the enormous changes going on across society, doom it to failure and passivity in the face of an uprising?

Was it more personal? Did the Shah doom himself, or was he doomed by his illness and accompanying depression that clearly sapped any ability to make decisions, something at which he had not excelled at the best of times? He tended towards vacillation; behind the domineering figure he tried to present to the media was someone who often could not make up his mind. Did the Shah's own mystical ideas of being born to rule betray him when he sickened, undermining his confidence as his divine right faded? Was it the family who sapped popular support, undermining the "social welfare monarchy" that the Queen had promoted? Nikkie Keddie, one of the foremost historians of modern Iran, believed that the Pahlavi ideas about modernization were doomed because they came in the form of Westernization. But much of the ideology of the regime and many of its public statements were conspicuously anti-Western, and many were even draped in religious ideas and language. Did the Pahlavis themselves open the door to the black-eyed mystic and his religious rule?

The historian Ervand Abrahamian believed that it was the failure to modernize politics alongside the economy and society that undid the Shah. It was a genuinely progressive demand for democracy that Khomeini hijacked because he was the only one who held the fractious coalition together, mostly by telling everyone what they wanted to hear. A populist who has no shame in the lies he tells—and they mostly do not—can go a long way when there is a desperate hankering for a leader. By 1982, the religious right dominated the political landscape, and

THE SHAH'S PARTY

the left-wing politics that had driven the Revolution were shattered. Iran, along with much of the world, abandoned the left in that decade.

Unusually, the Iranian Revolution did not come in the wake of a losing military engagement, as the Russian and Portuguese revolutions did. It did not come because of some long-standing occupation that roused the people, as was the case in China and Vietnam. There was little real external pressure on the Shah; Carter wished to see improvements in human rights, but the United States had no desire to see the regime gone.

Did oil cause the regime to collapse? The breakneck speed of industrialization, paid for by vast new oil revenues, undermined traditional economic sectors—agriculture, bazaar trading, and small-scale manufacturing were all crushed by the new oil economy of the 1970s, which washed in with the speed and power of a tsunami. Many, of course, benefited from this surge. The lives of more Iranians improved by a greater degree during the rule of the Shah than at any time in history. The petty bourgeoisie were on side until growth faltered. When the tide of petrodollars retreated, they were revealed to be swimming naked, a painful experience after decades of growth. It was the bazaaris, as traders were known, and minor landowners who financed the Revolution. Their children were the students, looking ahead towards unemployment and lacking the career-making connections of the elite, who were among those who took to the streets. The Shah had pumped billions into education; it was perhaps his most enduring legacy, and yet it contributed to his fall.

Many countries experienced these conditions and yet did not end up as theocracies. How could a modernizing country that seemed secular change in this way? But Iran had a history of a religious establishment being involved in politics and administration. It had been steadily pushed aside under Pahlavi rule; they no longer managed the legal or education systems, local leaders

THE BANQUET

paid them no heed, technocrats were unresponsive, indeed, even hostile, to their views.

After the removal of Mosaddeq and the weakening of the National Front, religious groups had been the only dissenting political force that was able to operate in the limited space available; political parties were populated by sycophants united in their obedience to the Shah and divided only by the degree of eagerness of their praise. But the mosque door remained open a crack. Khomeini was the most prominent critic, but tens of thousands of others operated in a more subtle and ultimately corrosive manner. Like many revolutionaries over the years, they mastered new technologies and put them to effective use. Cassette tapes were copied in their thousands. Khomeini's voice grew ever louder as the reedy tones of the Shah faded.

Changes were afoot in the 1970s. The attention of the world was on the emergence of Iran as a regional leader and the Shah as a prominent world figure, no longer the playboy prince with the wives and the embarrassing flight to Rome, but a figure of consequence. Below the surface, a new form of Shiism was developing that contained a pressing demand for change.

The religious networks that had been building for decades were ticking away in 1977 when a series of events occurred that seemed to have set the Revolution down an irreversible path, although it did not seem this way at the time. In October of that year, Khomeini's eldest son, Mostafa, died in Najaf aged 46. The apparent cause was a heart attack, but immediately the word went out that he had been poisoned by SAVAK. Mostafa was also a cleric and hewed closely to his father's views, living with him in exile in Najaf. His death seemed to signal to many back in Iran that the Shah would stop at nothing to stay in power, even killing religious men. When the ceremonies marking forty days since the death were held in Tehran, thousands gathered to mourn the ayatollah's son.

THE SHAH'S PARTY

By this stage, the Shah had recognized that he needed to reform, but his actions only created new dangers for him. There was a softening of press controls, and in the wake of Mostafa's death, newspapers published condolence notes referring to Khomeini as the "Great Ayatollah." Press controls and his long absence in Najaf had severely reduced the numbers who knew of him, but now he was back. No longer able to repress all discussion of Khomeini, the Shah went on the attack. In January 1978, the state newspaper *Ettilat* published an article accusing Khomeini of being the leader of the "Black Reaction." It included a number of falsehoods about the cleric: he was Indian and not even an Iranian citizen; he suffered from mental illnesses and, inevitably, he was an agent of foreign powers. Rumors soon spread that the actual author was none other than the Shah himself, although his then head of protocol, the diplomat Amin Aslan Afshar, denies that it could be possible. Whomever the author was, Khomeini was more than ever established as the unchallenged center of opposition to the Shah.

One unforced error by the Shah followed another. The government decided it would be better to force Khomeini out of Iraq and make him live in France, where he would be exposed to the press, which would reveal the harshness of his political and religious views. In October 1978, he left Najaf for France and moved to the drab Parisian suburb of Neauphle-le-Château. It turned out that the international media fell for Khomeini's disingenuous and evasive mutterings. The sophisticated exiles around him, including the future president Abolhassan Banisadr, were careful not to let his true views show. A Council of Revolution was formed, dominated by clerics, and the small band set about achieving what most thought was impossible: the overthrow of the Shah.

The group around Khomeini had mostly been in exile for years, but they were politically astute. They knew the main arguments against the Shah in Europe concerned human rights, and it would not do for Westerners to hear the Ayatollah's true views on women, democracy, or the decadence of France, his place of exile. Khomeini's highly effective campaign of dissimulation amplified the growing view that the Shah was a terrible despot and that Khomeini was fighting for the rights of all Iranians. The ayatollah had also tapped into his networks of clerics back in Iran, who fed him information on what was happening. Several senior clerics, even those who did not see eye-to-eye with him on all matters, endorsed him, giving him growing legitimacy as the leader of the Revolution.

* * *

By the mid-1970s, the ubiquity of the Shah in the media had become suffocating to many Iranians. No front page was complete without photographs or articles about the royal family, many of them touting some triumph or promising some future achievement that was almost certainly unattainable. Imperial panegyric inevitably made claims for the benefits of Pahlavi rule that were not felt on the streets. "Man's Exploitation by Man Abolished" was the headline above one such story about the Shah's achievements in what seems like an article from a satirical newspaper. Reality was rarely a subject for journalism. Instead, the focus was on grandiosity. The Shah had told Fallaci: "Believe me, in Iran we're far more advanced than you and really have nothing to learn from you." His frequent prediction was for the collapse of the West under the weight of its moral degradation and the inevitable rise of Iran, China, and Brazil. It was a vision out of a futuristic comic book: electric cars and monorails would sweep through Tehran by 1984; people would have three or four days off each week as automation took over. It was all just a decade away. For the next few years, the targets were all just a decade away.

THE SHAH'S PARTY

In 1977, the economy was in such poor shape, and public resentment had surged to such a degree that a retrenchment was in order. Obscene amounts of money had been squandered in the rush for development; in 1975 and the following year, the state is said to have paid two billion dollars in demurrage fees for shipping that was lined up in the Persian Gulf waiting sometimes for months to offload imports at the clogged ports. In the previous years, a number of new regulations had deepened anger, particularly among two groups who would prove central to the Revolution, clerics and bazaaris. The latter had been particularly inflamed by efforts to stem inflation and land speculation. They had their revenge by providing funds to religious groups.

By this stage the strange coalition that would oust the Shah was coming together. It included the Tudeh Party, the leftist guerrillas of the Fadaiyan-e Khalq, and the leftist-religious combine of Mujahedin-e Khalq. It brought in organizations from ethnic minorities such as the Kurds, as well as various nationalist forces. And of course, it included the populist religious right of Khomeini. Without all of these components coming together, it is not clear that the Revolution would have succeeded; the left played an essential role as they were doing all over the world during what came to be known as "the Red Decade." Students had led the way; just as the killing of Benno Ohnesorg had galvanized German students, others around the world rallied against authoritarian governments from 1967 onwards: Mexico around the Olympics and France with *les evenements* of May 1968, Italy with the *autunno caldo* of 1969; Greece, Spain, Portugal and Japan saw a rise in student rebellion and leftist violence. In 1973, students at the University of Athens and the Polytechnic School took on the military junta known as The Colonels. Iranian students were early participants in this global movement of opposition, driven by the young and the left-wing.

None of it was to last; by 1980, a massive backlash to the left had spread around the world, ushering in the era of Thatcher

THE BANQUET

and Reagan, neoliberalism and the repressive religious state created by Khomeini.

In the dusty Iraqi town of Najaf the Ayatollah spent his days sitting on the floor of his simple house, his back resting against the wall, writing and receiving the handful of visitors who made it from Iran to see him. He had been abroad since he was exiled in 1964 for protesting against a law that would have given immunity to United States military personnel stationed in Iran. "I cannot express the sorry I feel in my heart," he told a protest in the religious center of Qom at the time.

> If some American's servant, some American's cook assassinated your Grand Marja (the leading ayatollah) in the middle of the bazaar or runs over him, the police do not have the right to apprehend him! The dossier must be sent to America so our masters there can decide what to do.

This law tapped into a well of indignation among Iranians about the unequal treatment demanded by foreigners, something that had been emphasized by nationalists for decades. The exploitative arrangements agreed by Qajar monarchs for oil and tobacco concessions had inspired the constitutional movement. A popular demand was that shahs be prevented from selling the family silver so they could squander the money in the fleshpots of Europe. A few days after his inflammatory speech, Khomeini was arrested and put on a plane to Turkey, then the most secular of Middle Eastern countries and a place that Khomeini loathed. There he was forbidden from wearing a turban and clerical robes.

After a year, SAVAK made the mistake of letting him go to Najaf, alongside Karbala one of the two holiest cities for the Shia faith. Exile freed Khomeini from the restraints of his peers back in Iran and allowed him to emerge as a political force. On arrival, he did not receive a warm welcome from his fellow religious leaders. They tended to regard those from Qom as intellectual arrivistes as the city had only developed as a major religious center since the 1920s, whereas Najaf had a thousand-year history of scholarship. They also did not view his writing highly, nor were they aligned with his confrontational approach to politics. Although they disdained the White Revolution for undermining their powers, they were against a direct clash with the Shah, fearing that they would be blamed for any resulting public crackdown.

Khomeini's success in Najaf was by no means certain, but he quietly and patiently established the ideas and networks that would eventually bring him to power. He spent his time teaching and writing, only occasionally putting his head above the parapet. In 1971, Khomeini published his seminal work known as *Islamic Government*. This laid out his novel ideas for *vilayat-i faqih*, or government by the faithful. There were three main precepts: government must be subordinate to Islam; religious scholars had a duty to bring about an Islamic state; and thirdly, the religious establishment in Iran needed to undergo reforms if it were to reach its goals. Khomeini describes government by religious scholars as "self-evident," "necessary," and something that everyone would agree on as soon as they read or heard about it. That was not the case. For many centuries, clerics had restricted themselves to a narrow religious mandate, focusing on areas such as family law and education.

Khomeini's writings had a strong populist slant. He was quick to tap into anti-Semitic ideas and was always eager to criticize the privileged or the foreign. His world view was narrow, xenophobic and racist, with no curiosity about anyone else's life. He was entirely certain in these solipsistic views; no shadow of doubt ever moves over them. He was also quick to declare sympathy for those wronged by the government in Iran, for those trying to get justice in an increasingly bureaucratic system. Khomeini was on the side of those "wasting their time in corridors or standing in front of some official's desk, and in the end, they will still not know what has transpired." He wrote: "Anyone who is more cunning and more willing and able to give bribes, has his case settled expeditiously but at the cost of justice."

His words took on a powerful resonance. He was enormously prescient about what would inflame the crowd—talk of agents of imperialism, the murky intentions of the Americans and the British, the growing resentment at both corruption and the harsh punishments of the state that fell increasingly on the bazaaris, as well as the urban poor and the rural landless. In his world, imperialists produced hostile propaganda against religion and denied that Islam has a place in government, Khomeini thundered. This would have been music to the ears of many of those who hated the Westernization that would only accelerate in Iran in the 1970s. Sexuality, jealousy, corruption, resentments, and widening gaps between the rich and poor were stirring society.

He spent his days in his small house, eating his meagre breakfast and then settling down to write, enraptured by his own piety and devotion. When he published his book on Islamic government and issued his declaration against the Persepolis celebrations, it was more of an echo than a shout back home, but that would change. He was kept under watch by the Iranian Embassy in Baghdad, which occasionally pressed the Iraqi regime to rein him in. From 1965 until the early 1970s, he had been quiet, mostly sticking to teaching and writing and rarely commenting on politics.

The 1971 events were an opportunity to attach himself to an issue that he knew would inflame Iranian nationalism, just as the law on United States forces had done in 1964. Khomeini marked the occasion with a stony letter on the incompatibility of monarchy and Islam. It was, as were most of his writings, calculated to arouse anger.

People in Iran were starving, he wrote, and yet the country was spending vast amounts on decorating Tehran. "Experts have been invited from Israel to take care of the arrangements—from Israel, that stubborn enemy of Islam and the Koran…" Israel played no role in organizing or provisioning the events, and no representative had been invited, to the slight irritation of the government and commentators there, whose own commemoration of Cyrus the Great had in part inspired the event. Israel may have been involved in intelligence sharing, given the Shah's fears of disruption by Iraq or local militant organizations, but that was the limit of it. Reality did not stop Khomeini from a lengthy anti-Semitic rant. After stating that Israel was planning to occupy Muslim lands and destroy the holy shrines of Shiism, he wrote: "That state is now to arrange the celebrations of the Iranian monarchy, and that state is supplied with oil by tankers."

He went on to list a series of violent abuses by Persian monarchs, particularly against the religious community. "God only knows what disasters the Iranian monarchy has given rise to since its very beginnings and what crimes it has committed." The ceremonies should be boycotted. "I proclaim to the governments and heads of state that mean to take part in this abominable festival that it has no connection with the people of Iran and that to participate in it is to participate in the murder of the oppressed people of Iran."

He was not shy about issuing edicts.

> Let all Muslim heads of state take note in particular that this festival is anti-Islamic and that it is being arranged by Israeli experts and engineers; they should therefore shun all participation in it. … The monarchy in Iran, from its inception to this day—God be my witness—has inflicted miseries and perpetrated enormous crimes. The crimes of Persian shahs have blackened the pages of history,

he wrote. "Who but these very shahs of Iran ordered massacres of people and piled their severed heads into pyramids? The very best of these shahs were ruthless ruffians." Nuance was not for

THE BANQUET

him. His aim was to squeeze out others by focusing relentlessly on his singular message against the Shah.

> It is the duty of the Muslim people of Iran to refrain from participation in this illegitimate festival, to engage in passive struggle against it, to remain indoors during the days of the festival, and to express by any means possible their disgust and aversion for anyone who contributes to the organization or celebration of the festival.

It was calculated to irritate, and it did. Asked by the *Le Monde* correspondent Eric Rouleau what he thought of Khomeini's complaints, the Shah was dismissive. "Why should I have to answer to Khomeini?" he asked. Rouleau persisted, saying he was just asking for the Shah's opinion. "I will not answer your question because Khomeini is neither Iranian nor Persian. He is Indian and I do not answer to Indians."

* * *

Khomeini was not Indian. He was born in Khomein, in central Iran, in September 1902. His father was an impoverished imam whose family had lived in India but was of Persian origin. His forebears had been part of a long tradition of religious scholarship, a key part of the Twelver Shia faith, and his family claimed descent from the Seventh Imam, Musa al-Kazim. Some of the family had migrated to Lucknow, India, in the late eighteenth century, a time of significant exchanges between the Persian and Mughal empires. However, his grandfather returned to live in Iran after making a pilgrimage to the holy city of Najaf. Although the family's ties to India never resumed, his grandfather was sometimes known as Hindi, and his descendants either carried this name or, like Khomeini, used it occasionally as a pen name.

His father was murdered when he was a small child. Much would be made of this story as an ever-expanding mythology grew around the cleric: his father was said to have been killed by

THE SHAH'S PARTY

Reza Shah, which explained the longstanding antipathy Khomeini held for the Pahlavis. But the future king was a Cossack cadet at the time and was not involved. Another story was that Khomeini's father died defending impoverished peasants. In fact, his death was the result of a feud, and a member of a rival local family was hanged for the crime.

His mother died when he was a teenager. He left home and began a lengthy education at madrassas around the country, eventually ending up in Qom. The city was undergoing a resurgence as a religious center after being overshadowed by the holy cities in Iraq. Reza Shah, no fan of clerics, preferred that they all be concentrated in one place where a close eye could be kept on them. Khomeini became a product of the intense and often claustrophobic religiosity of the city as it became increasingly like a Shia version of the Vatican. "Wherever I may be, I am a citizen of Qom and take pride in the fact. My heart is always with Qom and its people," he would later write. After the Revolution, he moved back to the city, which he regarded as the epicenter of the faith and the Revolution.

Shia Islam is a complex faith with multiple strands of thought and many clerics whose job is to interpret it for the times. By one reckoning, there are at least 200 distinct variants of the religion. The hierarchy of religious thinkers was not centralized or controlled by some authority but driven by individuals dependent on intellectual prowess, teaching ability, and the publishing of books of guidance on religious practice and law. Shia clerics are essentially religious lawyers who teach students and issue guidance. Khomeini did well in this world, but his eventual position at the top of the faith was by no means a foregone conclusion. He was one of a great many students in Qom and then became one of many teachers, all competing in various ways for the favor of those above and emulation by those below.

As a young man, Khomeini did not engage much in politics, although the first twenty years of his life were a time of dramatic

THE BANQUET

change with the end of the Qajar dynasty at home and the Russian Revolution next door. His early adulthood was a time of intense pressure on the *ulema*. Reza Shah had diminished their role in society and was adopting the sort of secular policies introduced in neighboring Turkey by Kemal Ataturk. Khomeini's interest was mainly in studying Shia forms of gnosis, or knowledge of the self. Shiism has always had an inward-looking, apolitical aspect; it was permissible to focus on an inner spiritual world. As a junior religious teacher, this was the position Khomeini took. Only in his private poetry did he express the hatred of the Pahlavis that he would nurture for decades.

In 1944, he published a book, *The Discovery of Secrets*. It was a polemic against the increasingly secular state and challenges such as those from Ahmad Kasravi, a politician and historian who campaigned to eliminate Islamic and Arabic influences from Persian culture. Khomeini wanted people to "wipe out these shameless sinners with an iron fist." Kasravi was assassinated in 1946 by the Fedaiyan-e Islam, a religious death squad responsible for several high-profile murders, including the killing of two prime ministers and an attempt on the Shah's life in 1949.

A major shift came in 1962, by which time Khomeini was a middle-ranked cleric, respected as a teacher of philosophy rather than the higher status religious law. He had surrounded himself with many of the figures who would emerge as leaders after the Revolution, but he still deferred to more senior clerics who did not challenge the Shah. But as Mohammad Reza exerted increasing power after the removal of Mossadegh in 1953, he began a series of reforms that antagonized the *ulema*. In 1962, the government passed a law that would have allowed elected officials to swear their oath of office on any book. This would have opened the door for Bahais to stand for election. It was an idea that outraged Khomeini, a fanatical hater of these supposed apostates.

Khomeini's emergence as the pre-eminent figure in the Revolution did not occur until after 1977. For many years before that, he was barely on the radar screen of most of his countrymen. Unusually, his was a political life lived in old age. He was 79 before he became an immensely powerful, world-changing figure, whereas so many others in the twentieth century had seized their moment when young.

He elevated the notion of Islamic government with a deep cunning. Firstly, he made himself inseparable from his doctrine. Although he did not name it Khomeinism, it came only from him, and not from a group of scholars or theoreticians. There was no question that he would be the leading figure in any government of jurists. More importantly, he blurred the line between the idea of the Hidden Imam—the Twelfth Imam who had gone into hiding and would reappear as a messiah—with his own return to Iran. His flight back to Tehran on an Air France 747 as his magical chariot was an unlikely way for the Imam to return, but when it happened, millions gathered to welcome him home.

Khomeini was a master of survival and invention. He was never the most senior or most respected religious figure, but he was supremely skilled at blending widespread popular anxieties about modernity, opposition to the Shah, leftist politics, and Shia notions of the return of the Imam. He conjured up a modern theological justification for an Islamic state, but promised democracy until he got into power. His ambitions were boundless; the rule of the clerics, i.e., him, was not just something for Iran but represented the future for all Muslims, indeed all mankind.

10

AFTER THE PARTY

16 OCTOBER 1971

Those running the tent city must have breathed a collective sigh of relief as the royals and politicians got into their Mercedes limousines for the drive to Shiraz and their departure. Some flew off on their own planes. Air Force Two took Spiro Agnew to Tehran briefly and then to Greece, his ancestral home, where he was to meet with the colonels who had seized power and ousted King Constantine. Haile Selassie's plane headed towards Tehran, where he would again be the guest of honor.

The Shah flew back to Tehran, where he was to inaugurate the Shahyad Aryamehr Monument, a towering inverted Y-shaped archway that would be the new gateway to the capital. To evoke continuity between the ancient monument of Persepolis and the bustling center of Iranian politics and business, guests had been invited to attend both events. A spokesman for the government described the Tehran events as a jump "out of history into the nation's future."

Crowds of hundreds of thousands could be mustered in Tehran, and so the events, which included the opening of a new national stadium, had a much more popular feel than those in the high-security confines of Persepolis. Tehran and its people were finally allowed to play a role in the performance of modernity and political power. The Shahyad monument would be a central architectural symbol of the Pahlavi era. It had started life as the Gate of Cyrus before becoming the Imperial Gate and then the Shahyad Gate, or the Gate of the Remembrance of Kings. After the Revolution, it was smoothly repurposed to serve the new regime, which renamed it the Azadi Monument.

From taking the throne in 1941 until the celebrations in 1971, the Shah had mostly steered clear of grandiose architectural gestures. Most of what had been built in that time was functional, modernist, and fairly empty of massive political gestures. The state had mostly focused on dams, universities, hospitals, and ministry buildings. This monument was the first move into an area that others in the region had long employed to political ends. Saddam Hussein, Nasser, and Ataturk in particular had already tapped into megaprojects as a way to express the power, grandeur, and modernity of their regimes. Since the 1950s, the Middle East and South Asia have been an epicenter for the Edifice Complex. Leaders hankered for the massive modernist architectural statement, such as the Indian city of Chandigarh, designed by the Swiss-French architect Le Corbusier. The Shah only showed an interest in ceremonial architecture relatively late in his reign, when he had the resources to build on an enormous scale.

At the ceremony to open the Shahyad Arch, a quiet young man was taken in hand by the Shah and introduced to Haile Selassie and the other guests who had stayed on for the Tehran events. Hossein Amanat was just 22 years old and a recent graduate of Tehran University when he won an open competition in 1966 to build a monument that would serve as a gateway for the capital and an enduring emblem of the city. He was still sleeping

AFTER THE PARTY

in his childhood bedroom in his parents' house when, in a matter of weeks, he came up with an extraordinary design that won over ideas from far more established architects.

His marble arch—indefinably a mix of sculpture, building, museum, triumphal space, and public park—was to survive political upheavals and generational shifts to remain at the heart of the city's image. Up to then, Tehran had lacked a truly identifiable monument; by the time of the Revolution, the arch was well established as its emblem. The fluted marble-clad structure with its mix of traditional and modern geometries and its garden of fountains and lawns was to become not just the main space for the Shah's glorification but the place where crowds gathered to demand the end of his reign.

Amanat managed to create a modern monument from various ancient influences, ranging from Parthian fire temples to ancient tomb towers. It combines the parabolic arches of Sassanian Dynasty palaces with a pointed arch reminiscent of Islamic architecture and a cornice resembling the Seljuk-era Tughrul Tower, a twelfth-century building in the city of Rey. Inside, it laid out the history of Iran as seen through the Pahlavi lens with a heavy investment in culture before the Arab conquest. As is so often the case, it was completed hours before the opening ceremonies, with the last exhibits installed in the underground museum.

The building was astonishingly complicated in technical terms and surprisingly thoughtful for a design by such a young architect. His vision survived almost intact from the early drawings, thanks to the direct intervention of the Shah, who allowed him to hire the world's leading engineering company. London-based Ove Arup and Partners was pioneering the use of computer-aided design that allowed the construction of complex shapes, vital for an arch in which the curves bend in two directions. The arch had no ground-level opening so as to look as though it had grown up from the earth; the interior museum was reached through a long tunnel that was lined with display cases for artefacts from ancient Iran to the present day. A viewing platform at the top allowed spectators to look out over the surrounding garden, reminiscent of the traditional *paradis* with its complex geometry of lawns, fountains and paths.

From the start, the monument met with some unsurprising criticism, as did every public project connected to the events. In the 1972 satirical movie, *Secrets of the Jinni Valley Treasure*, an impoverished farmer discovers buried treasure while ploughing his fields and ends up building a vast phallic monument to himself as part of a wild spending spree. A massive earthquake destroys his monument and reburies his treasure. Rumors abounded, as they always did in Tehran at that time, of massive corruption involved in the building of the Shahyad Tower. Amanat later denied that the bill was more than a million dollars, a remarkably modest cost.

As a number of writers have noted, the tower captured a moment when Tehran was rushing into the future, and it has gone on to embody the promise of those times, particularly among new generations of city dwellers who have grown up under the Islamic regime. Something in the design managed to capture optimism, a forward-looking sense of Iranian identity that transcended politics. "It creatively bridged the city's tormented past to its triumphant mood about its future," wrote the historian Abbas Milani.

The monument established Amanat's reputation as an architectural wunderkind, and he was soon offered an array of commissions, including one to build a new Iranian embassy in Beijing. This modernist structure carefully blends ancient and modern forms, yet remains distinctly Iranian. He also built several major buildings for the Bahai faith. Amanat's family were adherents to this offshoot of Islam whose followers were brutally persecuted after the Revolution. Amanat fled the country just

AFTER THE PARTY

before the Shah's departure and as a Bahai has been shunned since by the government in Tehran despite being one of the most important architects to come out of Iran.

* * *

On 7 September 1978, hundreds of thousands of people marched on Shahyad Square to demand a new government, taking up Khomeini's message that the Shah must go. SAVAK leaders had warned people not to attend the rally, but fear of the regime had broken like a fever; the people of Tehran marched from across the city, encouraged by a belief that the Shah would not gun them down while the Japanese prime minister was visiting the city. They also knew that the moment would soon come when they would be victorious.

* * *

Nearly a year after the party, Asadollah Alam was seeing the Shah and Shahbanou off as they left for a state visit to the Soviet Union. He asked the Empress if he could take the Crown Prince to the premiere of the documentary about the event. "For goodness' sake, leave me alone," she snapped at him. "I want our names to be utterly dissociated from those ghastly celebrations." Alam, always the deferential courtier, did not state the obvious. It was far too late for that now.

Almost everyone has thrown a disaster of a party and word always gets out. One of the most damaging royal events was that for the coronation of Nicholas II, also the last of his dynasty and a man, like the Shah, cursed with terrible judgment under pressure. His coronation in Moscow would become a byword for disasters, casting a pall over his rule from the start.

Four days after his elaborate coronation with the immense diamond crown of Catherine the Great, Nicholas was to throw a party for the people of Moscow at Khodynka Field, a large area

THE SHAH'S PARTY

of land just outside the city that was used for horse racing and county fairs. The field was next to the Petrovskii Palace, where Tsars traditionally spent the nights before their coronation in the Kremlin cathedral. The Imperial Family had moved up to Moscow from St Petersburg en masse for days of celebrations.

Nicholas had ordered that the celebration for the people of Moscow should be as generous as possible, and word quickly got out that the gifts traditionally on offer would be worth traveling for. Railway lines had opened up across the region, drawing in thousands for the party to be held on one square kilometer of land right in front of the palace. It was unusually warm for May, with many of the spectators soon finding themselves overcome by the heat.

Several stands were set up—for the Imperial family, aristocrats, and those willing to pay for a seat. A large crowd was expected, attracted by the promise of gifts from the monarch: gingerbread, pretzels, sausages, and a commemorative mug. Crowds were larger than expected, with some accounts putting the number at half a million. Inevitably, rumors swelled that they had run out of gifts, causing shoving to start among the crowd. The police force of 1,800 men lost control, and hundreds of people fell into a ditch cut across the land.

The dynamics of crowds are complicated, and they can easily turn into death traps. Surges tend to be fed by people pushing towards something rather than trying to get away in a panic. Inevitably, the victims themselves are blamed, but once there is a certain density of people in a place, physics, or more specifically, fluid dynamics, takes over. If densities get to seven people per square meter, the crowd becomes fluid, with pressure often being applied from one side as more join the group. At that density, people are lifted off their feet, losing shoes and even clothing as they are carried forward. Commonly, their arms are pinned to their sides, so they have no way to climb upwards if they start to go under. People exhale, often in panic, but the crush prevents them from taking in another breath. They die from compressional asphyxiation, either standing or on the ground, when finally, something gives way and the crowd collapses.

As many as 4,000 people died that way on Khodynka Field, although the numbers are uncertain. People had crowded into the space where the gifts were handed out throughout the night. Many were exhausted from long journeys and had not eaten. An early heatwave had engulfed Moscow, making conditions unbearable. At around six in the morning, word went out that distribution had begun. They pressed forward. Attendants tried to divert the direction of the pressing mass of people, but by then, the pressure was too great to do anything. Eventually, the barriers collapsed, and hundreds were crushed under the wooden shoes of those behind them.

"No such holocaust of human victims has been caused by a crowd in the open air, and probably no such ghastly disfigurement of the dead has ever been seen on any modern battlefield," according to the account in *The Times* of London. The crush lasted ten minutes, but it took days to clear the bodies from the ditches and wells that covered the field. But the deaths had occurred in a small area of the large celebration, and by the time the Tsar arrived at about 2 pm, the crowd was back to about half a million people. As the Emperor and Empress appeared on the high balcony of one of the stands, there was a roar of enthusiasm from the crowd; this may have been organized, as was often the case with Russian festivities. The front of the crowd was made up of traditionally dressed peasants, whose representatives joined the Imperial family for lunch in the Petrovskii Palace after the Tsar and Tsarina had waved from the balcony for fifteen minutes.

Conflicting accounts have the crowd dispersing in silence after the deaths. Others have them filling their caps with shit and throwing them at the Tsar, but that is unlikely. It is only mentioned by one Soviet historian writing long after the event. But resentment certainly brewed up from people angered at the lack of preparation and security for the event. While those events involving the Imperial family and aristocrats were all tightly protected, there had not been nearly enough security on the field, even though large numbers of soldiers had been camped nearby.

Even more troubling for many was the fact that the Tsar ordered the parties to continue. On the night of the tragedy, he attended the ball held by the French Ambassador Count Louis-Gustav de Montebello at his residence in the center of Moscow. He had dithered, as usual, over the decision, torn between the advice of his conservative uncles and those who had more concern for what this would mean for the people. His first instinct had been not to attend, encouraged by some of his family, as recorded in the autobiography of his brother-in-law. "Remember, Nicky," said Grand Duke Nikolai Mikhailovich,

> the blood of those five thousand men, women, and children will remain forever a blot on your reign. You cannot revive the dead, but you must show sympathy with their families. Do not let the enemies of the regime say that the young Tsar danced while his murdered subjects were taken to the Potter's Field.

But he did dance, and his enemies took note. Soon pamphlets appeared denouncing the government for failing to hold anyone responsible and for the meagre compensation offered to the families of the dead. "If the people truly managed themselves, would they really permit the waste of two hundred million rubles on the coronation, tsarist feasts, balls, and other such things?" one read. The secrecy of the official investigation inflamed many who, quite rightly, suspected a cover-up. The mismanagement of everything, much of which ultimately came down to decisions made by the Tsar, was a dismal foretaste of his reign.

The tragedy hit educated Russians as yet another sign of their backward, unsympathetic system of government. A careless and exploitative aristocracy ruled over this vast country with no consequences for their seemingly endless stupidity and greed. A man who was ill-equipped for the job in every way was handed absolute power. Many other Russians, more superstitious in their outlook, took it as a terrible augury for the future. Anger slowly built, particularly at the behavior of the Imperial family in the wake of the tragedy. This was compounded by the arrest of around 1,500 students and workers who had gathered at a cemetery six months later to hold a traditional commemoration of the dead. Priests refused to carry out a ceremony, and a detachment of Cossacks was sent to break up the crowd. It was to be a foretaste of the rulers' poor decisions and indifference to the plight of the Russian people.

* * *

Sadegh Khalkhali enjoyed power. The portly ayatollah, a cheerful man with a short beard and a sunny laugh, a fondness for ice cream and kangaroo courts, was the most feared man in Revolutionary Iran. He oversaw the trials and swift executions of hundreds of people, including the former prime minister Amir-Abbas Hoveyda. He reveled in his reputation as a hanging judge. "I killed over 500 criminals close to the royal family," he boasted in his autobiography. "I feel no regret or guilt over the executions," he wrote. "I killed only a few. There were many more who deserved to be killed, but I could not get my hands on them."

Khalkhali had been in Khomeini's circle since the 1950s and was alleged to have run a death squad known as the Fedaiyan-e Islam. He was barely known to the public before the Revolution, perhaps due to his work in the Islamist underground, but he soon became famous when he was appointed the first head of the judiciary in the new regime within a month of its emergence. Khomeini ordered the sweeping away of the laws that had been

THE SHAH'S PARTY

in force for decades and their replacement with Islamic jurisprudence, which often took on novel forms. Hundreds were tried for the previously unknown crimes of "warring against God" or "spreading corruption on earth."

The portly mullah set up shop on what had been renamed Dr. Shariati Street in what had been a military court set up to try the opponents of the Shah. Now it went after his supporters, operating twenty-four hours a day to administer the new justice. On some nights, thirty or forty bodies were taken out through the blue gates of the compound. Photographs of these bodies lying out on a mortuary slab could sometimes be found for sale on the streets.

Hoveyda, Iran's longest-serving prime minister and one of the last ministers of the court under the Pahlavi dynasty, had been arrested by SAVAK in 1978 as the Shah intended that he absorb the blame for the unraveling situation. But the crowds that were spiraling out of control were not assuaged by the sacrifice of the Shah's loyal servant, and the arrest only prompted greater efforts to oust the king. Hoveyda was reluctant to leave Iran as his mother was too sick to travel, and he saw no benefit in heading into exile. When the Shah left, the SAVAK guards abandoned the former minister in the safe house where he was held, and he turned himself in to the new revolutionary guard, expecting to be found innocent of any wrongdoing.

He had not expected to face the law as interpreted by Khalkhali. Seventeen charges were brought against him, ranging from "Fighting God, God's creatures and the Viceroy of Iman Zaman" to smuggling opium. Most of the charges were unprovable in any way, but the court had little interest in evidence. As Abbas Milani, Hoveyda's biographer, wrote:

> It became clear that rules of evidence, notions of innocence until proven guilty, and a dispassionate judge, dispensing impartial judgments based on incontrovertible evidence, were all alien to this court

AFTER THE PARTY

... Gossip had the authority of fact ... and unsubstantiated rumors were taken as proof of guilt.

Pressure to allow him to go in to exile and spare him the ordeal of a trial was considerable, but to no avail. His trial was perfunctory and brutal. Eventually, he would be dragged into a courtyard in the school that was serving as a Revolutionary courthouse. He was shot several times by Hojatoleslam Hadi Ghaffari, known as the "machine gun mullah" due to his love of guns.

Khalkhali's fame grew as he directed the executions of once-powerful figures who had been close to the Shah. As the regime became more radical, he became its avenging angel and international provocateur. He came to international prominence when he was filmed opening the body bags of American servicemen killed in the botched effort to rescue the U.S. Embassy hostages. He poked at the charred bodies with a stick.

He was from a poor farming family and spent his childhood herding goats. A religious education was probably the only way out of a life of grinding rural hardship, and he went far, ending up at the heart of power in the new regime. He became close to Khomeini and was clearly one of the few colleagues who was capable of making the dour man laugh. When he was visited in Qom by the British writer V.S. Naipaul, his humor seemed to center entirely on executions and death; he crowed that his childhood years as a shepherd meant he knew how to behead a sheep.

Demolition became something of a passion for Khalkhali. Shortly after the Revolution, he led a mob of young men to destroy the mausoleum of Reza Shah in Ray, now a suburb of Tehran. The modernist structure, a solid 25-metre tower, was made of granite and reinforced concrete that resisted the sledgehammers. Khalkhali retreated and later sent in engineers with dynamite. It took them twenty days to destroy the building. He ordered the seizing of the most important Bahai religious building, the House of the Bab, in Shiraz. The building was razed along with the surrounding neighborhood, and a mosque was built in its place. It was one of many buildings that he tried to destroy. Among them was the Shahyad Arch. It survived, renamed as the Azadi Monument. He also ordered the closing of Ferdowsi's tomb and other memorials to great Iranians. Anything that revealed the history or diversity of Iranian culture or faith was to be erased.

A particular obsession was the Bahais. This religion was probably the second largest in Iran after Shiism at the time and was a particular source of antagonism for the *ulema*. The faith emerged out of a messianic movement in the nineteenth century known as Babism, which was violently put down in the 1840s. One of the followers of the Sayyed ʿAli-Moḥammad Sirazi, who had proclaimed himself the Bab, or the forerunner of the Twelfth Imam who was to deliver humanity on his return according to Shia beliefs, managed to survive the crackdown and fled to Iraq and then to Istanbul. In 1863, Mirza Hussein Ali Nuri Baha-Allah proclaimed himself the Messianic figure and that he brought with him a new revelation that superseded the Bab's message. In 1873, while under house arrest ordered by the Ottoman authorities, Baha-Allah wrote the Most Holy Book, which laid down the rules of the faith and how it should be organized.

The Shia establishment did everything possible to stem the rapid growth of the faith, which they regarded as heretical and a direct challenge to them. Reza Shah saw them as a potential threat to his administration, closing their schools and refusing to recognize their marriages. The first decade of Mohammad Reza's rule saw a rise in pogroms and attacks against Bahais as state security weakened, and in 1955, possibly to divert attention from an unpopular military alliance with Britain and the United States, the military destroyed the Bahai center in Tehran. Gradually, tensions eased, but the suspicions of the state continued; SAVAK monitored the religion closely. Bahais suffered from the worst of all worlds: they were seen by many as supporters of the Shah and yet still came under the thumb of his secret police.

Worse was to come after the Revolution. More than 200 of the most prominent members of the faith were killed, many on the orders of Khalkhali. All Bahai religious establishments were confiscated and their businesses closed. The state's confiscation of a central membership registry meant they knew all the members of the faith. Civil servants who belonged to the faith were sacked, and large numbers were driven into exile. People who engaged in Bahai marriages were prosecuted for promoting prostitution. Bahais were banned from passing on their religion to their children or sending them to schools. They were not permitted state ration cards. The regime have remained determined to wipe out the followers of this faith. Under international law, the Revolutionary Government's actions amount to an attempted genocide of the Bahais.

In what was seen as another of his greatest crimes, Khalkhali was also involved in the killings of large numbers of Kurds, seen by the Revolutionary Government as a threat because of their demands for autonomy or a federal system. One of those sentenced to death was a doctor there to treat the wounded after a clash between Kurds and the Revolutionary forces. Khalkhali had overstepped his powers and become an embarrassment for those who were trying to present the government as fair and just.

President Bani-Sadr, eager to present a more moderate face of the regime, removed him from his post in 1981 but was still willing to appoint him to be head of a drugs task force. Khalkhali was just as brutal there, executing more than 300 alleged traffickers in just three months, even though before the Revolution, Khomeini had complained of the Shah's brutality in killing such people. Khalkhali would later announce to a crowd an effort to impeach Bani-Sadr, making the gesture for a hanging as the crowd bayed for blood. Bani-Sadr fled the country, boarding an air force jet in

THE SHAH'S PARTY

Tehran dressed as a woman. The former president ended up living in Versailles under the close guard of the French police.

Naipaul interviewed Khalkhali just after the Revolution, when he was at the height of his powers. He saw him again six years later when he was adrift, "completely bald, baby-faced without his turban, head held down against his chest, looking up from below his forehead, eyes without mischief now and seemingly close to tears, as though he wished to dramatize his situation and needed pity."

One of the mullah's obsessions was that Cyrus the Great had been a criminal, a liar, and a homosexual. He should not, therefore, be revered by Iranians, who should look for their heroes only among figures from Islamic history. Before the party, Khalkhali had even written a pamphlet expressing his hatred of Cyrus, pointing out the unreliability of the Cylinder and the Bible as sources attesting to his greatness.

Years later, he decided that the connection that the Shah had tried to make to both Cyrus and Persepolis should be broken. Khalkhali set out for Shiraz, determined to destroy the ruins and burn down the tented city, already in a somewhat bedraggled state after several years of neglect. A crowd gathered to hear him speak about the evils of Cyrus and the need to bulldoze the site. The response was not what he was expecting. The citizens of Shiraz pelted him with stones, and he was forced to retreat. For once, Khalkhali would not get his way.

Khalkhali was a sinister emblem of the Revolution, the smiling, laughing murderer who was said to have taken up a machine gun to execute those he had sentenced. In his autobiography, published in 2000, he named sixty-seven people he had sentenced to death in one sitting. They were taken to the roof of the court and killed immediately. He was repeatedly elected as the representative to the Majlis from Qom, where he taught students at a madrasa.

AFTER THE PARTY

Khalkhali was the embodiment of the indiscriminate violence and terror inflicted on Iranians for decades. Here was a barely educated man with an extreme moral certitude and the power to enforce it. There is no doubt he was relentless in his violence, unrepentant and barbarous. It was all in direct contrast to his wide, cheerful face and sunny demeanor. His daughter later recalled her father as strict but never violent. He never spoke about his past, she said. Fatema Sadeghi admitted her father had "done many bad things to many people," but she had seen little of his violent nature at home. She grew up in a fairly liberal atmosphere, attending university and eventually earning a doctorate. She often espoused secular policies, writing a well-circulated essay against compulsory hijab. Just the sort of thing that might have had her facing a firing squad in her father's day.

* * *

Farah's anger at the press coverage of the party was still evident years later when she published an updated, and far more open, autobiography.

> Of all the tasks that fell to me in the preparation for the festivities, coping with (the press) was the most difficult and depressing, for just as I had predicted, a wave of acerbic criticisms about expenditures on luxuries slowly arose from the West. The journalists got on this hobbyhorse and rode it again and again. What kind of monarchy is dressed by Lanvin and eats at Maxim's when its people still sometimes lack food and schools? ... A final fireworks display was held on this occasion, and, in the last group photo, I can clearly be seen giving a sign of relief.

The decisions made in the planning of the event were a premonition of those to come in the 1970s. Security dominated everything, meaning that ordinary people were left out of the events, and the Imperial family became ever more isolated. The Shah's

323

THE SHAH'S PARTY

minions tended towards decisions that reinforced the ossified and brittle approaches of the court.

But many of the assessments at the time and those that came much later were fairly positive. "It could have been a disaster," the British Ambassador wrote. "The boldness of the challenge was hubristic and invited nemesis. The Shah would have suffered a monumental loss of face if only minor relations of monarchs, a posse of Sheikhs and colorless figures representing Heads of State had sat down to supper in tented splendor on 14 October." But with precise British superciliousness, he went on to muse that "The Persian is a poet, not an administrator."

* * *

The portrayal of the Persepolis celebration followed a pattern that would have been familiar to Greeks going back to Plato: Persia was all about luxury, femininity, decay, and decadence. The reversal of fortune, the end came like that of Darius, forced to wander in the desert, held in golden shackles, an emblem of defeat that was played out over and over. The coverage of the Shah, of Iran in the 1970s, of Persepolis, and of the coming of the Revolution echoes the language of Herodotus; indeed, a great many quoted his line saying, with admiration, that Persians were always the quickest to adopt foreign ways. "As soon as they discover a luxury, they are quick to make it their own."

Some of the most influential coverage was by Sally Quinn, the forthright society columnist of *The Washington Post*. Known for her insider take on the American capital, often derided as "Hollywood for ugly people," she was a skilled, if somewhat provincial, writer who was sent off to cover the events in one of her first forays into foreign coverage. The fact that *The Washington Post* sent her rather than a foreign correspondent showed what they thought of the event. This was not the Congress of Vienna. It was a party attended by Imelda Marcos and Cristina Ford.

AFTER THE PARTY

Quinn's first article, written in Washington, showed the utter lack of sophistication among the court media handlers. Instead of playing up the culture of Persia, the antiquity of imperial rule, the importance of discussions among those gathering in Persepolis, or any other positive aspect, an initial press briefing from the Iranian Embassy focused almost entirely on the extravagance of the event. Quinn wrote it up in minute detail, immediately grasping that the core of the story would be its excess. "You can just say that no common people will be there," she quoted an embassy spokesman as saying. "They will all be very high up."

The main stylistic device in Quinn's article was *accumulatio*, the piling up of detail in a way that mirrored the excesses of the event. It was a common approach of Greek writers, too, when describing the Persians. The article spread across five pages of the newspaper, pointing out the dimensions of the tents ("In the blue and white reception hall, 112 feet in diameter with a 20-foot domed ceiling covered in red silk, will hang 20 crystal chandeliers"), the yardage of trimming and canvas (12,000 and 20,000 respectively), and the requirements of the 30 hairdressers ("100 kilograms of hair pins, 3,000 rollers, 50 liters of concentrated shampoo, 2,000 bottles of lacquer, 200 bottles of plant brilliantine, 100 kilograms of wigs and 300 brushes and combs from Carita and Alexandre as well as 400 pairs of false eyelashes (which cost 10 dollars each) 30 liters of face cleansers and lotions and dozens of different foundations and eyeshadows from Elizabeth Arden.").

Including excess upon excess had the desired effect. The party looked grotesque, a sign of the appalling nature of a regime that had lost any sense of perspective. A sketched history of the Pahlavis made the point that this was all part of some nouveau riche striving. The last few paragraphs contained a less-than-subtle dig at the Shah and his pretensions, mentioning that historians believed the Cyrus Cylinder, the motto of the event, was pure propaganda and showed the skill of Cyrus in promoting his rule. "His Imperial Majesty will have his chance to prove he can hold his own against Cyrus come October."

The journalists hated being cooped up in Shiraz, so far from the tent city. The mishandling of the media by the inexperienced palace staff, who had never dealt with the rude, multi-headed beast that is the international media unleashed, made it all worse. Boasting about the extravagance of the event had set it up for failure, particularly in a country where inequality was so visible. The British historian, Robert Steele, has urged a reconsideration of just how useful the event was, saying that not only did it put the Shah and Iran on the map as his power was growing, but that bringing together international figures at a time of tensions was a worthwhile endeavor.

But few saw it that way at the time. Under the dismissive headline "Dust Settles on the Shah's Picnic," Patrick O'Donovan of *The Observer* wrote of all the guests packing their bags and returning home. "Yet nothing happened," he wrote.

> No one made any political statements. It can only be reported that the Kings and Presidents and the largest press corps I have ever seen were all at once, eccentrically, in the same country … It would be easy to hail this as the greatest non-event of our time, a creation of a royal despotism taking advantage of a bedazzled media.

It was no surprise that the Shah hated the British press. For them, he was a cartoonish figure who brought out the worst of British superiority. British journalists had so many reasons to take exception to the Shah: his Frenchified world; the gaucheness of his personality; his boastfulness about the future of Iran; his occasional brusqueness when confronted by the media. But what might have rattled them most was the realization that the Shah was focused on Iranian national interests, not on being a well-behaved puppet.

AFTER THE PARTY

"All this was not quite the vanity of a man who does not have kingly blood," wrote O'Donovan.

> It was an expensive and carefully crafted act of state. (The fact that it might help the tourist trade is incidental). It was a somewhat disturbing assertion of Iranian identity. Beneath the jeweled crown and the Islamic culture, the Shah has created a new type of nation. It is not on anyone's side.

O'Donovan was a well-regarded correspondent for *The Observer* in its heyday, an Anglo-Irishman educated at Ampleforth and Oxford who had enjoyed "a good war" in the Irish Guards. Not an Establishment voice but one that perhaps reflected the decline of the United Kingdom. Here, the Shah was announcing his presence on the stage just as Britain was exiting.

In an assessment of the event written for *The New York Times*, Charlotte Curtis also emphasized an emptiness at the heart of the events.

> The question is that was the Imperial encampment at Persepolis anything more than Iran's moment in the sun.
>
> The celebration worked despite high-level infighting—mostly concerning the French overlay to what Empress Farah had hoped would be a purely Persian anniversary—and a bureaucracy so incompetent that it dispatched Teheran taxi drivers to Shiraz to chauffeur distinguished visitors through what to the drivers was totally foreign territory.

The New York Times ponderously summed up its view in an editorial:

> The anniversary celebration opening today in Persepolis, the ancient Persian capital, is extravagantly overdone. The Shah has erected a Scheherazade dream world of air-conditioned tents for attending heads of state and their representatives from half a hundred countries. They will sit on velvet-covered "thrones" and be served food

THE SHAH'S PARTY

from Maxim's of Paris, by waiters in $800 uniforms airlifted from Switzerland. This may be in the best tradition of Persian potentates, but it hardly befits a modernizing nation still heavily in debt and afflicted with widespread poverty. Its current capital, Teheran, does not even have a sewage system.

Every effort is being made in connection with the celebration to identify the present Shah with the ancient "King of Kings." But Shah Pahlavi, who was put on the throne by the British during World War II and who retained it only after C.I.A. intervention during the Mossadegh uprisings in 1953, is no Cyrus. Nor should he aspire to be, beyond emulating the ancient ruler's reputation for tolerance and justice.

"What do we care what our critics think?" the Shah told the media at his only press conference during the celebration. "The important thing is the impression of my own people." That has always been difficult to ascertain. Many Iranians would have seen it on television, despite the efforts by left-wing guerrillas to blow up power lines. It must have seemed remote, cinematic, and foreign to many. Many grumbled that cities had been cleaned up only for visiting foreigners. Of course, opinions were divided depending on support for the Shah, but given the nationalism of Iranians, many must have felt a sense of pride after so many decades of humiliation. Although there had been royal visits and presidential stopovers, never before had such a large contingent of the great and the good descended on the country. Fifty years later, it is a source of pride among some Iranians on the internet, with hundreds of Pinterest sites dedicated to the elaborate displays of the Imperial family and the party.

"It was a Field of the Cloth of Gold without a purpose. It was the Congress of Vienna without any business. It was a picnic of unparalleled vulgarity," sneered O'Donovan. "By this fantastic gathering of the famous, we have been told there is a new power in the second rank of nations."

AFTER THE PARTY

The Shah might have liked the final line of O'Donovan's scornful judgment. The event had been aimed to show that Iran was back on the world stage and that it commanded both global respect and regional power in one of the most closely watched parts of the globe. The reporting emphasized the magnificence over the significance, mostly because there was no immediate or consequential diplomatic outcome. But it was almost certainly a success in the way the Shah intended; dozens of world leaders came to Iran, and the world's attention was focused on the ways in which the country was emerging as a regional force. By inviting the sheikhs of the newly independent nations on the southern coast of the Persian Gulf, mostly at the urging of the British, who were keen to promote their protégés, the Shah ensured that they were all seen to pay obeisance to him. Likewise the attendance of figures from so many of the world's geopolitical rivals—China, the Soviet Union, India, Pakistan, South Africa, Ethiopia, and others—showed how he was carving an independent way through the difficult politics of the time while signaling to rivals in such countries as Iraq that he was far ahead of them in terms of building international ties.

The Economist Intelligence Unit offered an upbeat take on the event.

> Despite foreign criticism of the expenditures incurred for the celebrations, the formalities were excellently presented and well received on the domestic front, where extravagance at the personal level is as marked among the peasants as among the monarchs and where the weighty considerations of reputation and hospitality are better understood than in the Western press. Overseas, the long-term impact has already emerged. Iran is now known by repute and location and may expect to be more seriously treated than in the past.

Inevitably, the costs pulled focus from the other aspects of the events, and this was not just a concern for the foreign reporters

THE SHAH'S PARTY

whose negative reporting was tainted by the view that the Pahlavis were parvenus with an inflated sense of themselves. Many correspondents drew on deep cultural prejudices about Iran: a land still seen through a classical lens as barbarous, extravagant, and excessive.

It took many years for the full domestic effects of the party to emerge, and even then, it was one factor among many on the growing list of problems that would affect the country as the 1970s progressed. Domestically, the event did little to promote a sense of national identity in the near term, although it did ultimately create an enduring connection between Iranians' ideas about themselves and their distant history. Cyrus and the Achaemenids are more a part of how people see themselves and their nation than at any time since, in part, because even the Islamic government has had to adopt nationalist symbols re-established under the Pahlavis.

The events were seen with a mix of pride at their celebration of the nation's long history and rich culture, and resentment at the exclusion of so many. The Pahlavi dynasty inspires a similar mixed view. Almost everything positive in Iran today—the many educated men and women, a developed sense of history and culture, infrastructure, even the strong sense of political autonomy and independence—originated under the last two Shahs. The push to create a modern, unified nation at a rapid pace came with some high costs: the lack of political development and the weakness of institutions opened the door to religious dictatorship when the Shah was overthrown, and the stifling of freedoms created an atmosphere of paranoia and conspiracies that stimulated the populism of Khomeini. Nevertheless, it would be hard to point to a period in Iranian history that raised living standards more or allowed a greater degree of freedom and security. The Pahlavis fell short in many ways, but not nearly to the extent of those who came before and after.

AFTER THE PARTY

International opinion only worsened with time, as the costs were exaggerated and the benefits diminished. C.L. Sulzberger, a journalist and a member of the family who owns *The New York Times*, packed in many easy stereotypes of Iran in an assessment of the Shah written in 1972: "One might offhand be tempted to think of the gaudy tent town, with its mushroom dwellings, butler's pantries and ivory dial telephones as farcical replicas of the cruel, hard monolith towering above in ruined splendor."

Perhaps the most coruscating view came from the American diplomat George Ball, who had attended the coronation in 1967. "What an absurd, bathetic spectacle! The son of a colonel in a Persian Cossack regiment play-acting as the emperor of a country with an average per capita income of $250 a year, proclaiming his achievements in modernizing his nation while accoutered in the raiment and symbols of ancient despotism," Ball wrote in his 1982 autobiography.

> No wonder we talked among ourselves about the fragility of an anachronistic structure that compounded the doubtful expectancy of an absolute monarch with wasteful display. It was, I thought, a deliberate insult to the wretchedly poor with whom the country abounded. Still, though the prodigality of Versailles had nothing on the Golestan Palace, the greatest affront was not to come until four years later. Then the Shah and his queen spent $120 million on an opulent pageant at Persepolis that enriched not Omar the Tentmaker, but Pierre the Tentmaker and the other luxury merchants of Paris who handled the arrangements. A few minor heads of state showed up to keep company with Spiro Agnew, but the world was either too polite or too humorless to laugh.

* * *

How much did the party cost? Well, should we include the airports and new roads, the satellite communications, the power plants and lines, and the building of more than 2,500 schools?

THE SHAH'S PARTY

Should we consider the donations from the many businesses that had done well out of Pahlavi rule and were perhaps strong-armed into making bigger donations than they otherwise might have given? What about the vast gate built in Tehran and the museum it houses? If one considers all expenditures in the years ahead of the celebration, then it might have run into tens of millions of dollars. Otherwise, it is hard to imagine some of the figures, which run into the billions in some cases, being anything other than exaggerations. But these figures emerged even before the party had taken place, in part because of the clumsy way in which the Iranian government handled the press and because they revealed far too much about some of the more ridiculous expenses—400 pairs of fake eyelashes from Elizabeth Arden at $10 each.

Most of the more realistic figures put the cost at less than $20 million, which would be around $140 today. That includes costs such as the immense security operation and the logistics of getting everyone to Persepolis and putting them up. The figures of a billion dollars or more are absurd, even when counting the airports, hotels, a stadium, roads, schools, and museums that were all part of a development plan that was much needed in a country lacking modern infrastructure. Almost all of them were necessary components in a plan to build tourism, an industry that was growing rapidly at the time.

Before the party had even been planned, there was muttering about extravagance. Academics who had been organized into committees ahead of what had been expected to be a quiet, mostly intellectual celebration of the anniversary were concerned about what it had become. By the time the party happened, *The Washington Post* and others were reporting costs in the hundreds of millions, which would be billions of dollars today.

Alam told reporters just after the event that the costs were $16.6 million. About a third went on the design and construction

AFTER THE PARTY

of the monument to the Pahlavis that still stands in Tehran today, but is now called the Azadi Monument. Entertainment costs were $2.3 million, which Alam said was about one quarter of one per cent of the state's budget at the time. Quite a lot to spend on a party, but nothing on the scale that was being alleged.

The tent city cost $6.3 million, of which one million was spent on the banqueting tent alone. It was supposed to recoup its expenses by being leased to Club Med as a tourist hotel. The French company withdrew from the deal when it was discovered that the sewerage and water system had barely coped with the three-day event and would not be able to meet the demands of a tourist hotel. The project had not been planned with tourism in mind and lacked many of the facilities that a hotel would need. The large tents that had been used for the banquets and receptions were put to use as a conference center on occasions, but soon the desert sands, the blistering sun, and the powerful winds that blew through the area took their toll on the blue and white canvas.

Alam remained on the defensive, telling a press conference: "The proud and glorious Iranian nation was, and shall always be, prepared to forego even its daily necessities in order to help restore the ancient grandeur of this proud land."

POSTSCRIPT

"... no memory remains of these kings except the words of men, who say that one had nobility of soul and that the other did not, who blame one and celebrate the other. In our turn, we too shall pass away."

Ferdowsi, *The Shahnameh*, Book 35

In early 2018, workmen digging up a site in Tehran near a shrine to a Shia saint found a mummified body. A workman posted a photograph of the corpse on social media, and word soon spread. Embalmed and wrapped bodies are unusual in Iran, where the custom is to bury the dead in a simple shroud without any measures to preserve them. Talk immediately turned to whether it might be the body of Reza Shah, the father of Mohamed Reza.

Nobody knows what happened to the remains of Reza Shah, whose body had been preserved after his death in South Africa in 1944. He was entombed in Egypt for a while before returning to Iran. He was re-buried in a large modernist mausoleum in 1951. This building would eventually be blown up after the Revolution, but his body was not found. This possible ghostly re-emergence set off nostalgia for his rule. What was needed, some in the neighborhood said, was a strong man like Reza Shah to come in and fix the chaos in the country. Iranians live in a state of permanent uncertainty brought about by a government that has failed them for decades. Population growth outstripped economic progress, inequality worsened, and the once growing middle class retreated into a life of penury and disappointment.

Growing resentment at the religious leadership and their security forces has led to a series of mass protests, starting with the Green Movement in 2009. The limits on democracy, personal freedoms, and economic failure have steadily expanded the numbers joining street demonstrations. In 2022, the killing of Mahsa Amini, a young ethnic Kurdish woman, who was taken into custody for not wearing her hijab in the prescribed manner, set off a wave of angry crowds demanding change. Each wave of protest has been different; this time, many demonstrations were led by women, and the chant, taken up across the country, was for *Zan! Zedagi! Azadi!*—Women! Life! Freedom!

In the 1970s, Khomeini would win the battle of slogans, but his successors have lost a more complex war, one that still leaves a dark shadow over Iran. The current system of religious dominance of the higher reaches of society has created a catastrophic gulf between the people and their rulers. A foreigner in Iran only has to wait a few moments before a stranger will sidle up to them and say how much they hate the mullahs. Everywhere you go, there are stories of deep disappointment: a business closed during difficult economic times; a job given to the less qualified but better-connected person; or a nasty and humiliating encounter with the religious police. Many visitors to Iran are struck by the astonishing hospitality and generosity of people not yet soured by mass tourism. But just as noticeable is the yawning rift between people—most notably the majority that live in cities—and the government.

Mohammad Reza was a flawed man who left behind some troubling legacies. His regime used torture; it allowed entrenched corruption; it stifled demands for a more open democratic system; it adopted a grandiose vision of Iran's place in the world

POSTSCRIPT

that worried its neighbors and overstretched its finances. These proved to be precedents, even examples, for much worse behavior by the Islamic Republic, which has far exceeded its predecessor in all manner of terrible acts, to the massive detriment of the Iranian people. A single example: the Iranian Supreme Leader Ayatollah Khamenei controls an organization that has amassed real estate and other assets worth $95 billion. The Headquarters for Executing the Order of the Imam, also known as *Setad*, is a vast and secretive business enterprise controlled by a single individual. Much of its wealth comes from confiscating property owned by minorities and Iranians living abroad. While Khamenei lives a fairly modest life by all accounts, this enormous empire of stolen wealth empowers him massively and creates a culture of corruption and state abuse that dominates the economy, obliterating opportunity for those without connections. It allows the supreme leader to operate outside the control of any elected official, and it gives him economic resources that dwarf those controlled by anyone else in the country.

Khomeini's system of religious rule is still firmly in place, but for how long? Anger burns across Iran. It is like a fire that smolders in a deep seam of coal, sometimes bursting above ground. Enormous wealth is held by very few, while the vast majority suffer economic collapse. Unfortunately, international sanctions have only contributed to this; only those with connections within the Islamic establishment stand a good chance of evading them. Shady dealings are now the defining aspect of the economy. State violence has far exceeded anything under the Pahlavis; currently, thousands are in prison, arrested in recent rounds of protests. Executions, carried out by hanging, are common; the country kills more of its citizens relative to its population than any other on the planet. Minorities are abused to the degree that a charge of genocide would be justified against Iranian leaders for their treatment of Bahais.

THE SHAH'S PARTY

The terrible violence to come was inevitable, given both the religious totalitarianism pushed by Khomeini and the populist rhetoric that only he could rule Iran. Alas, the Shah had opened the door to this and to other disasters under the Islamic Republic. His embrace of the idea that he had been chosen by God, rather than the people, was, in its way, mimicked by Khomeini's idea of the Guardianship of the Faithful. His bouts of xenophobia and embrace of conspiracy theories ultimately led down a path to the hostility and violence the Revolutionary Government showed to foreign governments and any of its citizens who wanted links to the wider world. The Shah's concentration of power was also replicated in a way by the new regime, with merely perfunctory nods to democracy and accountability. Likewise, the Shah's tolerance of corruption, particularly by his family, is now part of a system in which the children of clerics drive supercars and spend their weekends partying in Dubai. Those known sarcastically as *aghazadeh*, or "noble born," flaunt their wealth on Instagram through selfies with their customized Cadillac SUVs and pet tigers.

The rapid growth of cities and the lack of effective support for rural life contributed to the Shah's downfall and are still reflected in economic problems to this day. The White Revolution may have been worthy in its aims, but it was poorly designed and implemented, transferring wealth to landowners, rather than farmers, and not regenerating the systems that managed rural life. It contributed to industrialization, but it also led to a massive expansion of urban populations that lacked housing or other support. Sudden urbanization can be highly destabilizing: it was the urban poor that made up Khomeini's support base.

On the positive side of the ledger, Pahlavi rule created a number of enduring trends in the country. There is a strong belief in and general desire for education. A century ago, when the Pahlavi dynasty began, Iran had only a handful of very basic institutes of

POSTSCRIPT

higher education covering medicine, law, military studies, and political sciences. Tehran University was only founded in 1934. Today, there are fifty-four state universities and 289 private institutes of higher education. The Shah's embrace of education also involved the state paying for tens of thousands of students to study abroad. Many of those on government scholarships played key roles in his overthrow. The expansion of the student population was dramatic: it rose tenfold from 1953 to more than 150,000 by the time of the Shah's exile.

Iran's cultural life also burgeoned under the Shah, even with the bouts of heavy-handed and often absurd censorship. The roots of globally recognized worlds of literature, art, and film emerged from the mix of imperial patronage, wealth, and underground resistance. All contributed in their way to the emergence of a modern artistic identity that is unmatched in the Middle East despite the repression of the Islamic regime. Iran was decades ahead of its neighbors in recognizing the importance of museums and other cultural institutes in the development of a modern society, a national identity, and a diverse economy. As a result, it still has some world-class collections, internationally recognized artists, and a deep sense of its own heritage.

Far from being solely intoxicated by the West and ideas of modernization, the Pahlavis revived interest and knowledge of the long and rich history of Iran. Although much of this was driven by dynastic and nationalist imperatives, the development of knowledge of ancient Iran survived all attempts by the Revolutionary Government to minimize the importance of anything except Islam. Just after the revolution, an American historian, Richard Frye, who had lived in Iran for decades, said he believed that all the efforts put into the promotion of archaeology and history had no effect on anyone. That may have been the case at the time, but in the long run, it has had an impact. Today, this history brings Iranians together around the world in

THE SHAH'S PARTY

a sense of pride at their extraordinary achievements over the centuries. The Shah was ridiculed for comparing himself to Cyrus the Great, but by embracing this history, he had an enormous effect on the identity of Iranians. Increasingly, they are rejecting the Islamic identity pushed on them for more than four decades and seeing themselves in the more ancient sense of as Persians. It was always going to be impossible to stifle that part of the national identity. In recent years, the authorities have closed off the area around Cyrus's tomb in Pasargadae to prevent public commemorations during the Nowruz new year holidays. Embracing the past only goes so far.

Khomeini's intent from before the Revolution was to remake Iranians into a new, purely Shia people following only his vision. This was made clear in his writings, although it was ignored by many whose sole focus was on getting rid of the Shah. No aspect of life would remain untouched by his intrusion of Islamic law, his novel theological precepts, and his personal prejudices. He had no time for the idea of a government that simply maintained order on the streets and allowed people to do whatever they wanted at home.

The result of this has been a society that has steadily turned its back on his beliefs and, in many cases, returned to traditional pre-Islamic ideas of faith and much more modern ideas of democracy. Iranians of all stripes have made it increasingly clear that they want to live in a "normal" country—one that does not interfere with its neighbors, trades with its friends, is allied to the West as well as other nations, and allows its people to live their lives in freedom. People want more economic and personal security. They want to live without having faith forced on them in a society that embraces diversity and modernity. They want to live without anyone insisting they hold a monopoly on the truth. Iran's population is simply too sophisticated and educated to want to live under autocratic rule any longer.

POSTSCRIPT

We do not have access to the polling and research that would be available in an open society, but there are ways of gleaning information about broad trends in Iran. A study by researchers at Stanford University found that many accounts that sent out supportive tweets about the regime were "Astroturf" writers—essentially fake accounts set up to give the impression of grassroots support for the government. Opposition accounts, many of them abroad, seemed to have a much greater reach. We do not know how much of this negative information about the regime spreads, but Iranian engagement on social media seems to be significant despite all the efforts of the government to limit it. We do know that many young Iranians have been willing to risk their lives to demand something more than the system as it is.

The fact that the widespread outrage over the killing of Mahsa Amini has united people of various ethnicities, classes, and religions in opposition to the clerics is potentially transformative in the longer term, as is the leadership of women in this uprising. The fact that much of the protesting has been inspired by women illustrates the extent of change in Iran, the seeds of which were planted under the Pahlavis. The recognition under their rule that a modern developing nation could not ignore half its population led to a massive expansion in educational opportunities. Women were admitted to the University of Tehran in 1937, some thirty-two years before they were allowed to study at Yale. Now, more women than men graduate from Iranian universities, but sadly, this is often the peak of their opportunities, given the sexism that pervades workplaces and government policies.

The decades of modernization under the Pahlavis were challenging and faced waves of resistance, large and small, culminating in their overthrow in 1979. But in the long sweep of history, were these two kings right to have pushed to drag their nation out of the doldrums? They had little choice if Iran was to survive as a nation. Afghanistan was in a similar economic and political state as Iran in 1925, but lacked a monarch with the drive and intensity of Reza Shah. By 1960, Iran's per capita GDP was four times that of Afghanistan. Now, for all its economic problems, Iran has a GDP ten times that of its neighbor, which has now seen a century of at best fitful development and seemingly endless conflict. Not only has Afghanistan endured tragic levels of violence for fifty years, but it has seen its neighbors and others interfere relentlessly. Autonomy has been a pipe dream. Afghanistan is a failed state in every possible way.

Iran might have suffered a similar fate. In 1925, there were fewer than twenty industrial plants in the country; by 1941, that number had risen to 800. Mohammad Reza's unreal vision in the 1970s of overtaking Britain and matching Japan as an industrial power was never going to be realized in a country with uneven development and shortages of well-trained people, but he still lifted Iran out of a quagmire and turned it into a nation that had great potential. Alas, it is heavily burdened by corruption and state mismanagement, two problems that emerged under the Shah and have only become much worse since. They will endure as long as democracy is smothered.

The level of freedom enjoyed by Iranians has risen and fallen, depending on the weakness of their leaders. Before 1925, they mostly lived at the whims of local aristocrats and tribal chiefs with little recourse to any law. Up until 1941, they were under the growing control of Reza Shah and his expanding state, although this also brought with it some security and predictability. The early years of his son's rule were fairly open until democracy ended with the 1953 coup. A decade later, Mohammad Reza was able to expand his control until it tipped into the grandiosity and wastefulness of the 1970s, in which he squandered many of the possibilities of the time by failing to open up the political space and allow Iranians more of a voice. By the time his regime was on the rocks and he began reforms, it was too late to

POSTSCRIPT

stem the Revolution. The greatest tragedy of his rule was the mistakes that led to this.

But the Shah's regime always contained within it the possibility of democracy through a constitutional monarchy, whereas the current system in Iran is designed to prevent any political opening, no matter how often the people take to the streets to demand change. Ultimately, power resides in the hands of one man, whatever infighting takes place below him. When the rule of mullahs is said to be handed down by God, it is difficult to reform, as successive attempts have shown. On top of this, it is designed to resist the sort of revolution that brought it to power, with several competing security agencies and mechanisms to limit the power of different institutions. The power to weed out any opponents from elections and the multiple networks of coercion and corruption make it hard to see a way out. Those who captured the Revolution from the mix of leftists, nationalists and others in 1979 learned from the mistakes of their predecessor by establishing coup-proof security and ensuring that economic opportunities and political power are sufficiently distributed among loyalists to ensure the system has some resilience. The regime is willing to kill a limitless number of people to stay in power, something the Shah found impossible. The government killed more than 500 people, including seventy-seven children, in 2022 alone, adding to a total over forty years that is a large multiple of all the violent deaths under Pahlavi rule. Iran executed 841 people in the first eight months of 2025.

More nuanced assessments of the Pahlavis have emerged in recent years alongside the nostalgia in Iran for a past that is remembered as much easier than the immensely challenging present of economic collapse, international opprobrium, and persistent political repression. Partly this is due to the horrors that followed Pahlavi rule: the mass murders, the Iran-Iraq war, the daily violence and humiliations at the hands of the religious

THE SHAH'S PARTY

police and others. But it is also to do with an ever-expanding recognition that, for all his many faults, Mohammad Reza allowed a far greater level of freedom and opportunity than Khomeini or his successor Khamenei. There was a far more diverse, cosmopolitan, and open expression of culture in all its forms. Women enjoyed a far wider array of choices about how to live their lives. Iran today is a warning to all those choosing populist leaders: the results will be violence, censorship, poverty, isolation, and profound regret.

Progress in the 1970s did not mean leaving the country, as so many young people in Iran now feel it does. There were far more possibilities, and far more people were able to take advantage of them. The Revolution failed in almost all its aims except the acquisition of power: Iranians are probably less religious and more engaged with Western culture than ever before, despite the efforts of the state. They have less freedom, less security, and fewer chances to improve their lives. The clerics have utterly discredited themselves with their violence, intolerance, intrusion, and, more than anything, their corruption. The cycles of protest accelerate, and the brutality needed to crush them intensifies. Most of the young no longer feel that they have anything to lose, so they may as well take to the streets, even if that means imprisonment, torture, or death. The fearless young women knocking the turbans off the heads of mullahs have the measure of their rulers. *Zan, Zendegi, Azadi*!

NOTES

PROLOGUE

Background on the Achaemenid world comes from Llewellyn-Jones, L. (2013), (2017), (2018), and (2022). The latter work covers the history from the view of the Persians rather than the Greeks. See also, Mallowan, M. and Gershevitch, I. (1985).

Relationship with the United States is from Alvandi, R. (2014). Afkhami (2009) mentions the women flown in from Madame Claude in Paris. Economic data is from Esfahani, H. S., and Pesaran, M.H. (2009). Philip Larkin's quote is from his poem *Annus Mirabilis*, first published in his 1974 collection *High Windows*.

Details of *Bunte* magazine from: "60 Jahre Bunte", Bunte (in German), 27 March 2008, and Köpf, P. (2002). More on Masoumeh Ebtekar at Azizi, A. (2019). Caryl, C. (2013), captures the strange confluence of political events in 1979/80. Shawcross (1988) covers the exile and death of the Shah. Events at Pasargadae: Housego, D. (1971), Rais, G. (1971).

1
BEFORE THE PARTY

Vick, B. E. (2014) and (2015) details the history of the Congress of Vienna. Davis, D. (2006) covers Truman Capote's Black and White Ball. Hyde,

NOTES

S. (2022) covered the Proust Ball held shortly after the Persepolis celebration. Bender. A (2020), Skelton, G. (1989) wrote of Malcolm Forbes' party in Tangiers.

Azizi (2010) writes of smallpox eradiation in Iran. Fenner, F. (2022) examines the global eradication. Ilic, I. and Ilic, M. (2022) recap the history of the Yugoslav outbreak. Arabian S. et al. (2025) examine the early history of the disease in Iran. Kotar S. L. and Gessler G. E. (2013) examine the global history of the virus. Hendersen D. A. (2009) recounts his role in the eradication.

Ansari A. M.'s PhD thesis (1998) and article (2001) cover the Shah's role in the White Revolution and some of the failures of the land reform. Craig, D. (1978), Majd, M. G. (2000). Milani, A. (2004), Keddie, N. (1971), Mahdavy, H. (1965), Ramazani, R. K. (1974), Theberge, R. (1973), Willcocks, M. J. (2016) and Summitt, A. R. (2004) looked at the U.S. pressure for reform. The Shah authored his own account of the White Revolution: Pahlavi, M. R. (1967). Saikal A. (1979) and Abrahamian E. (2018) both cover the period in detail. Razi, G. H. (1968) looked at the press and the White Revolution.

2
THE PARTY PLANNER

Steele R. (2020) provides much of the background and history of the celebrations, particularly the role of Shojaeddin Shafa. Afkhami, G. R. (2009), Alamir, D. (1971), Alam, A., and Alikhani, A. (1991), Browne, M. (1971), Hess, J. (1971), Granger, R. (2002), Green (2019), Kashfi (2021), Jenkins, L. (1971), MERIP Reports (1971), Randal, J. (1971), Rouleau, E. (1971), and Zia-Ebrahimi (2016) cover the Party. Shafa self-published his life story (Shafa, 2000). FCO (1971), written by the British Ambassador, contains many details of the celebrations, as does his interview with the Iranian Oral History Project at Harvard University. See: Ladjevardi, H. (1985).

NOTES

3
THE VENUE

Quote about the Greeks stripping wealth after the Battle of Platea is from Herodotus' *Histories*. 9:80. Herodotus (2009). Background on tents comes from Abbott, J. A. et al (2006), Apple. R. W. (1982), Burke, J. (2001), Mann, A. (1971), as well as interviews. The history of tents comes from Andrews, P. A. (1999), Bevan, R. (2015), Chowdhury, Z. (2015), Collins, A. W. (2017), Dode, Z. (2018), Durand-Guédy, D. (2018), Ferrero, G. (1901), Gervers, M., and Schlepp, W. A. (1997), Homan, M. M. (2000), Nibley, H. (1966), O'Kane, B. (2021), Pursey (2019), and Saidel, B. A. (2009), *New York Times* (1971), Wilber, D. N. (1979), Wright, G. R. H. (1958).

Russell, J. G. (1969) and Richardson G. (2013) write of the Field of the Cloth of Gold. Briant, P. (1982), Bahadori, A., and Miri, N. (2024), Naiden, F. S., Talbert, R. J. A. (2017), and Potts, D. T. (2013), write about the political nomadism of the Achaemenids.

Llewellyn-Jones L. (2013, 2018, 2022) writes extensively on Persepolis, along with Morgan, J. (2017), Babaie, S., and Grigor, T. (2015), Bahadori, A., and Miri, N. (2024), Canepa, M. P. (2010), (2018), Grigor, T. (2005), Spier, J. et al. (2022), Mallowan, M., and Gershevitch, I. (1985), and Mousavi, A. (2012). On Dawson's Field hijackings and the security situation in the early 1970s, see: Carlton, D. (2005), Department of State (1970), Hobson, A. (2020), Irving, S. (2012), Khaled, L. and Hajjar, G. (1973) Klenka, M. (2019), Porat, (2022), Sheehi, S. (2025), and Sohrabi, N. (2019).

The story of Sadiq Behdad's arrest comes from the Department of State (1972). On SAVAK: Afkhami, G. R. (2008), Cohen, R.A. (2015), Delannoy, C. (1990), Faroughy A. (1974), Ladjaevardi, H (1998), Nasr, V. (1991), Nematollahi, J., and Sayyad, A. (2024), Rahnema, A. (2023), Sale, R.T. (1977), Shannon, M.K. (2017) Wainwright, D. (2019). On Emadeddin Baghi, see: Kadivar, C. (2005), Martin Ennals Award (2009), Rubin, E. (2003), Tucker, S. C. (2017), Yong (2010).

On Siakhal and the Fadai, see: Vahabzadeh. P (2010) (2022), also Abrahamian, E. (1980), Ascherson, N. (1972), Moghadam, V. (1987),

NOTES

Rahnema, A. (2021), Randjbar et al (2023), *Washington Post* Foreign Service (1972). On security, see: CIA (1971) and Department of State (1971), *Financial Times* (1971), Marsden, E. (1971), Zabih, S. (1982).

4
THE GUESTS

On the arrivals, see: *Washington Post* (1971), (1971). On Chinese relations with Iran, see: Figueroa W. (2020) and (2024), Szulc, T. (1971). On Lin Biao, see: Teiwes, F. C., and Sun, W. (1996), Qiu, J. (2025), Yao, M., and Karnow, S. (1983). On Kuo Mojo, see Birch, C., et al. (1991) and Leys, S. (2013). Cristina Ford, see: *Life* Magazine, (1971). On Marcos, see: Curtis, C. (1971).

On relations with the United States, see Alvandi, R. (2014) for the most detailed study of this time. Also, Bayandor, D. (2018), Grenier, C. (1971), Herrera, E. J. (2007), McGlinchey, S. (2014), Randal, J. (1971), Department of State (1971) on India. Quotes about the Shah from Department of State (1972). *Centers of Power in Iran*. On Nixon: Kissinger, H. (1971), Department of State (1972). President's Visit: Joint Communique, Alvandi, R. (2014), Curtis, C. (1971).

On the United Kingdom and Queen Elizabeth II, see: Aldrich, R. J. (2021). Behravesh, M. (2012). Longinotti, E. (2015), FCO (1970), Gilby, N. (2015), Posnett, E. (2012). See oral history interviews with Ramsbotham. On France: Mann, A. (1971), Rouleau, E. (1971). *Le Monde* (1971). On Romania and Ceaușescu, see: Bowd, G. (2015). Bowd, G., and Anton, M. (2019). Campbell, J. C. (1990). Cavalcanti, M. (1997). Danta, D. (1993). On Tito: Hopkins M. (1971).

On Ethiopia: Haber, L. (1992), Kapuściński R. (2006), Levine, D. (1961), Marsden P. (2005), Steele R. (2021). On Senghor, see: Ndong, H. B. (2021), Steele, R. (2022), (2024). On the Soviet Union: CIA Directorate of Intelligence. (1969), Corfield, J. (2011). Meyer-Landrut, A. (1964). CIA Directorate of Intelligence. (1972), Pahlavi, A. (1980).

NOTES

5
THE GIFT

On the Cyrus Cylinder, see: Abdi, K. (2020), Curtis, J., MacGregor, N., et al. (2013), Finkel, I. L. (2013), Lyon, D. G. (1886), Mitchell, L. (2023), (2023), Sanadjian, M. (2011), St John. S., and Finkel, I. (2013). Targeted News Service, (2013), *The Economist*, (2013), (2013), *The Middle East*. (2013), van de Ven (2015), (2015), (2017), (2017), van de Ven, A. and Luciani, M (2018), Walker, C. B. F. (1972), Waters, M. W. (2022).

6
THE HOST

The most comprehensive biography of the Shah is Milani, A. (2011). Other biographies and sources include: Afkhami, G.R. (2009), Cooper, A. S. (2016), Gregory, L. (1959), Hoyt, E. P. (1976), Kapuściński, R (2006), Nahavandi, H. (2005), Saikal, A. (1980), Sanghvi, R. (1968), (1969), Shawcross, W. (1988), Taheri, A. (1991), Tayekh, R. (2021), Zonis, M. (1991), Villiers, G. (1975).

Alam, A. and Alikhani, A. (1991), Alvandi, R. (2014), Ansari A. M. and Ansari-Biglari, K.(2016), Arico, S.L. (201), Axworthy, M. (2008), Baraheni, R. (1977), Bostock, F. and Jones, G. (1988), CIA Directorate of Intelligence. (1972), CIA Directorate of Intelligence. (1972), Department of State (1972), Department of State (1972), De Steafan, C. and Harss, M. (2017), Diba, F. (1978), Diba, F. and Clancy, P. (2004), Fallaci, O. (2020), Fallaci, O. and Shepley, J. (1976), Green, J. (2019), Harney, D. (1988), Helms, C. (1981), Hoveyda, F. (1980), Meier, D. (2007), Milani, A. (2008), Oney, E. (1976), Pahlavi, A. (1980), Pahlavi, M. R. (1961), (1967), (1980), (1980), (2024), Parsons, A. (1984), Radji, P. (1983), Rahnema, A. (2021), Thompson, G. R. (2016), Zahedi, A. (1967), (2012), (2014).

On the paranoid view in politics and conspiracy theories, see: Blout, E. L. (2023), Clarke, (2002) Dentith, M. R. X., and Orr, M. (2018), Lange, P. A. M. van, and Prooijen, J.-W. van. (2014), Naghdipour, B. (2014), Peters, M. A. (2021), van Prooijen, J.-W. van. (2018), van Prooijen, J.-W. and van Vugt, M. (2018), van Prooijen, J., and Douglas, K. M. (2018), Raikka, J. (2009).

NOTES

On human rights and Amnesty International, see: Amnesty International (1976), Buchanan, T. (2020), House of Representatives, (1977), Moyn, S. (2010), Nikpour, G. (2018).

On Princess Ashraf, see: Alam, A. and Alikhani, A. (1991), Buchanan, R. (2018), Department of State (1971), Pahlavi A. (1980), (1983),

On the Shah's personality, relations with the media and censorship: Fallaci, O. (2020), Fallaci, O. and Shepley, J. (1976), Razavi, S. (2021), Walters, B. (2008). On Pahlavism, see: Bakhshandeh, E. (2015), Shakibi, Z. (2020), Steele, R. (2019), Zia-Ebrahimi, R. (2016).

On Jalal Al-e Ahmad and Westoxification, see: Al-e Ahmad, J. (1984), Ali, A. (2016), Avisahi, B. (2014), Deylami, S. S. (2011), Mirsepassi, A. (2019), Mishra, P. (2016), Omid, H. (1992), Rouhani, H. (2024), Schultz, D. (2022), Shakibi, Z. (2020), Sreberny-Mohammadi, A. and Mohammadi, A. (1994), Yavari, N., Zemmin, F., Dressler, M. and Stadler, N. (2024).

On Cyrus the Great and his importance in modern Iran, see: Ansari, A. (2021), Curtis, V. S. and Stewart, S. (2005). Bakker, E. J., Wees, H. van, and Jong, I. J. F. de. (2002), Friendly, A. (1971), Granger, R. (2002), Mallowan, M. (1972), Mallowan, M. and Gershevitch, I. (1985), Merhavy, M. (2015) (2021), Weeden, L. (2015), Xenophon (2009).

7
THE HOSTESS

Farah Diba produced a number of autobiographies: Diba, F. (1978), (2003), (2004), (2021). There is also a large amount of information on her life in the biographies of the Shah written after 1960.

On social movements: Penziner, V. L. (2006). On Niramund and Meinhof: Niramund, B. (1967). Meinhof, U. (1967). Stein, D. (2020) focuses on the empress and her role in the arts. On Parviz Tanavoli and Niavaran Palace, see: Bazyar, M., and Steele, R. (2023), Branigan, W. (1979), Daftari, F., and Diba, L. (2013), Jullian, P. (1977), Parsons, A. (1984), Pope, H. (1986), Radan, S. (2010). Randal, J.C. (1979), Tanavoli, P., and Rebick, S. (2023). Tuohy, W. (1979).

NOTES

On Warhol and the portraits of the Imperial Family: Colacello, B. (1990), Warhol, A. and Hackett, P. (2009). Also see: Blanch (1978), Morris, J. (1969).

On the Shiraz Festival of Arts: Afshar, M. (2015). Aghaie, (2005), K. S., Charney, J. J. (2020), Dabashi, H. (2005), Farhat, H. (2015), Gluck, R. (2007), Goss. L. (2018), Mahlouji, V. (2013), Nelson, P. (2025), Wardle, I. (1971), Xenakis, I. (2008).

8
GHOSTS AT THE BANQUET

On Mossadegh and the 1953 Coup, see: Abrahamian, E. (2013), Azizi, A. (2024), Behravesh, M. (2012), de Bellaigue, C. (2012), Hendelman-Baavur, L. (2024), Kinzer. (2003), Mokhtari, F. (2005), Rahnema (2014), Razavi, S. (2021), Westwood, A. (1965), Wilber, D.N. (2006), Zabih, S. (1982), Zahrani, T. (2002).

On young people in Iran: Breyley, G. (2010), Department of State (1971), FCO (1971), Fish, L. (2020), Hashemi, M. (2015), Hemmasi, F. (2017), Kalb, Z. and Hashemi, M. (2020), Mirsepassi, A. and Faraji, M. (2017), Morgan, E.P. (1975), Pareles, J. (2000), Sadeghi-Esfahani, A. (2021), Grigor, T. et al (2016).

On Khomeini: Akbar, A. (2022), Behdad, S. (1997), Abrahamian, E. (1993), Dorraj, M. (1990), Falk, R. (1979), Ferdows, A. (1983), Gellner (1979) (1981), Itzchakov, D. (2023), Moin, B. (2000), Monshipouri, M., and Dorraj, M. (2021). Mottale, M. (2011), Shahvar, S. (2009). Tayebipour, M. (2023), Yazdani, M. (2012), Zabeh, S. (1982).

On Ali Shariati and his role in political Islam, see: Aghaie, K. (2001), Ali, A. (2016), Byrd, D. J., Cope, Z., and Ness, I. (2021), Kanaaneh, A. (2021), Mansoori, N. (2021), Marashi, A., and Aghaie, K. S. (2014), Moaddel, M., and Talattof, K. (2000), Rahnema, A. (1998), Shariati, A. (1979), (1980), (1980), (1980), (2006).

On Evin Prison, see: Abrahamian, E. (1980), (1982), (1989), (1999), Elmer, G., and Neville, S. J. (2021), Elmer, G., and Neville, S. J. (2021), Gould,

NOTES

R. R. (2017), Irani, H. (2017), Messud, C. (2009), Naipaul (1981), (1997), Parvaz, N., and Namazie, M. (2003), Radio Free Europe/Radio Liberty. (2011), Sahimi, M (2009), Tajbaksh, K. (2008). Writing by prisoners includes: Abbas, M. (1996), Berkeley, B. (2006), Esfandiari, G. (2009), Ghamari-Tabrizi, B. (2016), Haj Hassan, H. (2005), Jahanbegloo, R. (2014), Nabavi, E. (2009), Nemat, M. (2012), Parvaz, N. (2018), Parvaz, N. and Namazie, M. (2003), Rahati, G. (2001), Rezaian, J. (2019). Prisons and sound: Bloch, S., and Olivares-Pelayo, E. A. (2025), Hemsworth, K., Morin, K. M., and Moran, D. (2015), Herrity, K. (2024), Howes, D., and Walfish, S. (2023), Jacobson, C., Jacobson, J., and Crowe, T. (1989), Johnston, N. B. (2000).

9
THE BANQUET

On the banquet, see: Adler, N. (2017), Bondy, F. (1971), Curtis, C. (1971), (1971), Giniger, H. (1972), Granger, R. (2002), Grenier, C. (1971), (1971), Fletcher, N. (2010), *Los Angeles Times*. (1971), Saffron, I. (2002), United Press International (1971)

On Alexander and the burning of Persepolis, see: Balcer, J. M. (1978), Bloedow, E. F., and Loube, H. M. (1997), Gabriel, R. (2013), Garstad, B (2018), Heidari, M., Torabi-Kaveh, M., and Mohseni, H. (2016), Liappas, J. A., Lascaratos, J., Fafouti, S., and Christodoulou (2003), McAuley, A. (2018) and G. N, Mínguez, V. and Rodríguez-Moya, I. (2024).

The relationship between the Greeks and the Persians was long and contentious; much of what we know about Persian history comes from Greek sources. See: Almagor, (2017), Brunelle. C. (2017), Frye, R. (1972), Gorman, R., and Gorman, V.B. (2014), Johnson. D. M. (2005) Llewellyn-Jones, L. (2013), (2017,) (2018), (2022), Marincola, J., Llewellyn-Jones, L., and Maciver, C. A. (2012), Morgan. J. (2016).

On the consulate bombing in San Francisco: Johnston, M. (1971), Moradian, M. (2022), United Press International (1971), (1971).

Khomeini, the Shah, and the Revolution: Abrahamian, E. (1989),

NOTES

(1991), (1993), (2009), Adib-Moghaddam, A. (2014), Ali, A. (2016), Almond. I. (2010), Amini, P. (2002), Amuzegar, J. (1991), Arjomand, S. A. (1989), Axworthy, M. (2013), Bayandor, D. (2018), Bhasin, G. (1994), Bibiyan. M. (2010), Boroujerdi, Mehrzad. Chehabi, H. E. (1990), Dabashi, H. (1993), Fardust, H. and Dareini. A.A. (1999), FCO. (1981), Gellner, E (1979), Green, J. (1980), Harney, D. (1998), Hegland, M. E. (2014), Hoveyda, F. (1980), Jervis, Robert. (2010) Keddie, N. R. (2003), Kurzman, C. (2004), Milani, A. (2008), Mirsepassi, A. (2019), Moradian, M. (2022), Nahavandi, H. (2005), Owen, D. (2008), Pahlavi, M. R. (1980), Parsons, A. (1984), Radji, P. (1983), Rahnema, A. (2023), Rouleau, Eric. (2012) Saikal, A. (1980), Takeyh, R (2021), Zabih, S. (1982), Zonis, Marvin. (1991).

10
AFTER THE PARTY

On the aftermath, see: Burke, J, (2001), Curtis, C. (1971), FCO (1971), (1971), (1971), 1972), (1972), *Guardian* (1971), *New York Times*, (1971), Quinn, S. (1971), (1971), Sulzberger, C. (1972). On the Azadi Tower and the close of the celebrations, see: Danaeifar, M., and Hartoonian, G. (2023) Dehgham, S. K. (2017), FCO (1971), (1971), (1972), (1972), Grigor T. (2003). Grigor, T., Christie, J., Bogdanović, J., and Guzmán, E. (2016), Mozaffari, A. (2014), (2020). On Khalkhali: Afshar, H. (2003), Branigan, W. (1980), Ghiabi, M. (2019), Hannah, N. (1982), Naipaul, V. S. (1981), (1997), Ross, J. (1980), Pahlavi, A. (1979), *The Economist* (2003), Trebach, A. S. (1983), *Tribune* (1980), (2020), Quinn, S. (1971), Soltani, Z. (2020) (2024), *The Guardian* (1971).On Khodynka Field, see: Baker, H. (2003).

Media responses to the event see: See Curtis, C (1971), Economist Intelligence Unit (1971), *New York Times* (1971), O'Donovan P. (1971), Quinn S. (1971). On the costs of the event, see: Associated Press (1971), Ball G. (1982), *Economist*. (1971), *Washington Post* (1971).

POSTSCRIPT

On the possible discovery of Reza Shah's body: Erdbrink, T. (2018). On Mahsa Amini and the protests, see: de Bellaigue, C. (2022), Horton (2023),

NOTES

Lob, E. (2024), Khosrokhavar, F. (2023). On social media, see: Azadi, P., and Mesgaran, M. B. (2021), and on the current economic situation, see Azadi, P., Mesgaran, M. B., Mirramezani, M. (2022).

BIBLIOGRAPHY

BOOKS

Abbott, J. A., Owens, M., Jansen, J.-H., and Maison Jansen. (2006). *Jansen*. New York: Acanthus Press.

Abrahamian, E. (1982). *Iran between Two Revolutions*. Princeton University Press.

——— (1989). *Radical Islam: The Iranian Mojahedin*. London: I.B. Tauris.

——— (1993). *Khomeinism: Essays on the Islamic Republic*. Berkeley: University of California Press.

——— (1999). *Tortured Confessions. Prisons and Public Recantations in Modern Iran*. Berkeley: University of California Press.

——— (2013). *The Coup: 1953, The CIA, and The Roots of Modern U.S.-Iranian Relations*. New York: The New Press.

——— (2018). *A History of Modern Iran*. Cambridge University Press.

——— (2021). *Oil Crisis in Iran: From Nationalism to Coup d'état*. Cambridge University Press.

Adib-Moghaddam, A. (2008). *Iran in World Politics: The Question of the Islamic Republic*. New York: Columbia University Press.

——— (2014). *A Critical Introduction to Khomeini*. Cambridge University Press.

Afary, J., Anderson, K., and Foucault, M. (2005). *Foucault and the Iranian Revolution: Gender and the Seductions of Islamism*. University of Chicago Press.

BIBLIOGRAPHY

Afkhami, G. R. (2009). *The Life and Times of the Shah*. Berkeley: University of California Press.

Alam, A., and Alikhani, A. (1991). *The Shah and I: The Confidential Diary of Iran's Royal Court. 1969–1977*. London: I. B. Tauris.

Aldrich, R.J. (2021). *The Secret Royals: Spying and the Crown from Victoria to Diana*. London: Atlantic Books.

Al-e Ahmad, J. (1984). *Occidentosis: A Plague from the West*. Berkeley: Mizan Press.

Almond. I. (2010). *The New Orientalists. Postmodern Representations of Islam from Foucault to Baudrillard*. London: I.B. Tauris.

Alter, J. (2020). *His Very Best: Jimmy Carter, A Life*. New York: Simon and Schuster.

Alvandi, R. (2014). *Nixon, Kissinger, and the Shah: The United States and Iran in the Cold War*. Oxford University Press.

——— ed. (2018). *The Age of Aryamehr: Late Pahlavi Iran and Its Global Entanglements*. London: Gingko Library.

Amuzegar, J. (1991). *The Dynamics of the Iranian Revolution: The Pahlavis' Triumph and Tragedy*. Albany: State University of New York Press.

Andrews, P. A. (1999). *Felt Tents and Pavilions: The Nomadic Tradition and its Interaction with Princely Tentage*. London: Melisende.

Ansari, A. M. (2003). *Modern Iran since 1921: The Pahlavis and After*. London: Longman.

——— (2006). *Confronting Iran: The Failure of American Foreign Policy and the Next Great Crisis in the Middle East*. London: Basic Books.

——— (2014). *Iran: A Very Short Introduction*. Oxford University Press.

——— (2014). *Perceptions of Iran: History, Myths and Nationalism from Medieval Persia to the Islamic Republic*. London: I.B. Tauris.

——— (2016). *Iran's Constitutional Revolution of 1906: Narratives of the Enlightenment*. London: Gingko Library.

——— (2019). *Modern Iran since 1797: Reform and Revolution*. London: Routledge.

——— (2024). *Iran*. Cambridge: Polity.

Ansari, A.M. and Ansari-Biglari, K. (2016). *The Shah's Iran—Rise and Fall: Conversations with an Insider*. London: Bloomsbury Publishing.

Arico, S. L. (2010). *Oriana Fallaci: The Woman and the Myth*. Carbondale: Southern Illinois University Press.

BIBLIOGRAPHY

Arjomand, S. A. (1989). *The Turban for the Crown: The Islamic Revolution in Iran*. Oxford University Press.

Asserate, A. (2015). *King of Kings. The Triumph and Tragedy of Emperor Haile Selassie I of Ethiopia*. London: Haus Publishing.

Atabaki, T. (2009). *Iran in the 20th Century: Historiography and Political Culture*. London: I. B. Tauris.

Atabaki, Touraj, and Erik Jan Zürcher. (2004). *Men of Order: Authoritarian Modernization under Atatürk and Reza Shah*. London: I.B. Tauris.

Avery, P., Hambly, G., and Melville, C.P. (1989). *The Cambridge History of Iran. Vol 7, From Nadir Shah to the Islamic Republic*. Cambridge University Press.

Axworthy, M. (2008). *A History of Iran: Empire of the Mind*. New York: Basic Books.

——— (2013). *Revolutionary Iran: A History of the Islamic Republic*. Oxford University Press.

——— (2017). *Iran: What Everyone Needs to Know*. Oxford University Press.

Ayatollahi, A. Y. (2022). *Political Conservatism and Religious Reformation in Iran (1905–1979). Reconsidering the Monarchic Legacy*. Wiesbaden: Springer Fachmedien.

Azadi, P., Mesgaran, M. B., and Mirramezani, M. (2022). *The Struggle for Development in Iran: The Evolution of Governance, Economy, and Society*. Palo Alto: Stanford University Press.

Azimi, F. (2008). *The Quest for Democracy in Iran: A Century of Struggle Against Authoritarian Rule*. Cambridge: Harvard University Press.

Babaie, S., and Grigor, T. (2015). *Persian Kingship and Architecture: Strategies of Power in Iran from the Achaemenids to the Pahlavis*. London: I.B. Tauris.

Bakhash, S. (2021). *The Fall of Reza Shah: The Abdication, Exile, and Death of Modern Iran's Founder*. London: I.B. Tauris.

Bakhshandeh, E. (2015). *Occidentalism in Iran: Representations of the West in the Iranian Media*. London: I.B. Tauris.

Bakker, E. J., van Wees, H., and de Jong, I. J. F. (2002). *Brill's Companion to Herodotus*. Leiden: Brill.

Ball G. (1982). *The Past has Another Pattern*. New York: W. W. Norton.

BIBLIOGRAPHY

Bang, P. F., Bayly, C. A., and Scheidel, W. (2021). *The Oxford World History of Empire*. Oxford University Press.

Baraheni, R. (1977). *The Crowned Cannibals: Writings on Repression in Iran*. New York: Vintage Books.

Bayandor, D. (2018). *The Shah, the Islamic Revolution and the United States*. Basingstoke: Palgrave Macmillan.

Bayne, E. A. (1968). *Persian Kingship in Transition. Conversations with a Monarch Whose Office Is Traditional and Whose Goal Is Modernization*. New York: American Universities Field Staff.

Berry, C.J. (1994). *The Idea of Luxury: A Conceptual and Historical Investigation*. Cambridge University Press.

Bibiyan. M. (2010). *Secrets of the Iranian Revolution*. Bloomington: Xlibris Publications.

Blout, E. L. (2023). *Media and Power in Modern Iran. Mass Communication, Ideology, and the State*. London: I.B. Tauris.

Bomati, Y. and Nahavandi, H. (2013). *Mohammad Réza Pahlavi, Le Dernier Shah: 1919–1980*. Paris: Perrin.

Boroujerdi, M (1996). *Iranian Intellectuals and the West: The Tormented Triumph of Nativism*. New York: Syracuse University Press.

Bostock, F. and Jones, G. (1988). *Planning and Power in Iran: Ebtehaj and Economic Development under the Shah*. London: Cass.

Briant, P. (1982). *Etat et pasteurs au Moyen-Orient ancient*. Cambridge/Paris: Cambridge University Press/Editions de la Maison des sciences de l'homme.

Briant, P. and Kuhrt, A. (2012). *Alexander the Great and His Empire: A Short Introduction*. Princeton University Press.

Buchanan, T. (2020). *Amnesty International and Human Rights Activism in Postwar Britain, 1945–1977*. Cambridge University Press.

Burke, R. (2010). *Decolonization and the Evolution of International Human Rights*. Philadelphia: University of Pennsylvania Press.

Canepa, M. P. (2018). *The Iranian Expanse: Transforming Royal Identity through Architecture, Landscape, and the Built Environment, 550 BCE-642 CE*. Berkeley: University of California Press.

Caryl, C. (2013). *Strange Rebels: 1979 and the Birth of the 21st Century*. New York. Basic Books.

BIBLIOGRAPHY

Chehabi, H. E. (1990). *Iranian Politics and Religious Modernism: The Liberation Movement of Iran under the Shah and Khomeini*. Ithaca: Cornell University Press.

——— ed. (2025). *Political, Social and Cultural History of Modern Iran: Essays in Honour of Ervand Abrahamian*. Edinburgh University Press.

Chelkowski, P. J., and Dabashi, H. (1999). *Staging a Revolution: The Art of Persuasion in the Islamic Republic of Iran*. New York University Press.

Chin, C.M. and Moulie, V. (2015). *Late Ancient Knowing: Explorations in Intellectual History*. Berkeley: University of California Press.

Colacello, B. (1990). *Holy Terror: Andy Warhol Up Close*. New York: Harper Collins.

Collier, D. R. (2017). *Democracy and the Nature of American Influence in Iran, 1941–1979*. New York: Syracuse University Press.

Cooper, A.S. (2016). *The Fall of Heaven: The Pahlavis and the Final Days of Imperial Iran*. London: Macmillan.

Cronin, S., ed. (2003). *The Making of Modern Iran: State and Society under Riza Shah, 1921–1941*. London: Routledge.

——— (2010). *Soldiers, Shahs and Subalterns in Iran: Opposition, Protest and Revolt, 1921–1941*. Basingstoke: Palgrave Macmillan.

Curtis, J., MacGregor, N., Finkel, I. L., Arthur M. Sackler Gallery, Museum of Fine Arts, Houston, and J. Paul Getty Museum. (2013). *The Cyrus Cylinder and Ancient Persia: A New Beginning for the Middle East*. British Museum.

Curtis, V.S. and Stewart, S. (2005). *Birth of the Persian Empire Vol 1*. London: I.B. Tauris.

Dabashi, H. (1993). *Theology of Discontent: The Ideological Foundations of the Islamic Revolution in Iran*. New York University Press.

——— (2007). *Iran: A People Interrupted*. New York: New Press.

——— (2011). *The Green Movement in Iran*. London: Routledge.

——— (2011). *Shi'ism: A Religion of Protest*. Cambridge: Harvard University Press.

——— (2015). *Persophilia: Persian Culture on the Global Scene*. Cambridge: Harvard University Press.

——— (2016). *Iran Without Borders. Towards a Critique of the Post-Colonial Nation*. London: Verso.

BIBLIOGRAPHY

——— (2016). *Iran: The Rebirth of a Nation*. Basingstoke: Palgrave Macmillan.

——— (2019). *Europe and Its Shadows: Coloniality After Empire*. London: Pluto Press.

——— (2021). *The Last Muslim Intellectual. The Life and Legacy of Jalaa Al-e Ahmad*. Edinburgh University Press.

——— (2023). *An Iranian Childhood: Rethinking History and Memory*. Cambridge University Press.

Daryaee, T. (2013). *Cyrus the Great: An Ancient Iranian King*. Santa Monica: Afshar Publishing.

David, C., Carrol, N.A., and Selden, Z. (1993). *Foreign Policy Failure in the White House: Reappraising the Fall of the Shah and the Iran-Contra Affair*. Lanham: University Press of America.

Davis, D. (2006). *Party of the Century: The Fabulous Story of Truman Capote and His Black and White Ball*. Hoboken: John Wiley.

de Bellaigue, C. (2004). *In the Rose Garden of the Martyrs: A Memoir of Iran*. London: HarperCollins.

——— (2007). *The Struggle for Iran*. New York Review Books.

——— (2012). *Patriot of Persia: Muhammad Mossadegh and a Very British Coup*. London: Bodley Head.

——— (2017). *The Islamic Enlightenment: The Struggle between Faith and Reason: 1798 to Modern Times*. New York: W.W. Norton.

Delannoy, C. (1990). *Savak*. Paris: Stock.

Dentith, M.R.X. (2014). *The Philosophy of Conspiracy Theories*. Basingstoke: Palgrave Macmillan.

De Stefano, C., and Harss, M. (2017). *Oriana Fallaci: The Journalist, the Agitator, the Legend*. New York: Other Press.

Diba, F. (1978). *My Thousand and One Days: An Autobiography*. London: W.H. Allen.

——— (2003). *Mémoires*. Paris: XO.

Diba, F. and Clancy, P. (2004). *An Enduring Love*. New York: Miramax.

Diba, F. and Viens, T. (2021). *1001 Days: Memoirs of an Empress*. Vanishing Pictures Press.

Dikötter, F. (2019). *How to Be a Dictator: The Cult of Personality in the Twentieth Century*. London: Bloomsbury Publishing.

BIBLIOGRAPHY

Domoslawski, A. (2012). *Ryszard Kapuściński: A Life*. London: Verso.

Dorraj, M. (1990). *From Zarathustra to Khomeini: Populism and Dissent in Iran*. Boulder: Lynne Rienner Publishers.

Fallaci, O. and Shepley, J. (1976). *Interview with History*. New York: Liveright.

Fardust, H. and Dareini. A.A. (1999). *The Rise and Fall of the Pahlavi Dynasty: Memoirs of Former General Hussein Fardust*. Delhi: Motilal Banarsidass.

Farmanfarmaiyan, M. and Farmanfarmaian, R. (1999). *Blood and Oil: Inside the Shah's Iran*. New York: Modern Library.

Fazeli, N. (2006). *The Politics of Culture in Iran*. London: Routledge.

Finkel, I. L. (2013). *The Cyrus Cylinder: The King of Persia's Proclamation from Ancient Babylon*. London: I.B. Tauris.

Firouz, M. (1971). *L'Iran face à l'imposture de l'histoire*. Paris: Editions de Herne.

Fisher, W. B., and Boyd, J.A. (1968). *The Cambridge History of Iran*. Cambridge University Press.

FitzGibbon, C. (1963). *The Autobiography of H.I.H. Princess Soraya*. Translated by Constantine Fitzgibbon. London: Arthur Barker.

Fletcher, N. (2010). *Caviar: A Global History*. London: Reaktion Books.

Fraser, J. (2023). *Luxury and Power. Persia to Greece*. London: The British Museum.

Gellner, Ernest. (1981). *Muslim Society*. Cambridge University Press.

Ghamari-Tabrizi, B. (2016). *Remembering Akbar: Inside the Iranian Revolution*. New York: OR Books.

Ghani, S. (1998). *Iran and the Rise of Reza Shah: From Qajar Collapse to Pahlavi Power*. London: I. B. Tauris.

Gil Guerrero, J. (2016). *The Carter Administration and the Fall of Iran's Pahlavi Dynasty: US-Iran Relations on the Brink of the 1979 Revolution*. Basingstoke: Palgrave Macmillan.

Gorman, R., and Gorman, V. B. (2014). *Corrupting Luxury in Ancient Greek Literature*. Ann Arbor: University of Michigan Press.

Green, J. (2019). *Devotion. The Memoirs of Mehrdad Pahlbod. Serving the Last Shah of Iran*. Pulp Hero Press.

Gregory, L. (1959). *The Shah and Persia*. Orpington: Orpington Press.

BIBLIOGRAPHY

Grigor, T. (2009). *Building Iran: Modernism, Architecture, and National Heritage under the Pahlavi Monarchs*. Reading: Periscope Books.

Hafiz. (2003). *The Garden of Heaven: Poems of Hafiz*. Dover Thrift Editions. Originally published as *Poems from the Divan of Hafiz*, translated by Gertrude Bell.

Haj Hassan, H. (2005). *Face à la bête: des Iraniennes dans les prisons des mollahs*. Paris: Picollec.

Halliday, F. and Sadeghi-Boroujerdi, E. (2024). *Iran: Dictatorship and Development*. London: Oneworld Academic.

Handley-Taylor, G. (1969). *Bibliography of Iran*. London: St James Press.

Harney, D. (1998). *The Priest and the King: An Eyewitness Account of the Iranian Revolution*. London. I.B. Tauris.

Harris, David. (2004). *The Crisis: The President, the Prophet, and the Shah—1979 and the Coming of Militant Islam*. New York: Little, Brown.

Hegland, M.E. (2014). *Days of Revolution*. Palo Alto: Stanford University Press.

Helms, C. (1981). *An Ambassador's Wife in Iran*. New York: Dodd, Mead.

Henderson, D. A. and Preston, R. (2009). *Smallpox: The Death of a Disease: The Inside Story of Eradicating a Worldwide Killer*. New York: Prometheus Books.

Herodotus (2009). *The Histories* Edited by Robert Strassler. New York: Anchor Books.

Herrity, K. (2024). *Sound, Order, and Survival in Prison: The Rhythms and Routines of HMP Midtown*. Bristol University Press.

Homan, M. M. (2000). *To Your Tents, O Israel! The Terminology, Function, Form, and Symbolism of Tents in the Hebrew Bible and the Ancient Near East*. Leiden: Brill.

Hoveyda, F. (1980). *The Fall of the Shah*. London: Wyndham Books.

Hoyt. E.P. (1976). *The Shah. The Glittering Story of Iran and Its People*. New York: Paul Eriksson.

Irving, S. (2012). *Leila Khaled: An Icon of Palestinian Liberation*. London: Pluto Press.

Jahanbegloo, R. (2014). *Time Will Say Nothing: A Philosopher Survives an Iranian Prison*. University of Regina Press.

Jervis, Robert. (2010). *Why Intelligence Fails: Lessons from the Iranian Revolution and the Iraq War*. Ithaca: Cornell University Press.

BIBLIOGRAPHY

Johnston, N. B. (2000). *Forms of Constraint: A History of Prison Architecture*. Champaign: University of Illinois Press.

Kadivar, Cyrus. (2017). *Farewell Shiraz: An Iranian Memoir of Revolution and Exile*. The American University in Cairo Press.

Kamrava, M. (2008). *Iran's Intellectual Revolution*. Cambridge University Press.

Kapuściński, R. (2006). *Shah of Shahs*. London: Penguin Classics.

——— (2006). *The Emperor*. London: Penguin Classics.

Kashani-Sabet, F., and Steele, R. (2023). *Iran and the Global Decolonization: Politics and Resistance after Empire*. London: Gingko.

Katouzian, H. (1990). *Musaddiq and the Struggle for Power in Iran*. London: I.B. Tauris.

Keddie, N.R. (2003). *Modern Iran: Roots and Results of a Revolution*. New Haven: Yale University Press.

Khaled, L. and Hajjar, G. (1973). *My People Shall Live: The Autobiography of a Revolutionary*. New York: Hodder and Stoughton.

Khomeini, R, (1981). *Islam and Revolution: Writings and Declarations of Imam Khomeini*, trans. by Hamid Algar. Berkeley: Mizan Press.

Khosrokhavar, F. (2023). *Iran: la jeunesse démocratique contre l'État prédateur: essai*. Paris: Fauves éditions.

King, D. (2008). *Vienna 1814: How the Conquerors of Napoleon Made Love, War and Peace at the Congress of Vienna*. New York: Three Rivers Press.

Kinzer, S. (2003). *All the Shah's Men: The Hidden Story of the CIA's Coup in Iran*. Hoboken: John Wiley.

Köpf, P. (2002). *Die Burdas*. Hamburg: Europa Verlag.

Kotar, S. L., and Gessler, J. E. (2013). *Smallpox: A History*. Jefferson: McFarland.

Kurzman, C. (2004). *The Unthinkable Revolution in Iran*. Cambridge: Harvard University Press.

Isfandiyari, H. (2009). *My Prison, My Home: One Woman's Story of Captivity in Iran*. New York: Ecco.

Ladjevardi H. ed, (1998). *Memoirs of Fatemeh Pakravan*. Maryland: Ibex.

Laing, Margaret. (1977). *The Shah*. London: Sidgwick and Jackson.

Langford, M. (2019). *Allegory in Iranian Cinema: The Aesthetics of Poetry and Resistance*. London: Bloomsbury.

BIBLIOGRAPHY

Larkin, P. (1974). *High Windows*. London: Faber and Faber.

Lange, P. A. M. van, and Prooijen, J.-W. van. (2014). *Power, Politics, and Paranoia: Why People Are Suspicious of Their Leaders*. Cambridge University Press.

Leonard, A. J. (2024). *Meltdown Expected: Crisis, Disorder, and Upheaval at the End of the 1970s*. Brunswick: Rutgers University Press.

Leys, S. (2013). *The Hall of Uselessness: Collected Essays*. New York Review Books.

Llewellyn-Jones, L. (2013). *King and Court in Ancient Persia 559 to 331 BCE*. Edinburgh University Press.

——— (2018). *Designs on the Past: How Hollywood Created the Ancient World*. Edinburgh University Press.

——— (2022). *Persians: The Age of the Great Kings*. New York. Basic Books.

Majd, M. G. (2000). *Resistance to the Shah: Landowners and the Ulama in Iran*. Gainesville: University Press of Florida.

Maloney, S. (2020). *The Iranian Revolution at Forty*. Washington, Brookings Institution Press.

Mankoff J. (2022). *Empires of Eurasia. How Imperial Legacies Shape International Security*. New Haven: Yale University Press.

Marashi, A. and Aghaie, K. S. (2014). *Rethinking Iranian Nationalism and Modernity*. Austin: University of Texas Press.

Marcovici, O. (2018). *From Paris to Tehran: The 'Forgotten King.'* Danaster, Iasi (Romania).

Marsden, P. (2005). *The Chains of Heaven: An Ethiopian Romance*. London: Harper Collins.

Marincola, J., Llewellyn-Jones, L., and Maciver, C. A. (2012). *Greek Notions of the Past in the Archaic and Classical Eras: History without Historians*. Edinburgh University Press.

Matin-Asgari, A. (2002). *Iranian Student Opposition to the Shah*. Costa Mesa: Mazda Publishers.

——— (2018). *Both Eastern and Western: An Intellectual History of Iranian Modernity*. Cambridge University Press.

McGlinchey, S. (2014). *Arms Policies towards the Shah's Iran*. Abingdon: Routledge.

BIBLIOGRAPHY

Merhavy, M. (2019). *National Symbols in Modern Iran: Identity, Ethnicity, and Collective Memory.* Syracuse University Press.

Milani, A. (2004). *Lost Wisdom: Rethinking Modernity in Iran.* Washington: Mage Publishers.

——— (2008). *Eminent Persians: The Men and Women Who Made Modern Iran, 1941–1979.* New York: Syracuse University Press.

——— (2009). *The Persian Sphinx: Amir Abbas Hoveyda and the Riddle of the Iranian Revolution.* Washington, DC: Mage Publishers.

——— (2011). *The Shah.* New York: Palgrave Macmillan.

Mirsepassi, A. (2019). *Iran's Quiet Revolution: The Downfall of the Pahlavi State.* Cambridge University Press.

——— (2010). *Democracy in Modern Iran: Islam, Culture, and Political Change.* New York University Press.

——— (2011). *Political Islam, Iran, and the Enlightenment: Philosophies of Hope and Despair.* Cambridge University Press.

——— (2019). *Iran's Troubled Modernity: Debating Ahmad Fardid's Legacy.* Cambridge University Press.

——— (2023). *The Loneliest Revolution: A Memoir of Solidarity and Struggle in Iran.* Edinburgh University Press.

Mitchell, L. G. (2023). *Cyrus the Great: A Biography of Kingship.* London: Routledge.

Moaddel, M., and Talattof, K. (2000). *Contemporary Debates in Islam: An Anthology of Modernist and Fundamentalist Thought.* London: Macmillan.

Moradian, M. (2022). *This Flame Within: Iranian Revolutionaries in the United States.* Durham: Duke University Press.

Morgan. J. (2016). *Greek Perspectives on the Achaemenid Empire: Persia Through the Looking Glass.* Edinburgh University Press.

Moser, K., Gösken, U., and Hayes, J., eds. (2019). *Heidegger in the Islamicate World.* London: Rowman and Littlefield International.

Mousavi, A. (2012). *Persepolis: Discovery and Afterlife of a World Wonder.* Leiden: De Gruyter.

Moyn, S. (2010). *The Last Utopia: Human Rights in History.* Cambridge: Harvard University Press.

Mozaffari, A. (2014). *Forming National Identity in Iran: The Idea of Homeland Derived from Ancient Persian and Islamic Imaginations of Place.* London: I.B. Tauris.

BIBLIOGRAPHY

———— (2020). *Development, Architecture and the Formation of Heritage in Late-Twentieth-Century Iran: A Vital Past.* Manchester University Press.

Nabavi, N. (2003). *Intellectual Trends in Twentieth-Century Iran: A Critical Survey.* Gainesville: University Press of Florida.

Naficy, H. (2011). *A Social History of Iranian Cinema (Vol 1–4).* Durham: Duke University Press.

Naiden, F. S., and Talbert, R. J. A. (2017). *Mercury's Wings: Exploring Modes of Communication in the Ancient World.* Oxford University Press.

Naipaul, V. S. (1981). *Among the Believers: An Islamic Journey.* New York: Knopf.

Nahavandi, H. (2005). *The Last Shah of Iran: Fatal Countdown of a Great Patriot Betrayed by the Free World, a Great Country Whose Fault Was Success.* Slough: Aquilion Ltd.

Naraghi, E. (1994). *From Palace to Prison: Inside the Iranian Revolution.* London: I.B. Tauris.

Nasr, V. (2025). *Iran's Grand Strategy: A Political History.* Princeton University Press.

Ndong, H.B. (2021). *Senghor: un prêtre sans étole.* Dakar: L'Harmattan Sénégal.

Nemat, M. (2012). *Prisoner of Tehran.* Toronto: Penguin Canada.

Nikpour, G. (2024). *The Incarcerated Modern: Prisons and Public Life in Iran.* Palo Alto: Stanford University Press.

Niramund, B. (1967). *Persia, A Model of a Developing Nation or the Dictatorship of the Free World (Persien, Modell eines Entwicklungslandes oder Die Diktatur der Freien Welt).* Rowohlt, Reinbek.

Owen, D. (2008). *In Sickness and in Power: Illness in Heads of Government During the Last 100 Years.* Westport: Greenwood Publishing Group.

Pahlavi, A. (1980). *Faces in a Mirror: Memoirs from Exile.* New York: Prentice-Hall.

———— (1983). *Jamais résignée.* Paris: Table Ronde.

Pahlavi, M.R. (1961). *Mission for My Country.* London: Hutchinson.

Pahlavi, M.R. (1967). *The White Revolution of Iran.* Tehran: Imperial Pahlavi Library.

———— (1980). *The Shah's Story.* London: Michael Joseph.

———— (1980). *Answer to History.* New York: Stein and Day.

BIBLIOGRAPHY

Pahlavi, M.R. (Steele, R. and Ansari, A. M.). (2024). *Towards the Great Civilization*. London: I.B. Tauris.

Parker, G. (2014). *Power in Stone: Cities as Symbols of Empire*. London: Reaktion Books.

Parker, G., and Parker, B. (2016). *The Persians: Lost Civilizations* (1st ed., Vol 3). London: Reaktion Books.

Parsi, K, and Villarreal, P. (2016). *Accused #13 in the Shah's Iran: A Memoir of Injustice*. Jefferson: McFarland and Company, Inc.

Parsons, A. (1984). *The Pride and the Fall: Iran, 1974–1979*. London: Jonathan Cape.

Parvaz, N. (2018). *One Woman's Struggle in Iran. A Prison Memoir*. Uttoxeter: Victorina Press.

Pizishkzad, I., and Davis, D. (1996). *My Uncle Napoleon: A Novel*. Washington DC: Mage Publishers.

Popescu, L., Seymour-Jones, C., and PEN. (2007). *Writers under Siege: Voices of Freedom from Around the World: A PEN Anthology*. New York University Press.

Potts, D. T. (2013). *The Oxford Handbook of Ancient Iran*. Oxford University Press.

Radji, P. (1983). *In the Service of the Peacock Throne: The Diaries of the Shah's Last Ambassador to London*. London: Hamish Hamilton.

Rafizadeh, M. (1987). *Witness: From the Shah to the Secret Arms Deal, An Insider's Account of U.S. Involvement in Iran*. New York: William Morrow.

Rahnema, A. (2011). *Superstition as Ideology in Iranian Politics: From Majlesi to Ahmadinejad*. Cambridge University Press.

——— (2014). *Behind the 1953 Coup in Iran: Thugs, Turncoats, Soldiers, Spooks*. Cambridge University Press.

——— (2014). *An Islamic Utopian. A Political Biography of Ali Shariati*. London: I.B. Tauris.

——— (2021). *The Rise of Modern Despotism in Iran: the Shah, the Opposition, and the US, 1953–1968*. London: Oneworld Academic.

——— (2021). *Call to Arms: Iran's Marxist revolutionaries: Formation and Evolution of the Fadais, 1964–1976*. London: Oneworld Academic.

——— (2023). *The Political History of Modern Iran: Revolution, Reaction and Transformation, 1905 to the Present*. London: I.B. Tauris.

BIBLIOGRAPHY

Randjbar-Daemi, S., Atabaki, T., and Mohajer, N. (2023). *A Glance at the Organization of Iranian People's Fada'i Guerrillas (1976–9)*. In *Fada'i Guerrilla Praxis in Iran, 1970–1979*. London: I. B. Tauris.

Razoux, P. *The Iran-Iraq War*. (2015). Cambridge: Belknapp Press Harvard University.

Rezaian, J. (2019). *Prisoner: My 544 days in an Iranian Prison—Solitary Confinement, a Sham Trial, High-stakes Diplomacy, and the Extraordinary Efforts It Took to Get Me Out*. New York: Ecco.

Richardson, G. (2013). *The Field of the Cloth of Gold*. New Haven: Yale University Press.

Rostampour, M., Amirizadeh, M., and Perry, J. (2013). *Captive in Iran: A Remarkable True Story of Hope and Triumph Amid the Horror of Tehran's Brutal Evin Prison*. Carol Stream: Tyndale Momentum.

Rouleau, Eric. (2012). *Dans les coulisses du Proche-Orient. Memoires d'un journaliste diplomate*. Paris: Fayard.

Russell, J. G. (1969). *The Field of the Cloth of Gold*. London: Routledge and Kegan Paul.

Saffron, I. (2002). *Caviar: The Strange History and Uncertain Future of the World's Most Coveted Delicacy*. New York: Broadway Books.

Saikal, A. (1980). *The Rise and Fall of the Shah 1941–1979*. London: Angus and Robertson.

Sanghvi, R. (1968). *Aryamehr: The Shah of Iran: A Political Biography*. London: Macmillan.

——— (1969). *The Shah of Iran*. New York: Stein and Day.

Scott, James. (1998). *Seeing Like a State. What Certain Schemes to Improve the Human Condition Have Failed*. New Haven: Yale University Press.

Shafa, S. (2000). *Shojaeddin Shafa: In His Own Words*. Paris: Self-Published Manuscript.

Shakibi, Z. (2002). *The King, the Tsar, the Shah: Agency and the Making of Revolution in Bourbon France, Romanov Russia, and Pahlavi Iran*. University of London.

Shannon, M. K. (2017). *Losing Hearts and Minds*. Ithaca: Cornell University Press.

Shariati, A. (1979). *Reflections of a Concerned Muslim on the Plight of Oppressed Peoples*. Free Islamic Literatures.

BIBLIOGRAPHY

——— (1980). *Reflection of Humanity: Two Views of Civilization and the Plight of Man: Lectures.* Free Islamic Literatures.

——— (1980). *Martyrdom—Arise and Bear Witness.* Tehran: Ministry of Islamic Guidance.

——— (2006). *Civilization and Modernization: What's the difference?* Citizens International.

Shariati, A. and Algar, H. (1980). *On the Sociology of Islam: Lectures.* Berkeley: Mizan Press.

Shawcross, W. (1988). *The Shah's Last Ride: The Fate of an Ally.* New York: Simon and Schuster.

Sreberny-Mohammadi, A. and Mohammadi, A. (1994). *Small Media, Big Revolution. Communication, Culture and the Iranian Revolution.* Minneapolis: University of Minnesota Press.

Steele, R. (2020). *The Shah's Imperial Celebrations of 1971: Nationalism, Culture and Politics in Late Pahlavi Iran.* London: I.B. Tauris.

——— (2024). *Pahlavi Iran's Relations with Africa: Cultural and Political Connections in the Cold War.* Cambridge University Press.

Stein, D. (2020). *The Empress and I.* Milan: Skira Editore.

Stevenson, M., and Arnolfini Gallery. (2008). *Celebration at Persepolis.* Arnolfini. JRP/Ringier Kunstverlag.

Strassler, R. B. (1996). *The Landmark Thucydides.* New York. Free Press.

Solouki, M. (2010). *Fatwa de sang de mon quartier de Téhéran à la prison d'Evin.* Paris: Lafon.

Taheri, A. (1991). *The Unknown Life of the Shah.* London: Hutchinson.

Takeyh, R. (2021). *The Last Shah: America, Iran, and the Fall of the Pahlavi Dynasty.* New Haven: Yale University Press.

Talattof K. ed., (2015). *Persian Language, Literature and Culture: New Leaves, Fresh Looks.* London and NY: Routledge.

Tanavoli, P. and Rebick S. (2023). *Parviz Tanavoli: Poets, Locks, Cages.* Vancouver, BC and Munich: Vancouver Art Gallery. Hirmer.

Taverdi, R. (1971). *The Land of Kings.* Tehran: Information Ministry Press.

Thomas, C. G. (2007). *Alexander the Great in his World.* Oxford: Blackwell Pub.

Thompson, G.R. (2016). *All the Shah's Horses.* Self-Published Manuscript.

BIBLIOGRAPHY

Tucker, S. C. (2017). *The Roots and Consequences of Civil Wars and Revolutions: Conflicts That Changed World History*. London: Bloomsbury Publishing.

Vahabzadeh, P. (2010). *A Guerrilla Odyssey: Modernization, Secularism, Democracy, and the Fadai Period of National Liberation in Iran, 1971–1979*. New York: Syracuse University Press.

Teiwes, F. C., and Sun, W. (1996). *The Tragedy of Lin Biao: Riding the Tiger during the Cultural Revolution, 1966–1971*. Honolulu: University of Hawaii Press.

van Prooijen, J-W. (2018). *The Psychology of Conspiracy Theories*. London: Routledge.

Vick, B. E. (2014). *The Congress of Vienna: Power and Politics after Napoleon*. Cambridge: Harvard University Press.

Villiers, G. (1975). *L'Irrésistible Ascension de Mohammad Reza, Shah d'Iran*. Paris: Plon.

Walters, B. (2008). *Audition: A Memoir*. New York: Knopf.

Warhol, A. and Hackett, P. (2009). *The Andy Warhol Diaries*. New York: Grand Central Publishing.

Waters, M. W. (2022). *King of the World: The Life of Cyrus the Great*. Oxford University Press.

Weeden, L. (2015). *Ambiguities of Domination. Politics, Rhetoric and Symbols in Contemporary Syria*. University of Chicago Press.

Whooley, J. (2018). *Imagining Iran: Orientalism and the Construction of Security Development in American Foreign Policy*. New York: Peter Lang.

Wilber, D.N. (1975). *Riza Shah Pahlavi: The Resurrection and Reconstruction of Iran*. Hicksville: Exposition Press.

——— (2006). *Regime Change in Iran: Overthrow of Premier Mossadegh of Iran, November 1952-August 1953*. Nottingham: Spokesman.

Wolin, R. (2009). *The Seduction of Unreason: The Intellectual Romance with Fascism from Nietzsche to Postmodernism*. Princeton University Press.

Wolin, R. (2022). *Heidegger in Ruins: Between Philosophy and Ideology*. New Haven: Yale University Press.

Wright, D. (1977). *The English Among the Persians*. London: William Heinemann.

Xenophon, (2009). *Cyropaedia: The Education of Cyrus*. Digireads.com Publishing.

BIBLIOGRAPHY

Zahedi, Ardeshir. (1967). *A Memoir of His Imperial Majesty Mohammad Reza Shah Pahlavi, Shahanshah of Iran*. Royal Blue Book.

——— (2012). *The Memoirs of Ardeshir Zahedi. Vol One*. Bethesda: Ibex Publishing.

——— (2014). *The Memoirs of Ardeshir Zahedi. Vol Two*. Bethesda: Ibex Publishing.

Zabih, S. (1982). *The Mossadegh Era: Roots of the Iranian Revolution*. Lake View Press.

Zia-Ebrahimi, R. (2016). *The Emergence of Iranian Nationalism: Race and the Politics of Dislocation*. New York: Columbia University Press.

Zonis, Marvin. (1991). *Majestic Failure: The Fall of the Shah*. University of Chicago Press.

ACADEMIC ARTICLES, THESES AND CHAPTERS IN BOOKS

Abdi, K. (2020). "The Lucrative Business of the Cyrus Cylinder." In *Testing the Canon of Ancient Near Eastern Art and Archaeology*. Oxford University Press.

Abrahamian, E. (1980). "The Guerrilla Movement in Iran, 1963–1977." *MERIP Reports* No. 86. March–April. pp. 3–15.

——— (1991). "Khomeini: Fundamentalist or Populist." *NLR* 186. March–April.

——— (2001). "The 1953 Coup in Iran". *Science and Society*. (New York), 65(2).

——— (2009). "The Crowd in the Iranian Revolution." *Radical History Review*, 2009 (105).

——— (2009). "Why the Islamic Republic Has Survived." *Middle East Report* New York, 1988, 39 (1), pp. 10–16.

Afshar, M. (2015). *Festival of Arts Shiraz-Persepolis. 1967–1977*. New York: Asia Society. Published 2013, revised 2015.

Aghaie, K. S. (2001). "The Karbala Narrative: Shi'ite Political Discourse in Modern Iran in the 1960s and 1970s." *Journal of Islamic Studies*. 12(2), pp. 151–76.

——— (2005). "The Origins of the Sunnite—Shiite Divide and the Emergence of the Ta'ziyeh Tradition." *The Drama Review*, 49(4), pp. 42–7.

BIBLIOGRAPHY

Ali, A. (2016). "From Islamophobia to Westophobia: The Long Road to Radical Islamism." *Journal of Asian Security and International Affairs*, 3(1), pp. 1–19.

Almagor, E. (2017). "Plutarch and the Persians". *Electrum*. Vol 24. pp. 123–70.

Amini, P. (2002). "A Single Party State in Iran, 1975–78: The Rastakhiz Party—The Final Attempt by the Shah to Consolidate his Political Base." *Middle Eastern Studies*, 38(1), pp. 131–68.

Amnesty International (1976). "Iran: An Amnesty International Briefing". London: Amnesty International,.

Ansari, A. M. (1998). "Shah Mohammad Reza Pahlavi and the Myth of Imperial Authority." PhD Thesis. School of African and Oriental Studies, University of London.

——— (2001). "The Myth of the White Revolution: Mohammad Reza Shah, 'Modernization' and the Consolidation of Power." *Middle Eastern Studies*, 37(3), pp. 1–24.

——— (2021). "A Royal Romance: The Cult of Cyrus the Great in Modern Iran." *Journal of the Royal Asiatic Society*, 31(3), pp. 405–19.

Arabian, S., Sadr, M., Ayati, M. H., İnce, F., and Zargaran, A. (2025). "The Earliest Report of Smallpox Oral Vaccination by Baha' al-Dawlah Razi in the 16th Century." *Vaccine*, 52, 126949–126949.

Atwood, B. (2016). "When the Sun Goes Down: Sex, Desire, and Cinema in 1970s Tehran." *Asian Cinema* Vol 27. No 2.

Avisahi, B. (2014). "Among the Believers: What Jalal Al-e Ahmad Thought Iranian Islamism Could Learn from Zionism." *Foreign Affairs*. Vol 93. No. 2. March–April. pp. 115–24.

Azadi, P. and Mesgaran, M.B. (2021). "The Clash of Ideologies on Iranian Twitter." *Stanford Iran 2040. Working Paper No. 10*. June.

Azizi, A. (2024). "Communism, Cold War, and the 1953 Coup." *International Journal of Middle East Studies* 56 (2): pp. 295–99.

Azizi M.H. (2010). "A Brief History of Smallpox Eradication in Iran." *Arch Iran Med*. Jan;13(1): pp. 69–73.

Bahadori, A., and Miri, N. (2024). "The So-called Achaemenid Capitals and the Problem of Royal Court Residence." *Iran: Journal of the British Institute of Persian Studies*, pp. 1–31.

BIBLIOGRAPHY

Baker, H. (2003). "Monarchy Discredited? Reactions to the Khodynka Coronation Catastrophe of 1896." *Revolutionary Russia*. 16:1 pp. 1–46.

Balcer, J. M. (1978). "Alexander's Burning of Persepolis." *Iranica Antiqua*, 13, 119.

Barnett. R.D. (1957). "Persepolis." *Iraq*. Vol 19. No. 1. Spring.

Bayat, A. (2010). "Tehran: Paradox City." *NLR*. 66. November–December.

Bazyar, M., and Steele, R. (2023). "'The Shah's House Became the People's House': Narrating Iran's Modern History at the Pahlavi Dynasty Museum." *Iranian Studies*, 56(3), pp. 497–521.

Bedford, C. (2007). "An Analysis of the Use of Political Marketing by an Insurgent Group: A Case Study of the Mojahedin-e Khalq Organization." Vol 46, Number 3, ProQuest Dissertations and Theses.

Beglinger. M. (2014). "The Most Expensive Party Ever." *Tages-Anzeiger*. May.

Behdad, S. (1997). "Islamic Utopia in Pre-Revolutionary Iran: Navvab Safavi and the Fada'ian-e Eslam." *Middle Eastern Studies*. Vol 33. No 1. January. pp. 40–65.

Behravesh, M. (2012). "The Formative Years of Anglo-Iranian Relations (1907–1953): Colonial Scramble for Iran and Its Political Legacy." *Digest of Middle East Studies*. Vol 21. No. 2. pp. 386–400.

Berkeley, B. (2006). "Know Thine Enemy." *Columbia Journalism Review*. Vol 45, Number 3, p. 50.

Bevan, R. (2015). "In the Pursuit of Pleasure: The Not so Fleeting Life of the Pavilion and its Ilk." *Architectural Design*, 85(3), pp. 16–25.

Bharier. J. (1972). "The Growth of Towns and Villages in Iran. 1900–1966." *Middle Eastern Studies*. Vol 8. No. 1. January.

Bhasin, G. (1994). "Khomeini's Millenarian Vision and the Iranian Revolution." ProQuest Dissertations and Theses.

Biglari, M. (2016). "Captive to the Demonology of the Iranian Mobs: U.S. Foreign Policy and Perceptions of Shi'a Islam During the Iranian Revolution, 1978–79." *Diplomatic History*, 40(4), pp. 579–605.

Birch, C., MacFarquhar, R., and Fairbank, J. K. (1991). "Literature under Communism." In *The Cambridge History of China* (Vol 15, pp. 743–812). Cambridge University Press.

BIBLIOGRAPHY

Bloch, S., and Olivares-Pelayo, E. A. (2025). "Banging Them Out: An Affective Politics of Prison Sound." *Geoforum*, 164,.

Bloedow, E. F., and Loube, H. M. (1997). "Alexander the Great 'Under Fire' in Persepolis". *Klio* 79(2), 341.

Bowd, G. (2015). "Calling Planet Marx: Nicolae Ceaușescu's Cultural Revolution." *Twentieth Century Communism*, 9(9), pp. 136–147.

Bowd, G., and Anton, M. (2019). "Peak Dictatorship: Ceaușescu's State Visit to Great Britain, June 1978." *The Slavonic and East European Review (1928)*, 97(4), pp. 711–37.

Breyley, G. (2010). "Hope, Fear and Dance Dance Dance: Popular Music in 1960s Iran." *Musicology Australia*. 32:2 pp. 203–26.

Brunelle. C. (2017). "Alexander's Persian Pillow and Plutarch's Cultured Commander." *The Classical Journal*. 112.3.

Buchanan, R. (2018). "The Iran Album (1974): Some Sleeve Notes." *Archivaria* 85: pp. 124–54.

Butler, W.J. and Levasseur, G. (1978). "Human Rights and the Legal System in Iran." Geneva: International Commission of Jurists.

Byrd, D. J., Cope, Z., and Ness, I. (2021). "Ali Shariati (1933–1977)." In *The Palgrave Encyclopedia of Imperialism and Anti-Imperialism*. pp. 106–20. Springer International Publishing.

Campbell, J. C. (1990). "Nationalism and Communism in Romania: The Rise and Fall of Ceaușescu's Personal Dictatorship" [Review of *Nationalism and Communism in Romania: The Rise and Fall of Ceaușescu's Personal Dictatorship*]. *Foreign Affairs* (New York), 69(5), 202–202. Council on Foreign Relations.

Canepa, M. P. (2010). "Technologies of Memory in Early Sasanian Iran: Achaemenid Sites and Sasanian Identity." *American Journal of Archaeology*, 114(4),.

Carlton, D. (2005). "The 1970s: The West's Collective Response to Terrorism Following Dawson's Field." In *The West's Road to 9/11* pp. 39–46.

Cavalcanti, M. (1997). "Urban Reconstruction and Autocratic Regimes: Ceaușescu's Bucharest in its Historic Context." *Planning Perspectives*, Vol 12. pp. 71–109.

Charney, J. J. (2020). "The Shiraz Arts Festival: Cultural Democracy,

BIBLIOGRAPHY

National Identity, and Revolution in Iranian Performance, 1967–1977." ProQuest Dissertations and Theses.

Chatterjee, K. (2011). "Language of Opposition Politics in Late Pahlavi Iran." In *'Ali Shari'ati and the Shaping of Political Islam in Iran*. pp. 47–72. London: Palgrave Macmillan.

Chehabi, H.E. (2007). "How Caviar Turned out to be Halal." *Gastronomica: The Journal of Food and Culture*. Vol 7. No. 2.

Chowdhury, Z. (2015). "An Imperial Mughal Tent and Mobile Sovereignty in Eighteenth-Century Jodhpur." *Art History*, 38(4), 668.

Clarke, S, (2002). "Conspiracy Theories and Conspiracy Theorizing." *Philosophy of Social Sciences*. Vol 32. No. 2 pp. 131–50.

Clinton. J.W. (2016). "Al-e Ahmad, Jalal." *Encyclopædia Iranica*.

Cohen, R. A. (2015). "The CIA, SAVAK, and Mossad Connections with the Forqan." In *Revolution Under Attack*. pp. 101–14. London: Palgrave Macmillan.

Collins, A. W. (2017). "The Persian Royal Tent and Ceremonial of Alexander the Great." *Classical Quarterly*, 67(1), pp. 71–76.

Corfield, J. (2011). "Podgorny, Nikolai Viktorovich." In *The Encyclopedia of the Vietnam War: A Political, Social, and Military History*. Vol 2, pp. 918–918.

Craig, D. (1978). "The Impact of Land Reform on an Iranian Village." *Middle East Journal*. Vol 32 No. 2. Spring.

Dabashi H. (2005). "Ta'ziyeh as Theatre of Protest." *The Drama Review*. 49:4 Winter.

Danaeifar, M., and Hartoonian, G. (2023). "Shahyad Tower: Two Tendencies in One Ideological Symbol." In *The Visibility of Modernization in Architecture*. London: Routledge.

Danta, D. (1993). "Ceaușescu's Bucharest." *Geographical Review*. Vol 83. No. 2. April. pp. 170–82.

de Bellaigue, C. (2004). "What is Reasonable." *The Paris Review*. Issue 172. Winter.

Dentith, M. R. X., and Orr, M. (2018). "Secrecy and Conspiracy." *Episteme*, 15(4), pp. 433–50.

——— (2021). "Debunking conspiracy theories." *Synthese* (Dordrecht), 198(10), pp. 9897–9911.

BIBLIOGRAPHY

Deylami, S. S. (2011). "In the Face of the Machine: Westoxification, Cultural Globalization, and the Making of an Alternative Global Modernity." *Polity, 43*(2), pp. 242–63.

Dode, Z. (2018). "The Golden Tent Paradigm: Between the Mongols and Islam." *Revue Des Mondes Musulmans et de La Méditerranée*, 143.

Durand-Guédy, D. (2018). "Khargah and Other Terms for Tents in Firdawsi's Shah-namah." *Iranian Studies*, 51(6), pp. 819–49.

Elling R. and Harris, K. (2021). "Difference in Difference: Language, Geography, and Ethno-racial Identity in Contemporary Iran." *Ethnic and Racial Studies*. Vol 44. No 12. pp. 2255–2281.

Elmer, G., and Neville, S. J. (2021). "The Resonate Prison: Earwitnessing the Panacoustic Affect." *Surveillance and Society*, 19(1), pp. 11–21.

Esfahani H.S. and Pesaran M.H. (2009). "The Iranian Economy in the Twentieth Century: A Global Perspective." *Iranian Studies*, 42, pp. 177–211.

Fallaci, O. (2020). "Oriana Fallaci: The Art of Unclothing an Emperor." In Cott, J. *Listening: Interviews 1970–1989*. Minneapolis: University of Minnesota Press.

Farhat, H. (2020). Shiraz Arts Festival. Leiden, Koninklijke Brill NV.

Faroughy, A. (2006). "Repression in Iran." *Index on Censorship*. Vol 3, Number 4, pp. 9–18.

Fenner F. (1993). "Smallpox: Emergence, Global Spread, and Eradication." *Hist Philos Life Sci*.;15(3): pp. 397–420.

Ferdows, A. (1983). "Khomeini and Fadayan's Society and Politics." *Journal of Middle East Politics*. Vol 15. No. 2. May. pp. 241–57.

Ferrero. G. (1901). "The Evolution of Luxury." *International Journal of Ethics*. Vol 11, No. 3. April pp. 346–54.

Figueroa, W. (2022). "China and the Iranian Revolution: New Perspectives on Sino-Iranian Relations, 1965–1979." *Asian Affairs* (London), 53(1), pp. 106–23.

——— (2024). "Red Star Over Iran: Maoism and the Shah's Regime." In *Iran and Global Decolonisation*. Richmond: Gingko Press.

Fish, L. (2020). "Remixing Vulgarity: Reinterpreting the Legacy of Popular Iranian Cinema." *The Velvet Light Trap* Spring pp. 53–64. Austin: University of Texas Press.

BIBLIOGRAPHY

Frye, R. (1972). "Gestures of Deference to Royalty in Ancient Iran." *Iranica Antique.* Jan 1, 1979:9.

Gabriel, R. (2013). "Alexander the Monster." In *MHQ: The Quarterly Journal of Military History.* Vol 25, Number 4, p. 38. Weider History Group.

Gamez, P. (2019). "The Place of the Iranian Revolution in the History of Truth: Foucault on Neoliberalism, Spirituality and Enlightenment." *Philosophy and Social Criticism.* Vol 45(1) pp. 96–124.

Garstad, B. (2018). "Alexander the Great, the Disguised Dinner Guest." *Symbolae Osloenses, 92*(1), pp. 171–97.

Gellner, Ernest. (1979). "State and Revolution in Islam." *Millennium* 8 (3): pp. 185–99.

Gervers, M., and Schlepp, W. A. (1997). "Felt and 'Tent Carts' in The Secret History of the Mongols". *Journal of the Royal Asiatic Society,* 7(1), pp. 93–116.

Ghiabi, M. (2019). "Drugs, Revolution, War." In *Drugs Politics.* pp. 71–97.

Ghasemibarghi, A. (2024). "Persepolis, 1960–1971: Material Culture, State Ideology, and Melancholic Contemplation on National Identity." *MELA Notes,* 96, pp. 59–82.

Ghobadzadeh N. and Akbarzadeh S. (2020). "Religionization of politics in Iran: Shi'i Seminaries as the Bastion of Resistance." *Middle Eastern Studies.* Vol 56. No 4. pp. 570–84.

Gilby, N. (2015). "The 'Special Relationship': Britain and the Shah of Iran (1970–78)." In *Deception in High Places.* London: Pluto Press.

Gil Guerrero, J. (2024). "The Protestant Reformation as an Islamisation of Christianity in the Thought of Ziya Gökalp and Ali Shariati." *Religions.15*(7), 850.

Gluck R. (2007). "The Shiraz Arts Festival: Western Avant-Garde Arts in 1970s Iran." *Leonardo.* Vol 40 No. 1.

Goss. L. (2018). "You Are Invited Not to Attend: Answering the Call for a Cultural Boycott of the Shiraz Festival of the Arts." *Performance Paradigm* 14.

Gould, R.R. (2017). "Literature as a Tribunal: The Modern Iranian Prose of Incarceration." *Prose Studies* 39:1, pp. 19–38.

Grabicki, M. C. (2007). "Summering in Tehran." ProQuest Dissertations and Theses.

BIBLIOGRAPHY

Granger, R. (2002). "The Great King Invites You to Dine: Food and Ideology in the Achaemenid Empire." *Ancient History Resources for Teachers*. 32.2. January.

Green, J. (1980). "Pseudoparticipation and Countermobilization: Roots of the Iranian Revolution." *Iranian Studies* Vol 13. Nos 1–4.

Grigor, T. (2003). "Of Metamorphosis Meaning on Iranian Terms." *Third Text*, 17(3), pp. 207–25.

——— (2004). "Recultivating 'Good Taste': The Early Pahlavi Modernists and their Society for National Heritage." *Iranian Studies*, 37(1), pp. 17–45.

——— (2005). "Preserving the Antique Modern: Persepolis '71." *Future Anterior*, 2(1), pp. 22–9.

——— (2016). "Tehran: A Revolution in Making." In Christie, J.B., Bogdanović, H., and Guzmán, E. *Political Landscapes of Capital Cities*. Denver: University Press of Colorado.

——— (2021). "The Persian Revival as Iranian Modernity." In *The Persian Revival*. Philadelphia: Penn State University Press.

Grigor, T. and Chehabi, H.E. (2025). "Leisure Architecture and the Aesthetics of the Pahlavi 'Modern Middle Class.'" In *Political, Social and Cultural History of Modern Iran*. Edinburgh University Press.

Haber, L. (1992). "The Emperor Haile Selassie 1st in Bath, 1936–1940." The Anglo-Ethiopia Society.

Hashemi, M. (2015). "Waithood and Face: Morality and Mobility Among Lower-Class Youth in Iran." *Qualitative Sociology* 38:261–3.

Heidari, M., Torabi-Kaveh, M., and Mohseni, H. (2016). "Artificial weathering assessment of Persepolis stone due to heating to elucidate the effects of the burning of Persepolis." *Bulletin of Engineering Geology and the Environment*, 75(3), pp. 979–92.

Hemmasi, F. (2017). "Iran's Daughter and Mother Iran: Googoosh and Diasporic Nostalgia for the Pahlavi Modern." *Popular Music*. Vol 36/2. pp. 157–77.

Hemsworth, K., Morin, K. M., and Moran, D. (2015). "Carceral Acoustemologies: Historical Geographies of Sound in a Canadian Prison." In *Historical Geographies of Prisons*. pp. 17–33. Routledge.

Hendelman-Baavur, L. (2015). "The Odyssey of Jalal Al-Ahmad's

BIBLIOGRAPHY

Gharbzadegi—Five Decades After" in Kamran Talattof ed., *Persian Language, Literature and Culture: New Leaves, Fresh Looks*. London and New York: Routledge.

——— (2024). "A Man for All Seasons: Mosaddeq's Image and Legacy in Contemporary Iran." *International Journal of Middle East Studies* 56 (2): pp. 307–16.

Herrera, E. J. (2007). "Shaping Visions of the Middle East: Representations of the 1978–1979 Iranian Revolution in Mainstream United States Print Media." ProQuest Dissertations and Theses.

Hobson, A. (2020). "Creating a World Stage: Revolution Airport and the Illusion of Power." *International History Review*, *42*(5), pp. 930–50.

Hopkins M. (1971). "Tito on the Road." *New Leader*. Vol 54. Issue 23, November 29.

Horton, R. (2023). "Mahsa Amini—Never Forget." *The Lancet* (British Edition).

Hosseini, S. H. (1991). "Historical Profile of Iranian Higher Education from Antiquity to 1979: Its Challenges in Meeting Iran's Development Needs." ProQuest Dissertations and Theses.

Hourcade, B. and Matin-Asgari, A. (1993). "The Land Question and Islamic Revolution in Iran." *Comparative Studies of South Asia, Africa, and the Middle East*, 13 Nos 1 and 2, pp. 134–47.

Howes, D., and Walfish, S. (2023). "Litigating the carceral soundscape." *Osgoode Hall Law Journal*, *60*(1), pp. 175–219.

Ilic, I. and Ilic, M. (2022). "Historical Review: Towards the 50th Anniversary of the Last Major Smallpox Outbreak (Yugoslavia, 1972)." *Travel Medicine and Infectious Disease*. 48 102327.

Irani, H. (2017). "Torture Without Physical Pain: Inside Cell 24 of the Special Wing for Political Prisoners—Evin Prison, Iran." *Torture*. Vol 27. No. 2.

Ismael, J.S. and Ismael, T.Y. (1980). "Social Change in Islamic Society: The Political Thought of Ayatollah Khomeini." *Social Problems*. Vol 27. No. 5. June.

Itzchakov, D. (2023). "Ayatollah Khomeini's Approach to the Palestinian-Israeli Conflict and Its Longstanding Ramifications." *Israel Affairs* 29 (6): pp. 1094–1114.

BIBLIOGRAPHY

Jacobson C., Jacobson, J., and Crowe T. (1989). "Hearing Loss in Prison Inmates." *Ear and Hearing.* 10(3): pp. 178–83.

Kalb, Z. and Hashemi, M. (2020). "Tehran's Universal Studios." *NLR.* Vol 121. Jan-Feb.

Kanaaneh, A. (2021). "Ali Shariati: Islamizing Socialism and Socializing Islam." *Left History.* 24:1 Spring-Summer.

Kashfi, E. (2021). "The Politics of Calendars: State Appropriations of the Contested Iranian Past." *Religions. 2*(10), 861.

Keddie, N. (1971). "The Iranian Power Structure and Social Change 1800–1969. An Overview." *International Journal of Middle East Studies* Vol 2. No. 1 January. pp. 3–20.

Khodaei, S. M. (2017). "Solitary confinement, Section 350, Evin prison in Tehran." *Torture*, 27(2).

Khoshnood, A., and Khoshnood, A. (2016). "The Death of an Emperor—Mohammad Reza Shah Pahlavi and his Political Legacy." *Alexandria Journal of Medicine, 52*(3), pp. 201–8.

Klenka, M. (2019). "Major Incidents that Shaped Aviation Security." *Journal of Transportation Security*, 12(1–2), pp. 39–56.

Kurht, A. (1983). "The Cyrus Cylinder and Achaemenid Imperial Policy." *Journal of the Study of the Old Testament.* 25. pp. 83–97.

Levine, D. (1961). "Ethiopia: Myth or Reality?" *Africa Today.* Vol 8. No, 5. May.

Liappas, J. A., Lascaratos, J., Fafouti, S., and Christodoulou, G. N. (2003). "Alexander the Great's relationship with alcohol." *Addiction* (Abingdon, England), 98(5), pp. 561–7.

Little, D. (2004). "Mission Impossible: The CIA and the Cult of Covert Action in the Middle East." *Diplomatic History* Vol 28. No 5. November.

Llewellyn-Jones, L. (2017). "Persianisms: The Achaemenid Court in Greek Art, 380–330 BCE." *Iranian Studies.* Vol 50. No. 6. pp. 765–86.

Lob, E. (2024). "The Security-Development Nexus and the Jina Mahsa Amini Protests in Iran's Border Provinces." *Iranian Studies*, 57(2), pp. 317–22.

Longinotti, E. (2015). "Britain's Withdrawal from East of Suez: From Economic Determinism to Political Choice." *Contemporary British History*, 29(3), pp. 318–40.

BIBLIOGRAPHY

Lyon, D. G. (1886). "The Cyrus Cylinder." *Journal of the Society of Biblical Literature and Exegesis*, 6(1), p. 139.

Mahdavy, H. (1965). "The Coming Crisis in Iran." *Foreign Affairs*. 44:1 pp. 134–46.

Mahlouji, V. (2013). "Perspectives on the Shiraz Arts Festival: A Radical Third World Rewriting." In *Iran Modern*, edited by Fereshteh Daftari and Layla Diba. New York: Asia Society. pp. 87–91.

Mallowan, M. (1972). "Cyrus the Great." *Iran*, Vol 10. pp. 1–17.

Mallowan, M. and Gershevitch, I. (1985). "Cyrus the Great (558–529 B.C.)." In *The Cambridge History of Iran* (Vol 2, pp. 392–419). Cambridge University Press.

McAuley, A. (2018). "The Great Misstep: Alexander the Great, Thais, and the Destruction of Persepolis." In *Brill's Companion to the Reception of Alexander the Great*. Vol 14, pp. 717–38.

McDermott, R. (2007). "The Use and Abuse of Medical Intelligence." *Intelligence and National Security*, 22:4, pp. 491–520.

Mansoori, N. (2021). "Things Unheard: Popular Silence and the Popular Voice in Revolutionary Iran." *Theory and Event*. Vol 24. No 2. April.

Marcy, A. (2010). "Incapacitated by Education: The Role of Education in the Fall of Mohammed Reza Shah." ProQuest Dissertations and Theses.

Martin Ennals Award (2009). "2009 Laureate Emadeddin Baghi.".

Matin-Asgari, A. (1991). "Students as the vanguard of opposition in Iran and abroad (1960–78)." *Middle East Studies Association of North America*.

——— (2004). "The Intellectual Best-Sellers of Post-Revolutionary Iran: On Backwardness, Elite-Killing, and Western Rationality." *Iranian Studies*, Vol 37. No. 1. March.

——— (2006). "Twentieth-century Iran's Political Prisoners." *Middle Eastern Studies*, 42(5), pp. 689–707.

——— (2007). "Modern Iran's Ideological Renegades: A Study in Intellectual Accommodation to State Power." *Critique*. Saint Paul, Minnesota., 16(2), pp. 137–53.

——— (2023). "This Flame Within: Iranian Revolutionaries in the United States." *Diaspora* (New York), 23(1), pp. 147–50.

——— (2024). "Iranian Identity and National Oppression: Crafting the Modern Iranian Nation–State." *Iranian Studies*, 57(2), pp. 311–16.

BIBLIOGRAPHY

Matin-Asgari, A., and Daryaee, T. (2012). "The Pahlavi Era Iranian Modernity in Global Context." In *The Oxford Handbook of Iranian History*. Oxford University Press.

Matin-Asgari, A. Marashi, A. and Aghaie K.S. (2014). "The Berlin Circle: Iranian Nationalism Meets German Countermodernity." In *Rethinking Iranian Nationalism and Modernity*. Austin: University of Texas Press.

Meier, D. (2007). "Between Court Jester and Spy: The Career of a Swiss Gardener at the Royal Court in Iran." *Critique: Journal for Critical Studies of the Middle East*. 9:16. pp. 75–87.

Merhavy, M. (2015). "Religious Appropriation of National Symbols in Iran: Searching for Cyrus the Great." *Iranian Studies*. 48:6 pp. 933–48.

MERIP Reports. (1971). "A Celebration of Power." No. 4. November.

Meyer-Landrut, A. (1964). "Portrait: Nikolai Viktorowitsch Podgorny." *Osteuropa* (Stuttgart), 14 (7+08), pp. 537–8.

Mottale, M. (2011). "Iran's Clerical Regime's 'Jewish Problem.'" *Democracy and Security* 7 (3): pp. 258–70.

Nikpour, G. (2018). "Claiming Human Rights: Iranian Political Prisoners and the Making of a Transnational Movement, 1963–1979." *Humanity* (Philadelphia) 9 (3): pp. 363–88.

Milani, A. (2010). "Zoroaster and the Ayatollahs." *The National Interest*. December 16.

Millward. W.G. (1971). "Traditional Values and Social Change in Iran." *Iranian Studies*. Vol 4. No. 1 Winter.

Mínguez, V., and Rodríguez-Moya, I. (2024). "Alexander in the Palace: Scenes from Court Life." In *The Visual Legacy of Alexander the Great from the Renaissance to the Age of Revolution*. pp. 127–37. London: Routledge.

Mirsepassi, A., and Faraji, M. (2018). "De-politicizing Westoxification: The Case of Bonyad Monthly." *British Journal of Middle Eastern Studies*, 45(3), pp. 355–75.

——— (2017). "Iranian Cinema's 'Quiet Revolution' 1960–1978." *Middle East Critique*. 26:4. pp. 397–415.

Mishra, P. (2016). "The Entrapments of Top-Down Modernity." *Raritan*. 36:2. Fall.

Moghadam, V. (1987). "Socialism or Anti-Imperialism? The Left and the Revolution in Iran." *NLR*. 166. November–December.

BIBLIOGRAPHY

Mokhtari, F. (2005). "No One Will Scratch My Back: Iranian Security Perceptions in Historical Context." *The Middle East Journal*. Vol 59, Issue 2.

Monshipouri, M., and Dorraj, M. (2021). "The Resilience of Populism in Iranian Politics: A Closer Look at the Nexus between Internal and External Factors." *Middle East Journal*, 75 (2), 201–21.

Morgan, J. (2017). "Who Has the Biggest Bulls? Royal Power and the Persepolis Apadana." *Iranian Studies*. 50–6.

Mitchell, L.G. (2023). "Appendix A: Translation of the Cyrus Cylinder" (Irving Finkel). In *Cyrus the Great*. Taylor and Francis.

Morrison, G. (2001). "Alexander, Combat Psychology and Persepolis." *Antichthon* 35.

Muller, L. (1997). "Iran and the Persian Gulf in the Pahlavi Era." ProQuest Dissertations and Theses.

Naghdipour, B. (2014). "Jokes in Iran." *Folklore* (Tartu, Estonia), 59(59), pp. 105–20.

Nasrabadi, M., Matin-Asgari, A., Kirasirova, M., Jian, C., Klimke, M., Nolan, M., Young, M., and Waley-Cohen, J. (2018). "The Iranian Student Movement and the Making of Global 1968." In *The Routledge Handbook of the Global Sixties*. pp. 443–56. Routledge.

Neary, B. U. (1986). "Shah Mohammed Reza Pahlavi and Ayatollah Khomeini: In Light of Shi'i History." ProQuest Dissertations and Theses.

Nelson, P. (2025). "Iannis Xenakis's Persepolis. By Aram Yardumian." *Music and Letters*.

Nematollahi, J., and Sayyad, A. (2024). "The Omnipresent Gaze: Exploring Surveillance in Amir Naderi's 'Goodbye Friend'" (1971). *Journal of Film and Video*, 76(4), pp. 19–30.

——— (2025). "Displaying Modern Life: Experiencing the Promises, Desires, and Perils of Mohammad Reza Pahlavi's Tehran through Window-Shopping in 'Crossroad of Events' (1955), 'Mr. Naïve' (1971), and 'Under the Skin of Night' (1974)." *Iranian Studies*, pp. 1–15.

Nibley, H. (1966). "Tenting, Toll, and Taxing." *The Western Political Quarterly*, 19(4), pp. 599–630.

O'Kane, B. (2021). "From Tents to Pavilions. Royal Mobility and Persian

Palace Design." In *Studies in Persian Architecture*. Edinburgh University Press.

Omid, H. (1992). "Theocracy or Democracy? The Critics of 'Westoxification' and the Politics of Fundamentalism in Iran." *Third World Quarterly*. Vol 13. No 4. pp. 675–90.

Palma, M. C. (2000). "The 1979 Iranian Revolution: A Study in the Role of Culture in the Modernization of Traditional Societies." ProQuest Dissertations and Theses.

Parham, B. (2005). "Dialogue between Michael Foucault and Baqir Parham." *Daedalus*. 134, 1. Winter.

Parvaz, N. and Namazie, M. (2003). "Beneath the Narcissus: A Woman's Experience of Iranian Prisons and Beyond." *Feminist Review*. pp. 71–85.

Penziner, V. L. (2006). "Selective Omission: Inserting Farah Pahlavi and Jehan Sadat into the Women's Movements of Iran and Egypt." ProQuest Dissertations and Theses.

Peters, M. A. (2021). "On the Epistemology of Conspiracy." *Educational Philosophy and Theory*. 53(14), pp. 1413–17.

Pliskin, K.L. (1980). "Camouflage, Conspiracy and Collaborators: Rumors of Revolution." *Iranian Studies*. Vol 13. No. 1/4.

Porat, D. (2022). "The Hijacking of El Al Flight 426: The Advent of Air Terrorism." *Journal of Contemporary History*, 57(4), pp. 1072–88.

Posnett, E. (2012). "Treating His Imperial Majesty's Warts: British Policy towards Iran 1977–79." *Iranian Studies*, 45(1), pp. 119–37.

Potts, D. T., (2014). "Iranian Nomads in the Achaemenid, Seleucid, and Arsacid Periods", in *Nomadism in Iran: From Antiquity to the Modern Era*, Oxford Academic.

Pursey, L. (2019). "Tents, Towns, and Topography: How Chinese-Language Liao Epitaphs Depicted the Moving Court." *Journal of Song-Yuan Studies*, 48(1), pp. 177–206.

Qiu, J. (2025). "Mao's Tour to the South and the Lin Biao Incident." *East Asia* (Piscataway, N.J.).

Raikka, J. (2009). "On Political Conspiracy Theories." *The Journal of Political Philosophy*, 17(2), pp. 185–201.

Ram, H, (1992). "Crushing the Opposition: Adversaries of the Islamic Republic of Iran." *Middle East Journal* Vol 46. No. 3. Summer.

BIBLIOGRAPHY

Ramazani, R. K. (1974). "Iran's 'White Revolution': A Study in Political Development." *International Journal of Middle East Studies*, 5(2), pp. 124–39.

Randjbar-Daemi, S. (2021). "The Tudeh Party of Iran and the Land Reform Initiatives of the Pahlavi State, 1958–1964." *Middle Eastern Studies*. 58:4, pp. 617–35.

Razavi, S. (2021). "Rocks and Hard Places: Gender, Satire, and Social Reproduction in Pre-Revolutionary Iran." *Review of Middle East Studies* (Tucson, Ariz.) 55 (1): pp. 69–90.

——— (2024). "Refracted: Mohammad Mosaddeq and Iranian National Identity." *International Journal of Middle East Studies* 56 (2): pp. 300–6.

Razi, G.H. (1968). "The Press and Political Institutions of Iran: A Content Analysis of 'Ettelat' and 'Keyhan'." *Middle East Journal*. Vol 22. No. 4 Autumn. pp. 463–74.

Reising, M. K. (2024). "The King's House or the Tyrant's Palace? Rethinking Persia in Herodotus's History." *Polis*, 41(2), pp. 203–26.

Rice, T. (2016). "Sounds Inside: Prison, Prisoners and Acoustical Agency." *Sound Studies*. August 18.

Rodley, Nigel. (2005). "Ennals, Martin." *Encyclopedia of Genocide and Crimes Against Humanity*.

Rouhani. H. (2024). "Comparing Martin Heidegger's and Jalal Al-e-Ahmad's Views on Technology." *PizhūhishÊ¹hā-Yi Falsafī* (Tabrīz.), 18(48), pp. 249–60.

Ryle, J. (2001). "Tales of Mythical Africa. Review of *The Shadow of the Sun* by Ryszard Kapuściński." *Times Literary Supplement*.

Sadeghi-Boroujerdi, E. (2024). "Al-e Ahmad's Faustian Bargain? Antonio Gramsci, the 'Progressive Clergy,' and the Search for Hegemony in Late-Pahlavi Iran." *The South Atlantic Quarterly* 123 (3): pp. 505–27.

Sadeghi-Esfahani, A. (2021). "Allegories Beyond Subalternity: The Transformation of Cinematic Expression during the 1970s in Iranian Film." *Quarterly Review of Film and Video*. 38:5 pp. 453–72.

Sadeghpour, A. (1973). "Leadership Pattern of a Contemporary Monarch: The Shah of Iran." Dissertation: Los Angeles. University of Southern California.

BIBLIOGRAPHY

Saffari, S. (2013). "Reclaiming Islam and Modernity: A Neo-Shariati Revisiting of Ali Shariati's Intellectual Discourse in Post-revolutionary Iran" (Vol 75, Number 6). ProQuest Dissertations and Theses.

Saidel, B. A. (2009). "Coffee, Gender, and Tobacco: Observations on the History of the Bedouin Tent." *Anthropos*. 104(1), pp. 179–86.

Saikal, A. (1979). "The Emergence of a State from Dependence to Regional Power: The Case of Iran, 1953–1979." ProQuest Dissertations and Theses.

Salehi-Isfahani, (2009). "Poverty and Inequality Since the Revolution, The Iranian Revolution at 30." Washington, DC: Middle East Institute.

Saleth, T. (2008). "May 68 and the Iranian Left." *Critique*. 36:2 pp. 303–5.

Samii, A. W. (1994). "The Role of Savak in the 1978–1979 Iranian Revolution." ProQuest Dissertations and Theses.

Sanadjian, M. (2011). "Islamic Rule and the pre-Islamic Blessing, the 'homecoming' of the Cyrus Cylinder." *Dialectical Anthropology*, 35(4), pp. 459–74.

Schayegh, C. (2018). "Mohammad Reza Shah Pahlavi's Autocracy: Governmental Constraints, 1960s-1970s." *Iranian Studies*, 51(6), pp. 889–904.

——— (2010). "Seeing Like a State: An Essay on the Historiography of Modern Iran." *International Journal of Middle East Studies*, 42(1), pp. 37–61.

Schultz, D. (2022). "Revolutionary Spectatorship and Subalternity: Foucault in Iran." *History and Theory* 61 No. 1 March. pp. 71–95.

Scullion, R. (1995). "Michel Foucault the Orientalist: On Revolutionary Iran and the 'Spirit of Islam.'" *South Central Review* Vol 12. No. 2. pp. 16–40.

Shahvar, S. (2009). "The Islamic Regime in Iran and Its Attitude towards the Jews: The Religious and Political Dimensions." *Immigrants and Minorities* 27 (1): pp. 82–117.

Shakibi, Z. (2013). Pahlavīsm: "The Ideologization of Monarchy in Iran." *Politics, Religion and Ideology*, 14(1), pp. 114–35.

——— (2018). "The Rastakhiz Party and Pahlavism: The Beginnings of State Anti-Westernism in Iran." *British Journal of Middle Eastern Studies*, 45(2), pp. 251–68.

BIBLIOGRAPHY

——— (2020). "Pahlavism." In *Pahlavi Iran and the Politics of Occidentalism*. London: Bloomsbury.

Shannon, M.K. (2011). "Contacts with the Opposition. American Foreign Relations, the Iranian Student Movement, and the Global Sixties." *The Sixties*. 4:1. pp. 1–29.

Sheehi, S. (2025). "Intimacies of Guerrillas: Palestinian Liberation and the Cold War Revolutionary Image." *Journal of War and Culture Studies*, *18*(2), pp. 184–202.

Sohrabi, N. (2018). "The 'Problem Space' of the Historiography of the 1979 Iranian Revolution." *History Compass*. 2018: 16.

——— (2019). "Remembering the Palestine Group: Global Activism, Friendship and the Iranian Revolution." *International Journal of Middle East Studies*. Vol 51. pp. 281–300.

Soltani, Z. (2020). "Tehran: A Symptomatic Rendering of Public Architecture." ProQuest Dissertations and Theses.

——— (2024). "(Un)Settled Monument: Tehran's Shahyad Square in the Revolutionary Crucible." *Journal of Planning History*, *23*(2), pp. 126–49.

Spier, J., Potts, T. F., Cole, S. E., and J. Paul Getty Museum (2022). *Persia: Ancient Iran and the Classical World*. Los Angeles: J. Paul Getty Museum.

St John, S., and Finkel, I. (2013). "The Cyrus Cylinder: Display and Replica." In *The Cyrus Cylinder* pp. 69–84. London: I.B. Tauris.

Steele, R. (2021). "Crowning the 'Sun of the Aryans': Mohammad Reza Shah's Coronation and Monarchical Spectacle in Pahlavi Iran." *International Journal of Middle East* Studies, 53(2), pp. 175–93.

——— (2021). "The Keur Farah Pahlavi Project and Iranian-Senegalese Relations in the 1970s." *Iranian Studies*, 54(1–2), pp. 169–92.

——— (2021). "Two Kings of Kings: Iran-Ethiopia Relations Under Mohammad Reza Pahlavi and Haile Selassie." *International History Review*, 43(6), pp. 1375–92.

——— (2022). "Iran's Golden Age of Tourism: The Development of the Travel Industry in the Late Pahlavi Period (c. 1960–1979)." *Journal of Tourism History*, 14(3), pp. 239–62.

——— (2019). "The Pahlavi National Library Project: Education and Modernization in Late Pahlavi Iran." *Iranian Studies*, 52(1–2), pp. 85–110.

BIBLIOGRAPHY

———— (2018). "The 2500th Anniversary Celebrations and Cultural Politics in Late Pahlavi Iran." ProQuest Dissertations and Theses.

Summitt, A. R. (2004). "For a White Revolution: John F. Kennedy and the Shah of Iran." *The Middle East Journal*, 58(4), pp. 560–75.

Takeyh, R. (2021). "Did the US Intelligence Community Lose Iran?" *Survival*. 63:2 pp. 155–70.

Tayebipour, M. (2023). "Ayatollah Khomeini Through the Lens of the Iran-Iraq War." *Studies in Iranian Politics*. Springer International Publishing.

Theberge, R. (1973). "Iran: Ten Years after the 'White Revolution'." *MERIP Reports*. No. 18. June.

Trebach, A. S. (1983). "The Lesson of Ayatollah Khalkhali." *Journal of Drug Issues*, 13, 287.

Trisno, R., Husin, D., Lianto, F., and Hartoyo, C. E. (2025). "The Concept of Tent as a Temporary Architecture in the Millennium Era." *Space and Culture*, 28(2), pp. 252–62.

Unal, Yusuf. (2016). "Sayyid Qutb in Iran: Translating the Islamist Ideologue in the Islamic Republic." *Journal of Islamic and Muslim Studies* Col 1 No. 2 November pp. 35–60.

Vahabzadeh, P. (2022). "Event and Myth: Preparatory Considerations for the Study of Parallel Movements." In *The Art of Defiance* pp. 13–51. Edinburgh University Press.

van de Laar, A. (2018). "Complications: The Maestro and the Shah: Mohammed Reza Pahlavi." In *Under the Knife*. St. Martin's Press.

van de Ven. A (2015). "(Re-)Awakening the Power of Persepolis." *AASV Bulletin*. September.

———— (2015). "Objects of Displacement: The Affective Journey of the Cyrus Cylinder" *ASOR Annual Meeting*.

———— (2017). "The Many Faces of the Cyrus Cylinder: Displaying Contested Objects as Constellations." PhD dissertation. School of Historical and Philosophical Studies.

———— (2017). "(De-)Revolutionising the Monuments of Iran." *Historic Environment*. 29 (3): 16–29.

van de Ven, A. and Luciani, M (2018). "Persepolis—Fantastic Site, and Don't Forget the Tent City." In *Proceedings of the 10th International Congress on the Archaeology of the Ancient Near East*, Volume 1, 539.

BIBLIOGRAPHY

van Prooijen, J-W. (2020). "An Existential Threat Model of Conspiracy Theories." *European Psychologist*, 25(1), pp. 16–25.

van Prooijen, J-W., and Douglas, K. M. (2018). "Belief in conspiracy theories: Basic principles of an emerging research domain." *European Journal of Social Psychology*, 48(7), pp. 897–908.

van Prooijen, J-W. and van Vugt, M. (2018). "Conspiracy Theories: Evolved Functions and Psychological Mechanisms." *Perspectives on Psychological Science*. Vol 13(6). pp. 770–88.

Vasunia, P. (2009). "Herodotus and the Greco-Persian Wars." *PMLA*. Vol 124. No 5. Special Topic War. October.

Vataman, D. (2018). "Romania During Ceaușescu's Dictatorship: First Period in Power. (1965–1971)." *Romanian Journal of Historical Studies*, 1(1), pp. 29–38.

Vick, B. (2015). "The Vienna Congress as an Event in Austrian History: Civil Society and Politics and the Habsburg Empire at the End of the Wars against Napoleon." *Austrian History Yearbook*. 46. pp. 109–33.

Vitriol, J. A., and Marsh, J. K. (2018). "The Illusion of Explanatory Depth and the Endorsement of Conspiracy Beliefs." *European Journal of Social Psychology*, 48(7), pp. 955–69.

Wainwright, D. (2019). "Equal Partners? The Information Research Department, SAVAK, and the Dissemination of Anti-Communist Propaganda in Iran, 1956–68." *British Journal of Middle Eastern Studies*, 46(3), pp. 404–24.

Walker, C. B. F. (1972). "A Recently Identified Fragment of the Cyrus Cylinder." *Iran: Journal of the British Institute of Persian Studies*, 10, pp. 158–9.

Watson, K. (1976). "The Shah's White Revolution. Education and Reform in Iran." *Comparative Education*. Vol 12. No. 1 March.

Westwood, A. (1965). "The Politics of Mistrust in Iran." *Annals of the American Academy of Political and Social Science*, 358. pp. 123–35.

Wilber, D.N. (1979). "The Timurid Court: Life in Gardens and Tents." *Iran*. Vol 17 pp. 127–33.

Willcocks, M. J. (2016). "Agent or Client: Who instigated the White Revolution of the Shah and the people in Iran, 1963?" ProQuest Dissertations and Theses Global.

BIBLIOGRAPHY

Wright, G.R.H. (1958). "Tents and Domes in Persia." *Man* Vol 58. October. pp. 159–60.

Xenakis, I. (2008). "Open Letter by Xenakis to 'Le Monde'", December 14, 1971. In *Music and Architecture*. pp. 223–4. Hillsdale: Pendragon Press.

Yazdani, M. (2012). "The Islamic Revolution's Internal Other: The Case of Ayatollah Khomeini and the Bahais of Iran 1." *Journal of Religious History* 36 (4): pp. 593–604.

Yavari, N., Zemmin, F., Dressler, M., and Stadler, N. (2024). "Jalal Al Ahmad: 'Westoxification' (1962)." In *The Middle East and North Africa: Vol II* pp. 337–43. Walter de Gruyter GmbH.

Zabih, S. (1982). "Aspects of Terrorism in Iran." *The Annals of the American Academy of Political and Social Science*. Vol 463. September.

Zahiri, A. (2021). "Frantz Fanon in Iran: Darling of the Right and the Left in the 1960s and 1970s." *Interventions*. 23:4 pp. 506–25.

Zahrani, T. (2002). "The Coup That Changed the Middle East: Mossadegh V. the CIA in Retrospect." *World Policy Journal* 19 (2): pp. 93–9.

Zarrinnal, N. (2024). "From The Creators of Knowledge to the Specialists of Spirit: Anti-Clericalism in Iran's Modernist Intellectual Discourse (1925–1941)." *The Harvard Theological Review*, 117(4), pp. 820–36.

Zia-Ebrahimi, R. (2016). "The Road to Officialdom." In *The Emergence of Iranian Nationalism*. New York: Columbia University Press.

GOVERNMENT DOCUMENTS

Ball, G. (1978). Report to President Carter, *Issues and Implications of the Iranian Crisis*, Washington: National Security Archive. December 12.

CIA. (1971). *Presidential Daily Briefing*. October 8.

CIA Directorate of Intelligence. (1969). *Brezhnev's Struggle for Power*. 5 December.

CIA Directorate of Intelligence. (1972). *Centers of Power in Iran*. May.

CIA Directorate of Intelligence. (1972). *Moscow and the Persian Gulf*. May 12.

CIA Office of National Estimates. (1971). *Nothing Succeeds Like a Successful Shah*. October.

BIBLIOGRAPHY

Department of State (1968). *Background Paper: Visit of Amir Abbas Hoveyda, Prime Minister of Iran, December 5–6, 1968*. Iran's Relations with Communist Countries.

Department of State (1970). *Youth in Iran: Assessment by Embassy Youth Committee*. CA 322. February 22.

Department of State. (1970). 204. Paper Prepared by the NEA Working Group in the Department of State Operations Center. Washington, September 7.

Department of State (1971). *Students, Youth Groups, Iran*. NEA/IRN, Office of Iran Affairs, Lot File 75D351, Box 6, POL 13–2.

Department of State (1971). *Conversation Between President Nixon and the President's Assistant for National Security Affairs (Kissinger)*. Office of the Historian, Washington, May 26.

Department of State (1971). *Telegram 4816 From the Embassy in Iran to the Department of State*. (A) Tehran 671: (B) Tehran 4306. Office of the Historian, Washington, August 30.

Department of State (1972). *Centers of Power in Iran*. Intelligence Report 2035–72. Office of the Historian, May.

Department of State (1972). *Iran: Internal Dissidence—A Note of Warning*. Bureau of Intelligence and Research. June 12.

Department of State (1972). *Corruption in Iran: A Problem for American Companies*. June 20.

Department of State (1972). *Continuing Terrorist Violence*. Pol 23–8 IRAN. Tehran 5055. Office of the Historian, Washington,.

Department of State (1972). *President's Visit: Joint Communique*. Telegram 3254 From the Embassy in Iran to the Department of State. Office of the Historian. May 31.

Department of State (1972). *Journalist Argues that Unchecked SAVAK Power Constitutes Long-Term Danger to Iranian Regime*. Ref: Tehran 4789. Office of the Historian, Washington, September 9.

FCO (1971). *Visit of Duke of Edinburgh to Iran for 2500th Anniversary of Iranian Monarchy, October 1971*. 57/322.

FCO (1971). *Visit of Duke of Edinburgh to Iran for 2500th Anniversary of Iranian Monarchy, Including Details of Gifts Given by Shah*, October 1971. 57/323.

BIBLIOGRAPHY

FCO (1971). *2,500th Anniversary of Monarchy of Iran Celebrations in Persepolis and Tehran, 1971.* 17/1528.

FCO (1971). *2,500th Anniversary of Monarchy of Iran Celebrations in Persepolis and Tehran: Loan of the Cyrus Liberation Tablet by the British Museum to Iran for the Celebrations Honouring the Foundation of the Persian Empire by Cyrus the Great, 1971–1972.* 17/1529.

FCO. (1971). *2,500th Anniversary of Monarchy of Iran celebrations in Persepolis and Tehran: loan of the Cyrus Liberation Tablet by the British Museum to Iran for the celebrations honouring the foundation of the Persian Empire by Cyrus the Great.* NEP 26/1.

FCO. (1971). *Demonstrations by Students in Iran.* File No. NEP 1/7.

FCO. (1971). *Iran in 1971.* File No. NEP 1/1. December 29.

FCO. (1972). *Visit of Shah of Iran to UK, 21–25 June* (folder 1) 1972.

FCO. (1972). *Conspiracies against the Family and Life of Shah of Iran.* FCO 8/2288.

FCO. (1974). *Discussions between Mr A D Parsons, UK Ambassador in Tehran, and Shah of Iran* 1974.

FCO. (1975). *Discussions between Sir Anthony Parsons, UK Ambassador, and Shah of Iran* 1975.

FCO (1979). *Position of the Shah of Iran and Pahlavi Family: Question of Entry into the UK* 1979.

FCO. (1980). *The Shah of Iran and His Family.*

FCO. (1981). *British Policy in Iran 1974–1978.* NBP 020/28.

FO (1967). *The Shah's Coronation.* London. 248/1637,.

FO (1970). *Celebration of the 2,500th Anniversary of the Iranian Monarchy.* 248/1637,.

Iranian Government Documents Collected by the Revolutionary Government: (1998): *'Pahlavi-ye Dovvom va Nemuneh-ye Andishehhā-ye Bāstāngerāyāneh: negāhi be asnād-e mahramāneh-yejashnhā-ye 2500 sāleh-ye shāhanshāhi'* [The Second Pahlavi and some Elements of Archaic Thoughts: A Look at the Secret Documents Relating to the 2500th Anniversary Celebrations], Tārikh-e moʿāser-e irān, 2:5 (1377/1998).

Iranian Government Documents Collected by the Revolutionary Government (1998–2000): *Bazm-e Ahriman: jashnhā-ye 2500 sāleh-ye shāhanshāhi ba revāyat-e asnād-e sāvāk va darbār* [The Devil's Feast: The

BIBLIOGRAPHY

2500th Anniversary Celebrations according to SAVAK and Court Documents], four volumes (Tehran: Markaz-eBarrasi-ye Asnād-e Tārikhi-ye Vizārat-e Etelaʿāt, 1377–1378/1998–2000).

Kissinger, H. (1971). *Memorandum from the President's Assistant for National Security Affairs (Kissinger) to President Nixon.* Foreign Relations of the United States 1969–1976. Vol E-4. Washington, April 6.

Oney, E. (1976). *Elites and the Distribution of Power in Iran.* Central Intelligence Agency Research Study. February.

U.S. House of Representatives, (1977). *Human Rights in Iran*, Hearing Before the Subcommittee on International Organizations of the Committee on International Relations House of Representatives. October. Washington: U.S. Government Printing Office.

MEDIA ARTICLES

Adler, N. (2017). "Als der Schah zur größten Party auf Erden lud." *Spiegel.* 14 February.

Apple. R.W. (1982). "Guns Displace the Grandeur that was Persepolis." *The New York Times.* 17 November.

Ascherson, N. (1972). "Firing squads kept busy." *The Observer.*

Associated Press (1971). "Iranian Minister Says Fete Cost $16.6 million." 25 October.

Afshar, H. (2003). "Ayatollah Sadeq Khalkhali." *The Guardian.*

Alamir, D. (1971). "Persépolis accueille avec un faste sans precedent des dizaines de chefs d'État et de gouvernement de très importantes mesures de sécurité ont été prises." *Le Monde.* 12 October.

Azizi, A. (2019). "Sister Mary and Her Hostage, 38 years Later." *Iranwire*, 3 February.

Bakhash S. (1986). "A Big Bungle." *The New York Review of Books.* 8 May.

Baraheni, R. (1976). "Terror in Iran." *The New York Review of Books.* 28 October.

Bender. A (2020). "Remembering Malcolm Forbes' 70th Birthday, where 1980s Excess Peaked." *Insidehook.com.* 17 September.

Bondy, F. (1971). "Tehran: Pageantry of a Dynastic Era." *The New York Times.* 21 June.

BIBLIOGRAPHY

Branigan, W. (1979). "The Shah's Palace: Luxury, Simplicity." *The Washington Post*. 18 January.

Browne, M. (1971). "A Spectacle in Fall to Mark Persia's 2,500 Years." *The New York Times*. 27 July.

Buruma, I. (2005). "The Indiscreet Charm of Tyranny." *The New York Review of Books*. 12 May.

Burke, J, (2001). "Shah's Opulent Tent City Awaits Rebirth in Desert" *The Observer*. 9 September.

Cockburn, A., Ridgeway, J. and Albert, J. (2020). "Beautiful Butchers: The Shah Serves Up Caviar and Torture: The Social Success of the Shah in the Galaxy of International Despots Is the End Result of a Careful Campaign, Premised on Two Vital Ingredients: Snobbery and Cash." *The Village Voice* (Online). 4 August.

Cooley, J.K. (1972). "Relations Between Iran, Iraq Tense." *The Washington Post*. 28 January.

Curtis, C. (1971). "Tent City Awaits Celebration: Shah's 'Greatest Show'", *The New York Times*, 12 October.

——— (1971). "First Party of Iran's 2,500-Year Celebration." *The New York Times*. 13 October.

——— (1971). "Mrs. Marcos is First Guest at Iran Fete." *The New York Times*. 14 October.

——— (1971). "A Persian Night of Kings, Queens, Sheikhs, Sultans, and Diamonds." *The New York Times*. 15 October.

——— (1971). "Neighbors Go Visiting in Iran's Tent City." *The New York Times*. 16 October.

——— (1971). "After the Ball: Has Shah Achieved Lasting Gains?" *The New York Times*. 19 October.

Dabashi, H. (2016). "Lady Macbeth or just Princess Ashraf Pahlavi." Chicago: *TCA Regional News*. 8. January.

Dehgham, S.K. (2017). "After Azadi: Man Behind Iran's Freedom Tower on how his Life Unravelled." *The Guardian*. 15 August.

Dowden. R. (1984). "In the Terror of Tehran." *The New York Review of Books*. 2 February.

Drew, E. (1980). "1980: Kennedy." *The New Yorker*. 4 February.

Diba, F. (1960). "The Diary of a Bride-to-Be." *The Washington Post*. 31 January.

BIBLIOGRAPHY

Economist. (1971). "Iran: By Invitation Only." London: *The Economist* 9 October.

——— (2003). "Sadeq Khalkhali, Iran's Hanging Judge." London: *The Economist*. Vol 369, Number 8354, p. 86.

——— (2013). "Diplomatic Whirl: The Cyrus Cylinder." London: *The Economist*. Vol 406, No. 8828, p. 93.

——— (2013). "Why is the Cyrus Cylinder Important? The Economist explains." London: *Economist* Online.

Economist Intelligence Unit (1971). "Iran Fourth Quarter Report." *EIU*.

Erdbrink, T. (2018). "A Mummy Turned Up in Iran. Could it be the Former Shah?" *The New York Times*. 3 May.

Esfandiari, G. (2009). "A Vanishing Breed, Iranian Satirist Pokes Fun from Exile." *Radio Free Europe*.

Financial Times (1971). "Contentious Issue." 12 October.

Friendly, A. (1971). "Cyrus: A King Fit for a 2,500th Anniversary." *The Washington Post*. 18 October.

Gellner, E. (1984). "Inside Khomeini's Mind." *The New Republic*. 18 June.

Hannah, N. (1982). "The Night of the Ayatollahs." *National Review*. 14 May.

Hyde, S. (2022). "Far from the Madeleine Crowd." London: *World of Interiors*. 5 December.

Giniger, H. (1972). "For Maxim's, Still Three Stars in the Michelin." *The New York Times*. 8 March.

Grenier, C. (1971). "Tent City for Iran Celebrations Has Echoes of Arabian Nights." *The Los Angeles Times*. 14 October.

——— (1971). "Iran: Catching a Bite to Eat at Anniversary Celebration." *The Los Angeles Times*. 17 October.

——— (1971). "Hairstyling at Persepolis: Judy Agnew First in Line." *The Los Angeles Times*. 18 October.

——— (1971). "Iran Melting Pot of Culinary Traditions." *The Los Angeles Times*. 21 October.

——— (1971). "2,500 years of Civilization Passing in Review." *The Los Angeles Times*. 31 October.

Guardian. (1971). "A Kingdom Remembered—2,500 years on." 12 October.

BIBLIOGRAPHY

——— (1971). "Iran in a Modern Setting." 13 October.

——— (1971). "Finale Saves the Cyrus Show." 16 October.

Hannah, N. (1982). "The Night of the Ayatollahs." *National Review*. 14 May.

Hess, J. (1971). "Made in France—Persia's Splendorous Anniversary Celebration." *The New York Times*. 5 October.

Housego, D. (1971). "Heavy Guard as Shah Inaugurates Pageantry." *The Times*. 13 October.

Jacobi, F. (1949), "New Boy." *The New Yorker*. 26 February.

Jenkins, L. (1971). "Iran's Birthday Party." *Newsweek*. Vol 78, No. 17.

Johnston, M. (1971). "When the Bomb Went Off ..." *California Living Magazine*. December.

Jullian, P. (1977). "Architectural Digest Visits the Empress of Iran." *Architectural Digest*. December.

Le Monde (1971). "M. Pompidou: Les relations entre France et l'Iran sont excellentes." 9 October.

LIFE Magazine (1971). "Cover Story on Cristina Ford." New York. 4 June.

Los Angeles Times (1971). "DeMille Outdone in Persian Spectacular." 16 October.

——— (1971). "Feast Boss Solved a Crisis—a Corker." 19 October.

Mann, A. (1971). "Paris Wins the Order of the Bath." *The Daily Telegraph*. 11 October.

Marsden, E. (1971). "Guerrillas at Shah's Feast." *The Sunday Times*. 10 October.

Meinhof, U. (1967). "Open Letter to Farah Diba." *Neue Revue*. June.

Messud, C. (2009). "In Evin Prison." *The New York Review of Books*. 3 December.

Middle East (magazine). (2013). "Cyrus Cylinder Travels the US.". IC Publications Ltd.

Mirabella, G. (1971). "Fashions in Living: Fete for a King: New Designs, New Ideas Sweeping West from Iran." *Vogue*. Vol 158. Issue 7. October.

Morgan, E.P. (1975). "The Persian Predicament." *The Washington Post*. 21 June.

Morris, J. (1969). "Shahbanou Farah Pahlavi. The Spirit of Modern Persia." *Vogue*. December Issue.

BIBLIOGRAPHY

Nabavi, E. (2009). "The Confession: Ebrahim Nabavi: Mohammad Ali Abtahi." YouTube. 7 July Archived from the original on 21 December 2021.

Naipaul, V.S. (1997). "After the Revolution." *The New Yorker*. 18 May.

New York Times (1971). "Iran's Tent City—Potentate Housing." 3 October.

——— (1971). "In the Footsteps of Cyrus?" 12 October.

——— (1971). "First Party of Iran's 2,500-Year Celebration." 13 October.

——— (1971). "After 'the Tumult and the Shouting Dies' and the Captains and the King's Depart.'" 25 November.

New Yorker. (1947). "Talk of the Town: Progressive." 25 October.

O'Donovan, P. (1967). "Is it not Passing Fair to be a King?" *The Observer*.

——— (1971). "Dust settles on the Shah's picnic." *The Observer*.

Pahlavi. A. (1979). "I Am a Mother Who Has Lost a Cherished Child." *The Washington Post*, A22.

Paton Walsh, N. (2003). "Real St Petersburg Forced into Hiding." *The Guardian*. 24 May.

Pareles, J. (2000). "Iran's Silenced Star Bridging a 21-year Gap." *The New York Times*. 28 August.

Pope, H. (1986). "Iranians Get Their First Look at Shah's Favorite Palace: Bulldog Edition." *The Los Angeles Times*. 6 July.

Quinn, S. (1971). "50 Monarchs—50!—and All the Shaikhs of Arabee: Shah to Entertain VIPs in 'Tent City.'" *The Washington Post*. 29 August.

——— (1971). "A Sumptuous Party of Parties by the King of Kings." *The Washington Post*. 11 October.

——— (1971). "Splendor in the Dust." *The Washington Post*. 13 October.

——— (1971). "Travail in Tent City." *The Washington Post*. 16 October.

——— (1971). "The Party's Over." *The Washington Post*. 16 October.

——— (1971). "Winding up in Tehran." *The Washington Post*. 19 October.

Radan, S. (2010). "Parviz Tanavoli's Affair with Nothingness." *McClatchy-Tribune Business News*. Washington: Tribune Content Agency LLC.

Rais, G. (1971). "Shah Honours Cyrus With Splendour and Simplicity." *The Daily Telegraph*. 13 October.

Rahati, G. (2001). "Marketing the Prison Experience in Tehran." *Cabinet*. Fall.

BIBLIOGRAPHY

Randal, J. C. (1971). "The Shah's Iran. Arms, Debts, and Repression are the Price of Progress." *The Washington Post.* 10 October.

Randal, J.C. (1979). "Iranians Mix Fact with Fiction in Long Crisis Over Shah." *The Washington Post.* 15 December.

Rouleau E. (1971). "L'absence de M. Pompidou aux fêtes de Persépolis est une 'Décision regrettable', nous déclare le chah d'Iran." *Le Monde.* 8 October.

Rubin, E. (2003). "The Millimeter Revolution." *The New York Times Magazine.* 6 April.

Sahimi, M (2009). "The Bloody Red Summer of 1988." *PBS Frontline.* 25 August.

Sale, R.T. (1977). "SAVAK: A Feared and Pervasive Force." *The Washington Post.* 9 May.

Skelton, G. (1989). "Forbes Dazzles a Who's Who of Americans": Home Edition. *The Los Angeles Times.*

Smith. A (1971). "Iran's Era of Trepidation." *The Guardian.* 29 July.

Sulzberger, C. (1972). "Still a King of Kings." *The New York Times.* 11 February.

Szulc, T. (1971). "Peking Reported in Drive to Play Key Role in Mideast and Africa." *The New York Times.* 17 October.

Targeted News Service. (2013). "J. Paul Getty Museum Extends Dates for Popular Exhibition: The Cyrus Cylinder and Ancient Persia: A New Beginning." In *Targeted News Service.*

Tribune (1980). "Ayatollah Khalkhali." *Tribune* (London). Vol 44, Number 21, p. 10.

Tuohy, W. (1979). "Tour of a Vacant Palace: Shah Left Behind Art, Jewels, Photos." *The Los Angeles Times.* 18 January.

United Press International (1971), "Kings and Presidents Anxiously Dine Under Swaying Chandeliers." 15 October.

——— (1971). "Iranian Consul Lays Blast to Emigres." San Francisco. 16 October.

——— (1971). "Bomb-blasted Iran Consulate Target of Rally." 16 October.

van England, C. (1982). "Brutal Punishments Mark Daily Life in Iran." *The Christian Science Monitor.*

BIBLIOGRAPHY

Variety (1972). "Emerging from 2,500th Anniversary, Iran Maturing as a Broadcaster." *Variety*. 12 January.
Wardle, I. (1971). "A Theater Without Precedent." *The Los Angeles Times*. 17 October.
Washington Post (1971). "Welcome to the Party." 14 October.
——— (1971). "Persepolis Pecking Order." 15 October.
——— (1971). "Defensive Shah." 20 October.
Yong, William. (2010). "Dissident Iranian Journalist is Jailed in a Continued Crackdown." *The New York Times*. 22 September.

ORAL HISTORY and ENCYCLOPEDIAS

Two main Iranian oral history projects cover this period: The Iranian Oral History Collection, Harvard University, and the Oral History of Iran Collection of the Foundation for Iranian.
Studies in Bethesda, Virginia.
Assar, S. (1986). Interview with Peter Ramsbotham Hampshire, January 20. Oral History of Iran Collection of the Foundation for Iranian Studies.
Ladjevardi, H. (1984). Interview with Denis Wright. Aylesbury, UK, October 10 and 11.
Iranian Oral History Collection. Harvard University.
Ladjevardi, H (1985). Interview with Peter Ramsbotham. London. October 18. Iranian Oral History Collection. Harvard University.
Nasr, V. (1991). Interview with Earnest R Oney. Oral History Program of the Foundation for Iranian Studies.
Encyclopædia Iranica (iranicaonline.org) is a vital resource for information about Iran.

INDEX

Abadan, 209, 210
Abbas Mirza (Crown Prince), 227
Abbas, Shah, 46
Abrahamian, Ervand, 260, 295
Abu Dhabi, 96
Abu Ghraib, 253
Achaemenid Empire, xiii, 37, 45, 46, 48, 49, 52, 142, 174, 271–2, 279, 288–9, 330
Achilles, 290
Acropolis, 285–6
Adams, Eddie, 57
Addis Ababa, 111
Adle, Parviz, 292
Afghanistan, 7–9, 92, 122, 341–2
Afkhani, Gholamreza, 181
Africa, 111, 154
African Union, 111
Afshar, Amin Aslan, 298
aghazadeh, 338
Agnew, Spiro, 79, 84–5, 140, 309
Agreement (1901), 214–15
Al-e Ahmad, Jalal, 171, 229–30, 244, 245

Ahmadinejad, Mahmoud, 126, 174, 174, 180, 263–5
Ahmed Khan, Sayyed, 177
Air Force Two, 84, 309
Air France (747), 308
Akkadian script, 127
Alam, Asadollah, 15–16, 21–2, 24–31, 95, 97, 132, 158, 161, 166, 173, 282, 313, 332–3
tent, 38–45, 47–8
Albania, 150
Albion, Perfidious, 21
Alborz Hills, 248
Alexander the Great, xiv, 5, 44–5, 50, 140, 143, 178, 289–91
Persepolis attacked by, 285–9
Alfred (King), 176
Algeria, 55, 154, 241
Algerian National Liberation Front, 241
Amanat, Hossein, 310–13
Amazons, 290
American Legation, 87

INDEX

American Women's Club Handbook for Tehran, 223–4
Americans, 208, 218, 236, 266–7, 303
Amin, Idi, xvi, 80
Amini, Ali, 16, 87, 159
Amini, Mahsa, 336, 341
Amnesty International, 148–52
Amsterdam Airport, 56
Amsterdam, 55
Ananta, Pramoedya, 261–2
Anglo-Iranian Oil Company, 208, 214–216
Ankara, 84
Anne (Princess), 94, 96–7, 218–19, 282, 283–4
Ansari, Ali, 211
anti-clericism, 244
anti-colonialism, 12, 215
Anti-Semitism, 234
Apadana, 285, 287
Apollo, 125
Arafat, Yasser, 57
Arctic, 199
Arda Viraf (Zoroastrian text), 289
Ardres, 41
Argentina, 151
Argo (film), 148
Arguello, Patrick, 56
Armenia, 229, 278
Arnaud, Pierre, 284, 285
Arnault, Bernhard, 47
Arrian of Nicomedia, 5
Arsanjani, Hasan, 16, 159
Art Basel (2007), 195

Aryan people, 79, 179
Arymehr University of Industry, 226
Asceticism, 234
Ascot, 95, 96
Ashraf (Princess), 30, 75, 118, 134, 136, 159, 160–1, 195–7, 219
Ashurnasirpal II (King), 272
Asia, xvii, 131
Al-Assad, Hafez, 80, 180
Assyria, 49, 272, 279
Ataturk, Kemal, 235, 307
Athenaeus, 44, 278
Athenians, 272
Athens, 45, 285
Austria, 78
AWC, 224
Ayadi, Abdul Karim, 99
Azad, Abul Kalam, 178
Azadi Monument, 320, 333
Azerbaijan, 60
Azerbaijan crisis, 153–4
Azeris, 258

Baader-Meinhof Gang, 189
Baath Party, 181
Baathism, 267
Babism, 320
Babylon, xiv, 23, 49, 121–3, 181, 285
Babylonian temple, 121
Badrutt's Palace Hotel (St. Moritz), 81, 200, 270–1, 280
Baghdad Treaty, 116
Baghdad, 90, 96, 303

INDEX

Baghi, Emadeddin, 64–5
Baghj-e Eram, 35
Baha-Allah, Mirza Hussein Ali Nuri, 320
Bahais, 139, 217, 232, 312–313, 307, 320–1, 320, 337
Bahamas, xxi
Bahrain, 56, 141
Bakhtiar, Teymour (General), 54, 59–61, 159
Baku, 144
Balfour Declaration, 123
Balkans, xiv
Ball, George, 331
Balochistan, 204, 229
Bandung Generation, 213
Bangladesh, xvi, 86
Bani-Sadr, Abolhasan, 298, 321–2
Baraheni, Reza, 135, 152–3, 260
Bardot, Brigitte, xx
Barzagan, Mohammad, 256
Basel, 197
Bastille, 253
Bathsheba, 6
Bazaaris, 236, 244–5, 296, 300, 303
BBC Persian Service, 95–6, 164
Beaton, Cecil, 2
Beekman Place, 196–7
Beetle, VW, 111
Behdad, Sadiq, 53–4
Beijing, xvi, 31–2, 73, 106, 312
Beirut, 55, 56, 223
Béjart, Maurice, 204
bejel, 190
Belgrade, 8

Belshazzar, 122, 123
Bemileke War, 154
Bengali nationalists, 85
Ben-Gurion, David, 123
Benthamite Panopticon, 248
Berenson, Peter, 148
Berlin, 87
Biafra, 148
Bible, 23, 122, 177
Billings, Lem, 145
Birjand, 282
Blanch, Lesley, 198
BOAC, 56
Boer Republic of the Orange Free State, 113
Bokassa, Jean-Bedel, 80
Bolsheviks, 234
Bonaparte, Napoleon, 23
Book of Wei, The (Book), 46
Bordeaux, 280
Borujerdi, Ayatollah Mohamed Hossein, 14, 234, 235
Bossom, Clive, 129
Boudin, Stephane, 38–9
Brazil, 13, 66, 299
Brezhnev Doctrine, 101, 116–17
Brezhnev, 117, 150–1
Britain, 42, 56, 75, 78, 95, 107, 110, 149, 189, 208, 327
British East India Company, 177
British Embassy, 160, 227
British Foreign Office, 78
British India, 85
British Museum, 121–2, 125, 128, 193

INDEX

British Navy, 214
British, 85, 95, 208, 209–10, 234–5
Brook, Peter, 204
Broz, Jovanka, 108
Bruni, Carla, 253
Bucharest, 105
Buddhists, 246
Bulgarian Communist Party, 33
Bundestag, 82
Bunte (women's magazine), xix–xx
Burebista, (Dacian king) 103
Burgundy, 280
Buru Quartet (Ananta), 261–2

Caesar, 18
Cairo, 30, 55, 56, 77
Calais, 40
California, xvi, 292
Caligula, 135
Cambodia, 151
Cambyses, 125
Canada, 71, 152, 174
capitalism, 240, 245, 248
Capote, Truman, 2, 87
Carl-Gustaf (Crown Prince), 284
"Carmina Burana", 284
Carter, Jimmy, xx–xxi, 259, 293–4, 296
Cartier-Bresson, Henri, 137
Casino Ab Ali Supper Club, 223
Caspian Sea, 43, 189–90, 273
Castelot, Andre, 284
Catherine of Aragon, 42
Catherine the Great, 313–15

Caucasus, 116, 234
Cave Argent, 223
caviar, 273–8
Ceaușescu, Nicolae, 4, 101–5, 108, 157
 protests, 105–6
Cecil B. DeMille, 142
Central Asia, 7, 9, 116
Central Bank, 63
Cervantes, Miguel de, 261
Césaire, Aimé, 244
Chaban-Delmas, Jacques, 98
Chalfont (Lord), 134
Chandigarh, 310
Charles (Prince), 94
Château de Ferrières, 2
Château Lafite Rothschild, 280–1
Chatham House, 214
Che Guevara, 57, 66
Chiang Kai-Shek, 76
Chile, 151
China, xvi, 4, 13, 57, 66, 86, 101, 102, 296, 299, 329
 Cultural Revolution, 73–7, 150
Chinese Academy of Sciences, 77
Chinese Communist Party, 73
Chinese government, 73
Chinese People's Liberation Army, 73
Christianity, xviii
Christians, 139
Christmas, 275
Churchill, Winston, 87, 118, 208, 210
CIA (Central Intelligence Agency), 60, 71–72, 210, 213

INDEX

Circus Ball (1938), 39
Claude, Madame, xiv, 161
Cleopatra (Queen), 291
Clergy, 247
Cointrin Airport, 160
Colacello, Bob, 195, 196–7
Cold War, xx, 4, 62, 86, 88, 90, 92, 115, 157, 240
The Colonels (Greek dictatorship), 300
colonialism, 80, 208, 244
communism, 58, 101, 103, 240, 247
Communist Party of Iran, 74, 76, 156
Confederation of Iranian Students, 292
Congress of Vienna, 1, 78, 283
Congressional Record, 151
Consolation of Philosophy, The (Boethius), 261
Constantine (King), 309
Copenhagen, 284
Cornwall, 71
cosmopolitanism, 229
Cossacks, 52, 95, 317
Cote d'Azur, 160
Council of Revolution, 298
Crash of '79, The (Erdman), xx
Crowned Cannibals (Baraheni), 135
Cuba, 87
Cultural Revolution, 57, 73–7, 220–1, 263
Curtis, Charlotte, 33, 40, 327
Curzon (Lord), 51

cynicism, 220, 221
Cyrus at Pasargadae, xiii–xiv, 5, 35, 173
Cyrus Cylinder, 325–6
Cyrus the Great, xiii–xiv, 1, 5, 23, 37, 48, 110, 121, 122–8, 156, 174–5, 271, 304, 322, 340
  Islamic history and Cyrus, 176–9
Czechoslovakia, 101, 140

D'Arcy, William Knox, 210
d'Estaing, Valéry Giscard, xxi, 167
Dabashi, Hamid, 136
Daftari, Fereshteh, 193
Daily Mail (newspaper), 207
Dalí, Salvador, 3
Damascus, 90, 279
Darab (Persian King), 289
Darius I (Emperor), 44, 48, 125, 175–6, 178, 279, 287, 289–90
Darius III (King), 279
Darwish, Hamid, 205
Dawson's Field, 55
de Gaulle, Charles, 77, 89, 97, 194
de Montebello, Louis-Gustav, 316
DeBakey, Michael, 108
Decebalus, (Dacian king), 103
Delbee, Pierre, 47
Democratic Party, 90
Deng Xiaoping, xxi
Dhaka, 86
Dhofar Rebellion, 141
Diba, Farah (Empress), 5, 31, 78, 83, 150, 163, 185–8, 189–90, 193–4, 282, 323

INDEX

rise and fall of, 202–3
role in development of cultural life, 198–9
struggles faced by, 200–2
Diodorus of Sicily, 50
Dior, 200
Discovery of Secrets, The (Khomeini), 307
Divine Comedy (Dante), 286–7
Dom Pérignon, 280
Dong Biwu, 76
Dr. Shariati Street, 318
Dryden, John, 287
Dubai, 338
Douro, Marquess of, 97
Duvalier, Baby Doc 151

East Bengal, xvi
East of Suez, 85
East River, 197
East Timor, 151
Eastern Bloc, 117, 150
Eastern Europe, 101, 105, 107, 116, 118
Ebtekar, Masoumeh, xx
Economist Intelligence Uni, The, xvii, 329
Edifice Complex, 310
Egypt, xxi, 43, 49, 62, 90, 106, 110, 116, 125, 141, 157, 175, 286, 291
Eisenhower, Dwight D., 217
El Al, 55
Elizabeth II (Queen), 24, 79, 93–4, 96, 104, 146, 156, 281

Engels, Friedrich, 103
Ennals, Martin, 148–50
Ernest Perron: The Husband of the Shah of Iran (book), 146
Ethiopia, 4, 110, 329
Ettilat (newspaper), 298
Europe, xviii, 9, 23, 41, 45, 52, 60, 61, 78, 188, 228–9, 270–1
European Economic Community, xvi
European Union, xvi
Evin House of Detention, 152, 248–9, 250–4, 255–7, 259–63, 265–6
Existentialism, 243
Eyes Wide Shut (film), 3

Fabiola (Queen), 282
Facebook, 156
Fadai, 66, 69–70
Fadaiyan-e Khalq, 300
Falk, Richard, 230
Fallaci, Oriana, 163–6, 299
Fanon, Frantz, 239, 241, 244
Faraghi, Mohsen, 193
Farah Abad, 46
Fardust, Hussein, 144
Farmafarmaian, Khodadad, 63
Farmanfarmaian, Abdol-Aziz, 193
fascism, 181
Fatema (Princess), 76
Fauchon, 27
Fawzia (Princess), 30, 147
Fedaiyan-e Islam, 307, 317
Fellinger, Karl, 99
Ferdowsi Square, 275

INDEX

Ferdowsi, 52, 136, 176
Field of the Cloth of Gold, 40–1
filmfarsi, 224
Financial Times (newspaper), 95
Finland, 140
Five-Year Plan I, 13
Flandrin, Georges, 99
Forbes, Malcolm, 3
Ford II, Henry, 83
Ford, Charlotte, 283
Ford, Cristina, 83, 112, 324
Foreign Affairs, xvii
Foreign Policy (magazine), 230
Forest Guard HQ, 67
Foucault, Michel, 245
Fouché, Jacobus (jim), 113
France, 27, 29, 40, 53, 98–9, 100, 107, 114, 154, 228, 241–2, 300
Francis I, 40
Frankfurt Auschwitz trials, 192
Frankfurt, 55
Franzetti, Dante, 270–1
Frederik IX (King), 281–2
French Cameroon, 154
Frye, Richard, 339
Furstenberg, Cardinal von, 81

G7 meetings, 71
Gainsbourg, Charlotte, xvii
Gandhi, Indira, 85–6
Gandhi, Mahatma, 234
Gaumy, Jean, 256–7
Gdansk, 138
Geneva, 160
Genoa, 41

George V, (King), 123
Georgians, 229
Germany, 10, 61, 82, 188, 189, 241
Gestapo, 63
Ghaffari, Hojatoleslam Hadi, 319
Gheorghiu-Dej, Gheorghe, 103
al-Ghifari, Abu Dharr, 239
Gierek, Edward, 138
Gilan mountains, 67
Giri, V. V., 112
Golden Imperial Caviar, 276
Golestan, 204
Golpayegani, Mohammad-Reza, 277
Google Maps, 248
Googoosh, 223, 284
Graham, Katharine, 2
Great Leap Forward, 13
Greece, 84, 107, 286, 300
Greeks, 272, 288, 324
Greeley, 242
Green Movement (2009), 264, 336
Greenhill, Denis, 93
Guangzhou, 74
guerrilla movements (1970), 199
Guerrilla Warfare (Che Guevara), 66
Guines, 41
Gulf sheikhs, 107
Gurion, David Ben, 123
Guyana, xix

Habash, 56
Habbash, Georges, 55
Haddad, Wadi, 55

INDEX

Haeri, Abdolkarim, 234, 235
Haifa, 57
Haiti, 151
Hamadani, Mohammed Ibn Mahmud, 51
Hamburg, 190
Hamid II, Ahmed, 80
Hanoi, 149
Harem of Xerxes, 51
Hassan, Hengameh Haj, 251
Hassel, Kai-Uwe von, 82
Heath, Edward, 129, 149
Hebrew, 122
Heech (sculpture), 192–193
Heidegger, Martin, 245
Heinemann, Gustav, 78
Hellenic League, 288, 291
Henderson, D.A., 10–11
Henry VIII, (king) 40
Hepburn, Audrey, 2–3
Heraclides of Cyme, 278
Herodotus, 38, 45, 174, 272–3
Herrera, Carolina, 196
Hessarak Institute, 47
Hindi, 305
Hitler, Adolf, 230
Hittites, 279
Ho Chi Minh, 80, 213
Homer, 290
Hong Kong, xvi
Hosseiniyeh Ershad, 227, 246–7
Hotel Crillon (Paris), 200
Hotel Darius (Persepolis), 187
Hoti, Ibrahim, 8
Hoveyda, Amir-Abbas, 28, 33, 165, 220, 317

Hoveyda, Fereydoon, 196–7
Hoveyda, Gisela, 197
Hughes, Robert, 276
Hughes, Ted, 204
Hungarian Squat Theatre Company, 205
Hungary, 101
Huso huso, 276
Hussein, Saddam, 61, 94, 167, 173, 180, 310
Hyatt Hotel, 248

I Dream of Jeannie (film), 83–4
imperialism, 303
In Cold Blood (Capote), 2
India, xiv, 85–6, 177–8, 228–9, 305, 329
Indian Muslims, 127
Indian Ocean, 85, 92
Indochina War I, 154
Indochina, 87, 149, 209, 241
Indonesia, 151, 162
Ingrid (Queen), 282, 284
intizar, 244
Iran Air, 32
Iran Student Association, 293
Iran, xiii, xiv, xv–xvi, xvii, xx, 2, 6, 7, 22, 49, 56, 84, 110, 186, 189
  Aryan people, 179
  caviar export to Russia, 275
  and China, 75–7
  complex prison structure, 248–53
  disease and vaccination, 8–11

INDEX

expansion of education in, 225–6, 227–30
human rights, 147–53, 153–8
inflation, 181–2
land reforms, 12–20
oil, 131
protocol, 78–81
SAVAK, 57–64, 64–5, 66–8, 71–2
Shah, biographies of, 133–5
western democracy, 166–76
See also Cyrus the Great; Pahlavi, Mohammad Reza
Iranian Constitution, 126
Iranian nationalism, 121
Iranian People's Fadai Guerrillas, 66
Iranian Women's Association, 160
Iranians, 188, 190, 197, 215, 219–20, 228–32, 320–3, 328–30, 335–41
 expansion in education, 228–9
 freedom struggles, 342–4
 life under Shah's rule, 296, 299
 relationship with the West, 243
 views on Mossadegh, 212–13
Iran-Iraq war, 121–2, 180
Iraq, xx, 61, 62, 72, 76, 90, 91, 92, 116, 139, 159, 253, 267, 291
 virus, 6–10
Isfahan, 46, 59
Iskandar (Prince), 289–90
Islam, xviii, 177, 178, 234, 237–40, 241–5, 276, 302–3, 339
Islamabad, 76

Islamic Government (Khomeini), 302
Islamic law, 170
Islamic Republic, 65, 199, 205, 256, 260, 276, 336–8
Israel, 23, 62, 106, 123, 126, 264, 283, 304
Istanbul, 320
Italy, 83, 110

Jahanbegloo, Ramin, 250–1
Jamshid (King), 176, 279–80
Jansen, Maison, 29, 38, 141
Japan, xvii, 11, 167, 300
Jaruzelski, Wojciech, 138
Javanfekr, Ali Akbar, 264
Jenner, Edward, 8
Jerusalem, 23, 122, 127
Jewish law, 277
Jews, xiv, 122–3, 23, 139, 177, 229, 232
Jiang Qing, 74, 76
Jobhani, Maz, 174
Johnson, Lyndon, 87, 92
Johnston, Moira, 292–3
Jones, Jim, xix
Jordan, 54, 141
Juan-les-Pins, 160
Juliana (Queen), 78

Ka Mountain (play), 204
Kabul, 7
Kachouyi, Mohammad, 263
Kapuściński, Ryszard, 109, 136–9
Karanjia, R.K., 132

INDEX

Karbala, 301
Karikatur (magazine), 220
Kasravi, Ahmad, 307
"Kayan" dynasty, 51
al-Kazim, Musa, 305
Keddie, Nikkie, 295
Kelardasht, 208
Kennedy, Edward, 65, 154–5
Kennedy, Jackie, 196
Kennedy, John, 12, 16, 61, 87, 145–6, 153, 163
Kerman, 78
Keusch, Hugo, 271
Khaled, Leila, 56–7
Khalkhali, Sadegh, 179, 317–23
Khamenei, Ayatollah, 264, 337
Khan, Yahya, 85, 86, 112
Kharg Island, 165
Khatami, Mohammad, 180
Khayyam, Omar, 51
Khmer Rouge, 149
Khodynka Field, 313–14, 315
Khomeini, Ayatollah Ruhollah, xv, xix, xx, xxi, 25–6, 58, 61, 81, 132, 135, 159, 179, 263, 297–9, 300–5, 317–18, 340
  early life, 305–7
  emergence in Revolution, 307–8
  opposed Farah, 198
  rise and failure of, 230–8
  western democracy, 166–76
Khomeinism, 308
Khorasan, 25–6
Khrushchev, Nikita 118–19

Kim Il-Sung, 80, 101–2, 151, 157–8
King Farouk of Egypt, 30
King Hussein of Jordan, 32, 55
King of Babylon, 122
King of England, 123
King of Kings (Kapuściński), 109
King of Pars, 46
King of Scotland, 80
King of Thailand, 157
King's Party, 171
Kish, island of, 43, 99, 156
Kissinger, Henry, xiv, 85–6, 153, 164, 167, 274
Koran, 24, 51, 177–9, 276
Korean War, 102
Kosovo, 8
Kubrick, Stanley, 3
Kuo Mojo (Guo Moruo), 77
Kurds, 300, 321
Kuwait, 141, 142

La Boheme, 223
La Chiminee, 223
Ladjevardi, Asadollah, 263
Lambton, Ann, 216
Lambton, Anne, 223
Lanvin, (fashion house) 33
Larkin, Philip, xviii
Latin America, 66, 149
Lausanne, 144
Le Corbusier, 310
Le Monde (newspaper), 160, 164, 305
Le Rosey, 144–7

INDEX

Lebanon, 49, 66, 228–9, 285
Lei Feng, 74
Lenin, 103
Leonidas (King), 45
Levant, 278
Leviticus, 276
Leys, Simon, 77
liberation theology, 12
Liberia, 83
Library of Congress, 29
Libya, xiv, 22
LIFE (magazine), 83, 156
"Light of the Aryans", 134, 173
Lin Biao, 73–4
Lion of Judah, 31–2, 109
Little Red Book (Mao Zedong), 75
Liu Shaoqi, 76
London, 41, 54, 56, 96, 104, 128, 129, 163, 193, 214, 223, 275–6
Los Angeles Times, The (newspaper), 282
Los Angeles, 121, 174
Louis XIV, 108
Lubyanka, 253
Lucknow, 305
Luther, Martin, 261
LVMH, 47
Lydians, 278

MacArthur Jr, Douglas, 68
Macbeth (Lady), 136
Macedonia, 278, 288
  Macedonian, xiv, 286, 287, 289
Mahlouji, Vali, 205
Maison Jansen, 39

Majlis, 14, 17, 213, 216–17, 228
Makkonen, Tafari. *See* Haile Selassie
Mancatcher's Manual (Lambton), 223
Manson, Charles, xvi
Mao Zedong, 4, 66, 73–4, 77, 102, 109, 140, 157, 213
Maoism, 75, 220–1, 227, 260
Marcos, Imelda, 82–4, 112, 324
Marcos, Imelda Maria (Imee), 82–3
Mardom (newspaper), 156
Marduk, 123–5, 127
Marighella, Carlos, 66
Martyrs' Foundation, 64
Marx, Karl, 238–9
Marxism, 12, 239, 243, 245, 247–8
Mashhad, 7–8
Master of Ceremonies, 96
Masters of Mediocrity, 223
Masumeh, Fatima, 234
materialism, 239–40
Maxim's, 29, 33, 270–1
McGill, 226
McGregor, Neil, 122, 126–7
measles, 8
Mecca, 43
Medea, 175
Medes, 124
Mehrabad Airport, 95, 254
Mein Kampf (Hitler), 258
Meinhof, Ulrike, 189–91
MEK. *See* Mojahedin-e Khalq

411

INDEX

Menderes, Adnan, 16
Mendl (Lady), 39
Mendoub Palace, 3
Mengistu, Haile Mariam, 151
Mesopotamia, 180–1, 279
"Messiah of Africa", 80
Messiah, 23
Metropolitan Museum, 193, 279
Mexico, xxi, 300
Michael of Kent (Princess), 79
Middle East, xiv, xv–xvi, 7, 9, 52–3, 62, 90–3, 96, 106, 115, 143, 173, 209, 222, 264, 310, 339
Mikhailovich, Nikolai, 316
Milan, 80
Milani, Abbas, 27, 145–6, 260, 312, 318–19
Miller, John, 96–7
Milosz, Czeslaw, 131
Minimanual of the Urban Guerrilla (Marighella), 66
Minnelli, Liza, 196
Mirsepassi, Ali, 169
Modell eines Entwicklungslandes oder Die Diktatur der Freien Welt (Nirumand), 189
modernization, 240
Mohammad Ali Jinnah, 177
Moinian, Nosratollah, 22
Mojahedin-e Khalq, 199, 263
Mona Lisa, 127
Monaco, 146
Mongols, 233
Mongolia, 73, 74
Monroe, Marilyn, 196, 253

Monrovia Bloc, 110
Montazeri, Ayatollah, 260, 262
Montevideo, xvii
Montreux Casino, xvii
Morier, James, 52
Morocco, xxi
Morris, Jan, 201
Moscow, 75, 76, 79, 86–7, 90, 104, 116, 258, 313–14
Mossadegh, Mohammad, 12, 22, 16, 53, 59, 132, 134–5, 159, 165, 169, 189, 245–6, 258, 275
  political career, 212–18
  tensions between Reza and, 207–12
Mostafa, 297–8
Muhammad (Prophet), 205, 239, 277
Mujahedin-e Khalq, 300
mullahs, 14–18
Mumbai, 132
Mumdzic, Latif, 8
Museum of Iran, 279
Musk, Elon, xvii
Muslim League, 177
Muslims, 177, 234, 244, 245
  seafood restrictions, 276–7
Mussolini, Benito, 80, 110, 230

Nabavi, Ebrahim, 253
Nabonidus, 123–5
Naipaul, V.S., 248–9, 319, 322
Najaf, 297–8, 301–2, 305
Namzie, Maryan, 261
Napoleonic wars, 78

INDEX

Al-Nasser, Gamal Abdel, 62, 110
National Front, 53, 211, 216, 297
National Security Advisor, xiv
Nazi Germany, 255, 258
Nazis, 192, 284
Neauphle-le-Château, 298
Nebuchadnezzar, 127
Negritude movement, 113–14
Nehru, Jawaharlal, 213
neoliberalism, xviii, 301
Nerat, Marina, 249–50
Neue Revue (magazine), 189
New Delhi, 86, 250
New York Review of Books, 135–136
New York Times, The (newspaper), 33, 40, 327–8, 331
New York, 2, 54, 55, 128, 161, 193, 196, 264
New Yorker, The (magazine), 144
Newsweek (magazine), xiii, 150
Niavaran Palace, 94, 193–4, 293–4
Nicholas II (Emperor), 313–15
Nigeria, 162
Nile, 175
Nimrud, 272
Nirumand, Bahman, 189, 190–2
Nixon, Richard, xiv xviii, 35, 71, 78–9, 84–6, 87–92, 149, 153, 163, 164, 166–7, 221
Nkrumah, Kwame, 80, 110, 213
Normandy, 114
North Korea, 80, 101, 102, 150, 151, 157, 158
North Tehran hills, 194

North Tehran, 54, 223
Nowruz, 49, 52
Nyerere, Julius, 213

O'Donovan, Patrick, 326–9
Observer, The (newspaper), 326, 327
Ohnesorg, Benno, 188–9, 300
Old Testament, 122
Olympics, 300
Oman, xvii, 92
Omid (magazine), 164–5
Operation Dark Gene, 116
Operation Genghis Khan, 86
Operation Searchlight, 85
Orff, Carl, 284
Organization of African Unity, 111
Orlando, xvi
Oval Office, 87
Ovanessian, Arby, 204
Ove Arup and Partners, 311
Owen, David, 99–100
ozun borun. See sturgeon

Pahlavi dynasty, xv, xviii–xix, 27, 30, 155, 174, 227, 338–9
Pahlavi University, 227
Pahlavi, Keur Farah, 114–15
Pahlavi, Mohammad Reza, 5, 12, 53, 79, 88, 89, 91, 94, 97–9, 131–2, 144–5, 153, 154, 156–7, 167, 172–3, 204, 206, 216, 307
attacks against Bahais, 320
failures of, 215, 342–3
Le Rosey, life at, 144–7

413

INDEX

Moscow, 117–19
Nixon presidency, 87–96
oil prices, 111
party, idea for, 21–31
regime, 336–7
role in education expansion, 228–9
Shah, biographies of, 133–5
student opposition to, 241
tensions between Mossadegh and, 207–12
violence, 147–53, 153–8
western democracy, 166–76
Pahlavis, 127, 136, 185–6, 193, 196, 211, 306–7, 330, 341, 343
"Pahlavism", 19–20, 23–4, 156, 169, 203, 245
Pahlbod, Mehrdad, 22, 33
Pakistan, xvi, 85, 86, 116, 117, 177, 329
Palestine Liberation Organization, 55
Pan Am 747, 56
Panama, xxi
Pangaea, 273
Paon a l'Imperial, 270
Papon, Maurice, 241
Paris, 38, 98–9, 200, 223, 275–6
Parsons, Talcott, 13
Party of Donkeys, 165
Parvaz, Nasrin, 266
Pasargadae, 37, 38, 48, 271, 289, 340
Paul VI, Pope, 81
pavo real, 270

Pazeller, Rudolf, 280
People's Temple, xix
Peoples' Republic of China. *See* China
Pepsi, 101–2, 104
Peress, Gilles, 255
Permenion (general), 286
Perron, Ernest, 145–6, 216
Persepolis Fortification Archive, 278–9
Persepolis, 1, 11–12, 15, 21–2, 24, 31, 36–9, 41, 45, 46, 50, 51–3, 187–8, 255, 271–2
  attacked by Alexander, 285–9
  tents, 47–8
Persia, 6, 35–6, 43, 44, 45, 142, 289, 324
Persian Empire, xiii, 1, 5, 22, 30, 37, 48, 51–2, 127, 143, 171, 173, 28 285, 288, 291
Persian Gulf, xiv, 43, 94, 141, 283, 300
Persians, 272, 278, 324, 325
Persica, 278
Petrovskii Palace, 314, 315
PFLP, 55–6
Philip (Prince), 94, 96, 129, 146
Philippines, 82–3
Piero Georgetti Combo, 223
Pig, Child, Fire (play), 205
Pinochet, Augusto, 149, 151
Place de la Madeleine, 27
Plataea, Battle of (479 BCE), 37, 272–3

414

INDEX

Plaza Hotel (New York), 2
Plutarch, 285–6
Podgorny, Nikolai, 112, 116–17
Poland, 138
Polish United Workers' Party, 138
Politburo, 104
Pollock, Jackson, 101
Polo, Marco, 261
polytheism, 243, 244
Pompadour, Madame de, 108
Pompidou, Georges, 35, 97–9, 100
Pony Express, 48
Pope, Arthur, 29
populism, 211, 231, 233, 237, 330
Portugal, 300
"Power of the Trinity", 80
pragmatism, 231
Precht, Henry, 230
Presidential Daily Briefing, 71
Presidio Heights, 292
Prince Makhosini Dlamini of Swaziland, 33
Prince of Spain, 107
Private Eye (magazine), 95
pro-Soviet Marxism, 113
Prussia, 78
Ptolemy, 286, 291
Pyongyang, 101, 105, 106

Qajar dynasty, 19, 199, 209, 210, 229, 275, 307
Qalibaf, Mohammed Baqer, 265
Qatar, xvii, 141
Qazwin, 46
Qom, 25, 234, 265, 277, 301–2, 306

Qotbi, Reza, 203–4
Quebec, 71
Queen Mother, 5
Queen of Sheba, 110
Quinn, Sally, 10, 201, 324–5
Qutb, Sayyad, 242

Rabin, Yitzhak, 55–6
Radji, Parviz, 134
Rafsanjani, Akbar Hashemi, 179
Rahati, Golmohammad, 249
Rahnema, Ali, 247
Ramsbotham, Peter, 94–5
Rastafarianism, 109
Rastakhiz Party, 181–182
Reagan, Ronald, 301
Red Army, 103
Red Guards, 76
Revolution (1979), 218, 248, 343
Revolution Airport, 55–6
Revolutionary Government, 262, 263, 321, 338, 339
Revolutionary Guards, 262
Rey, 311
Reynolds, Joshua, 286–7
Reza (Prince), 140
Reza the Biker (film), 224
Reza, Abdul, 82, 220
Reza, Fazlollah, 226
Reza, Gholam, 220
Reza, Imam, 7
Rezaian, Jason, 266–7
Al Rhazes, 8
Rolle, 144
Romania, 101, 102, 104, 140

INDEX

Rome, 134, 207
Roneo Vickers, 240
Roosevelt, Franklin D., 87, 118
Roosevelt, Kermit, 61
Rothschild, Marie-Hélène, 2–3
Rouleau, Eric, 305
Royal Institute for International Affairs. *See* Chatham House
Royal Mews, 96
Royal Tehran Hilton, 196, 223
Rumi, 192, 242
Rushdie, Salman, 137, 232
Russia, 74, 78, 189, 275
Russian Empire, 258
Russian Revolution, 307
Russians, 208, 234–5, 275, 316–17

Sachs, Gunter, xx
Sadchikov, Ivan, 275
Sade, Marquis de, 261
Sadeghi, Fatema, 323
Safdie, Moshe, 114
Saint Laurent, Yves, 197
Sainte Freres, 46
San Francisco, 292
Saqqa-Kana School, 192
Sartre, Jean-Paul, 241
Sassanians, 177, 291, 311
Satanic Verses, The (Rushdie), 232
Saudi Arabia, 9, 139, 162, 214
Saudi monarchy, 62
Saul, 127
SAVAK (Sâzmân-e Ettelâ'ât va Amniyyat-e Kešvar or The Bureau for Intelligence and Security of the State), 10, 54, 57–61, 62–5, 66–70, 72, 75, 138–9, 152, 157, 159, 178, 182, 189, 203, 204, 220, 225, 260, 293, 320
   blamed for Shariati's death, 247–8
   control over Evin, 252, 254
   Hoveyda arrested by, 318
   Shariati and, 247–8
Seattle, Battle of, 71
Secrets of the Jinni Valley Treasure (movie), 312
Seine, 154, 241
Seko, Mobutu Sese, 4
Selassie, Haile, 4, 31, 78, 80, 107, 109–11, 115, 138, 140, 151, 273, 281, 309
Senghor, Léopold Sédar, 107, 113–15, 213
Sepah Avenue, 33
Setad, 337
Shafa, Shojaeddin, 6, 22–3, 29–30, 172
Shafrazi, Tony, 195
Shah of Shahs (Kapuściński), 136–8, 139
Shah, Reza, 13–14, 28, 87, 132, 137–8, 164–5, 186, 235, 258, 262, 305–7
   Anglo-Iranian agreement with, 214
   control over Iranians, 342
   death of, 335–6
   Mossadegh and, 211, 213

INDEX

opposition to Bahais, 320
secularization policies, 240
ta'ziyeh banned by, 206
Shah's Last Ride, The (Shawcross), xxi
Shahnameh (Book of Kings) (Ferdowsi), 51–2, 136, 176, 177, 284, 289
"The Shah-People Revolution", 12
Shahram (Prince), 72
Shahyad Arch, 128, 309, 312, 313
Shakibnia, Abolqassem, 239
Shamaqdari, Javad, 173–4
Shams (Princess), 33
Shapur II, 51
Sharia, 14
Shariati, Ali, 229–30
  role in islamic revolution, 238–48
Sharif-Emami, Jaafar, 1
Shawcross, William, xxi, 129
Shi'ism, 206
Shia communities, 7, 18, 26
Shia Islam, 65, 142, 171, 276, 306
Shia motifs, 192
Shia spiritualism, 206
Shiism, 170, 192, 238–9, 244, 246–7, 297, 307, 304, 320
Shiraz Airport, 54, 101
Shiraz Arts Festival, 204–5
Shiraz, 4, 10, 24, 38, 53, 56, 71, 72, 73, 82, 227, 234
Shouki, Lina, 223
Siakhal, 65, 67–70, 72

Siculus, Diodorus, 286
Silva y Figueroa, Don Garcia de, 50
Sirazi, Sayyed 'Ali-Moḥammad, 320
Six-Day War, 86, 91
Six Decrees, 13
Smallpox, 7–11
"Smoke on the Water" (song), xvii
Societal Security Law (1952), 258
Solomon (King), 6, 51
Soong Ching-ling, 76
Soraya (Queen), 60, 198, 207–8, 210–11
South Africa, 4, 117, 148, 329, 335
South Asia, 9, 79, 310
South Korea, 83
Soviet Bloc, 104
Soviet Union, 13, 62, 66, 87, 91–2, 101, 107, 111, 112, 115, 150–1, 166, 189, 239, 329
  occupation of Caucasus, 234
Soviets, 275
Spain, 97, 300
Spanish Inquisition, 260
Sparta, 290–1
St Cyr, 59, 98
St Michael, 41
St Petersburg, 314
St. Moritz, 43, 81, 131, 150, 156, 167, 200, 270
Stalin, Joseph, 80, 87, 102, 107, 112, 117, 118, 119, 156, 263
Standing Committee of the National People's Congress, 77

INDEX

Stanford University, 341
Stasi, 63
Steele, Robert, 110, 114, 326
Stewart, Michael, 21
Straits of Hormuz, xvii
sturgeon (fish), 273–8
Suez War, 62
Suharto, 151
Sukarno, 213
Sultan of Oman, 142
Sulzberger, C.L., 331
Sun Yat-Sen, 76
Sunset Boulevard, 174
Susa, 37, 38, 45, 48, 53
Swaziland, 83
Sweden, 13
Switzerland, 98, 133, 144–7, 169, 199, 270–1
Syria, 10, 55, 62, 91, 116, 149, 267, 291

ta'ziyeh, 206
al-Tabari, Mohammad ibn Jarir, 51
Tabatabaei, Ziaeddin, 255
Tafari, Ras, 109
Tajadod, Mahin, 204
Taj al-Moluk, (Queen Mother) 30–1
Takht-e Jamshid, 50
Taleghani, Ayatollah Mahmoud, 254–5
talismans, 192
Tamil People's Liberation Front, xvii

Tanavoli, Parviz, 192–3
Tangiers, 3
Tawfiq (newspaper), 164–5, 220
Tawfiq, Mohammad-Ali, 164–5
Tehran Central Prison, 265
Tehran College of Decorative Arts, 192
Tehran University, 225, 310, 339, 341
Tehran, 1, 23–4, 29, 33, 43, 53–4, 59–61, 65–6, 72, 77, 78–9, 87, 90–1, 116, 121, 128, 196, 223–4, 297, 309–10
See also Iran
Temple in Jerusalem, 122
Temple of Solomon, 122
Tenerife, xix
Thailand, 107
Thaïs (concubine), 286
Thatcher, Margaret, xxi, 16, 300–1
Thermopylae, Battle of, 173
Throne of Jamshid, 51
Tigray, 111
Times, The (newspaper), 150, 218, 315
Timisoara, 105
Tito, Josip Broz, 4, 24, 28–9, 106–8, 112, 140, 213
Tjecknavorian, Loris, 284
Tocqueville, Alexis de, 111
Today (TV show), 283
Torah, 23
Triassic Age, 273
Trinity Cathedral, 111

INDEX

Trojan Wars, 290
Trucial States, xvii, 141
Trump, Donald, 230
Tudeh Party, 12, 59, 61, 63, 75, 116, 209, 211, 217, 220, 258–9, 300
Tudeh publications, 156
Tughrul Tower, 311–12
Tupamaros, xvi–xvii
Turkey, 61, 84, 92, 93, 116, 186, 159, 228–9, 285
Turks, 234–5

U.S. government, 10
Uganda, xvi
Ukraine, 116
ulema, 235, 307, 320
Umayyad Caliphate, 239
UN Human Rights Commission, 161
UNESCO (United Nations Educational, Scientific and Cultural Organization), 22
Unit 209, 248, 251–2, 257
United Arab Emirates, xvii, 94, 142
United Kingdom (UK), 56, 75, 93, 107, 149
United Nations General Assembly, 264
United Nations Security Council, 128
United Nations, xvi, 148, 160
United States Capitol, xvii
United States Constitution, 127

United States Embassy, 28, 63, 219, 220, 264
United States policy, 86
United States (US), xiv, xvii, xviii, 12, 48, 55, 60, 62, 86–7, 90, 92–3, 107, 152, 174, 189, 217, 229, 253, 301, 320
  emergence as the Western superpower, 208
  involvement in coups, 210
  Iranian opposition to, 221
United States governments, 85
Universal Declaration of Human Rights, 149
University of Athens, 300
University of Coimbra, 148
University of Mashhad, 242
University of Tehran. *See* Tehran University
Ur, 124

Variety (newspaper), 223
Velayat e-faqih, 168–71, 302
Venezuela, 162
Vennes, 144
Versailles, 38, 322
Vichy government, 154
Vienna Protocol, 82
Vienna, 99
Vietnam War, 148
Vietnam, 87, 90, 92, 150, 192, 221, 296
Village Voice, The (newspaper), 197
Villiers, Gerard, 137

419

INDEX

Vogue (magazine), 201
von Furstenberg, Diane, 196

Waithood, 222
Waldenstrom's Syndrome, 99–100
Walt Disney World, xvi
Walters, Barbara, 163
Wang Guangmei, 76
Warhol, Andy, 195–7
Warsaw Pact, 101
Washington Post, The (newspaper), 2, 10, 201, 266, 324, 332
Washington, 28, 56, 60, 79, 85, 87, 90, 118, 153, 163, 208, 209, 275–6, 293
Welles, Orson, 173
West, Mae, 3
Western Europe, 220–1
Westernization, 246, 295, 303
Westoxification, 171, 202, 205, 244
White House, 195
"White Revolution", 12, 14–19, 23, 203, 222, 225, 235, 338
  Reza resistance to, 237
Wilson, Robert, 204
Windsor, 95
wine, 278–81
Winnie Hovler Dancers, 223
Winston, Harry, 281
Wolfe, Elsie de. *See* Mendl, Lady
Wollo, 111

Wolof, 114
Wolsey, Thomas (Cardinal), 42
World Health Organization (WHO), 9, 10–11
World Today, The (journal), 214
World Trade Organization (WTO), 71
World War I, 234–5
World War II, 39, 55, 87, 107, 113, 132, 148, 241

xenophobia, 215
Xenophon, 286
Xerxes (King), 37, 45, 48, 50, 125, 173, 272–3, 285

Yadegar-e Eman, 256
Yahya, 86
Yamani, Sheikh, 150
Yemen, 76, 92.
Yugoslavia, 4, 8–10, 24, 107–8

Zahedi, Fazlollah, 159
Zaire, (Congo), 4
Zappa, Frank, xvii
Zhang Tong, 77
Zhivkov, Todor, 33
Zhou Enlai, 74–5, 109
Zionism, 123
Zoroastrianism, 49, 290
Zurich, 55, 167